D

AQA

AS

Rosie McGinley
Julia Willerton
Jane Willson
James Bailey

Series editor
Simon Green

Published in 2008 by:
Nelson Thornes Ltd
Delta Place
27 Bath Road
CHELTENHAM
GL53 7TH
United Kingdom

12 / 10 9 8 7 6 5

A catalogue record for this book is available from the British Library

ISBN 978 0 7487 9823 0

Cover photograph by Photolibrary

Illustrations include artwork drawn by Angela Knowles, Peters and Zabransky UK Ltd,
Harry Venning and Wearset Ltd

Page make-up by Wearset Ltd, Boldon, Tyne and Wear

Printed in China by 1010 Printing International Ltd

The authors and publisher would like to thank the following for permission to reproduce
material:

p3: Alamy / Steve Teague; p27: Elizabeth Loftus; p43: (left to right) Alamy / Picture
Partners; Alamy / Ken Welsh; Alamy / Ian McKinnell; Alamy / Mary-Ella Keith; Alamy
/ stephen bond; p46: Getty Images / Thomas D. McAvoy / Stringer; p52: Science
Photo Library / Science Source; p54: **Drik**NEWS / Tanvir Ahmed; p71: © BBC; p77:
Alamy / Steve Benbow; pp87, 88, 89: Alamy / Aflo Foto Agency; p137: Alamy / Stock
Connection Distribution; p162: Digital Vision / Pushstock Tin; p185: Alamy / Iain
Masterton; p186: (top to bottom) Alamy / Hemis; Getty Images / Tim Graham; p191:
Getty / MGM Studios / Handout; p194: (top to bottom) Philip G. Zimbado, Inc.; © BBC /
Stuart Wood; p203: From the film Obedience (c)1968 by Stanley Milgram, © renewed
by Alexandra Milgram, and distributed by Penn State Media Sales; p213: Getty /
Orlando/Stringer; p221: Getty / Sahm Doherty/Contributor; p222: Getty / Scott Barbour/
Stringer; p229: Science Photo Library / Simon Fraser

p5: Fig. 1, 'How information is processed in the memory' from 'Model of Memory', by
R.C. Atkinson and R.M. Shiffrin, *The Psychology of Learning and Motivation*, 2, Academic
Press, 1968, pp89–195. Reprinted with permission; p9: Fig. 5, 'Free recall as a function
of serial position and duration of the interpolated task' adapted from 'Two storage
mechanisms in free recall', by M. Glanzer and A.R. Cunitz, *Journal of Verbal Learning
& Verbal Behaviour*, 5, 1966, pp351–60. Reprinted with permission of Elsevier Limited;
p20: Fig. 6, 'Working Memory: the Multiple-Component Model' A. D. Baddeley and R.H.
Logie, Chapter 2 in A. Miyake, P. Shal (eds) *Models of Working Memory: Mechanisms of
Active Maintenance and Executive Control*, Cambridge University Press 1999. Reprinted
with permission of Cambridge University Press; p21: Fig. 7, 'Folding flat shapes to
form a cube stimulus', R.N. Shephard and C. Feng, 'A Chronometric Study of Mental
Paper-Folding', *Cognitive Psychology*, 3, 1972, pp228–43. Reprinted with permission of
Elsevier Limited; p34: Fig. 2, graph of Geiselman *et al.*'s results from *An Introduction to
Applied Cognitive Psychology* by A. Estgate and D. Groome, 2004, p55. Reprinted with
permission of Taylor & Francis Books (UK); p36: extract from 'Contextual prerequisites
for understanding: some investigations of comprehension and recall', by J.D. Bransford
and M.K. Johnson, *Journal of Verbal Learning & Verbal Behaviour*, 11, 1972, pp717–26.
Reprinted with permission of Elsevier Limited; p100: use of the BPS Code of Ethics ©
British Psychological Society. Reprinted with permission; p113: Tables 4 and 5, by John
Crane from http://cranepsych.com. Reprinted with permission of the author; p139: Fig.
1 and p143: Fig. 6, *Psychology for A Level*, 2nd edition by Cardwell, Clark and Meldrum,
Collins Educational, 2000. Reprinted with permission of HarperCollins Publishers; p158:
Table 1, adapted from T.H. Holmes and R.H. Rahe, 'The Social Readjustment Rating
Scale', *Journal of Psychosomatic Research*, 1967, pp213–18. Reprinted with permission
of Elsevier Limited; p169: Table 4, COPE table, *Measure in Health Portfolio* © Weineman,
Wright, and Johnston, 1995. Reproduced by permission of NFER Nelson Publishing
Limited; p246: Fig. 1 'Ellis's ABC Model' from 'The revised ABC's of rational emotive
therapy (RET)', by A. Ellis, *The Journal of Rational-Emotive and Cognitive Behaviour
Therapy*, 9, 3, 1991, pp139–72. Reprinted with permission of Springer.

Contents

AQA introduction

Nelson Thornes has worked in partnership with AQA to ensure this book and the accompanying online resources offer you the best support for your A level course.

All resources have been approved by senior AQA examiners so you can feel assured that they closely match the specification for this subject and provide you with everything you need to prepare successfully for your exams.

These print and online resources together **unlock blended learning**; this means that the links between the activities in the book and the activities online blend together to maximise your understanding of a topic and help you achieve your potential.

These online resources are available on **kerboodle!** which can be accessed via the internet at **http://www.kerboodle.com/live**, anytime, anywhere. If your school or college subscribes to this service you will be provided with your own personal login details. Once logged in, access your course and locate the required activity.

For more information and help visit **http://www.kerboodle.com**

Icons in this book indicate where there is material online related to that topic. The following icons are used:

Learning activity

These resources include a variety of interactive and non-interactive activities to support your learning.

Progress tracking

These resources include a variety of tests that you can use to check your knowledge on particular topics (Test yourself) and a range of resources that enable you to analyse and understand examination questions (On your marks …).

Research support

These resources include WebQuests, in which you are assigned a task and provided with a range of web links to use as source material for research.

Audio stimulus

Each chapter has a podcast summarising the important points.

How to use this book

This book covers the specification for your course and is arranged in a sequence approved by AQA.

The book content is divided into two units – Unit 1 and Unit 2 – which match the two units of the AQA Psychology A AS specification. It is then divided into sections matched to the six sections of the specification – Cognitive psychology, Developmental psychology, Research methods, Biological psychology, Social psychology and Individual differences. Each section introduction contains a table mapping the section content to the specification so you can see at a glance where to find the information you need. Sections are then further divided into chapters, each with its own summary, and then topics, making them clear and easy to use.

The content of the book is designed to meet the requirements of How science works by giving you the necessary skills and information to plan your own psychological investigations.

The features in this book include:

Learning objectives

At the beginning of each topic you will find a list of learning objectives that contain targets linked to the requirements of the specification.

Key terms

Terms that you will need to be able to define and understand.

Hint

Hints to aid your understanding of the content.

Links

This highlights any key areas where sections relate to one another.

Research study

Certain studies are described in more detail. These research studies are designed to represent the research methods and findings typical of a particular area of psychological research. They also act as a focus for discussing methodological and ethical issues in psychological research, and there are links from them to the Research methods chapters.

You will need to know details of studies and concepts specifically mentioned in the specification, but in addition you should also know additional studies and concepts in outline to use in discussion and evaluation.

How science works: practical activity

At the end of each chapter there is a practical activity for you to undertake. Actually designing investigations, collecting data and analysing and interpreting the findings of your own research will bring the subject to life and will help you to develop a more thorough understanding of how science works.

Summary questions

Short questions that test your understanding of the subject and allow you to apply the skills you develop to different scenarios. The final question in each set is designed to be a stretch and challenge question and to require more thought. Answers are supplied free at www.nelsonthornes.com/psychology_answers.

Nelson Thornes is responsible for the solution(s) given and they may not constitute the only possible solution(s).

AQA Examiner's tip

Hints from AQA examiners to help you with your study and to prepare for your exam.

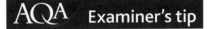 Examination-style questions

Questions in the style that you can expect in your exam. The Research methods questions are tested in the Cognitive and Developmental psychology sections and so there are no separate examination-style questions pages at the end of the Research methods section.

AQA examination questions are reproduced by permission of the Assessment and Qualifications Alliance.

Key points

A bulleted list at the end of each topic summarising the content in an easy-to-follow way.

Web links in the book

As Nelson Thornes is not responsible for third party content online, there may be some changes to this material that are beyond our control. In order for us to ensure that the links referred to in the book are as up-to-date and stable as possible, the websites are usually homepages with supporting instructions on how to reach the relevant pages if necessary.

Please let us know at **kerboodle@nelsonthornes.com** if you find a link that doesn't work and we will do our best to redirect the link, or to find an alternative site.

Introduction for students

Although you have decided to study psychology at AS Level you may not have come across the subject before. You may think you know what psychology is – most people have the idea that it is about understanding why people do things. Although this is an aim of psychology, a more formal definition sees psychology as the *scientific* study of brain and behaviour.

Today psychology is seen as a science, and studying psychology will give you a real understanding of 'How science works'. You will be introduced to the scientific method in the introduction to the Research methods section, but essentially it means using the methods of science such as observation, measurement and experimentation to study behaviour. Throughout this book you will be introduced to many examples of psychological studies and learn how contemporary psychology works.

Because human behaviour is complicated, psychology has used a number of different *approaches* in trying to explain behaviour. These include the biological, the cognitive, the behavioural and the psychodynamic approaches. A key aim of the AS Units 1 and 2 is to provide a solid grounding in these approaches that will also serve as a background for those of you going on to A2.

Structure of the book

This book is designed specifically for students new to psychology who are following the AQA specification A. All the authors are experienced teachers and examiners. Besides being introduced to the scientific method and approaches, you will also be introduced to the *core areas* of psychology. In Unit 1 these are Cognitive psychology and Developmental psychology, and in Unit 2 Biological psychology, Social psychology, and Individual differences. Each core area is illustrated by a specific topic, such as *Memory* for Cognitive psychology and *Early social development* for Developmental psychology. Throughout each topic there is reference to relevant approaches and research studies.

Unit 1 also covers *Research methods*. As a science, it is critical that you understand the methods that are used in psychology to investigate behaviour and experience, and that you develop the skills to plan and carry out practical investigations. This topic covers the basics of the scientific approach. However, as research methods underpin all topics in psychology, throughout the topics in both units there is discussion of research methods issues and specific links to the Research methods chapters. One of the best ways of developing your understanding of Research methods is by carrying out practical investigations in class, and you will be given guidance on the sorts of studies you might try.

Assessment objectives and skills

During your course you will need to develop skills relating to the assessment objectives. These are: knowledge and understanding of psychological theories and findings (AO1); the ability to analyse and evaluate psychological theories and findings, and to apply your knowledge to unfamiliar situations (AO2); knowledge and skills in relation to How science works and research methodology (AO3).

You will need to develop the ability to analyse and evaluate psychological theories, concepts, studies and findings. This may involve what we call *methodological* evaluation of studies to determine whether they are valid and whether the findings are reliable. In addition the *significance* of findings for our understanding of behaviour is a major issue in evaluating studies. Finally you will need to be able to apply your knowledge and understanding to unfamiliar situations. For instance, can you apply your knowledge and understanding of methods of stress management to a real world situation such as examinations?

Throughout the specification there is an emphasis on How science works, and your understanding of this will be assessed in the examination. However, you will acquire this understanding gradually as you progress through Units 1 and 2. It involves such skills as relating research findings to theories and models, understanding how to carry out psychological investigations, and the ability to select appropriate methods. Additional skills include evaluation of research methods in terms of, for instance, validity and ethics, and the application of psychological findings to the real world. As you can see, many of these skills relate to the Research methods topic in Unit 1. Others overlap with the analytic and evaluative assessment objectives mentioned earlier. This is why it is important not to worry too much over which assessment objective you are dealing with at any particular time; the examination is designed so that if you answer the question set you will automatically be satisfying the various assessment objectives.

Assessment

Across both examinations all questions will be compulsory, therefore you will need to have covered all of the specification in each Unit.

The examinations for Units 1 and 2 will use a variety of question styles, from multiple-choice to short essays. Some questions will use *scenarios*, a short description of some aspect of behaviour that will be followed by brief questions. This variety of question style is intended to give you the opportunity to use your psychological knowledge and understanding effectively. Remember that in many areas of psychology there is no one right answer. It is essential that you develop the ability to weigh up evidence in order to identify the most appropriate explanation.

The sequence of topics in the book follows the specification precisely and the unit examinations are organised in the same order. The Unit 1 examination covers Cognitive and Developmental psychology. Research methods will be tested in this unit using *contextualised* questions. This means that they will be set in the context of the cognitive and developmental material you have covered for this unit. So, for instance, you might be given an outline of a study of memory, and asked to comment on the methods used, the results obtained, and how the results relate to the theories and concepts you have studied.

The Unit 2 examination will have questions on Biological psychology, Social psychology, and Individual differences. Across both examinations there will be some assessment of How science works built into the questions.

You have come into psychology at a time when it has become one of the fastest growing subjects in schools, colleges, and in higher education. Psychology studies the most fascinating of all areas – human behaviour and experience. We hope that besides preparing you for the AS examinations, this book also shows you that psychology is a varied and exciting subject. And A2 Psychology is even more exciting…!

Cognitive psychology – memory

Introduction

◼ What is memory?

Memory is central to all our cognitive activities because we use it whenever we need to maintain information over time. For example, you can hold the first few words of this sentence in your memory until you get to the end – without this ability, we would not be able to read for meaning.

These days, we have organisers and diaries so we do not need to keep appointments in our heads. Similarly, calculators, computers and mobile phones have made rote-learned 'mental arithmetic' skills increasingly redundant. However, memory is still essential to our ability to function as human beings. It is not just a storehouse for facts but also contains everything we need to know about interacting with the world. Memory played a crucial part in your start to the day, for example, remembering where you keep your clothes, what the people who live in your house look like, how to tell the time, make the coffee, pack your bag, know your timetable for the day, etc.

On the whole we have amazing memories – we remember the names of thousands of people – not just friends and relatives, but people from our past and even people we only know from film and TV. We can name thousands of objects and remember countless facts, both about our personal experience and about the world in general. We can also recognise non-verbal sounds such as ambulance sirens or a piece of music. We have memories for the other senses as well, such as touch and smell. For example, we can remember how things feel, such as the touch of velvet or the sting of a nettle.

Memory can sometimes let us down – our minds can go blank in exams and we sometimes forget people's names or put something down and can't remember where it is. Such memory lapses happen to us all, but imagine what it would be like to lose the ability to use our memory. Clive Wearing was a gifted British musician, who suffered severe memory loss after contracting a viral infection. He can still talk, walk, read and write and also play the piano. However, he has dramatically reduced memory for personal events and for general knowledge. He does not read books or newspapers nor watch television or listen to the radio because he is unable to follow the thread. He recognises his wife and greets her emotionally when she comes to see him. However, within seconds of her leaving, he has no recollection of her visit. He has described his situation as 'Hell on earth'.

This kind of memory loss is tragic for the individual and difficult for the rest of us to imagine. Case studies such as his have, however, provided psychologists with important insights and helped them to understand normal memory functioning.

Memory has attracted vast amounts of research and continues to be the focus of huge interest among cognitive psychologists. We will now look at some explanations of how memory works and consider some of the practical applications of research.

1 Models of memory

The multi-store model

- Understand what is meant by the term 'model'.

- Describe the multi-store model of memory and understand the functions and limitations of its components (sensory memory, short-term memory and long-term memory).

- Describe and evaluate the evidence upon which this model is based.

- Understand the concepts of capacity, duration and encoding.

- Understand how these aspects of memory have been measured.

- Explain the strengths and weaknesses of the multi-store model.

Key terms

Short-term memory: a temporary store where small amounts of information can be kept for brief periods. It is a fragile store and information can be easily lost.

Long-term memory: a permanent store where limitless amounts of information can be stored for long periods of time.

Capacity: the amount of information that can be held in memory at any one time.

Duration: the length of time that memories can be held.

What is a model?

We have looked at some of the ways of defining what memory is and why it is so important to us. Cognitive psychologists have been interested in trying to explain *how* memory works. Early explanations were criticised for being vague and poorly detailed. Cognitive psychologists tried to meet these criticisms by developing computer programs to mimic human cognitive functioning. In order to work, these programs need to be highly specific and detailed. However, computer modelling is complex and time-consuming and, as a compromise, researchers have tended to use flow charts rather than fully developed computer programs to represent their theories. These theories based on information-processing systems are called models.

The information-processing models of memory all share similar features in terms of the structure of the memory system. For example, there is a temporary store where information can be briefly kept while some other operation is performed. This **short-term memory** store can handle only limited amounts of information at any one time. Once processed through the input buffer, the information is stored in a **long-term memory** store where it will remain permanently unless there is some damage or disruption to the system.

This is similar to the buffer store in a computer, which acts as a temporary memory area. This is where data queue while waiting to be transferred between devices or between programs operating at a different speed. A good example of this is the printing buffer that can hold several pages of text while earlier pages are being printed out. If the buffer is overloaded, information is lost. Once the information has been processed and passed on, the buffer has no record of it.

The Atkinson and Shiffrin model

The most well-known and influential multi-store model was proposed by Atkinson and Shiffrin (1968) and we will consider this model in more detail.

Atkinson and Shiffrin envisaged memory as a flow of information through an information-processing system. The system is divided into a series of stages as information passes from one store to another in a fixed sequence. At each stage of the process, there are constraints in terms of **capacity**, **duration** and **encoding**.

Atkinson and Shiffrin proposed that information enters the system from the environment and first registers on the **sensory memory** store where it stays for a very brief period of time before either decaying or passing on to the short-term memory store. The short-term memory store has a very small capacity, i.e. it can only hold very small amounts of information at any one time and the so-called memory traces held here are quite fragile.

Fig. 1 *The multi-store model of memory*

They can be lost within a few seconds if they are not rehearsed (repeated), i.e. the store has a short duration. Items in the short-term memory store are usually held as sounds although other kinds of encoding are possible. If the material is sufficiently rehearsed, it is passed on to the long-term memory. Once there, it can stay for a lifetime although it can be lost through damage to the hardware (i.e. the brain) and/or through the processes of decay or interference.

The Atkinson and Shiffrin model is called a structural model because it focuses on the storage components of the memory system. However, Atkinson and Shiffrin also described some of the control processes required to manipulate and transform the information as it flows through the system. These include encoding, retrieval strategies and rehearsal. One of the most important processes for their model is rehearsal whereby information can be circulated within the short-term memory store and passed on to the long-term memory store.

Researchers such as Atkinson and Shiffrin do not dream up models from their imagination – their model arose out of research studies, which provided evidence to underpin their theory. We will now look in a bit more detail at the components and processes of their multi-store model and consider some of the evidence on which they based their ideas.

■ Sensory memory

Stimuli coming into the memory system from the external environment first register in the sensory store. This holds information for fractions of a second after the physical stimulus is no longer available. Atkinson and Shiffrin proposed three separate sensory stores to accommodate different kinds of input:

- iconic store for visual input (things we see)
- echoic store for auditory input (things we hear)
- haptic store for tactile input (things we feel/touch).

It is the iconic store that has stimulated the most research interest so we will look at that more closely. According to Baddeley (1988), the purpose of the visual sensory store is to allow us to integrate visual information so that, at a conscious level, we experience a smooth, continuous visual experience instead of a jumbled set of jerky, disconnected images. You can understand this better by thinking of what happens when we watch a cartoon film. For example, we experience an episode of a cartoon series as a continuous visual scene but what is actually being presented is a quick-fire series of still images, one after the other. We have to hold in our sensory memory the information from one image during the few milliseconds it takes before the next image is presented. In this way, we make sense of the visual presentation and our conscious mind is not aware of the infinitesimally brief moments of darkness between the successive images.

For example, take a torch with a strong beam into a dark room and turn it on. Shine the beam on to a wall and quickly swing the hand with the

■ Key terms

Encoding: the way in which information is represented in the memory store, e.g. by sound, meaning or image.

Sensory memory: a set of limited capacity, modality-specific stores that hold information for a very brief period of time.

Fig. 2 *A strip of still frames from a cartoon*

torch round in a circular motion. If your arm movement is fast enough, you should see a complete circle of light. Your visual sensory memory has stored the beginning of the circle while you are looking at the end of the circle.

Another possible function of the sensory memory is to sift through huge amounts of incoming sensory information in order to avoid overloading the system. The sensory memory holds an image of the stimuli for a few milliseconds while they are scanned to decide which ones should be given attention and passed on through the system for further processing.

What is the evidence for sensory memory?

■ ### Research study: Sperling (1960)

The classic studies on sensory memory, which would have informed Atkinson and Shiffrin, were carried out by Sperling (1960). Sperling used a chart containing three rows of letters, which he displayed for very brief exposures (50 milliseconds) to his participants. See Figure 3 for an example.

Fig. 3 *Sperling's three rows of letters stimulus*

Participants were immediately asked to recall as many of the letters as possible and could usually only recall about four or five (whole report technique). However, they frequently reported having been aware of more letters even though they could no longer recall them. Sperling decided to test this by changing his procedure slightly (partial report technique). He trained participants to distinguish between three tones. He then exposed the chart for the same amount of time (50 milliseconds) but, this time, played one of the tones as soon as the chart had disappeared. Participants were instructed to recall the top row of letters in response to a high tone, the middle row in response to a medium tone and the bottom row in response to a low tone. Under these circumstances, participants were able to recall, on average, three items from whichever row had been cued by the tone. It is important to remember that participants did not know which row they would be asked to recall until after the display had disappeared. This suggests that, at that stage, they would have been able to recall an average of three letters in any of the three rows, because an image of the whole array of letters was available in their iconic memory. In other words, the number of items recalled in any one row can be multiplied by three (the number of rows) to give the number of items the participants had actually seen during the 50-millisecond display. Sperling estimated that participants had actually seen 9 to 10 items of a possible 12 on the chart. The reason why participants can only recall four items in the whole report technique is because the image of the whole array fades during the time it takes to report back these four items. It is a bit like trying to read the credits that roll up the screen at the end of a film – while you are paying attention to one name, others are disappearing off the screen.

Methodological issues

The advantage of a laboratory experiment like this is that there is a high level of control and that it can be replicated with similar results (i.e. it is reliable). However, the stimuli used were artificial and may not reflect how we use memory in everyday circumstances (i.e. the study might lack validity).

Sperling listened to what his participants had to say at the end of his first study, i.e. that they had actually *seen* more letters than they could then recall. This led him to generate a new hypothesis and devise a new method (the partial report technique) to test it.

Ethical issues

There are no serious ethical issues in a study of this nature. However, the investigator always has to gain the consent of participants and to debrief them afterwards. In a study like this, where participants might have felt frustrated by their inability to recall all the letters, the debriefing is important as a means of reassuring people that their performance was well within the normal range.

■ **Link**

For more information about laboratory experiments, see p107.

■ **Link**

For an explanation of reliability and validity, see p92.

■ **Link**

The results of Sperling's first study led him to formulate a new hypothesis. For an explanation of hypothesis formulation, see p90.

Later studies of sensory memory have confirmed Sperling's findings and allowed the following conclusions to be drawn:

- Items remain in sensory memory for a very brief period of time – probably less than two seconds (or even less than that in the iconic store).
- Information in sensory memory is in a relatively unprocessed form.
- Information is passively registered in sensory memory – in other words, we cannot really control what enters our sensory memory. We then actively select certain items for transmission to short-term memory by paying attention to them. Only a tiny fraction of the items is passed on – the rest are lost.
- There are separate sensory stores for the different senses, e.g. vision, hearing and touch.

■ Short-term and long-term memory

The central feature of the Atkinson and Shiffrin model is the distinction between short-term memory (STM) and long-term memory (LTM) and we need to consider some of the evidence supporting this claim.

They believed that the two stores were fundamentally different in terms of:

- how long they last (duration)
- how much information they can store (capacity)
- how they store information, e.g. as sounds or images (coding)
- how information is lost (forgetting).

Their basic ideas about the differences are set out in the table below:

■ **Key terms**

Displacement: a type of forgetting where the items currently in the limited capacity STM are pushed out before being transferred to LTM to make room for incoming items.

Interference: a type of forgetting where information stored in LTM is confused with similar information.

Table 1 *Differences between STM and LTM*

	Capacity	Duration	Encoding	Forgetting
STM	Very limited (approx. 7 items)	Very limited	Mainly acoustic (by sound)	Mainly **displacement**
LTM	Unlimited	Unlimited (up to a lifetime)	Mainly semantic (by meaning)	Mainly **interference**

What is the evidence for a distinction between STM and LTM?

One technique that has often been used to investigate STM and LTM is to ask participants to study long lists of words and then to recall as many words as possible in any order – this is called a **free recall** task. The researcher then plots on a graph the relationship between where the word appeared on the original list and the likelihood of recalling the word. Psychologists using this technique have found that free recall of a list of unrelated words produces a characteristic serial position curve. What this means is that words presented at the end of the list are recalled best, followed by reasonable recall of words presented at the beginning of the list. Words in the middle of the list have the lowest recall rate.

Researchers have interpreted these findings in terms of the distinction between STM and LTM. They reasoned that people can remember the last few words in the list (the recency effect) because the words are still circulating in the STM and can be easily retrieved. Words at the beginning of the list have been rehearsed (repeated) and so have been passed into LTM and can be retrieved at the time of recall (the primacy effect). Words in the middle (asymptote) are poorly recalled because they have had little time for rehearsal and have been displaced by later items in the list.

However, the existence of the serial position curve on its own does not prove that there is a distinction between STM and LTM. Later researchers argued that, if the different sections of the serial curve represent a genuine difference between STM and LTM, it should be possible to find ways of influencing one part of the curve but not the other.

■ ### Research study: Glanzer and Cunitz (1966)

A classic experiment by Glanzer and Cunitz (1966) illustrates this so-called functional dissociation.

They gave their participants lists of words presented one at a time and then tested their free recall.

There were two conditions in their experiment:

■ In Condition 1, participants were asked to recall the words immediately after they had been presented.

■ In Condition 2, participants were given a distractor task after the words had been presented and had to count backwards in threes for 30 seconds before they were asked to recall the words.

In Condition 1, Glanzer and Cunitz found the expected serial position curve. However, in Condition 2, they found that the distractor task had disrupted the recency effect and words from the last part of the list were not well recalled.

They explained this by suggesting that the task of counting backwards in threes had displaced the last few words in the list (the recency portion) from the fragile STM but that the task had not affected the earlier words (the primacy portion) because they had already been rehearsed and passed into the robust LTM.

Methodological issues

This was a highly controlled laboratory experiment and it has been replicated many times. However, the artificiality of the task means that it might not represent how memory works in everyday life.

Participants had to undertake several trials, i.e. they had to recall more than one list in each condition and their average score was recorded. This is done to avoid unrepresentative results.

■ ### Key term

Free recall: a way of testing memory where participants can recall items from a list in any order.

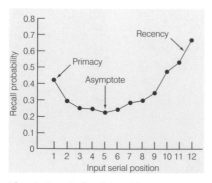

Fig. 4 *A typical serial position curve*

■ ### Link

A line graph is a good way of displaying the results of this kind of study as it clearly shows the difference between the conditions. For an explanation of graphs, see p129.

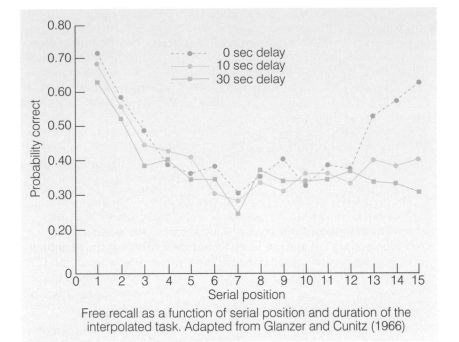

Free recall as a function of serial position and duration of the interpolated task. Adapted from Glanzer and Cunitz (1966)

Fig. 5 *Glanzer and Cunitz (1966) results*

Ethical issues

As with all studies, the investigators had to gain the informed consent of their participants and debrief them afterwards.

In a further series of experiments, Glanzer (1972) found other factors that affect one part of the serial position but not the other. For example, he found a number of factors that affected the primacy effect but not the recency effect:

- ▓ rate of presentation (the slower the presentation, the better the performance)
- ▓ age of the participant (elderly people remember fewer items than younger people)
- ▓ familiarity of the words (more familiar words are better remembered).

These are all examples of functional dissociation and provide good support for the idea that STM and LTM are separate stores. However, there are other types of evidence to consider.

Neuropsychological evidence

Some of the strongest evidence for a distinction between STM and LTM comes from the study of people who have suffered brain damage. The loss of memory among such people is usually selective, i.e. it affects one type of memory but not another.

💡 There are several case studies of people with severe memory loss, including that of Clive Wearing. Milner (1966) has reported on another famous case study of a young man known only by his initials, HM. He suffered from severe epilepsy and underwent brain surgery to remove parts of his temporal lobes and hippocampus. The operation alleviated his epilepsy but left him with severe memory deficits although his IQ remained above average. He was able to recall events in his early life but was unable to remember events for about ten years before the surgery

▓ Link

These are examples of case studies that can be very useful when an experiment would be impossible for ethical or practical reasons. See p121 for a discussion of case studies.

and could not learn or retain new information. He could remember approximately six numbers in the order they had been presented suggesting that his STM was relatively intact. However, he repeatedly read the same magazine without realising that he had read it before and was unable to recognise the psychologists who spent long periods with him. This suggests that HM had a normal STM but that his LTM was now defective and it was no longer possible for him to lay down new memories in LTM or, if he could, that he was unable to retrieve them.

Another case study provides evidence for a more unusual dissociation, i.e. an impaired STM working alongside a fully functioning LTM. Shallice and Warrington (1970) reported on the case of KF, a young man who sustained brain injuries after a motorcycle accident. He appeared to have an intact LTM in that he was able to learn new information and recall stored information. However, his STM was affected so that he had a recency effect of only one item.

Another source of evidence comes from the study of people with Alzheimer's disease. This is a serious disorder of the brain and early symptoms include severe memory impairment. Researchers have been interested in investigating some of the specialised chemicals in the brain called neurotransmitters, which are involved in brain processes. Patients with Alzheimer's disease have been found to have low levels of one of these neurotransmitters – acetylcholine – compared to controls. This suggests that acetylcholine might have an important function in memory. Drachman and Sahakian (1979) investigated this by administering a drug to a group of participants that blocks the action of acetylcholine in the brain. They then gave the participants various memory tasks that tested either LTM or STM and compared their performance with a control group. They found that the experimental group performed at normal levels on the STM tasks but significantly more poorly in the LTM task. This, again, suggests that STM and LTM work as separate stores.

Modern brain-scanning techniques such as positron emission tomography (PET) and functional magnetic resonance imaging (fMRI) scans have provided more support for the existence of two separate memory stores. Squire *et al.* (1992) found that the hippocampus is active in LTM tasks whereas areas in the pre-frontal cortex are activated for STM tasks.

We have shown that there is evidence for STM and LTM being separate stores. We now need to look at some research concerning the characteristics of the two stores described by Atkinson and Shiffrin.

■ Capacity

LTM

It is generally accepted amongst researchers that LTM has an unlimited capacity. It is possible to lose things from LTM through processes such as decay and interference but the loss does not occur because of capacity limitations. In this section, therefore, we will concentrate on STM.

STM

A central characteristic of STM, according to Atkinson and Shiffrin, is its limited storage space, i.e. its capacity. You are probably aware of the difficulty you have in trying to keep items in your immediate memory. A good example is when someone leaves you a message on your phone asking you to call them back on their mobile number. If the caller speaks very rapidly, you cannot keep up and find it impossible to note down the whole 11-digit number. It seems as if the later digits in the string are pushing out the first ones so that we cannot remember them. This type of forgetting is called displacement. Fortunately, with a phone message, you can replay it until you get it right. This replaying is a bit like the process of rehearsal where you repeat things in your head to keep them circulating in STM. However, if new information is trying to get in, this rehearsal process breaks down and you have to lose current information in order to find room for new items. You will be aware of these limitations if you try to do complicated mental arithmetic or decode complex sentences.

Try working out these problems in your head – do not write anything down or use a calculator:

1 $4 + 9 =$

2 $6 + 17 \times 3 =$

3 $7 + 2 + 8 \times 46 =$

It is likely that you had no difficulty with problem (1); problem (2) was a bit more challenging, but quite possible; the problem (3) almost certainly tested you beyond the limits of your STM.

This kind of activity demonstrates the limited capacity of STM and shows that we can only hold and manipulate a small number of items at any one time.

Psychologists have been interested in finding out exactly how big the capacity of STM is. This sounds like quite a straightforward task but, as we shall see, it seems to depend on the way it is measured.

One of the earliest systematic attempts to measure the capacity of STM was carried out in 1887 by Jacobs. He devised a method, which has since been used extensively by psychologists, called the **digit span technique**.

Jacobs found that, on average, people could recall about seven digits in this immediate **serial recall** task and his findings have been supported in many subsequent studies. George Miller wrote a famous article in 1956 called 'The Magical Number Seven, Plus or Minus Two', in which he proposed that we can hold about seven items in our STM, but that there is a range of capacity between five and nine items.

The question arises: 'What do we mean by items?' Miller believed that our immediate memory span is determined by the number of 'chunks' of information we can hold rather than the number of individual letters or numerals.

For example, read the following list of letters quickly, then cover them up and write them down in the same order as they appear on this page.

X G U W Z S P J Q L T B F M K

Now do the same with the following list

B A Q   K I B   M E P   G U J   V O F

Now do the same with the following list

B I T   K E G   S U N   L A W   T O Y

You probably found the first list impossible – there are 15 letters in the list, which is beyond the normal digit span. However, the second list, which also contains 15 letters, might have been more manageable and the third list was probably easy. What is the difference? The second list has grouped the letters into five three-letter sets. Although these groupings are not meaningful, they impose a rhythm on the list that seems to make recall easier. The third list has grouped the letters into five recognisable three-letter words. So, instead of learning 12 separate letters,

Key terms

Digit span technique: a way of measuring the capacity of STM. Participants have to repeat back strings of digits in order of presentation. The number of digits in the string is gradually increased until the participant can no longer recall the sequence of digits correctly.

Serial recall: a way of testing STM where participants are required to recall items in the order of presentation.

Link

See pp35–38 for more information on how to improve your memory.

it is possible to group them into 5 meaningful 'chunks'. This means that memory span can be increased by chunking.

Miller thought that the chunk was the basic unit in STM and that we can recall 7 +/–2 chunks of information at any one time. Other researchers have questioned this assumption and criticised Miller's term 'chunk' for being too vague. Simon (1974), for example, found that the span as measured in chunks depends on the amount of information contained in the chunk. He experimented with immediate serial recall of one-syllable, two-syllable and three-syllable words, and for two-word and eight-word phrases. He found that the span in chunks was less with larger chunks, i.e. eight-word phrases, than with smaller chunks. Glanzer and Razel (1974) used the recency effect rather than the digit span as a measure of the capacity of STM. They found that the recency effect was 2.2 items when the stimulus material consisted of single, unrelated words, but increased to 1.5 sentences (i.e. considerably more single words) when unfamiliar sentences were presented and to 2.2 proverbs when familiar proverbs (e.g. 'a stitch in time saves nine') were used.

Factors that affect the capacity of STM

It should now be clear that it is not easy to demonstrate the exact capacity of STM because it will vary depending on the nature of the material to be remembered and on certain other factors. The capacity of computer storage systems such as CD-ROMs or memory sticks can be accurately gauged because information is loaded into them in the form of basic units (e.g. the capacity of a memory stick might be 1Gb or a million 'bits' of information). There is, as yet, no way of defining a basic unit of information to be stored in human STM. It is also possible that STM is not the unitary store described by Atkinson and Shiffrin (see p19 for an account of working memory). In that case, the task of defining the capacity of STM becomes even more difficult.

There are a number of other factors that appear to affect the capacity of STM.

■ Influence of long-term memory: Cowan (2000) believes that Miller might have overestimated the number of chunks that can be held in STM. He thinks that performance on span tasks is often affected by rehearsal and long-term memory and does not reflect the capacity of 'pure' STM. He has estimated that the capacity of STM is actually four chunks when such factors are controlled. Bower and Winzenz (1969) found that digit strings that were repeated within a series of immediate memory span trials become easier for participants to recall. This suggests that the strings have been gradually rehearsed and stored in LTM, which temporarily increases the capacity of STM.

■ Reading aloud: digit span increases if participants read the digits aloud instead of reading them subvocally. Baddeley (1999, p22) suggests that this is because the digits are also then stored briefly in the echoic store (see p5), which strengthens the memory trace.

■ Pronunciation time: a number of studies have shown that the capacity of STM is determined by time constraints rather than structural limitations. Naveh-Benjamin and Ayres (1986) compared memory spans for speakers of English with speakers of other languages. They found a direct relationship (correlation) between size of digit span and pronunciation time. For example, digit span was less for speakers of Arabic because their digits take longer to pronounce than English digits. Similarly, Hitch, Halliday and Littler (1984) found that the immediate memory span of young children was related to the length of time it took

■ **Link**

For more information about correlation, see p116.

them to articulate words. Other researchers, for example Schweickert and Boruff (1986), have found that people can recall the number of items that can be articulated in 1.5 seconds (see p19 for more on working memory).

■ Individual differences: there is some evidence that individual differences affect STM capacity. For example, people who are highly anxious appear to have shorter spans (MacLeod and Donnellan, 1993).

■ Duration

STM

Whatever the problems in measuring the exact capacity of STM, it is generally accepted that it can only hold a very few items at any one time. It is also clear that STM can only hold items for a brief period of time although there has not been as much research interest in this aspect of STM. STM is a temporary store and anything we need to retain for longer periods has to be transferred to LTM. According to Atkinson and Shiffrin, the way we do this is to rehearse (or repeat) the information to ourselves. Repetition keeps the material in STM by continually reinserting it into the STM loop. Rehearsal strengthens the memory trace so that it can be lodged permanently in LTM.

■ Research study: Peterson and Peterson (1959)

Peterson and Peterson wanted to find out how long items would remain in STM without rehearsal. They presented participants with a consonant trigram (i.e. three consonants that do not form a pronounceable unit such as CXK or LDH). Participants were then asked to count backwards in threes from a specified number, e.g. 451. This was to stop them rehearsing the trigram. After intervals of 3, 6, 9, 12, 15 or 18 seconds, participants were asked to stop counting and to repeat the trigram. This procedure was repeated several times (trials) using different trigrams on each presentation.

Participants were able to recall about 80 per cent of trigrams after a 3-second interval without rehearsal but their recall became progressively worse as the time intervals lengthened until, after 18 seconds, they could recall fewer than 10 per cent correctly.

Peterson and Peterson concluded that information disappears or decays very rapidly from STM when rehearsal is prevented.

Methodological issues

This was a laboratory experiment carried out in controlled conditions. This study used a repeated measures design to avoid individual differences.

However, there are some problems of interpretation with this study:

■ Trigrams are artificial things to remember and may not be a good way of testing how we remember things in everyday life.

■ It is possible that the loss of information was more to do with capacity limitations than duration. The subsequent counting task might have pushed out (displaced) the trigram.

■ It is also possible that trigrams presented on earlier trials caused confusion (**proactive interference**) for the participants and so later trigrams are incorrectly recalled.

Link

See p109 for an explanation of repeated measures design.

Key term

Proactive interference: where things that have already been learned make it harder to learn new things.

Ethical issues

There are no serious ethical issues in this kind of study but investigators always have to gain consent from participants and to debrief them afterwards.

Factors affecting duration in STM

As discussed above with respect to capacity, the accurate measurement of the duration of STM seems to depend on other factors.

■ Rehearsal: we can extend the duration of STM by rehearsing information. For example, if we look up a phone number in a directory, we tend to repeat it over in our heads in order to hold it in our memory for long enough to dial it correctly.

■ Intention to recall: it seems to make a difference whether we are making a conscious effort to recall material or not. Sebrechts *et al.* (1989) tested serial recall for sets of three familiar English nouns. In the condition where participants were not expecting to be asked to have to remember the words, correct recall fell to 1 per cent after only four seconds.

■ Amount of information to be recalled: Murdock (1961) adopted the Peterson and Peterson technique but used either a single, three-letter word such as cat or a set of three unrelated words such as pen, hat and lid. When he used three words as the stimulus, he found the same pattern of decline in recall as in the original Peterson and Peterson study. However, when he used three letters (that formed a recognisable single word), recall was remarkably resistant to decay. Even though rehearsal had been prevented, accurate recall level was at about 90 per cent after 18 seconds. It seems, then, that the important factor is the number of chunks rather than the number of individual items, e.g. letters.

LTM

Long-term memory can hold limitless amounts of information for anything from a few minutes to almost a lifetime. It is difficult to measure the duration of LTM exactly but there is one well-known study in which Bahrick *et al.* (1975) attempted to explore the length of time memories can be retained. This study had a very complicated design so only a brief summary can be included here.

Bahrick *et al.* (1975) tested the memory of 392 graduates of an American high school for their former classmates. They used various memory tests including the recognition of classmates' pictures, matching names to pictures and recalling names with no picture cue. Participants performed remarkably well up to about 34 years although performance was better on recognition tasks than on recall tasks. There was a dip in performance on all types of memory test after 47 years but it is difficult to decide whether this deficit is due to the passage of time or to the ageing effects in the brains of older participants.

Factors affecting duration in LTM

■ Experimental techniques: people seem to be able to remember things from the distant past much better if they are given certain cues instead of being asked to recall from scratch. As you can see from the Bahrick study, accuracy increased when measured by a recognition rather than a recall test.

■ Depth of learning: people are likely to remember things for longer if they have learned it very well in the first place. Bahrick and Hall

---

■ **Link**

The researchers asked participants about their own memories and did not use artificial stimuli. This might have improved the validity of their results. See p92 for an explanation of validity.

■ **Hint**

Bahrick's study is particularly useful because it was carefully controlled and yet looked at how memory functions in real life rather than in artificial, laboratory settings.

(1991) tested long-term memory for algebra and geometry. People who had only taken maths courses up to secondary school level showed steady decline in their recall accuracy over the years. However, students who had gone on to take a higher course in maths showed high levels of accurate recall as much as 55 years later.

■ Pattern of learning: Bahrick (1987) looked at people who had learned Spanish and found that vocabulary items learned over spaced sessions were retained for longer than vocabulary learned in intensive sessions.

■ Nature of material to be learned: some types of material are retained for longer than others. Conway *et al*. (1991) tested Open University psychology students and found that certain subject topics were recalled more accurately over time. Statistics was an area that seemed to be particularly well retained possibly because it involves the acquisition of skills rather than facts.

■ Encoding

STM

When information arrives in sensory memory, it is still in its original form, e.g. as a visual image or as sound. The sensory store, as we saw earlier, has separate stores for different modalities (a modality is a particular form of sensory experience such as vision, sound or touch). Atkinson and Shiffrin envisaged STM as a unitary store, i.e. as a single storage space with no separate compartments. Psychologists have been interested in finding out what happens to the stimulus once it arrives in STM and it seems likely that it is recoded into a form that the STM can recognise and manipulate.

There are three main types of encoding used in memory:

■ acoustic coding: the sound of a stimulus

■ visual coding: the physical appearance of a stimulus

■ semantic coding: the meaning of the stimulus.

Research has shown that the main way of encoding in STM is by sound. Much of the evidence on encoding has come from studies into so-called substitution errors. These occur when people substitute a different item for a similar one on the list to be learned. The rationale for this is that people are likely to confuse items that sound alike if they are using an acoustic code, whereas they will confuse items that look similar if they are using a visual code or items that mean the same thing if they are using a semantic code.

■ Research study: Conrad (1964)

Conrad showed participants a random sequence of six consonants. He projected them in very rapid sequence on to a screen. There were two conditions in his study:

■ the letters were acoustically similar (e.g. B, G, C, T, D, V)

■ the letters were acoustically dissimilar (e.g. F, J, X, M, S, R).

Immediately after the presentation, participants were asked to write the letters down in correct serial order.

Remember that the normal digit span is about seven (see p11) so participants should have found the recall task quite easy. However, Conrad found that participants frequently made errors of recall. The majority of errors involved the substitution of a similar-

■ Link

The selection of participants can have an important effect on validity. See p98 for an explanation of sampling and p92 for validity.

Cognitive psychology

sounding letter (e.g. a V for a D). Participants found it more difficult to recall strings of letters that sounded the same than letters that sounded different. Remember, too, that the letters had been presented visually. Conrad concluded that we must convert visually presented material to an acoustic code in STM and that we then find it difficult to distinguish between words that sound the same, i.e. there is acoustic confusion.

Methodological issues

This was a well-controlled laboratory experiment. However, it used artificial stimuli – we do not have to remember strings of consonants in everyday life. He used students as his participants who might not be representative of the general population.

Ethical issues

There are no serious ethical issues in this kind of study but investigators always have to gain consent from participants and to debrief them afterwards.

His ideas were supported by Posner and Keele (1967), who showed participants pairs of letters such as B–B, B–b A–B with a very brief time delay between the two letters. Participants were simply asked to say whether the two letters had the same name or not. If we code by sound, we should be as quick responding to B–b as to B–B. However, if we code visually, we should take slightly longer to respond to B–b because we would have to translate the different symbols into their appropriate names. Posner and Keele found that people did indeed take longer to respond to B–b than B–B if the delay between the two letters was less than 1.5 seconds, but took the same amount of time if the delay was longer than 1.5 seconds. They concluded that the visual code had been stored in STM for a very brief period but that this fragile code is soon translated into an acoustic code.

LTM

Research has demonstrated that semantic coding, i.e. coding based on the meaning of the items, is the preferred method in LTM.

Research study: Baddeley (1966)

Baddeley constructed a pool of short, familiar words for each of four categories:

- acoustically similar words (e.g. mad, map, mat, cad, cap, cat)
- acoustically dissimilar words (e.g. pen, cow, pit, sup, day)
- semantically similar words (e.g. tall, high, broad, wide, big)
- semantically dissimilar words (e.g. foul, thin, late, safe, strong).

For each category, he presented a random sequence of five words and asked participants to write them down immediately after presentation in serial order. He found that the words that sounded similar were much harder to remember than words in any of the other three categories. He concluded, like Conrad, that STM codes acoustically.

Baddeley then modified his experiment to test LTM. He extended the length of the word lists from five words to ten and prevented the participants from rehearsing by interrupting them after each presentation. Each list was presented four times and then recall was tested after a 20-minute interval. Under these conditions, he found that acoustic similarity had no effect on recall but that words that were similar in meaning were poorly recalled. He concluded from this that LTM codes were mainly semantically.

Methodological issues

This was a laboratory experiment. Although still an artificial setting, Baddeley used familiar words rather than consonants (as Conrad had done).

Ethical issues

There are no serious ethical issues in this kind of study but investigators always have to gain consent from participants and to debrief them afterwards.

> ■ Link
>
> Baddeley used familiar words in all four conditions. This was a control to make sure that no single list was easier to remember. See p95 for an explanation of how to control extraneous variables.

It seems, then, that LTM uses semantic coding as its preferred method, but this is not the only type of encoding. We know from our own experience, for example, that we can easily recognise sounds such as ambulance sirens or phones ringing, which shows that we can store long-term memories acoustically. We can also easily bring to mind visual images of familiar places or people, suggesting that visual coding is also possible in LTM.

■ Strengths and weaknesses of the multi-store model

We have considered the various components of the multi-store model and looked at research evidence that has contributed to our understanding of how they work. We will now weigh up the strengths and weaknesses of the model.

The multi-store model has made an important contribution to memory research. The information-processing approach has enabled psychologists to construct testable models of memory and provided the foundation for later important work. Most modern researchers would agree that there is a basic distinction to be made between a short-term, temporary, limited-capacity store and a more robust and permanent long-term memory and, as we have seen, there is plenty of evidence to support this distinction.

However, the major problem with the model is that it is over-simplified. It is generally regarded as good scientific practice to explain things in the simplest possible way that can account for all the known facts. However, the multi-store model is too simple and fails to reflect the complexity of human memory.

For example, it takes no account of the different types of things we have to remember. It places great emphasis on the amount of information we can handle at any one time but disregards the nature of the information. Some things are easier to remember than others because they are more interesting, more relevant, funnier, etc.

The role of rehearsal in transferring material from STM to LTM is central in the multi-store model. However, there is considerable evidence that simple repetition is one of the least effective ways of passing on information. For example, Craik and Lockhart found that things are remembered better if they are processed semantically (i.e. in terms of their meaning). Kulik and Brown have described a special type of remembering called 'flashbulb memory', which is where the insignificant details surrounding highly emotional and shocking events (e.g. the destruction of

■ **Key term**

Pseudo-word: a combination of letters that sounds as though it could be an English word, but actually does not exist (e.g. nym).

✓ **Summary questions**

1 Describe what is meant by the terms sensory memory, short-term memory and long-term memory.

2 Explain how evidence from brain-damaged patients has helped to support the multi-store model.

3 Explain some of the ways in which psychologists have tried to measure the capacity of STM and explain some of the strengths and weaknesses of these methods.

4 'Peter was trying to remember the name of his first teacher at primary school without success. Then his mother managed to find an old class photo, which she showed Peter. The name of his teacher then popped into his mind.' Explain why Peter was suddenly able to remember.

5 'The multi-store model was very influential at one time but it has outlived its usefulness.' What is the evidence for this claim?

the twin towers in New York) are imprinted directly in LTM without any rehearsal. We also develop various strategies to help us remember things (see later section on improving memory, pp35–38) and the multi-store model cannot account for this.

Atkinson and Shiffrin believed that information flows through a one-way system and that STM has to process information before it reaches LTM. However, it is clear that information from LTM must sometimes be activated before certain stages of processing in STM occur. For example, consider Conrad's experiment (p15) – participants were shown the letters visually and yet they translated the visual image into an acoustic code. They can only have identified the letter 'B' as the sound 'bee' by getting this stored information from LTM. Ruchkin *et al.* (1999) measured brain activity in participants, who had been presented aurally with a set of words and **pseudo-words** and then asked to recall them in serial order. If people only process information acoustically in STM, there should be no difference in brain activity when processing words and pseudo-words. However, Ruckhin found that there were considerable differences, which suggests that semantic information stored in LTM was being used in this task.

Clinical evidence (see p9) supports the distinction between STM and LTM, but not necessarily other aspects of the multi-store model. KF, for example, had a severely impaired STM and yet his LTM appeared to work quite normally. This also suggests that the flow of information through the memory system is interactive rather than sequential as suggested by Atkinson and Shiffrin.

Much of the supporting evidence for the multi-store model comes from artificial, laboratory studies, which might not reflect how memory works in everyday life. It is sometimes possible to interpret the results of such studies in different ways. It is also sometimes the case that different experimental techniques can yield different results. For example, Brandimonte *et al.* (1992) showed that, when acoustic coding is prevented by asking participants to repeat a meaningless chant ('la-la-la') during the learning phase, visual coding can be used in STM and can, in fact, be more effective than acoustic coding.

Memory research data have accumulated that traditional multi-store models simply cannot explain. Researchers have, therefore, looked to new models in order to explain memory processes more fully.

Key points:

■ The multi-store model of memory was an influential theory of memory based on the information-processing approach.

■ Atkinson and Shiffrin proposed a structural model consisting of a series of stages: sensory, short-term and long-term memory. Information was thought to pass through these stages in a fixed sequence.

■ At each stage of the process, there are constraints in terms of capacity, duration and encoding.

■ There is a considerable body of evidence supporting the distinction between the different types of memory (i.e. sensory, short-term and long-term). Much of the evidence is based on laboratory studies but there is also important case-study research on people whose memories have been affected by disease or accident.

■ The multi-store model was important and influential when it was first proposed. However, subsequent research has revealed a number of weaknesses. The model is too simplistic and inflexible to explain fully the complexities of human memory.

The working memory model

Learning objectives:

Learning objectives:

- Understand what is meant by the concept of working memory.

- Describe the working memory model and understand the functions and limitations of its components.

- Describe and evaluate the evidence on which the working memory model is based.

- Understand the strengths and weaknesses of the model.

Key term

Dual task method: where participants are asked to carry out a primary task while also engaging in a secondary task. Performance is compared to performance on each of the tasks when done individually.

What is working memory?

In the early 1970s, there was huge interest in the topic of STM and many experimental techniques were devised to investigate it. The research became highly theoretical and laboratory based with little apparent relevance for everyday life. In addition, it was becoming clear that traditional multi-store models could not account for some of the things we know about memory.

Baddeley and Hitch (1974) decided to try and approach STM memory research in a novel way by asking the question: 'What is it for?' One feature central to Atkinson and Shiffrin's model was the idea of STM being a unitary store. Baddeley and Hitch contested this and pointed out that some of the research data undermined this idea. Specifically, they referred to the case of KF (see p10) who had a digit span of two and yet could transfer new information to his LTM. This suggested that there had been selective disruption to his STM. In other words, his digit span was impaired but other aspects of STM must have continued to function.

To test the idea that there is more than one component in STM, Baddeley and Hitch devised the **dual task method**. They asked participants to perform a reasoning task (a sentence-checking task) while simultaneously reciting aloud a list of six digits. If digit span really is a measure of maximum STM capacity, participants would be expected to show impaired performance on the reasoning task because their STM would be fully occupied with retaining the six digits. However, they found that participants made very few errors on either the reasoning or the digit span task although the speed of verifying the sentences was slightly slower than when the task was done alone.

Try this for yourself. Recite the six digit number 482917 aloud while ticking the True/False answers.

1	B is followed by A	BA	True/False
2	A is preceded by B	AB	True/False
3	A is not followed by B	BA	True/False
4	B follows A	AB	True/False
5	B does not follow A	BA	True/False
6	B is not followed by A	AB	True/False
7	A follows B	AB	True/False
8	B is not preceded by A	AB	True/False
9	A is not followed by B	BA	True/False
10	B does not precede A	AB	True/False

Baddeley and Hitch concluded that the short-term memory must have more than one component and must be involved in processes other than simple storage, e.g. reasoning, understanding and learning. They envisaged STM as a sort of workspace where a variety of operations could be carried out on both old and new memories. Crucially for the model, they concluded that two tasks can be carried out simultaneously in STM provided that they are being dealt with by

■ **Hint**

The working memory model does not deny the existence of sensory memory or long-term memory but it focuses on explaining STM.

different parts of the memory system. They envisaged LTM as a more passive store that maintains previously learned material for use by the STM when needed. They formulated their ideas into the working memory model.

💡 The components of the working memory model

According to Baddeley and Hitch, working memory is a complex and flexible system comprised of three main components.

■ There is a supervisory component called the central executive that has overall control. The central executive has limited capacity but can process information from any sensory system, i.e. vision, hearing, somatic sensation (touch), taste or olfaction (smell). It has responsibility for a range of important control processes, which include setting task goals, monitoring and correcting errors, starting the rehearsal process, switching attention between tasks, inhibiting irrelevant information, retrieving information from LTM, switching retrieval plans and coordinating the activity needed to carry out more than one processing task at a time. This core component is supported by two 'slave' systems, which can be used as storage systems, thereby freeing up some of its own capacity to deal with more demanding information-processing tasks. The slave systems have separate responsibilities and work independently of one another.

■ The phonological loop (sometimes called 'the inner voice') is a limited-capacity, temporary storage system for holding verbal information in a speech-based form.

■ The visuo-spatial sketchpad (sometimes called 'the inner eye') is a limited-capacity, temporary memory system for holding visual and/or spatial information.

■ Baddeley and colleagues (Baddeley and Logie, 1999) have refined aspects of the working memory model since it was first formulated in the 1970s. The phonological loop now consists of a passive storage system called the phonological store, which is linked to an active rehearsal system called the 'articulatory loop' whereby words can be maintained by **subvocal repetition**. Similarly, the visuo-spatial sketchpad consists of a passive visual store called the 'visual cache', which is linked to an active 'inner scribe' that acts as a rehearsal mechanism (see Figure 6).

■ **Key term**

Subvocal repetition: repeating something 'under your breath' or mentally so it's not said out loud.

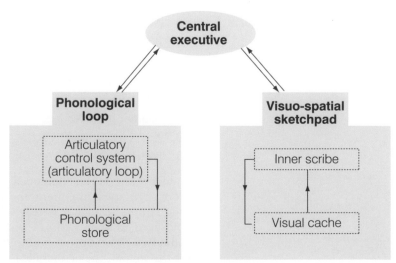

Fig. 6 *Phonological loop/model of working memory*

Evidence for the phonological loop

Research study: Baddeley, Thomson and Buchanan (1975)

The researchers gave visual presentations of word lists for very brief exposures and then asked participants to write them down in serial order. In one condition, the lists consisted of five words taken from a pool of familiar, one-syllable English words such as harm, wit, twice. In the second condition, the five words came from a list of polysyllabic words, e.g. organisation, university, association. Average correct recall over several trials showed a marked superiority for the short words. They called this the 'word length effect' and concluded that the capacity of the loop is determined by the length of time it takes to say words rather than by the number of items. They estimated this time to be 1.5 seconds.

Methodological issues

This was a laboratory experiment using a repeated measures design. It was well-controlled. However, one possible criticism is that longer words are simply less familiar than shorter words and are, therefore, harder to recall.

Ethical issues

There are no serious ethical issues in this kind of study but investigators always have to gain consent from participants and to debrief them afterwards.

Baddeley and his colleagues produced more evidence for an articulatory loop when they investigated the word length effect under conditions of **articulatory suppression**. They found that the word length effect disappeared (i.e. short words were recalled no better than long words). This suggests that the advantage in recalling short over long words depends critically on having a verbal rehearsal system, i.e. the articulatory loop. If this loop is filled up with irrelevant material i.e. 'la-la-la', then it seems likely that short and long words are being processed elsewhere, probably in the central executive.

Evidence for the visuo-spatial sketchpad

Like the phonological loop, the visual store also has limited capacity, although you need to remember that the limits of the two stores are

Key term

Articulatory suppression: a participant is given a task that would usually make use of the articulatory loop but they are simultaneously asked to repeat aloud a meaningless chant, e.g. 'la-la-la'.

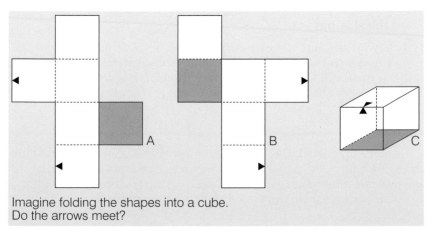

Imagine folding the shapes into a cube.
Do the arrows meet?

Fig. 7 *Shepard and Feng (1972)*

Cognitive psychology

independent. If you imagine trying to plan a room design on a small piece of paper, you are likely to make errors because you run out of space and do not represent the problem accurately. This is similar to the sketchpad.

There is a considerable body of research on the topic of visual imagery (see also the section on improving memory on pp35–38). One early experiment by Shepard and Feng (1972) used shapes such as those shown in Figure 7. Participants were asked to imagine folding these flat shapes to form a cube with the grey area as the base and then to decide whether, in the finished cube, the arrows would meet head on. They found that the time taken to make the decision was systematically related to the number of folds that would have been required if the participants had actually been doing the folding. In other words, visual images work in very similar ways to real-life perception.

It is believed that the visuo-spatial sketchpad is used in tasks like these for the temporary storage and manipulation of visual patterns and spatial movement. If this is the case, people are likely to find it difficult to do two tasks simultaneously if they both require the services of the visuo-spatial sketchpad.

Fig. 8 *Baddeley* et al. *(1973) stimulus*

Research study: Baddeley, Grant, Wight and Thomson (1973)

Baddeley *et al.* (1973) investigated this by giving participants a simple tracking task (following a spot of light with a pointer as it moved round a circular path) while carrying out a simultaneous visual imagery task. They had to imagine looking at an angular block capital such as H, T, F and E.

Participants were asked to hold the image in their heads and then, starting at the bottom left-hand corner, to respond to each angle as a 'yes' if it included the bottom or top line of the letter and as a 'no' if it did not. See Figure 8 for an example.

Participants had enormous difficulty in tracking the spot of light and accurately classifying the corners. This seems to be because the two tasks were competing for the same limited resources of the visuo-spatial sketchpad. This conclusion is supported by the finding that participants could successfully carry out the tracking task at the same time as performing a verbal task.

Methodological issues

This was a highly controlled laboratory experiment although the task was rather artificial. The investigators used a repeated measures design to eliminate the effects of individual differences.

Ethical issues

As with all studies, the investigators had to gain consent from their participants and to debrief them afterwards. Participants might have felt frustrated at being unable to complete both tasks effectively and it is important that they were given reassurance that this is perfectly normal.

■ Link

See p109 for an explanation of research designs.

It has been suggested (Logie, 1995) that the visual cache stores information about visual form and colour and that the inner scribe processes spatial and movement information. Klauer and Zhao (2004) supported this idea by asking participants to carry out one of two primary tasks:

■ a visual task
■ a spatial task.

At the same time as doing one of these tasks, they were asked to do either:

■ a spatial **interference task**
■ a visual interference task or
■ no secondary task (control condition).

They found that performance of the spatial task was much poorer for people who were simultaneously carrying out the spatial interference task than for people who were doing the visual interference task and vice versa.

Studies using positron emission tomography (PET) scans have also provided evidence for separate spatial and visual systems. There appears to be more activity in the left half of the brain of people carrying out visual working memory tasks but more in the right half of the brain during spatial tasks.

Evidence for the central executive

The central executive has a critical role in attention, planning and coordination, and is the most important and most flexible component of working memory. Baddeley himself accepts that this complexity 'makes it considerably harder to investigate' than the two slave systems (Baddeley, 1999, p67) and there is much less research evidence on the central executive. Research that has been carried out tends to focus on the different functions of the central executive (see p20).

For example, Baddeley (1996) investigated the functions attributed to the central executive of selective attention and switching retrieval plans. He asked participants to generate random strings of digits by pressing numbered keys on a keyboard.

Try this yourself. Think of a sequence of eight digits that show no systematic pattern. This is not as easy as it first seems because you have to pay close attention in order to avoid some kind of pattern emerging.

This task was carried out on its own or simultaneously with one of the following:

■ reciting the alphabet
■ counting from 1
■ alternating between letters and numbers (i.e. A 1 B 2 C 3 D 4 E 5 etc.).

The generated digit string became considerably less random in Condition 3 when participants were having to switch from alphabet to numbers at the same time.

Baddeley concluded that both the random number generation task and the alternation task were competing for the same central executive resources.

There have also been studies investigating the regions of the brain that are activated during central executive processing. Bunge *et al.* (2000), for example, gave participants two tasks to do either simultaneously or on their own. Under dual task conditions, which involve greater input for the central executive than single task conditions, there was significantly greater activation of the pre-frontal cortex.

■ Strengths and weaknesses of the working memory model

This model has been extremely influential and most cognitive psychologists now use the term working memory in preference to the

Cognitive psychology

Key points:

- The working memory model was proposed by Baddeley and Hitch as a way of explaining some of the research findings that could not be accounted for by the multi-store model.

- Working memory is essentially a multi-component short-term memory system. It consists of a central executive, which is a supervisory system in overall control, and two slave systems called the phonological loop and the visuo-spatial sketchpad.

- Evidence for the distinction between the components comes from studies based on the dual task technique where participants are asked to do tasks simultaneously and performance is then compared to performance when each task is undertaken alone.

- The model continues to be very influential and has a number of practical applications.

- Working memory can account for much of the research evidence into memory, but it is still not the full explanation and work continues to be carried out to refine the model.

✓ **Summary questions**

6 Explain why the case study of KF poses problems for the multi-store model.

7 Outline one study that has provided evidence for the visuo-spatial sketchpad.

8 Explain why researchers now think that there are separate spatial and visual systems within the sketchpad.

9 'The central executive is both the most important part of the working memory and, in some ways, its weakest link.' Explain what is meant by this statement.

10 Students often claim that they can take in programmes on TV and do homework at the same time. Using the working memory model, explain why this is not really possible.

---

term STM. It is a much more plausible model than the multi-store model because it explains STM in terms of both temporary storage and active processing. It also incorporates verbal rehearsal as just one optional process within the articulatory loop instead of being the sole means of transferring information as suggested by Atkinson and Shiffrin.

It is possible to apply the model to previous research data, e.g. the acoustic confusion effect, digit span etc. (see p11) and reinterpret it within the framework of working memory. It can also account for findings that are difficult for multi-store models to explain, e.g. some of the selective memory deficits that have been found in brain-damaged patients such as KF (see p10).

While the multi-store models are structural models, there is an attempt in the working memory model to explain how the memory functions. Baddeley *et al.* (1998) have presented evidence that the phonological loop, for example, plays a key role in the development of reading and that the phonological loop is not operative in some children with dyslexia. While it seems to be less crucial for fluent, adult readers, it still has an important role in helping to comprehend complex text. It also helps in the learning of new spoken vocabulary.

It can account for individual differences in memory processing. Turner and Engle (1989) devised a test to measure the capacity of working memory. They asked participants to hold a list of words in memory while simultaneously working out mental arithmetic problems. The number of words correctly recalled in a subsequent test was called the 'working memory span'. This measure of working memory capacity has been shown in a number of studies (Engle, Kane and Tuholski, 1999) to be linked to the ability to carry out various cognitive tasks such as reading comprehension, reasoning, spatial navigation, spelling, note-taking, etc. It has also been found that there can be individual differences within the components of working memory. For example, Shah and Miyake (1996) have shown that an individual can score high on spatial working memory yet low on verbal working memory and vice versa.

Similarly, the working memory model has been applied to various real-life settings. Because there is such a high correlation between working memory span and performance on various tasks, it has been suggested that working memory capacity might be used as a measure of suitability for certain jobs. Specifically, there have been investigations into its use as a recruitment tool for the US air force (Kyllonen and Christal, 1990).

However, working memory models do not offer a complete understanding of how memory works. The exact role played by the central executive remains slightly unclear and other researchers (e.g. Shah and Myake, 1996) have questioned whether it can be a single component or whether there are separate verbal and spatial working memory systems. Cowan (1998) has suggested that, in order to explain abilities such as text comprehension, working memory should also encompass some kind of long-term memory activation. Berz (1995) has also criticised the model for failing to account for musical memory because we are able to listen to instrumental music without impairing performance on other acoustic tasks.

Chapter summary

Cognitive psychology

Further reading and weblinks

A.D. Baddeley, *Your Memory: A User's Guide*, Carlton Books (2004)

This covers many of the topics covered in the two memory chapters and is written in a very accessible style.

A.D. Baddeley, *Essentials of Human Memory*, Psychology Press (1999)

This contains an overview of memory research and theory and is aimed at undergraduates but written in a way that should be accessible for A Level students.

D. Wearing, *Forever Today – A Memoir of Love and Amnesia*, Doubleday (2005)

This is an interesting book about the musician Clive Wearing who has severe memory loss.

www.psyonline.org.uk

This is a web resource for students and teachers of A Level psychology that is frequently modified and updated. It contains useful material on memory.

www.bbc.co.uk

The BBC Science and Nature: Human Body and Mind website is also a changing site, which has information about memory and various memory tests.

Links

For more about repeated measure design experiments, see p109.

For more on ethical issues, see p100.

For more on graphs and how to plot data, see p129.

- Early models of memory based on the information-processing approach were called multi-store models and focused on the structural aspects of memory.

- The most well-known of these models was proposed by Atkinson and Shiffrin. It consisted of a set of limited-capacity modality-specific sensory stores; a limited capacity short-term memory with a few seconds' duration; and a limitless long-term memory.

- The most important control process was thought to be rehearsal by which information was transferred from STM to LTM.

- There is considerable evidence supporting the distinction between STM and LTM.

- The multi-store model was important and had a major impact on memory research but the model is now outdated. Its accounts of both STM and LTM are oversimplified and its emphasis on the role of rehearsal is now known to be exaggerated.

- Baddeley's working memory model is the most influential recent explanation of how memory works. He has provided both a structural and functional model. He has replaced the idea of a unitary short-term memory with a multi-component, flexible memory system where rehearsal is simply one optional process.

- There is considerable research evidence to support the different components of the working memory model. However, it does not offer a complete explanation and the model is being regularly updated to accommodate new research findings.

How science works: practical activity

Try to demonstrate the primacy and recency effect for yourself. Ask other people in your class if they will act as participants (informed consent and right to withdraw are potential ethical issues here). Draw up five lists with 20 words in each list. Read each list out loud to your participants and, after each list, ask the participants to write down the words they heard in any order (i.e. a free recall task). For each list, count the number of words participants recalled correctly and note the serial position of the word. Then plot the results on a graph and see if you have demonstrated the serial position curve (see p8). Now relate your findings to the multi-store model of memory.

Things you will need to think about are: What kind of words should you use? Why do you need to give participants more than one list of words? How should you read out the words? What controls do you need to put in place?

You could go on to design an experiment to investigate whether delay in recall reduces the recency effect. Think carefully about the hypothesis, how to operationalise the variables, the investigation design, sampling and control of extraneous variables. You could use the investigation planning form on p104 to ensure that you have considered all the main issues.

When you have collected the data, summarise your findings, discuss your findings and outline your conclusions. In your discussion you should consider the methodology and consider how far the findings support memory theory and studies.

Eyewitness testimony

Learning objectives:

- Understand what is meant by eyewitness testimony (EWT).

- Be aware of some of the factors that affect the accuracy of EWT.

- Understand the impact of misleading information on EWT.

- Describe the cognitive interview technique and understand its rationale.

- Describe and evaluate evidence that underpins our understanding of EWT.

Key terms

Eyewitness testimony (EWT): the evidence given in court or in police investigations by someone who has witnessed a crime or an accident.

Leading question: a question phrased in such a way as to prompt a particular kind of answer. 'Was the man wearing a hat?' is an open question whereas 'What colour was the man's hat?' is a leading question since it suggests that the man was actually wearing a hat.

Link

We will return to this when we consider the role of the cognitive interview on p32.

As we have seen in the previous chapter, memory research can have valuable applications to everyday life. One type of memory that has particular relevance for real life is **eyewitness testimony (EWT)**. Juries appear to place great reliance on EWT as do British police officers according to a survey carried out by Kebbel and Milne (1998). However, there is a considerable amount of research evidence to suggest that this faith in the accuracy of EWT is misplaced.

Fruzzetti *et al*. (1992) have suggested that thousands of people are probably wrongly convicted every year on the basis of inaccurate EWT. Wells *et al*. (1998) have reported on 40 cases in the US where individuals convicted on the basis of EWT have since been cleared using DNA evidence. Even more alarming is the fact that five of these wrongly convicted individuals had been sentenced to death and were awaiting execution.

One of the foremost researchers in the field of EWT is Elizabeth Loftus. She and her colleagues have carried out extensive research over the last 30 years and have found that EWT is not always accurate and is vulnerable to many different types of influence.

The effects of misleading information on the accuracy of EWT

One of the main factors affecting the accuracy of memory for an event seems to be what happens after the event has taken place. The memories laid down at the time seem to be quite fragile and subject to distortion by post-event information. It appears that misinformation can introduce serious errors into eyewitnesses' recall of the event. Loftus (1992) called this 'misinformation acceptance' where people accept misleading information after an event and absorb it into their memory for the actual event. There is a greater tendency to accept post-event information in this way as the time since the event increases. This has important implications for the ways in which the police and lawyers question individuals in criminal investigations.

Loftus and her colleagues have typically used an experimental technique where participants are shown a film of an event such as a road traffic accident. They are then exposed to some kind of post-event information – this often takes the form of **leading questions** – and they are then tested for their memory of the original event.

False information given to witnesses after the event can serve to change the original memory by removing some elements and inserting others.

Research study: Loftus (1975)

Loftus showed participants a film of the events leading up to a car accident. After they had seen the film, participants were divided into a control group and an experimental group. The control group was asked questions consistent with what they had actually seen ('How fast was the white sports car going when it passed the Stop sign?'), whereas the experimental group was asked a question that included misleading information (How fast was the white sports car going when it passed the barn while travelling along the country road?'). There had been a Stop sign in the original film but no barn. All the participants were then asked more questions about the accident. Seventeen per cent of the participants in the experimental group reported seeing a barn in the original film but only 3 per cent of the control group made this error. Loftus concluded that some of the participants given the misleading post-event information had actually absorbed this with their original memory for the event and now really believed they had seen a barn.

Methodological issues

This was a controlled laboratory experiment. Loftus used realistic material, i.e. film footage of a car accident. However, the situation was still artificial because participants were aware that they had to pay attention. In a real-life eyewitness testimony incident, witnesses would not be pre-prepared.

Some critics of Loftus' studies have said that her participants were subject to demand characteristics. However, Loftus devised a new experiment to refute this criticism (see below).

Ethical issues

Investigators are always expected to obtain consent from their participants. However, in this case, Loftus could not obtain *fully informed consent* because she could not reveal in advance that she was going to ask misleading questions. Deception should normally be avoided in scientific studies but is sometimes necessary to avoid participants guessing the hypothesis. Where deception is used, debriefing is particularly important.

Researchers also have to avoid exposing participants to psychological harm. It could be distressing for participants to witness a car accident (although in this study, the accident was a minor one with no personal injuries).

It could be argued that there is no real change to the original memory, but that participants simply alter what they say, perhaps as result of demand characteristics. To test this idea, Loftus (1980) offered to reward participants with money if they could correctly recall details from a film of an accident. One group saw a film involving a pedestrian being knocked over after a car had stopped at a Stop sign. The other group saw the same incident except that the car had stopped at a Yield sign (the American equivalent of 'Give Way').

Two days later, participants were given a set of questions about the accident, one of which included some misleading information. In this critical question, participants who had seen the Stop sign in the film were misled by a reference to a Yield sign and vice versa. Loftus then asked all the participants to look at pairs of slides and point out, in each case, which one had been part of the original film. She divided up the participants into four groups:

1 offered no monetary reward
2 offered \$1 for each correct answer

■ **Hint**

Research into EWT has obvious real-life applications. However, Loftus's experimental technique does not exactly mimic real-life situations. In a genuine situation, onlookers are not expecting anything to happen and are, therefore, not paying attention in the way they would in an experimental set-up. They are also unlikely to be as emotionally affected by the experience as they would be by a real-life crime/accident.

■ **Link**

For an explanation of demand characteristics, see p96.

■ **Link**

For a more detailed discussion of ethical issues see p100.

AQA **Examiner's tip**

Be careful when you are reporting the results of such studies. Note that not all of the misled group were fooled by the post-event information.

Fig. 1 *The key difference in the visual materials used by Loftus*

3 offered $5 for each correct answer

4 $25 offered to the person in the group who scored the most correct answers.

She stressed the importance of giving correct answers.

Loftus found that, in spite of the financial incentive, over 70 per cent of the participants made an error on the crucial question in line with the misleading information they had been fed. This suggests that their original memory had been altered as a result of the misleading post-event information.

Interestingly, there do seem to be subtle differences in the accounts of people who have been misled and those who have not. Schooler *et al.* (1986) carried out a similar study using pairs of slides. They asked participants not just to identify the slide they had seen in the original presentation, but also to give more descriptive details. They found that people who had actually seen a Stop sign were able to give a far more detailed description of the scene than people who had been misled. This suggests that real events are associated with much richer perceptual detail than imagined events.

In other studies, Loftus and colleagues have shown that quite minor differences in the wording of a question can influence witness recall. For example, Loftus and Zanni (1975) showed participants a brief film clip of a car accident and then asked a series of questions. Half the participants were asked whether they had seen *'a'* broken headlight and the other half were asked if they had seen *'the'* broken headlight. Although there was no broken headlight in the film, 17 per cent of people asked about 'the' broken headlight reported seeing one as opposed to only 7 per cent of the group asked about 'a' broken headlight.

Similarly, Loftus and Palmer (1974) showed participants a film of a car accident and then asked them a series of questions about events leading up to the accident. One crucial question concerned the speed of the car on impact. One group was asked 'How fast were the cars going when they hit each other?' Other groups were asked the same question, but, in each case, the verb was changed to either 'smashed', 'bumped', 'collided' or 'contacted'. The verb used significantly affected speed estimates – 'smashed' produced the highest estimate and 'contacted' produced the lowest estimate. A week later, when questioned again, participants who had been asked the 'smashed' version of the question were more likely to report having seen broken glass at the scene of the accident, even though there had been none.

■ Other factors affecting accuracy of EWT

There are several other factors that seem to affect the accuracy of EWT. One simple reason that people often have poor memories for accidents or criminal incidents is that they do not register the information in the first place. In real life, unlike in staged laboratory experiments, people are usually not expecting such things to happen and are just not paying attention. Their testimony is then often distorted because they fill in the gaps in their memory with preconceptions. We have considered the effects of post-event information but EWT also seems to be susceptible to previously learned material. A very early memory researcher called Frederick Bartlett identified the idea of reconstructive memory in which, instead of storing an exact replica of events, we blend in elements of our own knowledge and experience to make it more memorable. This is called a schema.

Research study: List (1986)

List applied this idea to EWT by drawing up a list of elements that might occur during a shoplifting scenario. She asked people to rate these events in terms of how likely they were to occur in a typical shoplifting incident. She then compiled a video showing eight different shoplifting incidents and included some elements that people had rated as high probability and some that people had rated as low probability. She then showed the video to a new set of participants and asked them, a week later, to recall what they had seen. She found that participants were more likely to recall high probability events than low probability events and that they often reported seeing high probability elements that had not actually been included in the video at all.

Methodological issues

This was a laboratory-based experiment, but List took trouble to try to make her video realistic. This is, however, not the same as a real-life incident where witnesses would not be expecting anything to happen.

List used a pilot study to find out what elements people most commonly associate with shoplifting.

Ethical issues

As with any study, List needed to obtain the consent of her participants and to debrief them afterwards.

Link

See p106 for an explanation of pilot studies.

Imagine you walked into your bank one day when a robbery takes place. Just jot down the images you have in your mind when you conjure up the scene. This is your 'bank robbery schema'.

Tuckey and Brewer (2003) found that most people think the following:

- bank robbers are male
- they wear some kind of disguise
- they wear dark clothes
- they demand money from the cashiers
- they have a getaway car waiting outside the bank
- the getaway car has a driver sitting in it.

When they showed people a video of a staged bank hold-up, the participants had better recall for elements of the film that conformed to their schema than to elements that did not.

More recently, Lindsay *et al*. (2004) read accounts to participants of either a palace burglary or a school field trip to a palace. On the next day, all the participants were shown a video of a museum burglary and then asked to recall events from the video. Participants who had previously heard the account of the palace burglary made more errors in recall than people who had heard the account of the school trip. This suggests that memory for events can be distorted by previous knowledge of a similar topic.

We will now consider some of the other factors that seem to influence our recall for events.

Anxiety

There is conflicting evidence about the effect of stress and anxiety on witness recall. Laboratory-based studies have generally shown impaired

Cognitive psychology

recall in people who have witnessed particularly unpleasant or anxiety-inducing situations. In a study by Loftus and Burns (1982), some participants were shown a particularly violent version of a crime in which a boy was shot in the face. These participants had significantly impaired recall for events running up to the violent incident. Loftus (1979) also reported on a phenomenon known as the 'weapon effect'. Participants were asked to sit outside a laboratory where they thought they were hearing genuine exchanges between people inside the laboratory. In one condition, they heard an amicable discussion about an equipment failure. A man with greasy hands then came out of the laboratory holding a pen. In the other condition, they heard a hostile discussion, followed by the sound of breaking glass and overturned furniture. A man then emerged from the laboratory holding a knife covered in blood. Participants were then given 50 photos and asked to identify the man who had come out of the laboratory. People who had witnessed the peaceful scene were more accurate in recognising the man than people who had witnessed the more violent scene. Loftus believed that the anxiety elicited by the weapon (i.e. the blood-stained knife) narrowed the focus of attention for the witness and took attention away from the face of the man.

However, such laboratory studies might not reflect what happens in real-life events. Christianson and Hubinette (1993) reported that in real incidents involving high levels of stress, memory can be accurate, detailed and long lasting. They carried out a survey among 110 people, who had witnessed between them 22 genuine bank robberies. Some of these people had been bystanders in the bank at the time of the hold-ups while others had been directly threatened by the robbers. The victims, i.e. the people who had been subjected to the greatest anxiety, showed more detailed and accurate recall than the onlookers.

Age of witness

When we talk about EWT, we probably usually have adult witnesses in mind. However, in some court cases, often those dealing with sensitive issues such as abuse, quite young children have to act as witnesses. Psychologists have been interested in finding out if the same factors that affect accuracy in adults also operate in children.

Witnesses are sometimes called upon to identify a criminal in an identity parade and they are often reluctant to make a positive identification. Children have been found to be more willing than adults to make a positive identification but they are often of the wrong person (Dekle *et al.*, 1996).

Children also seem to be more susceptible than adults to absorbing post-event information into their original memory representation.

Hint

This shows the importance of collecting data from real, naturally occurring events where possible. Laboratory simulations cannot, for ethical reasons, reproduce the levels of stress generated by real events and are unlikely to have the same impact as real events.

Research study: Poole and Lindsay (2001)

Poole and Lindsay engaged children aged three to eight in a science demonstration. The parents of the children then read them a story, which contained some of the elements of the science demonstration but also included novel information. The children were then questioned about the science demonstration and it was found that they had incorporated much of the new information (i.e. from the parents' story) into their original memory. In another phase of the experiment, the children were asked to think very carefully about where they had got their information from (this is called source monitoring) and some of the older children then revised their account of the science demonstration and extracted the post-event information. However, the younger children did not seem able to do this. This has important implications for measuring the accuracy of small children's testimony since they seem very poor at source monitoring.

Methodological issues

This was an experiment but more difficult to eliminate extraneous variables than one using artificial stimuli in a highly controlled laboratory setting.

Investigators have to be particularly careful when using children, particularly those as young as 3 and 4 to make sure they understand instructions and that they are paying attention.

Ethical issues

There are particular factors to be taken into account when using young children who may not be able to give informed consent on their own behalf. Parents must give informed consent but, in this case, it was helpful that the parents were involved as well and so the children were with familiar people and less susceptible to investigator effects.

■ Link

See p96 for an explanation of investigator effects.

It seems to be the case that EWT becomes less accurate over time and that this decline is more marked in children. Flin *et al.* (1992) questioned children and adults one day after an incident and then again five months later. There were no differences in the amount and accuracy of recall after a single day but there was significant forgetting in the children after five months. This is very important given the long delays that often occur between a crime being committed and the subsequent court proceedings.

In a review of child witness research, Gordon *et al.* (2001) concluded that young children can provide detailed and accurate witness statements, but that they are particularly susceptible to suggestion and their accounts should be viewed with caution. Davies (1994), however, believes that some of the differences between child and adult witnesses have been overstated and that that children can provide very valuable testimony provided care is taken in the interviewing process.

There is also some evidence that elderly people are more prone to errors of recall than younger adults. Yarmey (1984) found that, when asked questions about a staged event, 80 per cent of elderly participants compared to 20 per cent of younger adults failed to mention that the attacker had a knife in his hand. Cohen and Faulkner (1989) showed a film of a kidnapping to groups of middle-aged and elderly participants. They then read a narrative account of the scene they had just witnessed. For half the participants, the narrative account was consistent with what they had seen in the film and for the other half the narrative contained some misleading information. In a subsequent recall test, elderly participants were found to have been much more susceptible to the effects of misleading information.

Consequentiality

It is clear from our discussion so far that much of the research into EWT has been carried out in laboratory conditions. However well the studies are controlled, participants are usually aware that they are in an artificial situation and that their responses will not have serious consequences for anybody. Foster *et al.* (1994) tried to see whether witnesses were more likely to be accurate if they believed that their evidence would influence a conviction. Participants watched a video of a bank robbery and were then asked to pick out the robbers from an identity parade. Half the participants were told that it was a genuine robbery and that their responses would influence the trial, while the others were led to believe that the film was a simulation. Participants were more accurate in the condition where they thought their testimony would have real consequences. This study could also be criticised for artificiality since it is very difficult in an experiment to make people believe that their testimony will have genuine importance. However, it is another indication that factors operating in real-life situations might be rather different from those in experimental situations.

Individual differences

Research has shown pretty conclusively that EWT is subject to all sorts of factors that reduce its accuracy. However, in all the studies we have discussed so far, it should be clear to you that not all participants have been adversely affected by misleading information, anxiety, etc.

Some people simply appear to be more susceptible to misinformation than others. It is not entirely clear why this should be so, but Tomes and Katz (1997) have suggested that people who are more likely to accept misinformation share the following characteristics:

- they have generally poorer recall for the event (i.e. not just the elements associated with misinformation)
- they score high on measures of imagery vividness
- they have high scores on measures of empathy (i.e. they are good at identifying with the mood of other people).

It also seems to be the case that people resist misleading information if it is blatantly incorrect. Loftus (1979) gave participants a set of slides that showed a red purse being stolen from a handbag. They were later given an account of the theft that included several errors including the 'fact' that the purse was brown. In a subsequent recall test, all but two of the participants resisted the misinformation about the colour of the purse although they were influenced by misinformation about less central elements of the theft. Loftus concluded that memory for information that is particularly striking or salient at the time is less susceptible to the effects of misinformation than memory for more peripheral details.

How to improve the accuracy of EWT

The cognitive interview technique

Because of the importance of EWT within the legal system and the serious repercussions when it goes wrong, cognitive psychologists have tried to develop methods for improving the accuracy of EWT. One suggestion is to improve the ways in which witnesses are questioned by police. Fisher *et al.* (1987) studied real interviews by experienced detective officers in Florida over a four-month period. They found that witnesses were frequently bombarded with a series of brief, direct and close-ended questions aimed to elicit facts. However, the sequencing of these questions often seemed to be out of sync with the witnesses' own mental representation of the event. Witnesses were often interrupted and not allowed to talk freely about their experiences. Fisher felt that these interruptions were unhelpful because they broke the concentration of the witnesses and also encouraged shorter answers with less detail.

On the basis of research such as this, Geiselman *et al.* (1985) developed the cognitive interview technique as a more effective tool for police investigators.

They identified four principles they believed would enhance accurate recall:

Table 1 *The main techniques used in the cognitive interview*

The cognitive interview	Instructions to witness
Context reinstatement (CR)	Mentally reinstate the context of the target event. Recall the scene, the weather, what you were thinking and feeling at the time, the preceding events, etc.
Report everything (RE)	Report every detail you can recall even if it seems trivial.
Recall from changed perspective (CP)	Report the episode in several different temporal orders moving backwards and forwards in time.
Recall in reverse order (RO)	Try to describe the episode as it would have been seen from different viewpoints, not just your own..

These techniques are all designed to enhance retrieval of the original memory. Although this kind of detail might seem trivial and poorly related to the actual witnessed event, it is designed to provide extra cues that might help to jog witnesses' memory for more central details. Subsequent research led to a version of the technique called the 'enhanced cognitive interview'. After looking at current police practice through detailed analysis of taped interviews, Fisher *et al.* (1987) suggested adding a few extra features. For example, they recommended that the interviewer should minimise distractions, actively listen to the witness, ask open-ended questions, pause after each response, avoid interruption, encourage the use of imagery, adapt their language to suit the witness and to avoid any judgemental comments.

Geiselman *et al.* (1985) tested participants by showing them videos of a simulated crime and then testing different groups with a cognitive interview, a standard police interview or an interview under the influence of hypnosis. They found that the cognitive interview elicited more information from the participants than either of the other two methods. A number of subsequent studies have confirmed these findings although Koehnken *et al.* (1999) found that witnesses questioned using the cognitive interview also recalled more incorrect information than those questioned using a standard technique. This is probably because the cognitive interview procedure elicits more information overall than other procedures.

Fisher *et al.* (1990) have also demonstrated the effectiveness of the cognitive interview technique in real police settings in Miami. They trained detectives to use the enhanced cognitive interview techniques with genuine crime witnesses and found that its use significantly increased the amount of information recalled. More recently, Kebbel *et al.* (1999) carried out a survey of police officers in the UK and found that there was quite widespread use of the cognitive interview. However, while officers generally found it useful, they expressed some concern about the amount of incorrect recall generated and the amount

Cognitive psychology

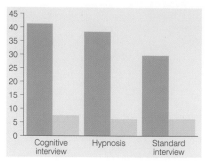

Fig. 2 *Geiselman* et al. *(1985) results. The number of correct (■) and incorrect (■) statements made by witnesses under three different interview conditions*

of time it took to complete an enhanced cognitive interview. In practice, it seemed that the officers were using the RE and CR instructions but rarely used the CP and RO instructions.

Psychologists have tried to test these police perceptions that certain elements of the cognitive interview are more useful than others. Milne and Bull (2002), for example, tested all the cognitive interview procedures either singly or in combination. They found that all four of the procedures used singly produced more recall from witnesses than standard interview techniques. However, the most effective combination appeared to be the use of CR and RE instructions, which is in line with what practising police officers had suspected.

One area where the cognitive interview has not proved particularly successful is in the questioning of young children. Geiselman (1999) reviewed a number of studies and concluded that children under the age of six years actually reported events slightly less accurately in response to cognitive interview techniques. This is probably because they find the instructions difficult to understand. The cognitive interview can be used quite effectively for children aged from about eight years upwards.

On balance, the cognitive interview technique has proved very useful in increasing the amount and the accuracy of eyewitness statements.

Key points:

■ Memory research can have very valuable applications to everyday life. One such application is eyewitness testimony (EWT). Police officers and juries attach great importance to EWT but psychological research has shown that it is often unreliable.

■ A leading researcher in this field is Elizabeth Loftus who has shown that EWT often lacks reliability.

■ There are several factors that affect the accuracy of EWT including anxiety, age of witness, consequentiality and individual differences.

■ One of the major factors to affect accuracy is the effect of misleading information given to the witness after the event. Accuracy can also be affected by previous knowledge or expectations that distort recall.

■ The cognitive interview technique has been devised by psychologists to improve the accuracy of witness recall in real-life cases.

✔ **Summary questions**

1 Explain why it is important for psychologists to research EWT.

2 What are the problems with investigating EWT in the laboratory?

3 Explain how anxiety might affect EWT accuracy.

4 How do children differ from adults in their witness statements?

5 Imagine that you are trying to get information from a friend who has been mugged and had her bag stolen. What sort of questions would you ask to encourage accurate recall? Why would these encourage accurate recall?

Strategies for memory improvement

Learning objectives:

■ Describe various strategies for improving memory.

■ Understand how such strategies are related to memory research.

Hint

Some people use verbal mnemonics to help them remember things where the order is important, e.g. they use first letter retrieval cues to recall the colours of the rainbow 'Richard Of York Gains Battles In Vain' (red, orange, yellow, green, blue, indigo, violet). Medical students who have to remember treatment routines or anatomical parts in exam conditions often use such techniques, e.g. a treatment for sports injures is PRICE (Position, Rest, Ice, Compression, Elevation).

As we saw on p2 most of us have amazing memory capacity and this can be supplemented by modern aids such as electronic diaries and mobile phones. Nevertheless, there are times when we would all like our memory to be better, i.e. to learn more quickly and to remember more accurately. We have looked at some theoretical perspectives on memory, but in this part of the chapter we are going to consider how theories can be applied to help us improve our memories.

The role of organisation

Organisation appears to be the key factor in using our memories to best effect. We will consider various ways in which we can use organisational strategies to improve our memory.

Mnemonics based on visual imagery

A number of techniques have been devised to improve memory and these are known as mnemonics. There are several different strategies but they all involve the same basic principle of organisation. Many of them depend on visual imagery, i.e. conjuring up a mental picture.

An example of one of these strategies is the so-called 'peg-word system'. Try this for yourself. First you have to learn the basic organisational structure, so read the following list and try to memorise it:

One is a bun	Six are sticks
Two is a shoe	Seven is heaven
Three is a tree	Eight is a gate
Four is a door	Nine is a line
Five is a hive	Ten is a hen

Then look at the following list of words and try to form a mental image of each word and then 'hang' it on one of the pegs. So, for example, if the first two words on the list are 'milk' and 'butter', imagine a bottle of milk balanced on top of a bun and a pack of butter resting inside a shoe – the stronger your mental image, the better you are likely to recall it.

■ Eggs	■ Cheese
■ Bread	■ Jam
■ Biscuits	■ Pasta
■ Tomatoes	■ Juice
■ Potatoes	■ Cornflakes

After you have completed the mental imagery task, close the book and don't look at it again. Then, in about an hour's time, see if you can write down the list of ten words.

A similar method is called the 'method of loci' where the memory pegs are places rather than rhymes. Think of a regular route you take – perhaps your journey to school or college in the morning and visualise ten key locations on the way (e.g. your front door, a post box at the end of your street, the bus stop, etc.). If you have a list of things you need to remember, associate each one with one of the locations on your route. When the time comes to remember, you just think about your familiar

Cognitive psychology

■ Key term

Concrete nouns: nouns that can easily be visualised, e.g. dog, tree.

Abstract words: words that can't be perceived with your senses, e.g. love, nice.

■ Hint

Another visual imagery technique is the keyword method for learning new foreign language vocabulary. This has been developed by Gruneberg and involves forming an image of a familiar English word with a foreign word that sounds similar. Take, for example, the German word for hedgehog, which is *igel* (pronounced 'eagle'). In order to learn the new German word, you could picture an eagle swooping down to carry off a hedgehog. Gruneberg and Jacobs (1991) reported on a group of English-speaking executives who were able to learn 400 new Spanish words in only 12 hours using the keyword system.

A similar method called the face–name system has been proposed by Lorayne and Lucas (1974) to help remember people's names. You think of an image that is similar to the person's name and then link that image to a prominent feature on the person's face. For example, you could imagine someone called Greene with a bright green nose.

Fig. 3 *Illustrating the keyword method*

landmarks on your journey and the associated word/topic becomes available as well.

Visual imagery has been shown in many studies to enhance recall. Paivio (1965) found that participants could recall **concrete nouns** better than **abstract words**. He explained his findings in terms of the dual coding hypothesis. This means that concrete words are encoded twice – once as a verbal code and then, again, as a visual image. More recently, De Beni and Moè (2003), while confirming the importance of visual imagery for improving memory, found that this kind of imagery is more helpful when applied to items that have been presented verbally rather than visually. In terms of the working memory system, it could be that visually presented items and an accompanying visual image would be competing for the same storage resources, i.e. the visuo-spatial sketchpad, whereas verbally presented items and visual images would be held in separate loops.

Organisation and understanding

So far we have been looking at memory for a rather restricted range of stimulus materials. You might be wondering what relevance they have to ordinary remembering. After all, how often do we need to remember lists of words like shopping lists? Usually, we can write such lists down so that we do not have to remember them by heart. In our everyday life, we usually want to remember more meaningful and complex material. However, the principles of organisation still seem to apply and, underpinning the idea of organisation, is the role of understanding.

Try this activity: ask someone to read the following passage at their normal reading speed and then take the book away from them. After a delay of about 30 minutes, ask them to jot down the main details from the passage:

> The procedure is actually quite simple. First you arrange items into different groups. Of course, one pile may be sufficient depending on how much there is to do. If you have to go somewhere else due to lack of facilities that is the next step; otherwise you are pretty well set. It is important not to overdo things. That is, it is better to do too few things at once than too many. In the short run, this may not seem important but complications can easily arise. A mistake can be expensive as well. At first, the whole procedure will seem complicated. Soon, however, it will become just another facet of life. It is difficult to foresee any end to the necessity for this task in the future, but then, one can never tell. After the procedure is completed one arranges the materials into different groups again. Then they can be put into their appropriate places. Eventually they will be used once more and the whole cycle will then have to be repeated. However, that is part of life.

■ *Bransford and Johnson, 1972*

This passage seems quite puzzling to most people and your participant probably struggled to recall much of the content accurately.

Bransford and Johnson gave this passage to participants but one group was given a title for the passage ('Doing the Laundry') before they read it and the other group was given no title. The first group performed significantly better on a later recall test than the group who had been given no context for the passage. This supports the idea that understanding material to be remembered is very important for later retrieval. In this case, people simply had to remember the title of the passage and that, coupled with their own stored knowledge about how to wash clothes, allowed them to retrieve the memory later.

Chunking

We considered earlier (see p11) the role of chunking in increasing STM capacity. If you think about this, you will see that chunking also involves organising material and making it more understandable. Understanding allows us to integrate and unify material and this, in turn, reduces the load on memory. Consider the following example first used by Katona over 60 years ago. He asked people to remember the following string of digits in serial order:

1 4 9 1 6 2 5 3 6 4 9 6 4 8 1 1 0 0 1 2 1

As you can see, this far exceeds the normal digit span so you won't be surprised to find that Katona's participants found this task impossible.

However, if we organise this list by inserting commas, i.e.:

1, 4, 9, 16, 25, 36, 49, 64, 81, 100, 121

you might see a pattern emerging (1^2, 2^2, 3^2, 4^2...11^2). Once you see this pattern, all you have to learn is that the digit string consists of the squares of the numbers 1 to 11. An impossible task has been reduced down to learning a simple rule.

Encoding and retrieval strategies

Have you ever been in the kitchen and realised you needed to get something from the garden? However, having got into the garden, you suddenly have no idea what you went for. You go back into the kitchen, which provides you with lots of cues (pans cooking on the stove, herbs in jars on the shelf, etc.), and realise immediately what you wanted from the garden (a sprig of parsley). This is an example of the encoding specificity principle whereby you recall things better if the retrieval context is like the encoding context. Geiselman and Glenny (1977) investigated this effect by asking participants to imagine a list of words being said aloud by a familiar person. Some participants were told to imagine a familiar female voice and others were asked to imagine a male voice. After a delay, participants were read a list of words that contained the previous list and some new words, and had to say which words they had been given before. Participants were more successful at this recognition task if the gender of the voice presenting it matched the gender of the voice they had imagined in the first phase of the experiment.

It has been shown that recall for information can be more successful if it is tested in the same room where it was learned. If that is not possible, it seems that simply imagining the original learning environment can help later recall (Jerabek and Standing, 1992).

It has also been suggested that your emotional or physical state at the time of encoding can affect the likelihood of recall. Ucros (1989) reviewed many studies of mood-state-dependent memory and found some evidence that recall is better if mood at the time of learning matched mood at the time of retrieval. However, the effect is only slight and it seems that, if material has been well learned, context is less important.

Active processing

It seems that we are more likely to remember material that we have actively processed. Simple repetition or rote rehearsal is not a very effective way to lay down permanent memories.

Craik and Lockhart (1975) suggested that memory depends on deep and meaningful processing at the point of learning. Craik (1977) investigated this idea by testing recall under different conditions. He presented a list of printed words to four different groups of participants and asked each of them to carry out a different task, as follows:

■ Links

Remember that context reinstatement is one of the successful techniques of the cognitive interview used to question eyewitnesses. See p32 for more details.

See information about the multi-store model on p4.

Cognitive psychology

- Group 1 had to answer a structural question (e.g. Is the word written in capital letters?).
- Group 2 had to carry out an acoustic task (e.g. Does the word rhyme with 'dog'?).
- Group 3 had to carry out a semantic task (e.g. Is it the name of a living thing?).
- Group 4 had no particular task to carry out. They were simply asked to try to commit the words to memory.

Note that it was only Group 4 that expected to be tested for their recall of the words. In a later recognition test, people in Group 3 performed significantly better than people in Groups 1 and 2 and at the same level as people in Group 4. This suggests that meaningful engagement with the stimulus material leads to better retention and it also shows that this learning is incidental – in other words, people do not have to be making a deliberate effort to remember. Craik and Lockhart believed that semantic processing is effective because it activates numerous associations within the LTM – this means that material is easier to retrieve because more retrieval routes have been set up.

■ The role of attention and practice

As we noted in the section on EWT, people will not remember anything if they are not paying attention in the first place. The effect of practice is less clear-cut.

Ericsson and Chase (1981) studied an individual called SF who was able to memorise lists of up to 80 digits. However, to do this, he had to practise for an hour a day over a two-year period. Interestingly, this skill was not transferred to other types of list and his memory span for words and letters was no better than average. However, practice does seem to be important for other types of learning such as revision for exams. It has generally been found that spaced learning is more effective than massed learning for long-term retention.

Many of the techniques outlined above are rather simplistic and have a limited range of application. Herrmann (1991) has suggested that we take a multi-modal approach to memory improvement. This involves developing a whole range of strategies that include maintaining our minds and bodies in optimum condition. Matlin (1998) has stressed the importance of meta-memory. This refers to your knowledge and awareness of your own memory and how it works. You need to recognise what strategies work for you and you need to be honest about your own strengths and weaknesses.

Key points:

- Memory theories can be used to help us improve our memories.
- Organisation is a key factor in using our memories effectively.
- Several techniques have been devised for improving memory. These are called mnemonics and include methods such as the peg-word system, the method of loci and the keyword system.
- Understanding plays a key part in accurate memory recall as it allows us to use our past knowledge and experience. Chunking is an example of how we use stored knowledge to increase our memory capacity.
- Effective retrieval of stored memories can depend on how they were encoded in the first place.
- Active processing seems to be more effective than rote learning.

✔ Summary questions

6 What is meant by the term 'mnemonics'?

7 What is visual imagery?

8 Why is it important for us to understand the material we are trying to learn?

9 Explain how the encoding specificity principle can help us to improve memory.

10 Imagine that you have been introduced to someone at a party and you want to remember his name – Harry Shaw. How might you try to commit this name to memory? Why would this be effective?

Chapter summary

✔ 🎧 Further reading and weblinks

A.D. Baddeley, *Your Memory: A User's Guide*, Carlton Books (2004)

This covers many of the topics covered in the two memory chapters and is written in an accessible style.

A.D. Baddeley, *Essentials of Human Memory*, Psychology Press (1999)

This contains an overview of memory research and theory and is aimed at undergraduates but written in a way that should be accessible for A Level students.

G.L. Wells and E.A. Olsen, 'Eyewitness testimony', *Annual Review of Psychology*, **54**, 277–295 (2003)

This article looks at some of the factors that affect the accuracy of EWT.

www.psyonline.org.uk

This is a web resource for students and teachers of A Level psychology that is frequently modified and updated. It contains useful material on memory.

www.bbc.co.uk

The BBC Science and Nature: Human Body and Mind website is also a changing site, which has information about memory and various memory tests.

Links

For more information about experimental control groups, see p106.

For more information about hypotheses, see p90.

For more information about independent groups design, see p109.

- Memory research can have valuable applications to everyday life, e.g. in improving the accuracy of EWT and of memory in general.
- EWT seems to be highly valued by juries and police officers but psychological research has shown that it can be subject to serious distortion.
- One factor that can impair accuracy is misleading post-event information.
- Loftus believes that such misinformation actually changes the original memory trace.
- There are other factors that can affect EWT accuracy. These include anxiety, age of witness, consequentiality and individual difference.
- Psychologists have developed the cognitive interview in an effort to elicit more accurate EWT.
- Psychological techniques have also been developed to improve memory in general.
- Many of these techniques reflect the importance of organising material in a meaningful way.

How science works: practical activity

Design an experiment to investigate whether misleading post-event information can distort recall. Find a photograph of a busy scene – a newspaper is probably a good source. Alternatively, you could find a short video clip. Find some participants who are willing to take part (be sure to consider ethical considerations here) and divide them randomly into two groups.

Compile a set of ten questions about the scene and ask both groups of participants the questions after they have viewed the scene. However, for one group (the experimental group), include *one* misleading question, e.g. 'What was the number of the bus waiting outside the *shoe shop*?', and for the other group (the control group), a congruent question, e.g. 'What was the number of the bus waiting outside the *clothes shop*?' Otherwise, all the questions should be in keeping with what was actually in the picture/video. After a delay of at least a day, go back to all the participants and ask them some more questions about the picture including, e.g. 'Did you see a shoe shop?' Your hypothesis would predict that more people in the experimental group would think they had seen a shoe shop than in the control group. You will need to think carefully about the kind of picture/video clip you choose, what kind of questions you ask, the hypothesis, the investigation design, sampling and control of extraneous variables. Use the investigation planning form on p104 to ensure you have considered all the main issues.

When you have collected the data, summarise your findings and discuss what your findings show. You should consider how far the findings support memory theory and studies.

Question 1

1   (a)   Using three of the four phrases listed below complete the table so that it correctly describes the component parts of the multi-store model.

          • Contains data stored for a fraction of a second

          • Information encoded mainly in terms of its sounds

          • Has no apparent limit to its capacity

          • Retains data in semantic form *(3 marks)*

Component parts of the multi-store model	Description of component part
Sensory memory	
Short-term memory	
Long-term memory	

       (b)   Outline how information is transferred from sensory memory to short-term memory in the multi-store model. *(2 marks)*

2   (a)   Identify two factors that affect the accuracy of eyewitness testimony and explain how each affects eyewitness testimony. *(6 marks)*

3   Trevor is a police officer. He is concerned that eyewitness statements he has taken have often proven to be incomplete and some contained false elements. When he interviews witnesses he generally asks lots of short, closed questions. Because he is always quite busy he avoids asking general questions and tends to interrupt if witnesses don't recall what he wants to know immediately. He claims his habit of asking questions 'in no particular order' ensures he keeps witnesses on their toes and stops them elaborating on what really happened.

Identify the problems with Trevor's current method of interviewing witnesses and suggest changes he could make to improve the accuracy of eyewitness testimony. *(6 marks)*

> **AQA** Examiner's tip
> For Question 1, part 3 it's important to analyse Trevor's behaviour in this scenario to bring out the key points in your answer.

4   (a)   (i)   Identify one strategy that will improve recall of information for an examination. *(1 mark)*

          (ii)   Explain why this strategy should improve recall. *(2 marks)*

       (b)   Strategies for memory improvement have generally been based on the findings of laboratory experiments. Explain some of the limitations of such laboratory based experiments as a basis for memory improvement. *(6 marks)*

> **AQA** Examiner's tip
> For Question 1, part 4(a) with questions that ask for a specific number of items, for example 'outline two factors …', always ensure that you do exactly as requested. Supplying too few points will restrict the number of marks available to you, while supplying too many points will not earn any extra credit.

5   It has been suggested that the phonological loop (a feature of the working memory model) is only able to hold the amount of information that can be said in two seconds. This in turn affects the capacity of working memory. This can then lead to a word-length effect where longer words are harder to remember than short words. A psychologist decided to investigate this word-length effect.

The following results were found (see Table 1 opposite).

The mean score for recall of short words was 6.5 items, while for long words it was 4.4 items.

       (a)   (i)   What is meant by the term mean score? *(1 mark)*

          (ii)   For the data described above explain why the median would be a better measure of central tendency. *(2 marks)*

(b) The experimental design was a repeated measures design. Tick which box below correctly describes this type of investigation.

☐ Each condition is completed by the same group of participants.

☐ Each condition is completed by a different group of participants.

☐ Each condition is completed by one of a pair of matched participants. *(1 mark)*

(c) Discuss what the findings of this study seem to show about working memory. *(6 marks)*

 AQA Examiner's tip For Question 1, part 5(c), you need to comment on both the features of the data and how the data relates to the working model of memory.

Table 1 A table to show the number of words remembered

Participant number	Number of short words recalled	Number of long words recalled
1	5	3
2	6	4
3	7	3
4	5	4
5	6	4
6	7	5
7	5	3
8	10	9
9	4	5
10	10	4

Question 2

1 Outline two characteristics of short-term memory. *(2 marks)*

2 (a) Explain one strategy for memory improvement. *(4 marks)*

(b) Evaluate this strategy in terms of research evidence. *(4 marks)*

AQA Examiner's tip Question 2, part 2(b) asks for an evaluation in terms of research evidence. Therefore you will not be awarded any marks unless your evaluation is specifically centred on evidence gained from research studies.

3 A psychologist wished to investigate the accuracy of eyewitnesses' recall of real-life incidents. Using a structured interview she questioned some witnesses to an armed robbery several months after the incident had occurred.

(a) Explain one advantage of using a structured interview to collect data. *(2 marks)*

The psychologist carried out a content analysis on the qualitative data from these interviews.

(b) Outline the processes involved in content analysis of these interviews. *(4 marks)*

AQA Examiner's tip If in preparation for the examination you have tried doing a content analysis, this would really help you to answer Question 2, part 3(b).

(c) Explain one strength of quantitative data. *(2 marks)*

Before interviewing the witnesses, the investigator conducted a pilot study.

(d) Explain what is meant by the term pilot study and explain why one was used in this investigation. *(1 mark + 2 marks)*

The investigator was aware that the research should be conducted in an ethical manner.

(e) (i) Identify one ethical issue that should have been considered in this research. *(1 mark)*

(ii) Explain why this is an ethical issue. *(2 marks)*

4 Outline and evaluate the working memory model of memory. *(12 marks)*

AQA Examiner's tip Question 2, part 4 is worth 12 marks; 6 of these are for the outlining of the model and 6 marks for evaluating it. You should spend an equal amount of time on both parts to create a balanced answer.

Developmental psychology – early social development

Introduction

This section of the course is concerned with developmental psychology. You are probably reading this book now as a young adult. However, the person you have become in all senses – your personality, friendships, hopes and ambitions – has been shaped by your earlier experiences and the people who have been important to you throughout your life so far.

Developmental psychologists are interested in how people develop and change from before they are born, throughout their life. This is why developmental psychology is often known as 'lifespan psychology' as changes continue throughout your life, even though we tend to talk about being 'grown up' as if it were some end point of development! The changes that take place are driven by biological factors (nature) and by environmental and cultural factors (nurture). For example, aspects of your physical make-up such as your height and weight are programmed by the genes you have inherited from your biological parents. However, even for something as 'biological' as this, the environment has an influence. The quality of your diet can affect how tall you grow and how much you weigh. Wider cultural influences and ideas about attractiveness such as the desirability of a 'size zero' body are also likely to affect how you feel about your body size and shape. It is for this reason that developmental psychologists are interested in both the innate (biological) factors that affect how we develop as well as the factors in our environment – the people who bring us up, the type of relationships we have with them, whether or not we have brothers or sisters, or attend nursery.

In this section of the course we will be looking at early childhood with a special focus on relationships and assessing how these early years influence our development and the kinds of people we become.

The formation of attachments in human babies

Learning objectives:

- Understand what is meant by the term 'attachment'.
- Describe the behaviours that show that an attachment has been formed.

Key term

Attachment: an emotional tie or relationship between two people shown in their behaviour.

What are attachments?

Think about the abilities of a newborn baby. Babies are physically helpless at birth: they cannot feed themselves or escape from danger. They can communicate only in a very simple way by crying. Babies are reliant on other people for their survival. Despite their apparent helplessness, babies do survive. They do this because they come into the world with the ability to get other people (generally their biological parents) to care for them, feed and protect them until they are able to do this for themselves. This section of the course looks at these early relationships and the strong emotions (or attachments) that bind babies and their parents together. These first relationships are important to babies as they ensure their survival during a relatively lengthy period of helplessness. As we shall see in this chapter, attachments are also important as they are the start of the connections that people form with others. Attachments and relationships are, for the majority of people, one of the most important aspects of their lives.

Although the terms 'attachment' and 'bond' are often used interchangeably there are differences between them. A bond is a set of feelings that ties one person to another: parents often feel strongly bonded with their newborn babies and we shall be considering later on in this section how this process of bonding takes place. An attachment is different to a bond as it involves two people (for example, both parent and baby) who have an emotional link between each other, which ties them together. It also takes longer to develop than a bond. While we cannot see the feelings people have for each other, attachments can be shown in the behaviour of the two attached people.

How can we see that two people have an attachment to each other?

While in this section we are most interested in the first attachments between babies and their parents, most people continue to have attachments throughout their lives, to family members, friends and partners. Maccoby (1980) argued that we can see that two people have an attachment by looking at their behaviours.

- Seeking proximity: the two people who have an attachment want to be near to each other and spend time together. A young baby will try to maintain proximity to the caregiver by watching them carefully, and howling when they go too far away. An older, more mobile baby will simply crawl after their attachment figure in hot pursuit!
- Distress on separation: the young infant will show distress when the caregiver leaves even for a short period of time. The older child may miss their parents and feel homesick on a school trip.

■ Joy on reunion: the baby will welcome back their attachment figure often by clinging to them and hugging them even when they have only been gone for five minutes.

■ General orientation of behaviour towards the other person: both baby and caregiver direct their attention to each other and try to engage each other in activities and interaction.

These attachment behaviours can also be seen in older people who have an attachment. Although adults have more sophisticated ways of maintaining proximity such as sending text messages, the underlying need to stay in touch is still the same. Distress on separation and joy on reunion can be seen on any railway station platform as can general orientation of an attached couple to each other.

Fig. 1 *Attachments: to parents, friends and lovers*

■ How do human babies develop attachments?

How are attachments formed? In many species of animal such as sheep and ducks, attachments are formed rapidly soon after birth. This process was first investigated by **ethologists**, including Konrad Lorenz. In his observations of animals, Lorenz noticed the tendency for newborn, orphaned animals to form an attachment to any animal that happened to be present and to follow it as if it were their real mother. This can often be seen on farms when orphaned lambs will attach themselves to the person who bottle feeds them and follow them happily around until they are very large sheep! This rapid attachment takes place in precocial (or mobile) species of animal, which are able to move around and follow their parents almost from birth.

In order to investigate this rapid formation of attachment, Lorenz carried out a series of studies with greylag geese in the 1930s, which yielded valuable information about the rapid formation of attachments. In a piece of research in 1935, he divided a number of fertile goose eggs randomly into two groups. Half were replaced under their mother and allowed to hatch naturally and the remaining eggs were kept in an incubator. Lorenz ensured that he was the first, large moving object seen by the incubator group. He found that the goslings formed a rapid attachment to him and would follow him around as if he were their mother. A short time after the geese had hatched Lorenz put all the goslings together in a container and then released them. They separated rapidly into two groups, each seeking their own 'mother'.

Lorenz called this formation of rapid attachments 'imprinting'. This is the tendency to form an attachment to the first large moving object seen after birth. In later studies he found that the strongest tendency to

AQA **Examiner's tip**

Be able to explain what is meant by an attachment.

■ Key term

Ethology: the study of animal behaviour. Ethologists observe how animals act and identify the purpose the behaviour is likely to have served in helping survival in the evolutionary past.

Developmental psychology

■ **Key term**

Critical period: a specific period of time in which something has to develop. For example, in an embryo limbs start to develop between 24 and 26 days after conception. Anything that interferes with the process during those days (for example drugs taken by the mother) will have a lasting effect.

imprint takes place between 13 and 16 hours after ducklings hatch out. By the time ducklings reach the grand old age of 32 hours the tendency to imprint has virtually passed and the attachment will not take place. Lorenz argued that imprinting had to take place within the 'window of development', which he called a **critical period.** If attachment does not happen by 32 hours then it will not happen at all. Imprinting clearly makes sense in terms of survival for mobile species of animal. As the mother moves around to forage and to escape from predators, the young must remain close to her in order to be protected and survive. Therefore behaviours involving following will promote survival of the young and have evolved via natural selection.

Fig. 2 *Konrad Lorenz – an unusual 'Mother Goose'!*

The formation of bonds between parents and babies

In contrast to precocial species, human babies are not mobile immediately after birth. They have a relatively long period of immaturity and only begin to crawl at about eight months of age. Because of their immobile state, human babies would have been extremely vulnerable to predators in the past. Therefore, the formation of an early protective bond from adult (and particularly mother) to baby would make sense in evolutionary terms. It would promote the survival of the infant by ensuring that the mother stayed close to them in order to protect them from predators. This has led some psychologists to look at the early period immediately after birth to see if this is an important or sensitive period for the formation of bonds from parent to infant.

Klaus and Kennell (1976) tested the hypothesis that early skin-to-skin contact led to closer bonds being formed between new mothers and their babies by studying women who gave birth in hospital. The usual practice before their field experiment was that babies would be removed from their mothers shortly after delivery and kept in a nursery unit to allow their mothers to rest and recover from the birth. (Consider how shocking this now sounds!) Klaus and Kennell took two groups of young mothers in a North American maternity hospital and followed them from birth until their babies were a year old.

■ The control group had routine contact: they saw their baby after delivery and when they were brought to them for feeds.

■ **Links**

For a reminder of what a field experiment is, see p107.

For a reminder about 'control' and 'experimental' groups see p106.

■ The experimental group had extended contact: they had one extra hour of 'skin-to-skin contact' after the birth and then an extra five hours of contact over the next three days.

Klaus and Kennell visited the mothers and their babies after one month and again after a year. They found a variety of differences in the behaviour of the routine and extended contact mothers. The extended contact mothers:

■ showed more soothing behaviours such as cuddling their babies when they were given a routine medical examination

■ maintained closer proximity to their babies and gazed at their babies more than the routine group.

Klaus and Kennell concluded that these behaviours seemed to indicate that the mothers had formed closer bonds with their babies, which produced noticeable differences in the closeness of the relationships up to one year after birth. This study indicated that there may be a special time or **sensitive period** immediately after birth that may be important for bonding to take place. These findings changed the established practices of Western childbirth in the mid twentieth century and most hospitals adopted the practice of 'rooming in' or keeping babies and their mothers together while in hospital. The findings also implied that it may be beneficial for fathers to be present at the birth of their children when this is possible to give them the opportunity to form early bonds with their children, which is largely taken for granted today.

Developmental psychology

Fig. 3 *A special time for the formation of bonds*

Some have criticised this study arguing that the two groups of mothers were young and unmarried and came from a disadvantaged North American inner city area. This may have meant that the closer bonds shown by the mothers may have been due to extra attention given to them in the experiment rather than the actual effects of the extra time they spent with their babies. However, other studies have replicated Klaus and Kennell's method and found the same effect. De Chateau *et al.* (1987) carried out a similar study using 42 middle-class Swedish mothers and their babies. Twenty were given routine contact and 22 extended contact. They found that the extended group held their babies more, and gazed at them at 36 hours after birth and at three months the babies themselves showed more laughing and smiling than the routine group who cried more. This implies that the differences seen in the original Klaus and Kennell study cannot simply be explained by the specific group of mothers studied but that early skin-to-skin contact can indeed facilitate the formation of bonds between mothers and their babies.

Developmental psychology

The formation of attachments

Even though the time after birth may be very special for parents to bond with their new baby, the overall process of the formation of attachments takes much longer in human infants and it is around seven or eight months before babies show their first real lasting attachments. This was noted by Schaffer and Emerson (1964) in their important study of 60 babies drawn from a predominantly working class area of Glasgow.

■ Research study: Schaffer and Emerson (1964)

This study looked at the gradual development of attachments. Schaffer and Emerson studied 60 babies in Glasgow, visiting them monthly for the first year of their lives and returning again at 18 months. They collected data on attachment by considering two types of behaviour:

- Separation anxiety: if the baby showed anxiety or distress when the caregiver left them. Separation anxiety indicates that the baby has formed an attachment to the person.
- Stranger distress: if the baby showed signs of distress when approached by someone who they did not know. Distress at strangers shows that the baby can recognise familiar people and feels anxious with those who are unfamiliar.

Schaffer and Emerson used a variety of methods to collect their data including observation and interviewing. During each visit, they would approach the baby and see if they cried, whimpered or showed signs of distress at a strange face. At each visit, they interviewed the mothers, asking them about the baby's response to various situations, for example,when the baby was left outside a shop, with a babysitter or when put in their cot at night. The mothers were asked to rate the baby's behaviour in each of these situations using a four-point scale from zero 'no protest shown' to three 'cries loudly every time'.

When does attachment take place?

Schaffer and Emerson found that attachment behaviours developed in stages which were loosely linked to age. Most babies started to show separation anxiety from their attachment figure at around 25–32 weeks (6–8 months) indicating that an attachment had been formed. Fear of strangers tended to follow about a month later. After their first attachment was formed, most babies went on to form multiple attachments with a variety of people they saw regularly such as grandparents, siblings, etc.

To whom do babies form their first attachments?

For most babies (65 per cent) the first attachment figure was their mother. This finding probably reflects the period when the study was carried out in which most child-rearing involved mothers who stayed at home to look after their children. By the same token, fathers were unlikely to be the first attachment figure with only 3 per cent of babies forming their first relationship with their father. Just over a quarter of babies (27 per cent) formed 'joint attachments' (i.e. to both mother and father) at the same time. Interestingly, babies did not necessarily form their attachments to the person who carried out most of the physical care such as feeding and changing

■ Link

You can read more about interviewing on p119 and observational research methods on p112.

nappies. In almost 40 per cent of babies, the person who cared for the child was not the first attachment figure.

Methodological issues

■ Schaffer and Emerson used a variety of methods of data collection here including observation and interview. These methods provide data that is very rich in detail. This use of different methods to study the same issue is known as 'triangulation'.

■ Babies were observed by the researchers in their own homes and mothers were asked to rate their babies' response to separation in a wide range of everyday situations. Both of these measurements make the study high in **ecological validity.**

■ This study has provided valuable information about the processes by which attachments are formed. The findings reflect the child-rearing practices of the mid 1960s where most childcare was carried out by mothers who were less likely to work outside the home. Today, fathers may be far more likely to be first attachment figures given their greater role today in child-rearing.

Ethical issues

As the research took place in the babies' own homes, the situation was relatively unstressful for the babies and their mothers. This is important as researchers should ensure that minimal psychological harm takes place. Later on in this section we shall consider research carried out by Ainsworth (1970) using the 'Strange Situation'. Here, babies and mothers attended a specially built laboratory 'playroom', which was unfamiliar to the babies and was likely to be a much more stressful experience.

■ **Key term**

Ecological validity: the extent to which the methods, materials and setting of the experiment approximate the real-life situation being studied.

■ **Link**

For more information about ecological validity, see p107.

Developmental psychology

Schaffer and Emerson's findings indicate that attachments take longer to form in human babies than in mobile species of animal. The stages suggested by Schaffer and Emerson's research are summarised in Table 1 below:

Table 1 *Stages in the development of attachments*

Stage and age	Characteristics
Asocial stage (0 to 6 weeks)	Babies produce similar responses to objects and people and do not prefer specific people to others. They have a bias towards human-like stimuli and prefer to look at faces and eyes. They rapidly learn to discriminate familiar people from unfamiliar by their smell and voice.
Indiscriminate attachments (6 weeks to 6 months)	Babies become more sociable. They can tell people apart and prefer to be in human company. They are relatively easily comforted by anyone and do not prefer specific individuals yet. They do not show fear of strangers.
Specific attachments (7 months onwards)	Two changes take place around seven months. The baby begins to show separation anxiety, protesting when their primary attachment figure leaves them. They also show fear of strangers.
Multiple attachments (10/11 months onwards)	Multiple attachments follow soon after the first attachment is made. The baby shows attachment behaviours towards several different people such as siblings, grandparents and childminders.

Key points:

■ This section has shown that the time taken for attachments to develop varies in different species.

■ In many mobile animals attachments are formed rapidly soon after birth, a process known as imprinting. This means that the young animal follows the parent, increasing their chance of survival.

■ There is likely to be a sensitive period soon after birth for new parents to form bonds towards their infants.

■ First attachments between babies and their caregiver are generally formed around the age of seven months and they are followed by multiple attachments to a range of significant people in the baby's life.

✓ **Summary questions**

1 What behaviours might indicate to psychologists that two people have an attachment?

2 Outline the stages of development of attachments in babies.

3 Explain what is meant by separation anxiety and stranger anxiety.

4 You baby-sit for your friend, looking after her baby once a week. When the baby gets to around seven months old, he starts to cry when your friend leaves and screams even louder when you pick him up. Use your knowledge of attachment to explain why the baby behaves like this.

Why do babies develop attachments?

✓ 💡

Learning objectives:

- Understand explanations that have been put forward for the development of attachments – the learning explanation and the evolutionary explanation.

- Evaluate these explanations of attachment in terms of research evidence.

Key terms

Positive reinforcement: something which increases the likelihood that the behaviour before it will be repeated.

Negative reinforcement: when a behaviour or response switches off something unpleasant. Taking a painkiller switches off the pain of a headache so the behaviour – painkiller taking – is likely to be repeated.

Unconditioned stimulus: an aspect of the environment which produces an automatic, unlearned response. For example, food produces salivation in a hungry dog.

Unconditioned response: an unlearned, reflex response to an unconditioned stimulus. Dilation of the pupil of the eye is an unconditioned response to the unconditioned stimulus of dim light.

Why are attachments formed? A range of explanations has been put forward to explain the process. Learning theories focus on the rewards provided by caregivers to babies in terms of food and comfort. Evolutionary theories focus on the adaptational advantages of attachments in ensuring that babies survive. This section will consider both of these explanations including the evidence on which they are based.

Learning theory

Learning theory argues that attachments are based on the principles of operant and classical conditioning. First attachments are quite often formed to the person who looks after the child, who feeds them, changes their nappy and cuddles them when they are afraid. First attachment figures are a powerful source of pleasure for the baby as well as removing physical and emotional discomforts including pain, cold and hunger. An early version of learning theory based on both operant and classical conditioning was proposed by Dollard and Miller (1950).

Operant conditioning

Skinner was a behaviourist who worked with rats and cats. He placed hungry animals in cages (called Skinner boxes) and found that they would explore their surroundings. When the animal accidentally pressed a lever that supplied a pellet of food, it quickly learned to repeat the behaviour in order to gain the food reward. According to the principle of operant conditioning, any behaviour that produces a reward (or **positive reinforcement**) such as food will be repeated. Behaviours that 'switch off' something unpleasant are also likely to be repeated (**negative reinforcement**). Behaviours that lead to an unpleasant outcome (or punishment) are less likely to be repeated.

How can this be applied to attachment? A newborn baby will cry in response to feelings of discomfort, which come from being hungry or cold. The sound of the baby crying is uncomfortable to the caregiver who will attempt to console the child by feeding and cuddling them. These behaviours are rewarding for the baby who is likely to settle down and stop crying. This acts as negative reinforcement for the parent and they are likely to repeat the feeding/cuddling when the baby cries the next time. As the crying has produced a reward or positive reinforcement, the baby is likely to repeat the crying behaviour. As the cuddling and feeding behaviour switched off the unpleasant crying, the parent learns to feed and cuddle the baby in order to stop the ear-splitting crying. It is a perfect system!

Classical conditioning

Classical conditioning is based on learning through association. Pavlov noticed how hungry dogs quickly learn to associate the sound of their keeper's footsteps with mealtimes. In terms of attachment, milk is an **unconditioned stimulus**, which provides an **unconditioned** (reflex) **response** in the baby of pleasure at relief from hunger. This reflex response is automatic and does not need to be learned. The baby associates the person who feeds them (the neutral stimulus) with the food and soon the person on their own comes to produce a learned or conditioned response of pleasure and relief. This is similar to the way in which your pet cat or dog shows you undying love and devotion when you pick up the tin opener and is sometimes known as the 'cupboard love' hypothesis. Initially it is the relief from discomfort or the pleasure of feeding that is rewarding for the baby but over time the caregiver comes to produce the same feelings of relief and pleasure via association or classical conditioning.

Does evidence support the learning account of attachment?

There is a strong body of evidence from human babies and studies of primates to suggest that attachment is not based on feeding.

- For example in Schaffer and Emerson's 1964 study, the first attachment formed by 39 per cent of babies was not to the person who carried out physical care, such as feeding and changing the baby's nappy. Attachments are more likely to be formed to those who are sensitive and rewarding to the baby and who play with them.

- Primate studies have also shown that attachment appears to be based on the need for comfort more than feeding. Mary and Harry Harlow (1958) and Harlow and Zimmerman (1959) carried out a series of experiments using young rhesus monkeys. They studied eight infant monkeys who were reared in isolation and deprived of their real mothers until they were eight months old. In each cage, there were two 'surrogate' mothers, one made of wire with a monkey-like face and an identical 'mother' covered with a soft, towelling fabric. A feeding bottle supplying milk was attached to the wire mother and the Harlows measured the amount of time the baby monkeys spent clinging to each mother. They checked to see if an attachment had been formed by putting a noisy mechanical toy in the cage to frighten the monkeys and to see which 'mother' they clung to. The Harlows found that the baby monkeys used the soft mother as their base, returning to her for comfort when they were frightened and only visiting the wire mother to feed. While this is clearly an animal study, which cannot be directly generalised to human babies, it provides strong evidence to suggest that there is much more to attachment than feeding and rewards.

- This explanation ignores the considerable evidence pointing to the importance of evolutionary (instinctive) aspects of attachment that are considered by Bowlby's theory, which is discussed opposite.

Fig. 4 *Cloth mum provides comfort and security in times of stress*

■ Social learning explanations

Rather than being a separate theory, the social learning explanation (Hay and Vespo, 1988) aims to develop the learning explanation to include an element of social learning in attachment. Social learning theory proposed by Bandura (1977) argues that children (and indeed adults) learn many of their behaviours through observation and imitation of the behaviour of other people who act as role models. Hay and Vespo argue that parents act as role models for their infants and teach them how to understand and carry out relationships by their own actions of looking after the child. Social learning involves a number of components including the following:

■ Role modelling: the parents show the child a range of affectionate behaviours such as holding and cuddling, which the child imitates.

■ Direct instruction: the parents teach the child to reciprocate affection, for example by saying 'Give me a kiss goodbye'.

■ Social facilitation: parents watch and help the child to carry out attachment behaviours, for example when they are playing with their friends and siblings.

Evaluation

■ This explanation of attachment takes into account the importance of parents as role models for their children. Clearly parents are very important in teaching their children about how to love and be loved as we shall see later when considering the 'continuity hypothesis'.

■ Hay and Vespo do not deny the importance of innate influences to attachment but draw attention instead to the importance of social influences on the development of attachment behaviours.

■ Hay and Vespo's theory does not explain why attachments are so emotionally intense for both people involved in them.

■ Evolutionary explanations

John Bowlby's theory

Perhaps the most influential explanation of attachment was presented by John Bowlby who began developing his ideas in the 1940s. Bowlby presented two key theories, namely the maternal deprivation hypothesis and his theory of attachment, which we shall consider here. The ideas behind these theories are closely linked.

Rather than locating the child's formation of attachment within the environment as learning theories do, Bowlby argued that attachment was an evolved mechanism that ensured the survival of the child. He drew on a variety of different influences to develop his theory.

■ The underlying basis of Bowlby's theory was the innate or instinctive nature of attachment. He argued that attachment behaviours in both babies and their caregivers have evolved through natural selection to ensure the baby survives to reach maturity and to reproduce. Babies possess instincts such as crying and smiling, which encourage the caregiver to look after them. Parents, especially mothers according to Bowlby, possess instincts designed to protect their baby from harm and to nurture them to ensure survival to maturity. Those babies and mothers who did not possess such behaviours have been less successful and therefore their genes are no longer in the gene pool!

■ A second important concept in Bowlby's theory was the idea of **monotropy** – a single attachment to one person who is most

---

AQA Examiner's tip

Make sure that you can explain and evaluate the learning theory of attachment.

■ **Key term**

Monotropy: the tendency of babies to form a primary attachment to one caregiver.

Developmental psychology

important to the baby. Bowlby did not deny that babies formed lots of attachments but he believed that for every infant, one relationship is more important than the rest and exists at the top of the hierarchy. This has been one of his more controversial claims.

■ Bowlby took up and developed Freud's idea of the mother–child relationship being important for future relationships. He argued that the first attachment between the baby and their caregiver provided the child with an **internal working model** or template for their future relationships. In this first attachment, the child is said to build up a model of themselves as lovable or not, a model of the caregiver as trustworthy or not and a model of the relationship between the two. Bowlby argued that the internal working model, begun in early childhood, influenced the child's later relationships through to adulthood. This is referred to as the continuity hypothesis. Bowlby also drew on the work carried out by the Harlows with rhesus monkeys who were showing the importance of the mother-figure providing comfort and security for the infant, a concept he developed into the idea of a 'safe base'.

■ Bowlby thought that the process of attachment took place within a sensitive period, during the first three years of the child's life. He borrowed this concept from the work of Lorenz and other ethologists who had pointed to the rapid formation of attachments in some animal species. From his research with troubled adolescents, he believed that the attachment between caregiver and child should not be disrupted or broken for any reason before the age of three years or there would be serious consequences. You can read more about this in the next sub-section on disruption of attachments.

Fig. 5 *Mother protecting child in times of danger.*

Evaluating Bowlby's theory

Bowlby's theory had a dramatic impact on ideas about how babies should be looked after and the importance of 'mothering'. Here, we shall consider the evidence for some of Bowlby's claims including the continuity hypothesis and monotropy. We shall also look at attachments to father and siblings, relationships that Bowlby largely overlooked.

The continuity hypothesis: broad support for Bowlby

According to Bowlby's theory, the internal working model gives a child an idea of themselves as lovable or otherwise and of other people as trustworthy or otherwise. This suggests that the type of relationships people have later on in their lives will be influenced by their first relationships with caregivers. Many studies have assessed if this is so and found support for this idea.

Hazan and Shaver (1987) set out to address the question 'Is love in adulthood directly related to the attachment type as a child?' Their research involved a 'Love Quiz' in their local North American paper, the *Rocky Mountain News*, which asked people to write into the paper reporting their experiences about two things:

■ Which of three descriptions best applied to their feelings/experiences about romantic relationships.

■ A simple adjective checklist which described their childhood relationship with their parents.

> I am somewhat uncomfortable being close to others; I find it difficult to trust them completely; difficult to allow myself to depend on them. I am nervous when anyone gets too close, and often others want me to be more intimate than I feel comfortable being.

> I find it relatively easy to get close to others and am comfortable depending on them and having them depend on me. I don't worry about being abandoned or about someone getting too close to me.

> I find that others are reluctant to get as close as I would like. I often worry that my partner doesn't really love me or won't want to stay with me. I want to get very close to my partner and this sometimes scares people away.

Hazan and Shaver tested two separate groups of people. The first included 215 men and 415 women randomly selected from the many responses to the paper advert. The second group consisted of 108 undergraduate students at their university. They found that there was a strong relationship between childhood attachment type and adulthood attachment type. 'Secure' types expressed a belief in lasting love. They found others trustworthy and were confident that they were lovable. 'Anxious avoidant' types were more doubtful about the existence of love, believing that it didn't happen in real life. They also felt that you don't need a happy relationship to get lots out of life. 'Anxious ambivalent' types fell in love easily and often but rarely found 'true love'. They felt insecure and experienced self-doubt in love.

A more recent study to test the continuity hypothesis was carried out by Black and Schutte (2006) using 205 young adults. They were asked to complete three measures to assess childhood and adult attachment types:

■ an 'adult attachment interview', which measured their feelings about current and previous adult relationships

■ a list of adjectives that described their childhood relationships with both parents

■ a description of childhood events and incidents such as birthday parties or Christmas that illustrated their relationships with their parents. This description produced rich, qualitative data.

Black and Schutte found a link between the types of childhood and adult relationships that Bowlby suggested. Those who recalled positive and loving relationships with their mothers were more trusting and more likely to open up to their partners and seek comfort from them. Those who had positive relationships with their fathers were more likely to rely on their partners. This study broadly supports Bowlby's claims of the continuity of attachment experiences.

■ Link

You can read more about secure and insecure attachment types in Ainsworth's research covered in the next sub-section of this chapter (see p58).

■ Hint

Note that both of these studies ask young adults to recall their childhood relationships with their parents. From a research methods perspective, it is important to be cautious when using this kind of evidence as it is difficult to assess how accurate these memories are.

Do early attachments always predict adult relationship experiences?

Not all studies have shown support for Bowlby's ideas of continuity. Some have pointed to the importance of other influences on later relationships and the need to be cautious when assuming that early childhood attachment experiences will always predict adult relationships. Zimmerman et al. (2000) carried out a longitudinal study of 44 children in Germany. Their attachment type as children was initially assessed between 12 and 18 months of age by seeing how they responded to separation and to strangers, and they were reassessed at the age of 16 years using interviews focusing on their relationship with their parents. Zimmerman et al. also recorded the life events such as parental divorce or death that occurred to the young people as they were growing up. They found that childhood attachment type was not a good predictor of attachments in adolescence. More important was the impact of serious life events such as parental divorce. This study suggests that continuity may only apply when serious life events do not have an impact on the child.

Others have pointed out that Bowlby's theory suggests that poor early relationship experiences 'sentence' a person to poor adult relationships. Main and Goldwyn (1984) argued that although some people have had difficult childhoods and insecure attachments, many have gone on to develop positive and secure relationships in adulthood, which they call 'earned security'. This may be due to positive school experiences or strong adult attachments, which have led them to develop feelings of security and trust later in their lives. Research by Rutter and Quinton in 1988 found that women who had had a range of difficult early experiences developed security if they had positive school experiences and strong adult relationships in later life.

Does monotropy really exist?

Many psychologists have criticised Bowlby's ideas regarding monotropy and argued that the babies' attachment to the first attachment figure (generally the mother) is not necessarily special or unique. Schaffer and Emerson's longitudinal study of 60 Glasgow babies found that multiple attachments seemed to be the norm for babies rather than the exception. By about seven months of age, just under a third (29 per cent) of babies had multiple attachments; by the age of 10 months, this figure had risen to almost two-thirds (59 per cent); and at 18 months 87 per cent of babies had multiple attachments. Schaffer and Emerson also found that the strongest bond was not necessarily to the mother as Bowlby had implied. At 18 months, only half of the sample were strongly attached to their mothers and about a third were strongly attached to their fathers.

Attachments to fathers and siblings

As we have seen, Bowlby's theory focused predominantly on the attachments between babies and their mothers and overlooked the importance of fathers and siblings. In fact he believed that fathers were of little importance in their children's lives. However, research shows that the children's relationships with their fathers are important in their own right. The relationship a child has with their father often depends on the amount of time the father spends with the baby and how involved he is in child-rearing. Some (e.g. Ross et al., 1975) have argued that there is a clear positive correlation between the number of nappies the father has changed and the strength of the child's attachment! Lamb (1983) has studied relationships of babies with their fathers and notes that fathers are often preferred as playmates to mothers as their play is more physical and unpredictable.

Link

You can read more about Rutter and Quinton's research in the section on institutionalisation (see p71).

Bowlby's theory also ignored relationships with siblings, which others have considered to be very important. Schaffer (1996) distinguishes between vertical relationships the child has with those who are older and more powerful such as parents and teachers; and horizontal relationships, which are attachments to someone with a similar level of power, usually a sibling or peer. Relationships with siblings are very long lasting and often very important in our lives. Bee (1995) has noted the different kinds of attachment between siblings such as 'buddies', often pairs of sisters, who try to be like each other and enjoy each other's company and 'caregivers' where an older sibling takes care of the younger, often behaving in a quasi-parental way. Bowlby's emphasis on the relationship between mother and baby led to these important attachments being ignored.

Conclusion: Bowlby's theory of attachment

Bowlby's ideas about the importance of attachments have produced substantial amounts of research. Most evidence suggests that early attachment experiences can have an influence on later adult relationships. However, it is important not to overestimate this influence and to consider other factors such as later life events, which influence adult relationships. Bowlby's idea regarding monotropy has been challenged and evidence supports the view that multiple attachments may be the rule rather than single and unique attachments.

> **AQA Examiner's tip**
>
> Make sure that you can outline the main features of Bowlby's theory of attachments and can discuss evidence for and against it.

Key points:

- Learning theories argue that attachments are formed on the basis of association and through observation and imitation of role models.

- There is little evidence to suggest that attachments are formed on the basis of rewards such as feeding.

- Bowlby's evolutionary explanation of attachment argues that attachment behaviours promote the survival of the infant.

- Bowlby claimed that attachments are monotropic and provide an internal working model or template for later relationships.

- This continuity hypothesis has received considerable support but there is less support for the idea of monotropy.

✓ Summary questions

5 Outline the learning theory explanation of attachments.

6 Give one piece of evidence which contradicts this explanation of attachment.

7 Outline Bowlby's theory of attachment.

8 Give one piece of evidence for and one against this explanation.

9 Discuss the differences between evolutionary and learning explanations of attachment. Which do you find most convincing and why?

Types of attachment including insecure and secure attachments

Developmental psychology

Learning objectives:

- Find out how babies differ in the types of attachment behaviours they show.

- Investigate what behaviours are shown by babies with secure and insecure attachment types.

- Explore two explanations given for these differences in attachment types.

Link

You can read about observation on p112.

💡 Variations in attachments

So far we have talked about attachments as if babies and caregivers behave in very similar ways. Clearly this is not so and there are considerable individual differences in the strength and type of attachments formed between babies and caregivers. These differences were explored by Mary Ainsworth who worked with Bowlby during the 1950s at the Tavistock Clinic in London. Ainsworth was interested in exploring the different types of attachment between babies and their caregivers and she developed an important procedure known as the 'Strange Situation' to do this. In the Strange Situation, babies and their mothers were observed in a range of situations, which allowed the researcher to see the different types of behaviours shown by infants.

Research study: Ainsworth (1970)

This study looked at individual differences in attachment. In Ainsworth's 'Strange Situation', infants aged one year to 18 months were observed through video cameras in a purpose-built laboratory playroom with their mothers. The room contained two comfortable chairs and a play area with a set of toys suitable for young children. The procedure in Ainsworth's research consisted of a series of situations, which were standardised for all the babies who took part.

1 Mother and infant enter the room. Mother sits in one of the chairs and reads a magazine. Child is placed on the floor and is free to explore the toys.

2 After about three minutes, a stranger enters, sits on the second chair and talks briefly with the mother.

3 The stranger approaches the infant and attempts to interact and play with them.

4 Mother leaves the room so the infant is alone with the stranger. The stranger comforts the baby if they are upset and offers to play with them.

5 After around three minutes mother returns and the stranger leaves.

6 Three minutes later mother departs again leaving the baby briefly alone in the room.

7 The stranger re-enters and offers to comfort and play with the baby.

8 Mother returns and the stranger leaves.

Using this procedure, Ainsworth was able to monitor the infant's behaviour in a variety of situations including the departure of the mother to assess separation anxiety, and the introduction of a stranger to measure stranger anxiety. She also examined the baby's behaviour towards the mother in a strange environment to assess whether or not the baby used her as a safe base to explore the room.

From her study, Ainsworth identified three broad types of attachment behaviour shown in the infants. These are shown in the table opposite.

Table 2 *Types of attachment in the Strange Situation*

Attachment type	Behaviour patterns
Secure infants (Type B attachment)	These babies used their mother as a safe base and were happy to explore the room when she was present. They showed distress by crying when she left, and welcomed her back on her return, settling back down to play fairly quickly. They were wary of the stranger and treated them very differently to their mother. 70% of babies fell into this category.
Insecure-avoidant attachment (Type A)	These babies did not orient their behaviour towards their mother in the same way. They showed some distress at her departure but did not seek comfort from her when she returned. They also rejected the stranger's attempts to comfort them. The relationship style of these babies involved keeping a distance and avoiding closeness. 15% of babies fell into this category.
Insecure-ambivalent attachment (Type C)	These babies were very upset at separation but were not easily comforted when the mother returned. They appeared to be angry and rejected her attempts to comfort them. These babies seemed to expect the relationship to be difficult and they alternated between seeking closeness and wanting distance. 15% of babies fell into this category.

Methodological issues

- The method used in the Strange Situation has been an extremely useful tool, which gives a great deal of information in a relatively short space of time about babies' attachments.

- The Strange Situation methodology is quite easy to replicate. This led to a rapid increase in the amount of research carried out into variations in attachment both within and between different cultures. Many studies have found similar results suggesting that the Strange Situation is a reliable method of studying attachment behaviours.

- Some critics have argued that Ainsworth's research lacks validity because of the strange and unfamiliar nature of the playroom, which was not the child's home. However, the situation itself is similar to many that children may experience such as being left with a baby-sitter or at playgroup or nursery suggesting that the method may provide a valid measure of the child's response to separations.

Ethical issues

- Ainsworth's research took place in an unfamiliar environment, which was not the baby's home. The departure of the mother in a strange place and the interaction with the stranger are likely to have been stressful for the infant although both the mother and researcher were instructed to stop the experiment and respond to the baby if they felt they were becoming very distressed. This situation was much more stressful than that used by Schaffer and Emerson (1964) in the baby's own home.

AQA Examiner's tip

Make sure you can explain the differences in behaviour shown by the secure and insecure infants in the Strange Situation.

What causes differences in attachment types – sensitivity of the mother or temperament of the baby?

Ainsworth's explanation for differences in attachment type rested on the sensitivity of the mother. Ainsworth argued that mothers who were sensitive to their infants' needs, who read their moods and feelings correctly, were likely to produce babies who were securely attached. In contrast, mothers who were less sensitive or responsive to their babies,

■ Link

You can read more about the method of correlation in the section on research methods (see p116).

■ Key term

Meta-analysis: a procedure in which researchers draw together and analyse the results of many different studies that have used a similar procedure. A meta-analysis uses only quantitative data.

who ignored them or who became impatient with them were said to be more likely to have insecurely attached infants. These babies would be likely to feel less safe and would be unsure if their needs would be met at any time. De Wolff and van IJzendoorn (1997) have carried out a **meta-analysis** to assess the relationship between parental sensitivity and the security of the babies' attachment. They analysed the results of 66 studies on over 4,000 families and found a correlation of 0.24 between sensitivity and attachment. This means that there is a weak positive relationship between sensitivity and attachment – generally more sensitive caregivers have more strongly attached babies. While this is not a very strong correlation, it does support the view that security of the babies' attachment type has some relation to how sensitive the caregiver is.

However, others such as Kagan have argued that Ainsworth's explanation places too much emphasis on the role of the mother and ignores the basic temperament of the infant. Temperaments are differences in babies that seem to be inbuilt and visible from birth. There are a number of different aspects to temperament including activity (how much time baby spends awake and alert), emotionality (how much they become upset or aroused by events) and sociability (how much the baby seeks human company). In Thomas and Chess's 1989 study of 138 American babies, they found three basic temperament types. Just under a half fell into the category of easy babies – they ate and slept regularly and accepted new experiences easily. About one in ten were classed as 'slow-to-warm-up' babies. These did not actively reject new experiences but took a while to get used to them, whereas difficult babies (15 per cent) ate and slept irregularly and actively rejected new experiences.

According to the temperament hypothesis, the attachment type formed by a baby may reflect their own basic temperament rather than how sensitive their caregiver is. If this is true, then the baby should show similar attachments to both parents. Fox (1991) found that there was a strong relationship between the attachment types of a child to both parents, which supports the claim that attachments may well relate to inbuilt temperaments. Easy babies may go on to be securely attached infants whereas slow-to-warm-up babies may go on to be avoidant. Difficult babies may turn into ambivalent toddlers. This provides a very different explanation of attachment types to that suggested by Ainsworth.

Belsky and Rovine (1987) argue that individual differences in attachment types may relate to both the inborn temperament of the baby as well as to the sensitivity of the caregiver. They argue that babies with different temperaments present different types of challenges to their caregiver. An extremely reactive or difficult baby may need to be soothed, whereas a slow-to-warm-up infant needs encouragement. This type of baby may go on to develop a secure attachment with a caregiver who is patient, encouraging and responsive. However, with an anxious caregiver, the attachment outcome may be very different.

Do all babies fit the three descriptions produced by Ainsworth?

Ainsworth provided a description of the main ways in which babies vary. Subsequent research indicated that not all babies fitted into Ainsworth's original three attachment types and a fourth type, D (disorganised attachment), was added by Main and Solomon (1986). The behaviour pattern of these babies did not fit any of the above categories but was inconsistent. For example the baby responded in different ways in the repeated episodes by crying the first time the mother left but not the second.

Key points:

■ The Strange Situation has been used to assess variations in the type of attachment behaviours shown by babies.

■ Secure attachments are the most common type. These babies show distress when the caregiver leaves and they settle down when they return.

■ Insecure attachments come in two types. Avoidant babies do not use the caregiver to provide comfort and tend to treat strangers in a similar way. Ambivalent babies show distress when the caregiver leaves but alternate between rejection and desire for closeness when she returns.

■ Ainsworth explained differences in attachment behaviour through the sensitivity of the mother. However, others have argued that temperament may be more important in how securely the baby attaches to the caregiver.

 Summary questions

10 Explain what is meant by secure and insecure attachments.

11 Give one strength and one criticism of the Strange Situation methodology.

12 Evaluate one explanation of differences in attachment types.

13 Compare the methods used to study attachment by Schaffer and Emerson (1964) and Ainsworth (1971) in terms of their ethics and validity. Which study do you consider to be better and why?

Cultural variations in attachments

Developmental psychology

Learning objectives:

- Explore how attachment types vary in different cultures.

- Understand how these differences relate to the ways in which children are brought up.

i Research from various countries

Attachments do not just differ between individual babies. They may also vary systematically across cultures. This is not surprising, as people bring up their children very differently in different parts of the world and encourage them to develop different abilities and qualities. For example, Fox (1977) studied child-rearing practices in kibbutzim, communal farms in Israel. Here, babies are placed into communal childcare when they are around four days old and cared for by a nurse who is called a 'metapelet'. The physical aspects of childcare such as feeding and nappy changing are carried out by the nurse and the parents visit the baby to play and cuddle, typically spending about three hours a day with their child after work. When they are around four months old, babies move to another nursery for older children and continue to be reared as a group together cared for by a nurse.

This approach to child-rearing shows important differences from those to which you may be accustomed. The child is likely to have less adult attention than in a family setting and much more contact with peers of similar ages. Both of these may be important influences on their attachments to parents and their later relationships.

Because of these variations in child-rearing practices, psychologists have been interested to see how babies vary between cultures in the types of attachment behaviours they show. Many of these studies have used the Strange Situation methodology devised by Ainsworth.

Research study: Van IJzendoorn and Kroonenberg (1988)

Link

This meta-analysis is based on Ainsworth's Strange Situation research which used observation. You can read more about observation on p112.

Two Dutch psychologists, Van IJzendoorn and Kroonenberg, carried out a meta-analysis in which they analysed the results of 32 separate studies carried out in eight different countries using Ainsworth's 'Strange Situation' to look at differences in attachment types both between and within cultures. In total, over 2,000 babies were studied making this a substantial piece of research. In each of these studies babies were classed using Ainsworth's system as Type A, B or C. A table of Van IJzendoorn and Kroonenberg's findings is shown below.

Table 3 *Comparisons of insecure and secure attachments in eight countries (adapted from Bee, 1995)*

Country	Number of studies	Secure (%)	Avoidant (%)	Ambivalent (%)
China	1	50.0	25.0	25.0
Great Britain	1	75.0	22.2	2.8
Japan	2	67.7	5.2	27.1
Israel	2	64.4	6.8	28.8
Netherlands	4	67.3	26.3	6.4
Sweden	1	74.5	21.6	3.9
US	18	64.8	21.1	14.1
West Germany	3	56.6	35.3	8.1

Table 3 shows that there are large difference between cultures, which are likely to reflect the different approaches to child-rearing in different places. Some of these differences are outlined below:

■ Secure attachments (Type B) were the most common form in all the cultures surveyed. The lowest proportion of secure attachments (50 per cent) was found in China and the highest (around three-quarters) in Great Britain and Sweden.

■ Type A (avoidant attachments) were more common in West Germany than in other Western countries. Avoidant attachments were very rare in Israel and Japan.

■ Type C (ambivalent attachments) were more common in Israel, China and Japan. Scandinavian countries such as Sweden had the lowest rate of ambivalent attachments.

As well as differences between cultures, Van IJzendoorn and Kroonenberg also found differences within cultures. Their three studies carried out in West Germany showed very different findings. In the two Japanese studies, one had no Type A babies whereas the second had around 20 per cent, which is roughly similar to Ainsworth's original findings. Van IJzendoorn and Kroonenberg noted overall that the intra-cultural variation (within cultures) was nearly one-and-a-half times the cross-cultural variation. This large variation within cultures demonstrates the common-sense point that it is an over-simplification to assume that all children are brought up in exactly the same way in a particular country or culture.

Methodological issues

■ This is a substantial meta-analysis considering the attachment behaviours of a very large number of infants. A large sample size is needed in order to generalise findings to the rest of the population.

■ However, over half (18) of the 32 studies were carried out in the US reflecting the dominance by America in research in this area. Twenty-seven of the studies were carried in **individualistic** cultures with only five taking place in **collectivist** cultures. Thus implies that the sample used may not be truly representative.

■ Ainsworth's Strange Situation method for studying attachment was developed in America and may be most suited to studying attachment in this type of culture. Goldberg (2002) argues that we can only make valid interpretations of the Strange Situation in cross-cultural studies if we understand the attitudes to child-rearing in that culture.

Ethical issues

As this is a meta-analysis, it involves bringing together the results of studies which have used similar methods. This means that there are no direct ethical issues associated with it as the data collection and analysis is secondary.

■ Key terms

Individualistic cultures: those where personal independence and achievement are valued. Examples of individualistic cultures in this study are North America and Germany.

Collectivist cultures: those where there is a high degree of interdependence between people. Examples of collectivist cultures in this meta-analysis are Japan, China and Israel.

■ How do these findings relate to child-rearing methods?

These results show that attachment types vary between and with different cultures. Babies are brought up in many different ways and different attributes and qualities may be encouraged in them depending on the values of the particular culture. The child's reaction in the Strange Situation reflects the methods of child-rearing prevalent in that culture. For example, in Japan, babies are very rarely separated from their mother, which explains why Japanese babies tended to react most violently with tears when the mother left, leading them to be classified as ambivalent. In contrast, babies brought up in Israel where they live in small groups and are rarely exposed to strangers, protested most violently when confronted with the stranger. Babies brought up in West Germany – where independence is highly valued and encouraged – showed little distress at separation, leading them to be classified as avoidant. It is important to recognise and understand cultural differences without necessarily assuming that the ways babies are reared in one part of the world is somehow superior to others. Babies have probably evolved to be fairly flexible and able to thrive in a variety of different arrangements.

However, one recent study that demonstrates the need for babies to spend time with their attachment figures was carried out by Aviezer *et al.* (1994) into babies living in the kibbutz system in Israel. In an extensive review of the effects of communal rearing, Aviezer and colleagues argued that the collective sleeping arrangements shown in kibbutzim, where babies and young children sleep together in large dormitories, may not be ideal for children overall and may be more likely to lead to insecure-ambivalent attachments. Following these findings, many kibbutzim are now changing this practice to make arrangements more family-like so children are cared for communally during the day but return to parents at night to sleep in the family house.

Key points:

- Attachment types vary across and within cultures.
- Secure attachments are the most common across all cultures.
- In places where babies rarely experience separation such as Japan they are more likely to be classed as insecure-ambivalent.
- Babies are more likely to be avoidant in Western European countries where independence is encouraged.

✔ Summary questions

14 Which is the most common attachment type across all cultures?

15 Give two examples of how differences in attachment types reflect child-rearing practices.

16 What is meant by inter- and intra-cultural variation?

17 Explain one criticism of van IJzendoorn and Kroonenberg's meta-analysis. Discuss methodological criticisms of meta-analysis research.

Disruption of attachment

Learning objectives:

- Understand what is meant by separation, privation and institutionalisation.

- Discover the range of effects these experiences have on children.

- Consider factors which influence whether these effects are permanent or temporary.

Key terms

Separation: takes place when the child spends some time away from their primary attachment figure. Separations may be for short or longer periods.

Separation anxiety: a longer-term effect of separation in which the child alternates between clinginess and detachment.

We have seen the importance of attachments to the development of the child and their later adjustment. In this section we shall consider some disruptions to attachment that can take place including **separations** and the lack of attachment, which may be experienced by children who have spent some time in institutional care.

The short- and long-term effects of separation

The immediate response to separation – protest-despair-detachment

Many children experience short-term separations from their attachment figure during their early childhood. These may be planned, for example if the child's mother goes into hospital to have another baby, or unplanned, such as if a parent falls ill. Most research in this area has focused on the separation of mother and baby, although more recently research has begun to consider father and child separations.

Once children have formed their first attachment at around eight–nine months, they are likely to respond to separation from their attachment figure with a behaviour pattern characterised by three stages (also referred to as PDD):

- Protest: the child cries, screams and protests angrily when the parent leaves. They are likely to try and cling to the parent and may struggle to escape from others who pick them up.

- Despair: after a while, the child's angry protest begins to subside and they appear calmer although still upset. The child is likely to refuse others' attempts to comfort them and they may appear to be withdrawn and uninterested in anything.

- Detachment: if the separation continues the child may begin to engage with other people again although they may be wary. They are likely to reject the caregiver when they return and show signs of anger.

This reaction to short-term separation was shown by the Robertsons in their study of John, a 17-month-old child who was placed in a residential nursery for nine days while his mother went into hospital to have a baby. You can watch a clip of the Robertsons' research on John in the film *Young Children in Brief Separation*.

The longer-term effect of separation

One longer-term effect of separation is **separation anxiety**. This may persist long after the separation is over and is shown by a range of behaviours:

- Extreme clinginess: the child may 'cling' whenever the parent attempts to leave them even in situations such as nursery where they have been happy to be left before. They may become clingy in anticipation of separation, for example when a baby-sitter is due to arrive.

■ Detachment: the child may appear to be detached from the caregiver and refuse to be cuddled or hugged. This behaviour may be designed to protect them from being hurt again if they are left. Many children alternate between detachment and clinginess, making it difficult for parents to predict how they will behave.

■ The child may be more demanding of their attachment figure.

What factors affect the child's response to separation?

Young children do not all respond in the same way to short separations – some become much more distressed than others. The precise response and amount of distress shown by the child depends on a number of factors:

■ The age of the child: the response to short-term separation is strongest between the ages of about 12 and 18 months. This was first noted by Schaffer and Callender (1959) who studied the behaviour of 76 babies aged between three and 51 weeks of age who were admitted to a children's hospital. They found that children younger than seven months showed minimal upset, adjusted to hospital well and showed little clinging. After this age, the strength of the child's response increased up to about 18 months with the most severe reaction being shown between 12 and 18 months. This may be related to development of the child's language skills as well as the ability to understand that the attachment figure will return (Maccoby, 1980).

■ The type of attachment between the child and the caregiver: a securely attached child is more likely to cope better with short separations than a child with an insecure-ambivalent attachment type. This may be because of their belief that the mother figure will return (Barrett, 1997).

■ The sex of the child: boys seem to respond more strongly to separation than girls although there are wide differences within as well as between sexes (Gross and McIlveen, 1997).

Fig. 6 *Separation – a stressful experience for small children*

- Whom the child is left with and the quality of the care they receive: we have noted that many children older than about ten months have multiple attachments. If the child is left with another attachment figure such as a grandparent, the effects may be minimal.
- Experience of previous separations: the child who is accustomed to brief separations such as being left at playgroup or with grandparents is likely to respond less strongly than the child who is very rarely separated from their attachment figure.

Some researchers such as Barrett (1997) have argued that the stages described by the PDD model are misleading. Barrett argues that the child's initial response to separation is not a 'protest' but is an effort to cope with the feelings produced by separation.

■ Lack of attachment: the effects of privation

As well as the fairly common experience of separation, a relatively small number of children experience **privation**, the lack of any attachment at all in early childhood. Privation can result from circumstances such as international conflict or civil war when many thousands of children may lose their parents and spend time in institutional care. Alternatively, privation can result from circumstances in which children experience neglect because their caregiver is unable to care for them.

There are two types of study that have informed us about the effects of privation:

- Case studies exist of children who have been brought up in extreme circumstances such as total isolation where they have been unable to form an attachment, for example Koluchova (1972) and Skuse (1984).
- Studies of children who have been raised in institutions and late adopted, for example, Tizard and Hodges (1978).

In this section of the course we shall examine the effects on children of early privation. Some of this research involves naturally occurring case studies where we shall consider the ethical issues involved in such case study research.

🔆 Case studies of privation

Koluchova (1972, 1977 and 1991) reported the case study of twin boys who were born in 1960 in Czechoslovakia and brought up in care after the death of their mother. At the age of 18 months they returned to live with their father and stepmother and suffered serious privation until the age of seven when they were discovered and taken into care. Between the ages of 18 months and seven years, they were locked in an unheated cellar away from human company, starved and beaten. When discovered, they had no speech, were terrified of people and had serious health problems from their early malnutrition.

Following discovery they attended a school for children with learning difficulties for intensive rehabilitation and were fostered then adopted by two sisters who provided a secure and permanent home for them. In this environment, they developed average intelligence and formed strong emotional bonds with their new family. When followed up by Koluchova in 1977, they were found to have attained average intelligence and to have developed into happy and sociable boys who were attending a mainstream school. In a follow-up in 1991 (the study began in 1969),

Key term

Privation: literally the lack of something. Emotional privation is the lack of attachment or love in a child who has been unable to form an attachment. Physical privation refers to the lack of basic physical needs such as food or shelter.

Developmental psychology

Koluchova reported that the early damage had been totally repaired and there were no signs of psychological problems.

Skuse (1984) reported the case of two sisters who suffered extreme social and emotional privation in early childhood. Their mother had severe learning difficulties and may have also had a mental illness. The children were kept in a small room, and tied to the bed with dog leads to keep the flat clean and prevent them from falling off the balcony. When they became too noisy they were covered with a blanket. The children were found by Social Services when they were aged 3½ (Louise) and 2½ (Mary), and put into care in a children's hospital. When found, they had no real speech and showed little evidence of play. Following speech therapy, Louise developed normal language and began to attend a primary school at the age of five. In contrast Mary did not develop language skills and was moved to a unit for autistic children aged 7½. A brother found with them was raised in a different family, remained autistic and had severe learning difficulties.

Evaluation of case study research

Ethical issues

Case studies of this nature provide serious ethical challenges and dilemmas for the researcher. Because the children involved are often seriously affected they may be unable to give their fully informed consent to take part in further study. Foster parents or carers may also feel under pressure from researchers to allow continued study of the children in their care. The ongoing follow-up of children in their later lives may be experienced by them as intrusive and some who have taken part in case studies have later suggested that the experience has been actively damaging to them, making them feel as if they are simply 'objects' of psychological interest. Researchers in this area tread a fine line in balancing the desire to study effects of privation against the needs of those directly involved.

Methodological issues: Lack of control

These case studies provide valuable information about the effects of early privation on children's emotional and cognitive development. However, the children involved have often suffered emotional and physical privation as well as physical maltreatment or abuse. It is difficult to assess the effects of each of these experiences on their overall development. In addition, case studies are retrospective: they involve looking back into the past to piece together what may have happened in the early life of the children. It is very difficult to establish this with accuracy and therefore it is difficult to draw conclusions from case study research.

These research problems were largely overcome in a natural experiment carried out by Tizard and Hodges (1984 and 1989) examining children raised in an institution. Their early childhoods were well documented, so there was no need to attempt to piece together the past. In addition, the children had all received a good standard of physical care and the only form of privation they had suffered was emotional privation.

Research study: Tizard and Hodges (1984 and 1989)

Tizard and Hodges carried out a natural experiment, which examined the long-term effects of emotional privation on 65 children brought up in a children's home until they were around four years old. During this time, the children were unable to form an attachment to any of the adults. Staff at the home were discouraged from forming relationships with the children to prevent the children becoming upset if the staff left their jobs. By the time the children were two years old, they had had on average 24 different carers and by the age of four around 50. The children were provided with good physical care and intellectual stimulation in the institution and showed no cognitive deficits.

At the age of two, the children showed a range of unusual 'attachment' behaviours. Rather than showing fear of strangers, they would run to any adult who entered the room and demand their attention in an indiscriminate manner. They would also cry when the adult left, despite the fact that they had no attachment with them. These behaviours are characteristic of children raised in institutions and are part of a behaviour pattern known as 'disinhibited attachment'.

A change took place when the children were around four years old. Twenty-five were returned or 'restored' to their biological parents who had given them up to care as babies. Another group of 33 were adopted and the remaining seven continued in care, being fostered for some periods of time and returning to the children's home at others. This was the naturally occurring independent variable. Tizard and Hodges visited the children with their families when the children were eight, and at 16 the children took part in interviews with a key adult (mother, father or careworker) present. Tizard and Hodges also asked for permission to contact the teenagers' schools and, if this was given, teachers and same-sex peers completed an assessment via a questionnaire to assess their attachment behaviour – the dependent variable.

Tizard and Hodges found that almost all of the adoptees (20/21) and some of the restored children (6/13) formed close attachment to their parents by the age of eight. This situation was similar at age 16 with more adoptees than restored children being close to their parents. This may have been due to the considerable effort made by adoptive families to form strong attachments with their children.

> ■ Link
>
> You can read more about disinhibited attachment behaviour patterns in the section on institutionalisation (see p70).

Table 4 *Tizard and Hodges's findings: attachments at age 8 and 16*

	Close attachment at age 8	Rejecting or hostile	Close attachment at age 16	Rejecting or hostile
Adopted children	20/21	1/21	17/21	4/21
Restored children	6/13	7/13	5/9	4/9

In terms of relationships with peers and siblings, the restored group had worse relationships with their siblings than the adoptees. However, all three groups raised in the institution had difficulties with peer relationships and were less likely to belong to a crowd. They were rated by teachers as more likely to seek attention from adults and members of the restored group were more argumentative.

Tizard and Hodges concluded that those who were adopted seemed to develop good family relationships. In contrast, the restored group continued to experience some problems and difficulties in their family relationships, notably with siblings. Both groups showed similar difficulties in relationships with peers. They continued to seem oriented to please adults but less able to form relationships with those outside the family.

Methodological issues

■ This study is commendable in the use of a range of research methods to collect information on the children's relationships including in-depth interviews, questionnaires to teachers and self-report measures.

■ One difficulty found with longitudinal research is participant attrition. This means that at each stage of the research, participants drop out of the study and do not wish to take part. In this study, 65 children were orignally in the sample but only 51 were studied at age eight. Those who continue to participate may not be a representative group.

■ This study is a natural experiment. The independent variable was the place in which the child was brought up from age four and this was not controlled by the researchers. This brings up the issue of how it was decided which children should be adopted and which should remain in the institution. It is possible that there may have been differences and perhaps the adopted group were more socially skilled, making them easier to place in adoptive families.

Ethical issues

This study involves the extremely sensitive area of family relationships. It was important for the researchers to ensure that families and children were placed under no pressure to continue to participate and for the researchers to respond in a sensitive and non-judgemental way during the follow-up interviews.

■ ## The effects of institutionalisation

Early experiences lead to some children spending a period of time in institutional care. This may be due to family breakdown or an inability of the caregiver to look after the child. While children in the UK are likely to be placed with foster parents, children in other parts of the world are regularly cared for in institutions. The civil war in Romania led to thousands of children being orphaned and many of these were raised in institutions in which the conditions were extremely poor. Film coverage indicates that these babies received minimum physical care, often being fed with bottles propped up in their cots. Due to the impoverished nature of the environment and the very small numbers of staff, there was minimal time for interaction or play and most of these babies spent all day in their cots.

Effects on emotional development

Tizard and Hodges's study (see above) pointed to an unusual pattern of behaviour in children raised without attachments in institutions. This **disinhibited attachment** behaviour pattern is being examined by Rutter *et al.* (2007) in their longitudinal study of Romanian orphans adopted by UK families.

■ **Link**

Tizard and Hodges' study is an example of a natural experiment.

You can read more about this kind of research on p107.

■ **Key terms**

Institutionalisation: refers to the behaviour patterns of children who have been raised in institutions such as orphanages or children's homes. In institutions children may have relationships with a variety of staff. However, they may not have a one-to-one attachment in the same way as a child raised in a family.

Disinhibited attachment: a behaviour pattern shown by some children who have been raised in institutions. Key features include attention-seeking behaviour towards all adults, even strangers, a lack of fear of strangers, making inappropriate physical contact with adults and lack of checking back to the parent in stressful situations.

Fig. 7 *Jacqueline Wilson's Story* 'Tracey Beaker' *explores institutionalisation*

Research study: Rutter *et al.* (2007)

Rutter *et al.* (2007) are carrying out an ongoing longitudinal study, comparing Romanian orphans who were adopted by UK families with UK-born adoptees who were placed with families before they were six months of age. The Romanian adoptees entered the orphanage as small babies between one and two weeks old. Conditions in the institutions were very poor. 58 babies were adopted before they were six months old and 59 were adopted between six and 24 months of age. 48 babies were classed as late placed adoptees (between two and four years of age). These formed the three conditions of the naturally-occurring independent variable. At the time of adoption, over half of the Romanian children showed evidence of severe malnourishment. They were in the bottom third of the population for weight and head size. Some of these children have been followed up at ages four, six and eleven years, using a range of measures including interviews and observations of the child's behaviour.

At age six, Rutter *et al.* found evidence of disinhibited attachment which they defined as 'a pervasive pattern of attention seeking behaviours with a relative lack of selectivity in social relationships' (p17). As Table 5 shows, disinhibited behaviour was most common in the late adopted Romanian group with over one-quarter (26.1 per cent) showing 'marked' disinhibited attachment behaviours. The behaviour pattern was extremely rare in UK adoptees (3.8 per cent) and early adopted children (8.9 per cent). This suggests that disinhibited attachments are more likely in children who have experienced longer periods in institutions.

■ **Link**

As with Tizard and Hodges' study, this is an example of a natural experiment.

You can read more about this type of experiment on p107.

Table 5 *Disinhibited attachment in Romanian and UK adoptees aged 6 years*

	No disinhibition	Mild disinhibition	Marked disinhibition
UK adoptees	21 (40.4%)	29 (55.8%)	2 (3.8%)
Romanian adopted ≤ 6 mths	24 (53.3%)	17 (37.8%)	4 (8.9%)
Romanian – adopted 6–24 mths	26 (29.5%)	39 (44.3%)	23 (26.1%)

In 2007, some of these children were followed up aged 11. Rutter found that the disinhibited behaviour pattern had persisted in many adoptees. Of the 83 Romanian children showing mild or

Developmental psychology

marked disinhibited attachment at age six, 45 (54 per cent) of these still showed this five years later. While this indicates a drop in the number of children showing this behaviour pattern at age 11, it is still well over half. Even more worryingly, Rutter found that many of the children showing disinhibited attachments were receiving help from either special educational and/or mental health services.

Methodological issues

- This study is using a range of measurements to assess the children's behaviour including semi-structured interviews and observation to see if the child makes inappropriate physcial contact. This makes the research rich and detailed.

- As with Tizard and Hodges's study, participant attrition is an issue in this longitudinal research study.

- Rutter *et al.* acknowledge that it has been difficult to obtain information about the quality of care in many of the institutions in Romania making it difficult to assess the extent of privation in the early environments of the children in the study.

Ethical issues

As with other longitudinal studies in this area, researchers need to be sensitive to the needs of both the children and their adoptive families in research of this nature. The extent of participant attrition shows that some families may wish to remove themselves from further study and to bring up their children outside the glare of research. Freedom to withdraw from a research study is an important ethical principle.

An in-depth case study of two Romanian children adopted into a Canadian family is being carried out by Chisholm (2000). These children were adopted aged three years three months and four years five months having spent their first years in an extremely deprived orphanage. Chisholm first interviewed the parents when the children had been in the adoptive home for eight months and eleven months respectively, and followed them up again three years later. As well as an interview with parents, the children have also been observed in a separation and reunion scenario similar to Ainsworth's Strange Situation. Chisholm has found that the children have adopted quite different attachment patterns with their adoptive family implying that there are likely to be individual differences in children's responses to early privation experiences.

Can children recover from institutionalisation and privation?

Studies on privation and institutionalisation suggest that children can recover from adverse early experiences. However, the extent of recovery depends on a number of factors.

- The quality of care at the institution: Dontas *et al.* (1985) carried out two studies on babies in a Greek orphanage to see if institutionally raised children could develop attachments in the normal way. In one study, they looked at 15 babies aged between seven and nine months (the important age at which attachments

Developmental psychology

are formed). Each child had been given a member of staff to care specifically for them and had formed an attachment with their carer. Dontas visited them after two weeks in their adoptive home. Dontas found that the babies adjusted well and by the end of the second week had started to form attachments to their new carers. In a second study at the institution, 16 babies aged between five and twelve months were observed playing with familiar and unfamiliar peers of a similar age. As in the above study, each of the babies had been able to form an attachment with a carer at the children's home. Their play behaviour showed none of the apparent effects of institutionalisation such as indiscriminate attention seeking that had previously been noted in Tizard and Hodges's study. This research shows how important it is for children in institutions to be able to develop attachments to staff at the normal age of between seven and eight months.

■ The age of the child when removed from privation or institutionalisation: children who are removed from privation when still young, such as the Romanian orphans adopted under six months, tend to make better developmental progress both cognitively and emotionally than those who have experienced privation for longer. Age is particularly important in relation to language development. While children show good language catch-up before puberty, they are much less likely to develop language skills after 11 or 12 years of age.

■ The quality of care after privation/institutionalisation: children are likely to do best when they are placed in a loving and supportive environment. They need the opportunity to form a one-to-one attachment with an adult who gives them sufficient attention as shown in research by Koluchova (1972 and 1991). Tizard and Hodges's study found that the adopted children were more strongly attached to their new parents than the restored group. This may be due to the quality of care provided by the adoptive parents.

■ The follow-on experiences in later life: there is evidence to suggest that adult experiences and relationships can go some way towards repairing early adverse circumstances. Quinton and Rutter (1984/1988) compared two groups of women in their twenties. Half had been brought up in care and spent several years of their childhood in children's homes. They were compared with a group matched for age that came from the same area but had not spent time in care. The care group was more likely to have relationship breakdowns, criminal records and more difficulties with parenting their children. However, there were dramatic differences *between* women who had been brought up in care. Those who had positive experiences at school and later good relationships or marriages fared much better. Quinton and Rutter argued that positive experiences in early adulthood led to different 'developmental pathways' for the two groups of women. By this they show that it is not just early experiences that influence later development. When they are followed by good experiences in later life, the early effects can be overcome.

Developmental psychology

Key points:

■ Protest-despair-detachment is a short-term response to separation. Separation anxiety is a long-term effect of separation. The strength of these responses depends on a range of factors including the age of the child and quality of the substitute care provided.

■ Emotional and physical privation can lead to cognitive and emotional problems. The longer the privation continues, the longer the effects are likely to last.

■ Children can form attachments after privation but some still experience problems with peer relationships.

■ One emotional effect of institutionalisation and privation is disinhibited attachment. Late adopted children appear to be most susceptible to this.

 Summary questions

18 Outline the behaviour of a child who is experiencing separation anxiety and disinhibited attachment.

19 Name two factors that affect the child's response to short-term separations.

20 Outline the findings of one study into the effects of privation on the child.

21 Outline one possible effect of institutionalisation.

22 Discuss factors that can influence how well children recover from early institutionalisation.

Chapter summary

Further reading and weblinks

H. Bee, *The Developing Child*, HarperCollins (1995)

J. Dunn, *The Beginnings of Social Understanding*, Blackwell (1988)

K. Durkin, *Developmental Social Psychology*, Blackwell (1995)

R. Schaffer, *Social Development*, Blackwell (1996)

P. Smith, H. Cowie and M. Blades, *Understanding Children's Development*, Blackwell (1998)

Films: you may wish to watch *Good Will Hunting* (1997), which tells the story of a young man with an attachment disorder.

Links

For more information about interviews, see p119.

For more information about reliability and validity, see p92.

For more information about qualitative and quantitative data, see p123.

For more information about data presentation, see pp123 and 129.

- Developmental psychologists are interested in the early relationships or attachments formed between young children and their caregivers.
- Bonds from parent to child are often formed quickly. Attachments take longer to develop.
- Attachments have been explained in terms of classical and operant conditioning.
- Attachments are adaptive as they help the baby to survive. They are also important for later adjustment and relationships.
- There are individual differences in the types of attachments formed, which may relate to the sensitivity of the parent and the temperament of the baby.
- Cultural differences in attachment patterns relate to child-rearing practices.
- Attachments may be disrupted through short- or long-term separations. Separations may have short-term effects and can lead to separation anxiety.
- The emotional impact of disruption depends on the age of the child and the quality of substitute care provided for them.
- Some children experience privation – the lack of any form of attachment. Some of these may go on to develop disinhibited attachment patterns.

How science works: practical activity

We have noted in this chapter that studying young children poses serious ethical questions for the researcher. For this reason, the activities in this section of the course require you to carry out interviews or questionnaires with adults, rather than to observe young children.

If you have contact with someone who has a pre-school child, devise and carry out a short interview asking them about how their child responds to a number of different situations involving short separations, such as being left with a baby-sitter or at playgroup. You will need to think about what type of interview to use as well as the number and types of questions (open/closed) to use. You can consider how to analyse the qualitative data produced by interview material. You may also like to think about devising a rating scale similar to that used by Schaffer and Emerson (1964) for parents to rate their child's responses to separation. You can then go on to discuss the relative advantages and disadvantages of quantitative and qualitative data in this type of research.

Reflect on this experience of collecting data and consider the strengths and weaknesses of interviews, the reliability and validity of the data and the relative advantages and disadvantages of quantitative and qualitative data in this type of research.

You could go on to do a more rigorous investigation of the stages in the development of attachment suggested by Schaffer and Emerson. Devise a short interview schedule as above but this time ensure the questions will give you data about the child's responses to separation at different ages from 0–15 months. Work as a group so that you can collect data about a number of children. Sample people whose children are just over 1 year old so that you would expect the interviewee to be able to recall their baby's response to separation at different ages.

Pool the data from your group's interviews. Consider how to analyse and present the qualitative and quantitative interview material and whether the interview data supports or challenges Schaffer and Emerson's findings about the age and/or sequence of development of attachment behaviour.

How does day care affect children's social development?

Developmental psychology

Learning objectives:

- Find out what day care is and what different types of day care are available.

- Explore the impact of different types of day care on children's positive social development, for example, their ability to make friends and cooperate with other children.

- Consider the impact of day care on negative aspects of social development including aggressive behaviour.

Key term

Day care: refers to care for children under school age, generally at a nursery or by a childminder.

AQA   Examiner's tip

Be able to name the different types of day care and explain the main ways in which family and nursery based care differ.

What is day care and what different types exist?

In this section we will examine research that looks at the effects of different day care settings on children's social development. Positive aspects of social development that have been studied include the child's relationships with their peers, their ability to mix and make friends, to cooperate, share toys and empathise with others. Negative aspects of social development, such as the child's use of aggressive behaviours, have also been considered. The main options for day care are as follows:

1   Nursery based care: parents are currently entitled to free nursery places for all children aged three years and above. Nurseries are staffed by trained workers, may be attached to a primary school and often benefit from use of school facilities. Nurseries are inspected by Ofsted (Office for Standards in Education) and are required to plan their activities.

2   Family based care:

- Registered childminders: here, the child receives care in the childminder's house rather than at their own home. The childminder often has young children of their own so the child is likely to have others to play with. Childminders need to be registered and are inspected by Ofsted.

- Nanny/au pair: this type of childcare involves an employee who looks after the child in the child's own home. The child is likely to be with their siblings rather than with children from other families.

- Informal arrangements including childcare by relatives or neighbours: this is often unpaid and has received little systematic research.

These settings differ in the number of children looked after by each adult and the amount of attention each child receives. Children are likely to receive the most attention in family based care settings and the least attention at nursery school. Another difference is the number of other children available to play with; this is highest in nursery settings and lower in family based care.

The effects of day care on social development

Children attending day care at nurseries or at a childminder generally have more contact with other children of a similar age than children who are cared for at home. This may provide them with increased opportunities to develop important social skills such as sharing and talking to others than children reared in a family setting.

Several studies have suggested that day care can be helpful for children's social development. Andersson (1989, 1992) carried out a variety of studies in Sweden, which found potentially good effects. In one study,

Andersson found that children who attended day care were able to get along with other children better, were more sociable and outgoing, and had better abilities to play with their peers than children who did not attend day care. Clarke-Stewart (1991) compared the progress of 150 children who had experienced different kinds of day care and found that children who attended nurseries had better social development than those who were looked after in family settings. More recently, Schindler, Moely and Frank (1998) found that children who spend more time in day care played more pro-socially with other children, implying that more time in day care produces helpful and cooperative toddlers. Field *et al.* (1988) have also argued that those children who attend full-time day care take part in more cooperative play than those who only attend part-time.

However, other studies have presented contradictory findings and argued that day care may have negative effects on social development. For example, DiLalla (1988) found a negative correlation between the amount of time children spend in care and their amount of pro-social behaviour. Children who spent more time in day care were less cooperative and helpful in their relationships with other children.

Why might these findings contradict each other? One suggestion by Campbell, Lamb and Hwang (2000) is that most of these studies have examined the quantity of care (how many hours the child attends) but have not considered the quality of care that children receive, which may be very important in relation to the overall effects on the child. It is possible that studies that report positive effects on social behaviour involve higher quality care than those that report negative effects. In addition Campbell has pointed out that many of the studies into the effects of day care are retrospective – rather than following a group of children across time they rely on memory and recall of day care experiences. In order to address these issues, Campbell *et al.* (2000) carried out a **longitudinal** research study, which looked at social development and related it to both quantity and quality of care.

Key term

Longitudinal: a study that follows the same group across a long period of time, returning to study them at regular intervals.

Research study: Campbell, Lamb and Hwang (2000)

Campbell *et al.* studied a group of children from Gothenburg in Sweden who all attended childcare continuously between the ages of 18 months and 3½ years of age. Of these, nine attended family based day care (e.g. childminder) and 30 attended nursery with a further nine switching from family based to nursery based care during the study. They were compared with a group of children whose parents had applied for day care places but who did not obtain them due to competition. At the age of around 18 months, before the children started day care, they were observed in their homes playing with familiar peers. The researcher assessed the standard of care the children were receiving at home using Caldwell's HOME inventory, a method of measuring the quality of a child's environment. After they had started day care, they were visited in the day care setting and observed playing with other children for 30 minutes. This gave the researchers a baseline condition at 18 months to see how socially skilled the children were before care started. These two assessments of the child in family and day care settings were repeated when the child was 2½ and 3½ years old.

At age 6½ the social competence of the children was assessed by asking the care provider to describe the child's social skills.

Fig. 1 *Children playing at a nursery*

■ Link

You can read more about observational research methods on p112.

Developmental psychology

At 8½, class teachers were asked to give their perceptions of the child's social behaviour. Finally, when they reached 15, each of the participants was visited at home where they completed two self-report measurements of social development, the friendship quality questionnaire (FQQ) and a social style questionnaire (SSQ), which included a range of questions such as 'How good are you at going to places where there are unfamiliar people?' and 'How good are you at listening while others let off steam about problems?'

Campbell *et al.*'s study produced a range of interesting findings. In terms of amount of care time spent in day care, children who spent long days in day care (for example, from 8am until 6pm) under the age of 3½ were found to be less socially competent. However, those who attended more days per week but had shorter days were more socially competent. While this appears contradictory it is probably explained by the length of the day – small children who experience long days in day care may become tired and frustrated at having to share adult attention for such a long time, leading to more negative interactions with other children. In contrast, those who attend more days but have shorter sessions gain more social benefit. In terms of quality of care, the findings were much clearer. Those children who attended high quality care before age 3½ developed better social abilities. Campbell also found that social competence was relatively stable between 3½ and 15 years of age. Children who were socially skilled at 3½ years of age also tended to be socially skilled at the three later intervals. This implies that children's social skills have largely developed by around age 3½ and then remain relatively constant across childhood. This study strongly suggests that good quality early childcare for children at least up to the age of 3½ years is important in the development of socially skilled children and that their level of social competence persists through childhood and adolescence.

Methodological issues

■ This study took a **prospective** approach, following the children from around the age of 18 months through to adolescence. This follow-up is much longer than many studies and allows us to see if day care has long-term effects.

■ All of the children who took part were assessed before they started day care providing a clear baseline of their social skills at the start of the study.

■ The researchers used a range of measurements to assess each child's social competence including reports from teachers and play workers and self-reports from adolescents. Using data from a range of different people including teachers and adolescents themselves provides a rich and detailed picture of the child's social abilities.

■ This research study considered day care in Sweden, which is very well funded. It may be difficult to apply these findings to day care in other countries where nurseries are less well funded.

Ethical issues

This study required considerable sensitivity from the researchers when dealing with both the children and their parents. The principle of fully informed parental consent is extremely important when working with young children.

■ Key term

Prospective: refers to the future. Prospective studies involve following participants over a period of time from the start of the study. An example would be studies of life stress and health.

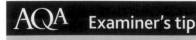

Examiner's tip

Be clear on the findings of Campbell *et al.*'s study and ensure you can explain the methodological strengths and limitations of this piece of research.

Can day care have negative effects?

Others have argued that day care can have potentially negative effects on the social development of children. Belsky has pointed to possible negative effects from a longitudinal study in the US, which has followed more than 1,000 children from birth. Belsky (2006) suggests that children who have experienced day care tend to show advanced cognitive and language development but may also show higher levels of problem behaviours including aggression towards peers. They may also be less obedient to authority figures such as adults as they grow older. This view has also been taken by Maccoby and Lewis (2003) who argued that the more hours spent in day care before the child was 4½ correlated with a range of negative social outcomes, including more behaviour problems at school, lower social skills and greater amounts of conflict with teachers. Field (1988) agreed with this view and argued that teachers rated children who had been to full-time day care as more aggressive and assertive with their peers.

However, while these findings can be interpreted negatively there are others who argue this may simply result from the need for the child who attends day care to develop greater independence at an earlier age. This can show itself in both positive and negative ways. On the one hand, children are more confident in dealing with social situations with peers but on the other hand this may lead them to be more challenging of adults. Clarke-Stewart (1990, 1992) argues that this is simply a sign that young children learn to look after themselves and think for themselves at an earlier age when they attend day care.

Other studies have indicated that day care does not always produce children who are more aggressive than home care and that the effect may sometimes be in the other direction! Borge *et al.* (2004) carried out a study using a representative sample of 3,431 two to three year olds living in Canada comparing home-reared with day care children. Maternal questionnaires were used to ask about the child's level of aggression, for example 'How often does your child kick, bite, or hurt another child?' (never, sometimes, often) and 'How does your child react when accidentally hurt by another child?' Borge *et al.* also took into account the role of family background by considering the occupational background of parents, mother's education, the number of siblings and family functioning. The findings showed that aggression was significantly higher in home-reared than in day care children. Once again, this implies that quality of care may be most important in determining the effects on the child.

■ Comparing different types of day care

Other studies have compared the outcomes for children's social development when they attend different types of day care. Melhuish (1990) carried out a **quasi-experimental** piece of research comparing three groups of children in London who started day care before they were nine months old. This study was unusual in its inclusion of informal day care arrangements, which have received very little attention by way of research. The three different day care settings were care by relatives, care by childminder and a private nursery. These care settings varied in the ratio of adults to children and in contact with other children. The adult–child ratio was highest when relatives cared for the child and lowest in the nursery setting where several children were cared for by each adult. In contrast, contact with other children was highest at nursery and lowest in relative care.

■ Key term

Quasi-experiment: an experiment that takes place in a field setting but the independent variable is already set, i.e. is not controlled by the investigator.

Developmental psychology

Melhuish assessed the children at 18 months and three years for their language skills and their ability to cooperate and share with other children. At 18 months, babies who had been cared for by relatives showed the highest levels of language skills and language was least developed in those children attending nursery. At three years, the nursery children were still slightly less advanced than the relative care group in language but they showed higher levels of pro-social behaviours such as sharing, cooperation and the ability to empathise with other children. This study suggests that choice of day care may be a case of 'swings and roundabouts': there may be different potential gains for children in each setting.

■ Assessing the effects of day care: evaluation

These studies have shown that it can be difficult to assess the effects of day care on children's social development for several reasons:

■ The variety of day care settings: day care arrangements vary and include family and nursery based care. These arrangements differ in terms of adult–child ratios and the number of other children present. Both of these can influence the child's experience of day care.

■ The time spent in day care: children start day care at different ages and the time they spend each week varies depending on the working pattern of their parents. It does not make sense to compare a child who starts day care at six months when maternity leave ends with one who starts at age three as we are not comparing like with like. The time spent in day care can also be complicated by the length of time for which the child attends, as shown in Campbell *et al.*'s study.

■ Day care settings vary in quality: as Campbell *et al.*'s study has shown quality is very important to the overall experience of the child.

■ Children have different temperaments and different attachment styles, meaning that some get more out of day care than others.

■ Families who use nursery based care may differ from those who use relatives for childcare. Melhuish *et al.* (1991) has compared the attitudes and choices of 255 women to work and childcare. Those who return to work after maternity leave tend to have higher status jobs and to believe strongly in the importance of maternal employment. Those who use family based care (i.e. relatives) tend to have stronger identities as mothers.

Key points:

■ Evidence has shown that good quality day care can have a range of beneficial social effects on children including their ability to play cooperatively with others, to mix and make friends.

■ Day care is a potentially stressful experience and poor quality care can be associated with less positive social outcomes such as increased aggression.

■ Evidence suggests that social skills develop early in childhood, before the age of about 3½, and then stabilise, pointing to the importance of high quality day care for very young children.

■ It is difficult to assess the effects of day care due to the variety of settings and individual differences in children's attachment styles and temperaments.

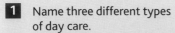

✔ Summary questions

1 Name three different types of day care.

2 Explain two possible effects of day care on social development.

3 What were the main findings of Campbell *et al.*'s study of day care?

4 Why is it difficult to assess the effects of day care on social development?

Implications of research into attachment and day care for childcare practices

Learning objectives:

- Explore how research into attachment has influenced childcare practices.
- Find out some characteristics of high quality day care.

In 1997, government policy ensured that all four year olds would be eligible for free nursery places, which could be taken at state or private nurseries. In 2004, the National Childcare Strategy was launched, which stated that free state nursery places were to be made available for all three and four year olds and provided guidelines for nurseries on what they should 'teach'. The strategy also introduced support and training for childminders. Finally, Sure Start programmes were set up to support families with children aged lower than three years old in economically deprived areas.

How has attachment research influenced childcare practices?

Research into attachments and specifically Bowlby's theory has suggested that:

- the child needs to have a secure attachment with an adult
- the child can have multiple attachments with a range of different adults
- the child needs to be able to use the attachment figure as a safe base to explore their environment and to seek security. They should be able to rely on their attachment figure in times of stress or when they are frightened.

Studies have indicated that day care can be a stressful experience for young children, because it involves separation from the attachment figure, an unfamiliar environment and strangers. Steele (2001) found that young children in the Strange Situation (see p58) have increased levels of cortisol (a stress hormone) up to half-an-hour after their parent returns from a brief separation. Watamura *et al.* (2006) compared the levels of cortisol in the same group of babies and toddlers on different days of the week as they attended nursery or stayed at home. They found that cortisol levels increased gradually from morning to afternoon when the babies were in the day care setting but not when they were at home. These increases were greatest for children aged 24–36 months and worse for toddlers who were shy or fearful.

In order to reduce stress and to make day care a positive experience for babies and toddlers, many nurseries have adopted a key worker approach (Goldschmied and Jackson, 1994). The key worker is a named person who acts as the significant adult for each child during their time at nursery. This adult is there to see to the needs of the child and for them to use as their attachment figure in times of stress, notably the beginning of the day when the parent drops off the child, and at collection time when children may be anxious about their parent's return. The key worker's job is to be emotionally available to the child and to provide warmth and security to help them to settle into the nursery day.

What constitutes good quality day care?

There is reasonable agreement among researchers about the characteristics of good quality day care. 'Structural' characteristics refer to how day care is organised, which is set out in government policies. Campbell *et al.* (2000) argue that structural characteristics of good quality day care include the following:

■ A low adult to child ratio to ensure each child can receive plenty of adult attention and stimulation. The recommended ratio varies depending on the age of the child.

■ A small sized group: small groups are easier for young children to deal with as there are fewer strangers.

■ A mixed age group of children combining older and younger children: research by Clarke-Stewart *et al.* (1994) notes that social development is improved when children are placed in mixed age groups. This is likely to be because this gives young toddlers the opportunity to observe their older peers' interactions and to copy their social behaviours.

■ Well-trained staff and a low staff turnover: this allows children to get to know staff and prevents feelings of insecurity when adults leave. This can be achieved by ensuring staff are trained and well paid.

Quality can also relate to the child's actual experiences of day care in terms of the emotional environment provided (termed 'process' characteristics). These include the following:

■ A secure attachment: good quality day care provides children with a stable attachment figure, a person with whom they can feel safe and secure in times of stress. The worker should be responsive and warm to the child. A good way to achieve this is in the form of a key worker system. Day care settings that have high staff turnover will be unsettling for the child.

■ A structured (rather than regimented) day: good quality day care should involve a structure to the day's activities with free time to play, some group time and some structured activities such as drawing. Routines help the child to feel that their environment is predictable and this is an important part of feeling safe.

Key points:

■ Attachment theory suggests that the day care environment should provide the child with a secure and warm attachment.

■ A key worker system is one way to achieve this.

■ Children do better in small groups comprising children of different ages.

✓ Summary questions

5 Explain one way in which day care practice has been influenced by research into attachment.

6 Outline two features of good quality day care.

7 Discuss the importance of structural and process characteristics in children's experience of day care.

Chapter summary

✔ 🎧

Further reading and weblinks

L. Dryden, R. Forbes, P. Mukherji and L. Pound, *Early Years*, Hodder & Stoughton (2005)

You can look at the government's childcare strategy by going to www.surestart.gov.uk

Links

For more information about the Campbell *et al.* study, see p77.

For more information about natural experiments, see p107.

For more information about experimental design, see p109.

For more information about designing observations, see p112.

For more information about reliability and validity, see p92.

- Day care can be family based or nursery based.
- High quality day care can have positive effects on social development including the ability to play and cooperate with other children.
- Lower quality day care or very lengthy days in care may foster the development of aggressive behaviour in younger children.
- High quality day care is characterised by the opportunity for attachment with a key worker in a stimulating environment.

How science works: practical activity

This activity will give you experience in designing an observational study. Campbell found that children who spent long days in day care (e.g. 8am–6pm) were less socially competent than those spending more, but shorter days in day care. One explanation of this is that those attending for long days became tired and frustrated, resulting in more negative interactions with other children.

Design a natural/quasi-experiment to investigate the association between social competence and patterns of day care attendance of pre-school children. Devise an appropriate observational schedule with clearly defined behavioural categories to measure social competence. You will need to think about behaviours that would indicate social competence in pre-school children and the appropriate number of behavioural categories. You will need to consider length of observation, how the behaviour would be sampled. Explain how you would ensure reliable and valid categorisation of behaviour. Pay particular attention to ethical issues and how you would address them. Provide full detail of the procedure for the study. Use the information in the investigation planning form (p104) to guide your planning and to record and explain all your design decisions.

Consider how you would go about summarising the data from the observation, displaying the data and drawing conclusions from the study. Remember this would be a natural experiment and this would limit the conclusions you would be able to draw from the data.

Question 1

1 Three of the following are descriptions of types of attachment:

A   Children who are not willing to explore, have high stranger anxiety and who seek and reject contact at the return of their caregiver.

B   Children who are willing to explore, have high stranger anxiety and who are enthusiastic at the return of their caregiver.

C   Children who are willing to explore, have low stranger anxiety and who avoid contact at the return of their caregiver.

D   Children who are not willing to explore, have low stranger anxiety and who seek and avoid contact at the return of their caregiver.

Type of attachment	Letter A, B, C or D
Secure	
Insecure-avoidant	
Insecure-resistant	

In the accompanying table, write down which example A, B, C or D matches each type of attachment listed in the table. *(3 marks)*

2 (a) Outline effects of disrupting attachment bonds. *(5 marks)*

(b) Explain what is meant by the term privation. *(2 marks)*

3 Some psychologists wanted to see the effects of separation upon children's development. They conducted a case study on a two-year-old child who was separated temporarily from her parents when she had to go into hospital. It was found that the child demonstrated protest, followed by despair and finally detachment.

(a) Explain one advantage of using a case study in psychological investigations. *(2 marks)*

(b) (i) Explain one difficulty in drawing conclusions about the effects of separation from this study. *(2 marks)*

(ii) Explain how this problem could be overcome. *(2 marks)*

AQA Examiner's tip For Question 1, part 3(b), read the whole question first, and make sure you choose a difficulty that can also be used for part (ii).

(c) (i) Explain one ethical issue that should be considered when undertaking psychological research that involves children. *(2 marks)*

(ii) Explain how this ethical issue would be dealt with. *(2 marks)*

AQA Examiner's tip Question 1, part 3c asks about ethical issues specific to the undertaking of psychological research that involves children. Ensure that your answer is therefore centred on ethical issues involving the use of children and nothing else.

There is a danger with case studies of investigator effects.

(d) (i) Explain one investigator effect that may have occurred in this case study. *(2 marks)*

(ii) Explain how this investigator effect could be reduced. *(2 marks)*

4 Outline and evaluate the evolutionary explanation of attachment. *(12 marks)*

Question 2

1   Psychologists have discovered that the occurrence of attachment types shows a great deal of consistency in Western cultures.

To illustrate these findings complete the table below using three of the four attachment types listed.

* Secure attachment type
* Insecure-avoidant attachment type
* Secure-resistant attachment type
* Insecure-resistant attachment type   *(3 marks)*

	Type of attachment pattern	Overall percentage of each attachment type
Most common attachment pattern		65%
Second most common attachment pattern		21%
Third most common attachment pattern		14%

2   The 'Strange Situation' has been used to investigate attachment.

Outline aspects of infants' behaviour that are recorded when using this research technique.   *(3 marks)*

3   (a)   Outline what psychological research has shown about the effects of institutionalisation on attachment behaviour.   *(6 marks)*

(b)   Discuss implications of research into the effects of institutionalisation on attachment behaviour.   *(4 marks)*

4   Lachmi is planning to provide day care facilities for pre-school children below the age of five years. She is keen to promote social development of the children attending.

Outline what practices Lachmi could introduce to encourage social development of the children attending.   *(6 marks)*

5   A group of students decided to perform a correlational study investigating the relationship between time spent in day care and aggressiveness. Time spent in day care was measured in hours per week. They asked parents to rate their child's aggression on a scale of 1 to 10.

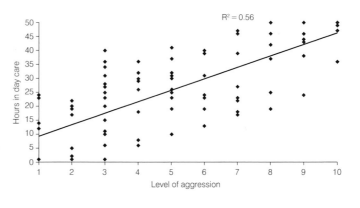

(a)   (i)   What type of relationship is depicted in the graph?   *(2 marks)*

(ii)   What does the scattergram suggest about the relationship between time spent in day care and aggressiveness?   *(2 marks)*

(b)   Explain one strength of using a correlational study in the situation above.   *(2 marks)*

(c)   Explain one limitation of using a correlational study in the situation above.   *(2 marks)*

6   To check the validity of the data the students decided to conduct an observational study of the children's aggressive behaviour.

(a)   Outline one strength and one limitation of using an observational study in the situation described above.   *(4 marks)*

(b)   Explain what is meant by a naturalistic observation   *(2 marks)*

(c)   Explain how quantitative data can be gained from observational studies.   *(2 marks)*

Research methods

Introduction

Psychology researchers will generally integrate the scientific method into their research process by breaking it down into a series of practical steps. Figure 1 outlines the main steps that are likely to be involved in any scientific psychology investigation.

The first stage in the scientific method is observational. The researcher will usually identify a problem or topic to research as a result of noting something that they would like to understand further. A key principle of the scientific method is that you can only study what you can observe; scientific research rejects any claims that are not based on observable, verifiable evidence.

As part of the process of trying to understand the issue or problem the researcher will gather as much relevant background information on it as possible. This will tell them what is already known and understood about the issue or problem.

The next step (step 3) is to develop some theoretical ideas that may explain the observed phenomena. However, simply theorising about behaviour or mental processes does not produce observable, verifiable evidence. The scientific method requires a psychologist to test their theoretical ideas to see if there is any evidence that may support them. The psychology researcher needs to form a hypothesis; this is a specific prediction about what will happen under certain conditions to the behaviour or the mental process that the researcher is investigating. The different types of hypothesis used in psychology investigations, together with a number of other issues central to investigation design, are outlined in Chapter 5.

Once the hypothesis has been formulated, the researcher has to select an appropriate method for collecting data that will be used to test the hypothesis. Psychologists use a number of different data collection methods. Each of these methods is discussed in Chapter 6.

With the hypothesis written and the research methods chosen, the next step is to collect the data (step 6). This generally involves following some well-specified procedures until enough data has been gathered for analysis (step 7). The researcher then uses the analysed data to draw conclusions about the hypothesis they are testing (step 8). If the data support the hypothesis, then it is possible to make some evidence-based claims about the subject under investigation. Knowledge of the subject will have grown and may form the basis for further investigation or contribute to the development of a broader theory. If the data do not support the hypothesis, then the hypothesis is refuted or rejected as false. Methods for presenting and analysing research data are outlined and discussed in Chapter 7.

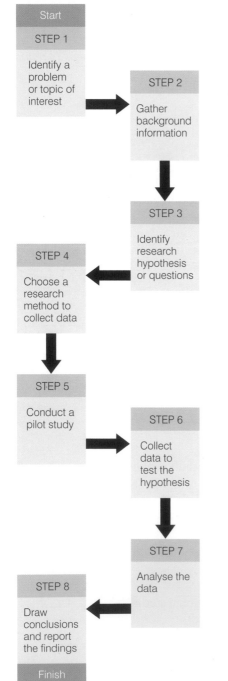

Fig. 1 *An eight-step version of the research process*

Specification	Section content	Page
Data analysis and presentation Candidates should be familiar with the following features of data analysis, presentation and interpretation:		
• Presentation and interpretation of quantitative data including graphs, scattergrams and tables	**Measures of central tendency** • Understanding data • Data tables	 123 123
	Graphs • The histogram • Bar chart • Scattergram	 129 129 130
• Analysis and interpretation of quantitative data. Measures of central tendency including median, mean, mode. Measures of dispersion including ranges and standard deviation	**Measures of dispersion** • Range • Standard deviation	 126 126
• Analysis and interpretation of correlational data. Positive and negative correlations and the interpretation of correlation coefficients	**Correlational methods** • Positive and negative correlation • Recognising and measuring correlation	 116 116
• Presentation of qualitative data	**Qualitative analysis** • Pure qualitative analysis	 132
• Processes involved in content analysis	**Qualitative analysis** • Content analysis	 131

Aims and hypotheses

Learning objectives:

- Formulate and recognise an experimental, alternative and null hypothesis.

- Formulate and recognise a directional and a non-directional hypothesis.

- Understand that at the end of your research investigation you will either accept or reject your null hypothesis.

- Understand the concepts of reliability and validity.

Key terms

Hypothesis: a precise, testable statement about the expected outcome of an investigation.

Aim: a general statement about the purpose of the investigation.

Experiment: a research investigation in which one specific variable is manipulated to observe its effect, if any, on another specific variable, while keeping all other variables controlled. In a true experiment, participants are randomly allocated to conditions or take part in all conditions.

Variable: a measurable characteristic or value that can differ from one person to another or have multiple values.

Experimental hypothesis: a hypothesis used in the context of an experiment.

Alternative hypothesis: any hypothesis that is not the null hypothesis.

The first steps in designing a research investigation involve identifying a topic or issue to study and carrying out a search and review of the existing or background literature on the area. When these preliminary stages have been completed the researcher is in a position to identify the aim and **hypothesis** of their investigation. We have already noted in the introduction that the scientific method involves the testing of hypotheses. In this section we will take a closer look at the different types of hypotheses that exist and the process of generating testable hypotheses.

Generating an aim and hypotheses

A research investigation always needs an **aim** to give it a clear focus. For example, the aim of an investigation into factors affecting children's behaviour might be 'To investigate the relationship between food additives and hyperactive behaviour'. In addition the researcher will need to state a hypothesis. The hypothesis should be expressed as a very specific statement or prediction about the outcome of the investigation. Usually, a hypothesis is based on some previous observations, such as noticing how children at a nursery behave during and after their morning snack break.

While a hypothesis is a testable statement, which may include a prediction, it is not a theory. Theories consist of complex sets of interrelated statements or hypotheses that, when taken together, offer a way of explaining observed phenomena. Metaphorically, a hypothesis is like a single brick in a larger theory wall.

For example, according to Baddeley (1966) the digit span of short-term memory can be increased if people read the digits out loud rather than sub-vocally. If this was investigated then the hypotheses to be tested would look something like the following:

- Experimental hypothesis: participants who read digits out loud will later recall a greater number of digits than participants who read the digits sub-vocally.

- Null hypothesis: there will be no difference between the number of digits recalled by participants who read digits out loud and those who read them sub-vocally.

As you can see from this example, a null hypothesis states that the results of an **experiment** will not show a difference or a relationship between two **variables**. The **experimental hypothesis** on the other hand is the statement that predicts that a difference or an expected relationship between two variables will be revealed by the research findings.

The term experimental hypothesis is used in the context of an investigation that uses the experiment as the main method. The term **alternative hypothesis** is often used to refer to all hypotheses that are not the null hypothesis. However, only some alternative hypotheses are also experimental hypotheses. Where a **correlational study** (exploring the possible association between parenting style and infant emotional development, for example) is conducted the hypothesis will not be an experimental hypothesis because it is not predicting a cause and effect relationship, but merely an association.

Many students are puzzled by the need to state a null hypothesis. However, sometimes the null hypothesis is what we are actually concerned about. For example, you may be actually challenging a theory and you do this by testing a hypothesis predicted by the theory and demonstrating that the null hypothesis is actually correct instead. In addition, Field (2004) points out that the null is very important as it is impossible to prove our experimental hypothesis correct but we can disprove our null hypothesis. If our analysis of data allows us to reject the null hypothesis, then this provides support for the experimental hypothesis.

In addition to understanding the difference between null, alternative and experimental hypotheses, you also need to understand that an experimental and an alternative hypothesis can each be directional or non-directional.

■ **Key term**

Correlational study: an investigation into the possible association of two variables.

■ **Hint**

When formulating or identifying a directional hypothesis look out for indicator words such as 'more', 'less', 'increased', 'decreased' and 'improved', for example. These words all indicate a direction to the results. Words such as 'difference' and 'affect' indicate a non-directional hypothesis. That is, you are saying that there will be a difference but you are not stating in what direction the difference will be.

Table 1 *Types of hypothesis*

Experimental/alternative hypothesis	Definition	Illustrative example
Directional	A directional hypothesis is more precise than a non-directional hypothesis and specifically states the direction of the results. This is also known as a one-tailed hypothesis because it predicts the nature or direction of the outcome.	Participants who read digits out loud will later recall a greater number of digits than participants who read the digits sub-vocally. Looking at this example we can see that the direction of the results is clearly stated, i.e. more digits will be recalled in one condition.
Non-directional	A non-directional hypothesis is one in which the direction of results is not predicted. This is also known as a two-tailed hypothesis because the direction of the result is not specified but could go in either direction – that is it could be 'more' or 'less'.	There will be a difference in the number of digits recalled in the reading out loud condition compared to the sub-vocal condition. The psychologist has predicted that there will be a difference but has not specified in which condition more or fewer digits will be recalled.
Null hypothesis	This tends to state that there will be no difference relationship between the variables being investigated. A null hypothesis is used because it makes a very precise prediction (nothing will happen) that can be disproved, thereby supporting the alternative hypothesis.	There will be no difference in the number of digits recalled in the reading out loud condition compared to the sub-vocal condition.

■ Operationalising variables

Once null and alternative hypotheses have been written, the researcher has to **operationalise** their variables. What this means is that the exact nature and means of measuring or observing the variables to which the hypotheses refer must be defined. When the variables have been defined clearly and objectively the researcher is said to have produced operational definitions. In the previous example, the psychology researcher was investigating memory and this was operationalised through the number of digits recalled. In addition the researcher would need to define clearly what 'reading out loud' is, and what is meant by 'sub-vocal'. The researcher would also need to identify how they intend to observe and measure the incidence of each of these variables in the research investigation. When this has been done, the hypotheses will actually be testable.

Research methods

AQA Examiner's tip

When writing a hypothesis, always remember to operationalise your variables and make it clear what the two conditions or variables are that are being compared.

■ **Key term**

Operationalising: the process of devising a way of measuring a variable.

The next step for the researcher is to carry out the research investigation. This will generate data that are then analysed. Analysis determines if the results verify or refute the experimental/alternative hypothesis. If, in our example, the results revealed that more digits were recalled in the reading out loud condition, then the experimental/alternative hypothesis would be supported and accepted. If there was no difference, the null hypothesis would be accepted and the experimental/alternative hypothesis refuted.

☑ Reliability and validity

Psychologists who are committed to using scientific methods in their research investigations try to design studies that can be replicated or repeated. To achieve this it is vital that the measurement tools used in an investigation are reliable and that the data they produce are valid.

Reliability means that two or more measurements or observations of the same psychological event will be consistent with each other. For example, imagine that two researchers are observing the same person at the same time in the same situation and are rating that person's behaviour using an observation checklist. There must be a high level of consistency between the two sets of observations if the observation checklist they are using is to be seen as reliable and effective at producing valid research data.

In addition to our measurements being consistent we also want our measurements to be valid. Validity means that we are actually measuring what we claim to be measuring. There are two broad categories of validity: **internal validity** and **external validity**.

Different methods are employed to measure the validity of tests, such as intelligence tests and personality tests. The following table summarises three ways of measuring validity.

Table 2 *Measuring validity*

Method of assessing validity	Explanation
Face validity	This is the most basic method of assessing validity and quite simply involves an 'eyeball test'. That is, does the test look as if it is measuring what it is supposed to measure?
Concurrent validity	This involves comparing the results yielded by a new test with those from an older test known to have good validity. For example, if a participant achieved an IQ score of 148 on an older IQ test but on the new test they scored 113, questions may be raised over the validity of the newer test.
Predictive validity	This is the ability of the test to predict performance on future tests. If it can do this then the test is said to have good predictive validity. Something you might like to consider is the predictive validity of GCSEs – do you think they predict performance at A Level?

Key terms

Internal validity: a research study or experiment has internal validity if the outcome is the result of the variables that are manipulated in the study.

External validity: the extent to which findings can be generalised to settings other than the research setting. This includes population validity, which is the question of whether the findings can be generalised to other people, and ecological validity, which is the question of whether the results can be generalised to other settings.

Hint

If you are asked what is meant by the term reliability, the key word to emphasise is consistency.

Key points:

■ A hypothesis is a testable statement, which makes a precise prediction about the outcome of the research.

■ A null hypothesis states there will be no difference between conditions or that there will be no relationship between variables.

■ A directional hypothesis is one in which the direction of difference or relationship is predicted.

■ A non-directional hypothesis is one where the direction of difference or relationship is not predicted.

■ On completion of research the results will indicate which hypothesis can be accepted and which can be rejected.

■ Reliability refers to the consistency of a measuring instrument.

■ Validity is the extent to which a test measures what it is intended to measure.

■ There are two main types of validity: internal and external validity.

✓ Summary questions

1 Look at the following hypotheses and indicate whether each is a null hypothesis or an experimental/alternative hypothesis. In addition, identify whether each is directional or non-directional.

Table 3

Hypothesis	Null or experimental/ alternative hypothesis	Directional or non-directional
There will be no difference in the number of trigrams recalled after 18 seconds compared to the number recalled after 3 seconds.		
The number of hours spent in day care as a child is negatively related to scores on a pro-social behaviour scale.		
There will be a difference in the number of Spanish vocabulary items retained after one year between participants who learned over spaced lessons compared to participants who learned in intensive sessions.		
Participants who are instructed to semantically process words will recall more words than participants who are instructed to visually process words.		
There will be a difference in the A Level grades achieved by a group of learners taught using active learning compared to those of a group taught using traditional methods.		

2 Read the following passage: a psychologist investigated the effects of the spacing of learning (see chapter 1, p15) on the later recall of material learned. Participants were randomly assigned to one of two groups. In the first condition they were exposed to four consecutive hours learning German vocabulary. In the other condition the students were also exposed to four hours learning German but over two two-hour sessions. Participants were later tested for the number of German words that they could recall correctly. The researcher's findings are summarised in the table below:

Table 4

Condition	Mean number of German words recalled
Intensive learning condition	36.5
Spaced learning condition	28

a Write a non-directional hypothesis for the research.

b Write a directional hypothesis for the research.

c Write a null hypothesis for the research.

d Which hypothesis would you accept, the null or the experimental/alternative hypothesis?

e Explain why the researcher needs to produce a null hypothesis in this piece of research.

3 Explain what is meant by reliability and outline one way in which the reliability of the investigation can be assured.

4 Explain what is meant by the term validity. Discuss the importance of validity in investigation design.

5 Look at the table below and evaluate the problem with the research in terms of reliability and validity.

Table 5

Study	Evaluation
Several studies have suggested that day care can be helpful for children's social development. Andersson (1989, 1992) carried out a variety of studies in Sweden, which found potentially good effects.	
Shallice and Warrington (1970) reported on the case of KF, a young man who sustained brain injuries after a motorcycle accident. He appeared to have an intact LTM in that he was able to learn new information and recall stored information. However, his STM was affected so that he had a recency effect of only one item.	

Variables

■ Key terms

Independent variable (IV): the
variable that the researcher
manipulates and which is assumed
to have a direct effect on the
dependent variable.

Dependent variable (DV): the
variable that is affected by
changes in the independent
variable.

Extraneous variables (EV): this is
a general term for any variables
other than the IV that might affect
the DV. Where EVs are important
enough to provide alternative
explanations for the effects, they
become confounding variables.

■ Independent and dependent variables

As we have seen in the previous chapter, psychology research focuses on the relationships between variables. A variable is simply the precise, technical term that psychologists use for something – a quality (attractiveness), characteristic (weight) or action (hyperactive behaviour), for example – that can change or vary. Where a researcher wants to establish the precise cause and effect relationship between two variables they will use an experimental method, which involves manipulating one variable to see how this affects another variable. We will look at this in detail shortly. Where the research simply wants to establish whether there is an association between two variables, they will use a correlational method. This doesn't require them to identify independent or dependent variables.

So, let us now consider what is meant by the terms **independent variable (IV)** and **dependent variable (DV)**. If we look back to our earlier examples of hypotheses (see p91) we can see that each hypothesis states that one thing (reading out loud) is affecting another thing (the digit span of short-term memory). Now consider a new research hypothesis that is part of a study into memory: 'There will be a difference in the number of words that participants can recall under organised and unorganised conditions'.

What is affecting what here? Hopefully you will see that the hypothesis is saying that the number of words that the research participants will be able to recall will be affected by the type of 'organisation' they experience. Using this example the variable that is doing the affecting (organisation or lack of it) is the IV and the variable that is affected (the number of words recalled) is the DV.

The easy way to understand IV and DV is to think about the IV as the cause and the DV as the effect. You are constantly identifying IVs and DVs; it is just that you do not use this technical jargon. For example, if I study for my exams and get good results, it is likely that I will assume that my success is due to my studying. That is, studying (IV) has had an effect on my success (DV). In an experimental research investigation it is always the case that the IV is manipulated and the DV is measured by the researcher.

It is very important to understand that an independent variable (IV) and a dependent variable (DV) are only used in an experimental hypothesis. If you consider that the experiment is the only method that allows us to draw conclusions about cause and effect, this should make sense!

■ Controlling extraneous variables

Looking at the definition of an experiment on p90 you will notice that it says 'while keeping all other variables controlled'. These other variables are known as **extraneous variables (EV)**.

In research we need to control EVs otherwise we cannot be sure that it is the IV that has affected the DV. Using our memory example we can start to identify possible EVs, which could interfere with the effect of our IV on the DV. If in our research we tested the organised condition in a quiet room and the unorganised condition in a noisy room then we would have

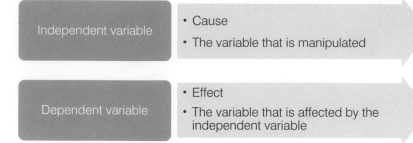

Fig. 1 *The independent and dependent variables*

an extraneous variable. That is, if a difference was found, we could not be sure that it was the IV of organisation that affected the DV of recall. It may be the level of noise (an EV) that brought about the difference. Obviously we should control this EV by ensuring that participants are tested under identical environmental conditions.

EVs need to be controlled – this may not eliminate the effect but will ensure it does not affect one condition of the IV and not the other. This is where good design comes into play.

There are a number of different types of extraneous (or confounding) variable that psychologists need to take account of when designing and implementing their investigations. These include the following:

- Situational variables: these are variables connected with the research situation. For example, temperature, instructions, time of day and lighting, materials used in the investigation are all situational variables. Situational variables are controlled through standardisation; that is ensuring that the only thing that differs between the two conditions is the IV, e.g. in the example above, making sure that the level of noise in the rooms was the same.

- Participant variables: those variables that are connected with the research participants. For example, intelligence, age, gender and personality are all participant variables. Participant variables are controlled through the experimental (or participant) design, such as the matched pairs design, where participants in one condition are matched with similar participants in the other condition, e.g. someone of similar intelligence or age. Randomly assigning participants to conditions also helps to control participant variables by reducing bias.

In addition to the broad categories of situational and participant variables there are other types of variable that need to be controlled to ensure that it is the IV that is bringing about the effect on the DV. These variables are known as **demand characteristics** and **investigator effects**. If these are not controlled we once again have a potential threat to the internal validity of the research. The demand characteristics of an experiment are those things that encourage or invite the participants to behave in a particular way. Typically these things are cues in the external environment that lead participants to think that they ought to act in a particular fashion. Investigator effects are those aspects of the researcher's appearance or behaviour that can also lead participants to think that they should act in a particular way.

These two potential threats to the internal validity of the research can be controlled using the following techniques:

- demand characteristics: **single blind technique**
- investigator effects: **double blind technique.**

Key terms

Demand characteristics: cues in the environment that help the participant work out what the research hypothesis is. This can lead to social desirability effects where the participant behaves in a way that the hypothesis will be supported or the 'screw you' effect where the participant purposefully disrupts the research.

Investigator effects: the influence of the researcher whereby their expectations of what the research outcome should be could lead to a self-fulfilling prophecy. The researcher may at an unconscious level behave in such a way as to bring about their prediction.

Single blind technique: a procedure in an experiment where the participants do not know the hypothesis and do not know which condition they are in.

Double blind technique: a procedure in an experiment where neither the participants nor the research assistant know the hypothesis or the condition that the participants are in. This involves a research assistant carrying out the data collection on behalf of the experimenter.

Key points:

- The independent variable is the variable that the researcher manipulates.
- The dependent variable is the measurable output of the research.
- It is very important that all variables are operationalised. That is, they must be defined in an objective, clearly measurable way.
- Extraneous variables need to be controlled otherwise they can confound the results. This would mean that we would be unsure whether it really was the IV that was affecting the DV. This would lower the internal validity of the research.
- Other variables that need controlling include demand characteristics and investigator effects.

✔ **Summary questions**

6 Revisit the hypotheses in question 1 (p93) and identify the IV and the DV.

7 Look at the following hypothesis and identify the IV and the DV: 'There will be a difference in the A Level grades achieved by a group taught to use mnemonics compared to a group who are not taught to use mnemonics.'

8 Read the following passage: 'Researchers were interested to see how the processing of material affects memory. In one condition the participants processed the words semantically, i.e. in terms of meaning. In the other condition the participants processed the words visually, i.e. in terms of how they looked. Participants were later instructed to free recall as many words from the list studied as possible.'

  a Identify the independent variable.

  b Identify the dependent variable.

  c Write a non-directional hypothesis for this study.

9 Explain how this hypothesis relates to psychological theories and/or studies.

Research methods

Sampling

Learning objectives:

- Understand what is meant by and recognise a target population.

- Understand what is meant by the term sampling.

- Recognise and describe different types of sampling.

- Understand the advantages and disadvantages of different types of sampling.

Links

See p58 for more on Ainsworth and the Strange Situation.

See p63 for an explanation of collectivist cultures.

Choosing a target population

In this topic we will consider how you decide who the people you study – known as the participants – will be. Or, to be more precise, who your sample will be. The number of participants taking part in your study is known as the sample size.

The first step is deciding who your target population is. This is the particular group of people you are interested in studying. For example, if you wanted to test a new approach to teaching literacy skills to pre-schoolers then your target population would be all pre-schoolers. This population would be fairly large in number so a researcher would not be able to study all the people in the target population and would therefore select a sample. It is important that the sample is representative of the target population so that the findings can be generalised from the sample back to the target population. If the sample is not representative of the target population then the sample is said to be biased.

Sampling is a key consideration when judging the external validity, in particular population validity, of research. There is a surprising amount of research in psychology that has been questioned over its population validity. For example, in Ainsworth's research using the Strange Situation, it has been argued that a larger sample size is needed in order to generalise findings to the rest of the population. In addition over half (18) of the 32 studies were carried out in the US, reflecting the dominance by America in research in this area. Twenty-seven of the studies were carried out in

Table 6 *Sampling*

Type of sampling	Definition	Method	Population validity
Random	A sample in which every member of the target population has an equal chance of being selected	Every member of the target population is identified and a random sampling technique is employed to select the sample. For example, names are drawn out of a hat or people are chosen from a numbered list using random number tables	This is a representative sample and has high population validity
Opportunity	A sample that consists of those people available to the researcher	The researcher would approach people and ask them to take part in the research. Basically the researcher takes advantage of whoever happens to be available and is willing to take part in the research	High chance that the sample will be biased leading to low population validity
Volunteer	A sample where the participants self-select. That is they volunteer to take part in the research	The researcher would advertise their research and the people who respond would be the sample	Research has found that a particular type of person is likely to volunteer for research; thus this type of sampling has a very high chance of bias. This means that we cannot generalise to the target population leading to low population validity

Western cultures with only five taking place in collectivist cultures. This implies that the sample used may not be truly representative.

■ Different types of sampling

There are different types of sampling that are employed in psychology research. The three we will consider are random sampling, opportunity sampling and volunteer sampling.

Key points:

- The group of people a researcher is interested in studying is known as the target population.

- In practical terms a researcher cannot usually study all the people in this population, therefore they will select a sample of people from the target population.

- A sample should be representative of the target population. If this is not the case then the sample is said to be biased.

- Sampling is integral to population validity. If a biased sample is employed then population validity is low.

- Different methods of sampling include: random sampling, opportunity sampling and volunteer sampling.

 Summary questions

10 A researcher needs to obtain a random sample of 15-year-old females to participate in her research into the effects of hormones on memory capacity. Explain how this sample could be obtained.

11 You are interested in the quality of day care nurseries in your neighbourhood. One nursery has published the results of their own questionnaire study of parents, and claims to find high levels of satisfaction with their nursery. What sampling issues would you investigate before deciding that the results were reliable?

Research methods

Ethical issues

Hint

The website for the BPS (http://www.bps.org.uk) should be checked for the most up to date 'Ethical Principles for Conducting Research with Human Participants' available in the 'Code of Conduct and Ethical Guidelines' section of the website.

💡 Ethics

Ethics in the conduct of research is extremely important. Research can directly or indirectly cause psychological, cultural or physical harm to a person, community or culture if it breaches the rights or disregards the best interests of those who participate in it. Psychology researchers have a responsibility to conduct their research in an ethical manner. The British Psychological Society has published a range of guidelines on ethical issues to which all psychologists should adhere.

British Psychological Society (BPS) guidelines for research with human participants

The British Psychological Society code of ethics, *Ethical Principles for Conducting Research with Human Participants*, covers nine different aspects of ethics that relate to research with human participants:

■ Consent: when someone consents to participate in research, their consent must be informed, i.e. the aims of the research should be made clear. In addition, anything that may influence their willingness to participate must be disclosed. Where the research involves children under the age of 16 years, then consent must be obtained from parents or guardians of the child.

■ Deception: information must not be withheld from participants, nor should they be misled, if they are likely to object when debriefed at the end of the procedure. Alternatives to deception should always be considered.

■ Debriefing: following an investigation, participants should be fully informed about the nature of the research. The participants' experiences of the research should also be discussed. Debriefing following an investigation does not justify the use of an unethical procedure.

■ Withdrawal from investigation: participants have the right to withdraw at any time, regardless of whether or not they were paid for their participation. They should be informed of this prior to commencement of the study. Participants can also withdraw at a later stage, after the study has been conducted. In this case, you are required to destroy any data or information collected from those who have elected to withdraw.

■ Confidentiality: participants have the right to confidentiality. If confidentiality cannot be assured, then this must be disclosed to participants before they consent to participate in the research. The Data Protection Act requires you to maintain the confidentiality of those people about whom you have collected information.

■ Protection of participants: psychologists have a responsibility for protecting their participants from physical or mental harm, including undue stress. The risk of harm to a participant must not be greater than that to which they are exposed in everyday life.

■ Observational research: observational studies must protect the privacy and psychological well-being of those observed. Where consent for observation has not been obtained, privacy is an important issue. Participants should not be observed in situations where they would not normally expect others to observe their behaviour.

- Giving advice: sometimes during the course of research (a) physical or psychological problems are identified by the researcher, and/or (b) participants solicit advice from the researcher. Great care must be taken in these situations. Where the problem may be serious, and you are unqualified to advise or help, then an appropriate source of professional advice should be suggested. If you are unsure about what such a source may be, then you should say so and not be tempted to offer any advice yourself.

- Colleagues: you are responsible for the ethical conduct of your own research, and that of your colleagues. Where you feel a colleague may be following an unethical procedure, then you should raise your concern with them and encourage them to re-evaluate what they are doing.

Some of the main **ethical issues** that occur in psychology research can be remembered by the mnemonic DIP (Deception, Informed consent, Protection of participants) (see Figure 2).

Link

The research study on obedience completed by Stanley Milgram (1963) is often cited as a piece of research that broke a number of ethical guidelines. Read this study on p202 and identify all the ethical issues raised.

Hint

There is a difference between an ethical guideline and an ethical issue. The guideline tells the researcher what they should do to conduct research that is ethically acceptable. On the other hand an ethical issue occurs when there is a dilemma between what the researcher wants to do in order to conduct the research and the rights and dignity of the participant.

AQA Examiner's tip

Avoid making the mistake of confusing ethical guidelines with ethical issues. A recent exam paper asked students to identify three ethical issues that have arisen in social psychological research (3 marks). If you remember the mnemonic 'DIP', answering the question should be very straightforward. In questions that ask you to identify ethical issues, simply name or briefly describe the issue – there is no need to explain. However, it is also common for there to be an exam question that asks you to explain why something is an ethical issue.

Key term

Ethical issues: these occur when there is a dilemma between what the researcher wants to do in order to conduct the research and the rights and dignity of the participants.

Deception	• Deception is an ethical issue because it prevents that participant from giving informed consent and the participant may find themselves in research against their wishes.
	• It is also an issue because the participants may start to become distrustful of psychologists in the future.
Informed consent	• Lack of informed consent means that the participant has not agreed to be in the research and may find themselves taking part in research against their wishes. The participant has not agreed to be in the research, which breaks ethical guidelines. It can also apply to participants who have volunteered to take part in the research but have not been fully informed about the aims of the study.
	• It is also an issue because the participants may start to become distrustful of psychologists in the future.
Protection of participants	• Participants have the right not to be harmed as a result of participating in a piece of psychological research. The participant should leave the research the same as when they entered it. If they are harmed they may suffer long-term effects which could impact on their future lives. In Milgram's research some of the participants were traumatised by the research, thus raising ethical issues.

Fig. 2 *Explanation of ethical issues*

Dealing with ethical issues

Ethical guidelines are the most obvious way in which psychologists deal with ethical issues. Let us now look at how each of the ethical issues identified in Figure 2 can be dealt with.

Table 7 *Ethical issues*

Ethical issue	Methods for dealing with ethical issues
Deception: very common in psychological research. Menges (1973) in a review of psychological research studies completed in America found that of the 1,000 studies reviewed, 80% involved not giving the participants full information about the study	• Debriefing: this is where on completion of the research the true aim of the research is revealed to the participant. The aim of the debriefing is to restore the participant to the state he or she was in prior to the research. A participant should leave a research study in the same state as when they entered. • Retrospective informed consent: once the true nature of the research has been revealed the participant should be given the right to withdraw their data.
Informed consent A further issue raised by research that involves children under the age of 16. The age of the participant may mean that the child does not fully understand what they are participating in, thus impacting on their ability to give informed consent	• Prior general consent: this solution involves obtaining the prior consent of participants to be involved in research that involves deception. If the participant agrees that they would not object to being deceived in future research studies, then in later studies where they participate it is assumed that they have agreed to being deceived. • Presumptive consent: this involves taking a random sample of the population and introducing them to the research, including any deception involved. If they agree that they would have still given their consent to the research then we can generalise from this and assume that the remainder of the general population would also have agreed. • Children as participants: this is resolved by gaining the consent of the parent or those *in loco parentis*, e.g. the headmistress of the school that the child attends.
Protection of participants	• The researcher should remind participants of their right to withdraw if at any point during the research the level of stress is higher than anticipated. • The researcher is responsible for terminating any research that results in psychological or physical harm that is higher than expected. For example, Zimbardo (see pp192–4) terminated his research after six days although it was intended to run for two weeks. Some argue that he should have terminated much earlier. • Debriefing is an important part of protection of participants.

Key points:

■ The BPS has published a set of guidelines that relate to research with human participants. Psychologists should adhere to these guidelines when conducting research.

■ The three main ethical issues in psychological research are: deception, informed consent and protection of participants.

■ Ways of dealing with deception are debriefing and retrospective consent.

■ Ways of dealing with lack of informed consent are presumptive consent and prior general consent.

■ Ways of dealing with protection of participants include debriefing and termination of the study.

Summary questions

12 Locate the studies listed in the table below and identify the ethical issues that occurred in research:

Table 8

Research study	Located on page	Ethical issues
Ainsworth (1970) 'The Strange Situation'	58	
Loftus and Burns (1982) Recall of a violent crime	30	

13 A researcher plans a piece of research where deception is required. Give advice as to how the researcher can deal with the issue of deception. Make one recommendation as to the best way to deal with it, and explain why they are ethical issues. How would you address these issues?

14 A friend is planning a psychological investigation and tells you that they plan to investigate the impact of stress on memory. A confederate will collapse in the corridor screaming in agony; simultaneously another confederate will run away from the supposed victim. In the other condition the confederate will collapse to the floor but with no screaming. They plan to interview witnesses after the incident to see whether they are able to pick the person running away out from a simulated identity parade. Identify as many ethical issues as you can see in the proposed research.

Chapter summary

- Researchers will state an aim for their research, which is a statement about the general purpose of the research.
- In addition they will also state a hypothesis, which is a more precise statement that is testable, and may involve a prediction.
- There are different types of hypothesis: experimental, alternative and null.
- Hypotheses can be further classified as directional or non-directional.
- For research to be meaningful it needs to be both reliable and valid. Reliability refers to the consistency of a measuring instrument. Validity means we are measuring what we are claiming to be measuring. Different types of validity include internal and external validity. External validity also includes ecological validity and population validity.
- An experimental hypothesis will make a statement about the relationship between the independent and dependent variable.
- To enable the researcher to conclude that it was indeed the independent variable that affected the dependent variable they must control extraneous variables.
- When carrying out research the researcher will study a sample. The sample is drawn from the target population that the researcher is interested in studying. It is crucial that the sample is representative of the target population if the researcher is to generalise the findings of the research.
- British researchers must adhere to the ethical guidelines set out by the BPS. If ethical issues do arise in the research, then the researcher must implement methods of dealing with them.

How science works: practical activity

This task is to plan and undertake a replication of part of Baddeley's research (1966) into encoding in memory. Read the outline of the investigation on p16. Use the investigation planning form below to record the details of Baddeley's study. This will then act as a plan for your research.

Investigation planning form

Experimental hypothesis	
Null hypothesis	
Justify why your hypothesis is directional or non-directional	
Independent variable (clearly operationalised)	
Dependent variable (clearly operationalised)	
Identify and justify the design selected	
Identify variables to be controlled and techniques to be employed to control them	
Detail of target population and sample (including sample size and how it will be selected)	
Ethical issues to be considered and steps taken to deal with them	
Procedure for carrying out the study (including sufficient detail to permit replication)	

Working in pairs, construct four lists of words (five words in each list) that you will present to the participants in your study:

■ acoustically similar words (e.g. mad, map, mat, cad, cap, cat)
■ acoustically dissimilar words (e.g. pen, cow, pit, sup, day)
■ semantically similar words (e.g. tall, high, broad, wide, big)
■ semantically dissimilar words (e.g. foul, thin, late, safe, strong).

Carry out your investigation with your chosen sample.

Keep your results safe as you will use them in a later activity in Chapter 7.

Research methods

6 Methods and techniques

Choosing a research method

Learning objectives:

- Outline the key features of a range of research methods used in psychology research.

- Describe different types of experimental, correlational, observational, interviews and case study methods for obtaining research data.

- Understand and explain the advantages and disadvantages of a range of data collection methods.

Key term

Control group: this is the group of participants who do not receive the experimental treatment or condition so that they can act as a comparison to the participants who do.

Examiner's tip

Remember all that you learn in research methods informs your critical thinking in relation to everything else you study in psychology. When you are evaluating a theory you will often look to the evidence that supports the theory – use your knowledge of research methods to judge the credibility of the evidence offered. This will significantly enhance your use of analytic and evaluative skills.

Pilot studies

Once a hypothesis has been written, and all of the variables to which it refers are operationalised, the psychology researcher is almost in a position to begin the research investigation. The next, critical step is to choose an appropriate research method. The method chosen must be capable of testing the hypothesis or research question that the researcher has produced.

Whatever the method selected, the researcher must trial it in a pilot study. This should be designed to test the reliability of the data collection tool and the researcher should make any necessary changes before carrying out their full investigation.

Experimental methods

Experimental methods provide the most rigorous way of testing hypotheses because they seek to establish cause and effect relationships. A true experiment has three key features:

- Manipulation of an independent variable: the independent variable (IV) is directly manipulated by the researcher to produce a change in the dependent variable (DV).

- Randomisation: a true experiment requires that participants are randomly allocated to conditions or that the participants take part in each condition of the independent variable.

- Control: efforts are made to control or hold constant all variables other than the independent and the dependent variable in an experiment. These other variables are known as extraneous variables (EVs). The aim of controlling EVs is to minimise their possible impact on the results of the investigation.

One way of imposing control within an experiment is to have an experimental group and a **control group**. For example, if we claim that people can retain material better if it is organised then it is very important to have a control group to establish the baseline of memory recall of information that is not organised.

There are different types of experiments in psychology. Each can be judged by the extent to which it meets the key features of the experiment.

💡 **Table 1** *Types of experiments*

Type of experiment	Description	Advantages	Disadvantages
Laboratory experiment	The method whereby all the key features of the experiment are met. That is, the IV is directly manipulated, all other extraneous variables are controlled and participants are randomly allocated to conditions.	High levels of control (both of the IV and EVs) Replicability – high Can conclude cause and effect	Can lack **ecological validity** Higher chance of investigator and participant effects Artificiality – the tasks in the experiment can sometimes lack **mundane realism**
Field experiment	The researcher controls the independent variable but the experimenter cannot control other extraneous variables to the same extent that one can in the laboratory. In addition participants are not necessarily randomly allocated to conditions.	Can conclude cause and effect Often has higher levels of ecological validity Reduction in participant effects (demand characteristics)	Less control over extraneous variables Often more time consuming Random allocation to conditions difficult
Natural experiment	The researcher does not manipulate variations in the independent variable and there is no random allocation of participants to conditions. This is a quasi-experiment, i.e. not a true experiment.	Useful where it would be unethical or impossible to manipulate the independent variable High levels of ecological validity	Problems with internal validity – many extraneous variables that cannot be controlled, meaning that we cannot conclude cause and effect No random allocation to conditions

■ *Research methods*

AQA Examiner's tip

You should be able to offer at least two advantages and disadvantages of the different experiments. Remember if two marks are available then mere identification of the advantage/disadvantage would only gain you one mark; you need to elaborate to gain the full marks. For example, stating a disadvantage of the laboratory experiment is that it lacks ecological validity would gain one mark. To gain the second mark for showing understanding you would need to elaborate and write 'It often lacks ecological validity meaning that due to the artificiality of the research situation it may be difficult to generalise the findings to other situations'.

Key terms

Laboratory experiment: an experiment that is carried out in a controlled environment where the independent variable is manipulated.

Mundane realism: the extent to which a study matches the real-world situation to which it will be applied.

Field experiment: an experiment that takes place in a natural environment: the independent variable is manipulated.

Natural experiment: the researcher takes advantage of a naturally occurring variable. Not a true experiment as variations in the independent variable occur naturally rather than through being manipulated by the researcher.

Ecological validity: the extent to which the methods, materials and setting of the experiment approximate the real-life situation being studied.

Table 2

Study	Page	Experimental/non-experimental	Type of experiment
Milner (1966)	9		
Peterson and Peterson (1959)	13		
Loftus and Burns (1982)	30		
Schaffer and Emerson (1964)	48		

Key points:

■ The experiment is the most scientific of all the research methods.

■ The experiment allows causal conclusions to be made.

■ The three criteria of what constitutes an experiment are: manipulation of IV, control of EVs and random allocation of participants to conditions.

■ There are different types of experiments: laboratory, field and natural.

■ Each of the above has advantages and disadvantages that can be judged along the common lines of ecological validity, artificiality, control of the IV, control of EVs and ability to make causal conclusions.

✓ Summary questions

1 Look at Table 2 above and identify whether the method used in the study was experimental or non-experimental. If it is experimental then identify what type of experiment was used.

2 Your friend claims that it is better to get up early and study for an exam rather than studying the night before. Your friend has been doing this for years and has advised that you should do the same for your forthcoming AS Psychology exam. Before taking his/her advice you decide to complete an experiment to determine whether your friend is giving good advice or not. What type of experiment would you use? What extraneous variables would you wish to control to ensure that it is time of studying that is affecting memory recall?

3 The mother of a friend of yours is a working mother with a small child who has just started primary school. She is finding arrangements for childcare difficult as her daughter is only at school for half a day for the first three weeks. You remember that when you started school you did half days only for the first week. You are interested in whether children entering reception class at school cope better with the first three weeks if they do half days for three weeks or one week. Design a natural experiment that you could carry out to investigate this question. How would you operationalise 'ability to cope'?

Experimental designs

Learning objectives:

- Understand repeated measures design, the independent groups design and the matched pairs design.
- Understand and explain the advantages and disadvantages of each of the designs.

Key term

Experimental design: the method of control imposed by the experimenter to control for participant variables. This is one of the major methods employed in an experiment to control extraneous variables (EVs).

Hint

The mnemonic RIM (Repeated, Independent, Matched) will help you to remember these three designs.

Hint

If you consider the table on p110 you will see that the advantages and disadvantages of the repeated measures design reverse with those of the independent groups. Therefore if you know the advantages and disadvantages of one it should be no problem remembering them for the other!

Different types of design

In a basic experiment there are two conditions: the experimental condition and the control condition. A decision has to be taken as to whether a participant will take part in both conditions or whether they will only participate in one. The decision taken will determine the **experimental design**. You are expected to know the following three experimental designs:

- repeated measures design
- independent groups design
- matched pairs design.
- Repeated measures design: in a repeated measures design every participant will take part in both conditions of the independent variable, in effect each participant acts as their own control. Thus if we were investigating the effect of organisation on memory, the participant would take part in both the organised and the unorganised condition.
- Independent groups design: in an independent groups design the participants take part in either the control or the experimental condition.
- Matched pairs design: in this design each participant in one of the experimental conditions is matched as closely as possible with a participant in the other condition. Examples of variables that they could be matched on include age, gender, intelligence and personality traits. When the matching pairs have been established they are randomly allocated to one or other of the conditions.

Table 3 *Advantages and disadvantages of experimental designs*

Design	Description	When should it be used?	Advantages	Disadvantages	Controls
Repeated measures design	The same participants are used in both conditions	When there is only a small number of participants – the same participants can be used for both conditions	• Participant variables are eliminated • Uses fewer participants: it is sometimes difficult to get people to participate in research. Identifying participants can be time consuming	• **Order effects** can occur, e.g. fatigue, learning, boredom • Increased chance of demand characteristics occurring • Cannot use the same stimulus materials	• Order effects can be controlled through **counterbalancing** • Demand characteristics – use single blind technique
Independent groups design	Participants are randomly allocated to either one or other of the conditions	This design is not affected as much by the number of participants, although in a small sample there's a risk that any differences between conditions could be due to individual differences of participants	• No order effects • Reduced chance of demand characteristics • Can use the same stimulus materials	• Least effective design for controlling participant variables • More participants required	Absolutely crucial that participants are randomly allocated to the different conditions
Matched pairs design	Participants are matched as closely as possible with another participant and then the pairs are randomly allocated to either one or the other conditions	When you have a lot of time, money and participants as they need to be carefully matched	• No order effects • Good attempt at controlling participant variables	• Difficult to match participants exactly • More participants required	Monozygotic twins (identical) provide researchers with a very close match for participant variables

■ Key terms

Order effects: a confounding effect that can occur when a repeated measures design is employed. If the participants always complete one condition first, by the time they get to the second condition they may experience order effects, such as practice, boredom and fatigue. This could then affect their performance in the second condition.

Counterbalancing: the method used to balance order effects in the repeated measures design. Half the participants would complete the experiment in one sequence – for example condition A first followed by condition B. The other half would do condition B first followed by condition A. The easy way to remember this is ABBA.

Research methods

Key points:

- Repeated measures design uses the same participants in both conditions.

- Independent groups design is where the participants are randomly allocated to either one condition or the other.

- Matched pairs design is where each participant is matched with another participant on relevant variables. The pairs are then randomly allocated to either one or the other condition.

- Each of the above have advantages and disadvantages – each design can be considered in terms of their ability to control participant variables, the number of participants required, vulnerability to demand characteristics and whether the same stimulus materials can be used.

✔ Summary questions

4 Read the following and decide which design is being employed:

a A natural experiment was completed that investigated the difference in social skills in five-year-olds. Children in one condition had attended day care while children in the other condition had been cared for at home.

b A researcher is interested in the effects of a new teaching method on the mathematical ability of Year 6 children. He has two conditions – in one condition the children are exposed to the new teaching method and in the other traditional teaching methods continue to be used. He matches children on their mathematical ability and then randomly allocates them to either the new method condition or the traditional method condition.

c A researcher presented participants with a list of 20 words. The words were presented one at a time and the participant was asked a question relating to the word. The question would prompt the participant to either process the word visually (e.g. Was the word in capital letters?), acoustically (Did the word sound like ...?) or semantically (What did the word mean?). On completion of the list participants were asked to recall as many of the 20 words presented as they could.

Research methods

Observational methods

Learning objectives:

- Describe the key features of observational methods of data collection.

- Define, describe and choose different types of observational method.

- Explain the advantages and disadvantages of different observational methods.

Key term

Observer bias: this happens when an observer makes their own particular interpretation of the behaviour they observe.

Link

See p58 for more information about Ainsworth's study.

AQA Examiner's tip

You may be asked to identify two factors that could affect the validity of an observation. This question is best answered by focusing on any extraneous variables that could affect the research. One of the main threats to observational research is observer bias – remember you need to explain what this means. Validity may also be affected by the sample being studied. If the sample is unrepresentative of the larger population then this is a threat to the population validity of the research. Another easy way of answering the question is to look at the positives of observational studies. For example, if it is a naturalistic observation then ecological validity is a strength because the behaviour is occurring in a natural environment.

What are observational methods?

Humans are constantly looking around and observing the behaviour of other people in their environment. However, most of these everyday observations are very different from those in a psychology investigation. Firstly, the observations in a scientific study will focus precisely on particular categories of behaviours or events. Secondly, these observations would be part of a research plan that would include the clear operational definitions of the behaviours or events to be observed. It is also very likely that a hypothesis would have been formulated to guide the observations. All of this is in sharp contrast to the more informal, casual observations that happen when we find ourselves 'people watching'.

When a psychology researcher decides to use observational methods to obtain research data, they will produce detailed guidelines for the people who will carry out the observations. An objective system for both observing and recording behaviours or events must be created before the research begins. The validity of the data produced by observational methods relies on the objectivity of the observers. As a result, steps need to be taken to minimise and ideally avoid any kind of **observer bias** affecting the observations.

Types of observation

There are different types of observations; the two we will focus on in this section are:

- naturalistic observation
- controlled observation.

Observational methods can be used for data collection within experiments as well as in purely observational research. The type of observation used will, in part, be determined by whether the investigation is based on a true experiment or not.

Naturalistic observation involves the researcher observing naturally occurring behaviour. This type of observation cannot happen in a true experiment where the researcher manipulates the independent variable to observe the effect on the dependent variable. However, naturalistic observation can be used in quasi-experiments, such as natural experiments. One of its strengths is that naturalistic observation offers an alternative to the artificiality of the laboratory experiment and can produce data with high ecological validity.

A controlled observation is one where the researcher attempts to control certain variables. Control of the environment can be achieved by carrying out an observation in a laboratory. A good illustration of a controlled observation is Ainsworth's (1970) research. She studied children under laboratory conditions where she controlled the environment in which the children reacted to separation from their mothers.

When discussing observation, further distinctions can be made along three main dimensions:

■ **participant** versus **non-participant observation**

■ **disclosed** and **undisclosed observation**

■ **structured** and **unstructured observation.**

The dimension of structured versus unstructured refers to how the data is collected in the research. In a structured observation the data would be gathered using a pre-written data collection grid and would mainly be quantitative (numerical) data. The first example of a structured data collection grid, shown below, illustrates a simple frequency count grid that is completed by an observer as they see examples of the specified behaviour occurring. Content analysis of documents and texts provides a second use for structured observation grids. An example of a structured observation grid to be used in a content analysis of gender stereotyping in children's books is illustrated in the second example below. In an unstructured observation it is likely that the data would be gathered in a more ad hoc, unplanned way with the researcher noting what they believed were important behaviours or events as they occurred. As a result unstructured observations are more likely to produce qualitative data that is more impressionistic and descriptive rather than numerical.

As we've already noted, a major problem faced by observational studies is observer bias. People can interpret what is apparently the same behaviour or situation differently and to some extent we all have expectations of other people's behaviour based on social stereotypes. As a result, if an observer is expecting to see something then their observations may be biased to the extent that they 'find' it in what they see. Various strategies can be used to increase the reliability of observational research. These include the following:

■ Use of double blind techniques: the researcher and the person completing the research should be unaware of the hypothesis.

Key terms

Participant observation requires the researcher to actually join the group or take part in the situation they are studying.

Non-participant observation: based on observations made from a distance or from 'outside' the group or situation being studied.

Disclosed observation: an observation in which the participants are aware that they are being observed. This is also known as overt observation.

Undisclosed observation: an observation in which the participants are not aware that they are being observed. This is also known as covert observation.

Structured observation: before the research begins the researcher determines precisely what behaviours are to be observed and will use a standardised checklist to record the frequency with which those behaviours are observed within a specified time period.

Research methods

Table 4 *An example of collection of data concerning an observation of aggressive behaviour in children*

Child	Hits or shoves unprovoked	Hits or shoves following peers	Hits or shoves in retaliation	Shouts at others unprovoked	Shouts at others following peers	Shouts at others in retaliation
A						
B						
C						

Table 5 *Example of coding gender stereotypes in children's books according to categories (stereotypes): content analysis*

	Nurturant		Emotional		Aggressive		Active	
	Male	Female	Male	Female	Male	Female	Male	Female
Book 1								
Book 2								
Book 3								
Etc.								
Total								
Percentage								

■ **Key terms**

Unstructured observation: the researcher uses direct observation to record behaviours as they occur; there is no predetermined plan about what will be observed.

Observation schedule: usually a structured form or grid that is completed in line with the researcher's instructions or guidance by an observer.

Inter-observer reliability: the extent to which a data collection tool used by a group of observers produces similar data.

■ Clear definitions of terms and concepts: for example, if you are observing 'aggressive behaviour' then a clear definition of 'aggression' will be needed to focus the observer on the precise behaviour that is being looked for.

■ A pilot study: this enables the observers to practise the use of the **observation schedule**, to check the appropriateness of the category definitions and to check whether all observers are categorising the behaviour in the same way.

■ Ensure that the observation is completed by more than one observer and compare their recordings. If quantitative data has been gathered then **inter-observer reliability** can be measured. This is measured using correlational techniques. If the observations are reliable (consistent) then we would expect a positive correlation between the scores.

Table 6 *Advantages and disadvantages of different types of observational studies*

Type of observation	Advantages	Disadvantages
Naturalistic	High levels of ecological validity. Participants may be unaware that they are being observed and therefore they may behave more naturally.	No control over EVs. If the participant is unaware that they are being observed, then this may raise ethical issues, e.g. lack of informed consent.
Controlled	Higher levels of control over EVs.	Participants may be affected by the fact that they know they are being observed. Behaviour may not be natural; this lowers the ecological validity of the research.
Participant	Very high ecological validity. Rich qualitative data can be yielded by the research. Easier to understand what the observees' behaviour actually means. A relationship based on trust can be established between those being observed and the observer.	Researcher has to rely on memory – unreliable. Observer may become too emotionally involved with the observees, meaning that observations can become subjective rather than objective. The presence of the observer may change the group dynamics.
Non–participant	Observees may not realise that they are being observed, meaning that behaviour may not be changed by the presence of the observer. The observer may be more objective as they are less likely to become emotionally involved with the participants. Observer can record their observations as they occur making them more reliable in terms of memory.	The actual meaning of the behaviour may not be so clear from a distance. A relationship is not formed between the observer and the observee with the consequence that there may be less trust.
Disclosed observation	Reduction of ethical issues – the observee knows they are being observed and thus has given their consent to the researcher doing so. Increases the trust between researchers and the public..	Increase in reactivity as the observee may change their behaviour as they know they are being observed. There will be an increase in demand characteristics.
Undisclosed observation	Reduction of reactivity as the participant does not realise they are being observed, meaning that there are less demand characteristics.	Ethical issues raised by the observation. When the observee realises that they have been observed they may come to distrust psychologists in the future.

Key points:

- A naturalistic observation is a type of observation where the researcher observes behaviour in the participant's own environment.

- A controlled observation is where the researcher exercises control over the environment.

- A participant observation is one where the observer takes part. A non-participant observation is one where the observer does not take part or play a role in the group observed.

- A structured observation is one where there is a clear framework for data gathering. For example, a data collection grid may be used.

- Observer bias is a major problem for observational studies.

- Inter-observer reliability can be measured using correlational techniques. It refers to the extent to which the observations completed by two observers are consistent.

✓ **Summary questions**

5 What types of observational study are represented below?

  a An investigation is carried out into whether there is a difference in the length of time a newborn baby spends looking at projected images of his or her mother or father. The observation is completed in a laboratory where the length of time spent gazing at enlarged images is measured using advanced technological techniques.

  b A researcher compares the behaviour of male and female two-year-olds when their parents say farewell to them at the beginning of the nursery day. The researcher has volunteered as a helper at the nursery for the day and notes the language and body language of the children at point of farewell.

6 Identify as many variables as you can that may affect the data collected from study (b), e.g. how long the child has been at nursery.

7 The researcher in study (b) is looking for advice on how to collect the data for this observation and improve the reliability of the study. What would the data collection grid look like? How could they improve the reliability of any observations made?

AQA Examiner's tip

If a question is asked on how to improve the reliability of observational research the easiest way of answering it is to focus on reducing observer bias and by suggesting ways in which this could be done.

AQA Examiner's tip

You need to know and be able to explain at least two advantages and disadvantages of observational research.

Research methods

Correlational methods

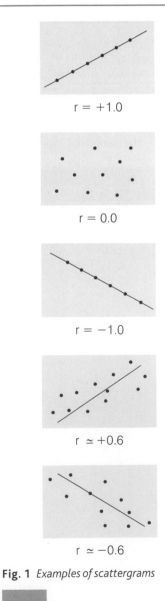

Fig. 1 *Examples of scattergrams*

Positive and negative correlation

The term correlation literally means co-relate and refers to the measurement of a relationship between two or more variables. The variables measured are known as the co-variables.

You should be able to recognise and describe the following types of correlation:

- Positive correlation: as one variable increases the other variable increases. For example, as the level of secure attachment increases, the number of smiles given increases.

- Negative correlation: as one variable increases the other variable decreases. For example, DiLalla (1988) found a negative correlation between the amount of time children spend in day care and the amount of pro-social behaviour they display. Children who spent longer in day care were less cooperative and helpful in their relationships with other children.

Recognising and measuring correlation

Correlational relationships are identified and demonstrated through the use of statistical techniques. This means variables have to be operationalised, that is given a numerical value. Using the example above, the amount of time children spend in care is quantitative as it can be measured in number of days/weeks etc. However, the amount of pro-social behaviour they display would have to be scored on some kind of rating scale, e.g. 1 = no pro-social behaviour; 10 = extreme pro-social behaviour.

The reason that correlation studies rely on quantitative data is because they actually measure the strength and direction of the relationship between two variables. They do more than simply state if two variables are related.

The following are examples of correlational statistical techniques:

- The scattergram: this provides a visual representation of a correlational relationship. It is a descriptive statistic and illustrates correlation through a special type of graph where one variable is placed on the x (horizontal) axis and the other variable is placed on the y (vertical) axis.

- A correlation coefficient is a numerical representation of the strength and direction of the relationship between two variables. The number below each graph in Figure 1 is the correlation coefficient. A correlation coefficient can range between –1.0 and +1.0. The number indicates the strength of the relationship, that is, the extent to which the two variables are related. The sign indicates the direction of the relationship – whether the correlation is positive or negative. Therefore +1 represents a perfect positive correlation and –1 represents a perfect negative: 0 means no relationship. The nearer the number is to +1 or –1 the stronger the correlation.

Table 7 *Correlation*

Advantages of correlation	Disadvantages of correlation
Can establish a relationship between two variables. They allow researchers to statistically analyse situations that could not be manipulated experimentally for ethical or practical reasons.	Correlation does not establish cause and effect; it only establishes a relationship between two variables. There may be a third variable that has not been identified that is creating the relationship. For example, in the relationship between amount of violent TV viewed by nine-year-olds and later aggression it may not be the violent television that is the key variable but rather that an already aggressive child chooses to watch such material. Correlations only identify linear relationships not curvilinear. For example, the relationship between temperature and aggression is a curvilinear relationship. The relationship between temperature and aggression is only positive up to a point, since at very high temperatures aggression begins to decrease. This is known as an inverted U relationship, which is not detected by correlation.

Key points:

- Correlation establishes relationships or associations between co-variables.
- There are different types of correlation. These are positive correlation and negative correlation.
- A positive correlation occurs where an increase in one variable leads to an increase in the other variable.
- A negative correlation occurs where an increase in one variable leads to a decrease in the other variable.
- A scattergram provides a graphical representation of correlation.
- The correlation coefficient is a number that tells us the strength and direction of the relationship between two variables. It always lies between +1 and −1.

✓ Summary questions

8 Identify whether the following statements indicate a positive or a negative correlation:
  a As the level of social deprivation increases, the physical health of the infant decreases.
  b The quicker a parent responds to a crying baby, the less the baby will cry when older.

9 Fill in the blanks to write some correlational statements of your own:
  a Positive correlations: as ___ increases, _____ increases.
  b Negative correlations: as ____ increases, _____ decreases.

10 Describe the direction and strength of the correlations indicated by the following correlation coefficients:
  a +0.95 b +0.22 c −0.33 d −0.67

11 Identify one piece of research which has made use of correlation. Identify the co-variables and state the conclusion. That is, indicate whether the researchers found no correlation, a positive correlation or a negative correlation.

AQA Examiner's tip

When writing a correlational hypothesis always operationalise the variables and if a directional hypothesis is asked for then use the terms positive or negative. Examiners like it! For example: 'There will be a significant positive correlation between the number of hours of violent television viewed and scores on an aggression questionnaire'.

Hint

Never make the mistake of thinking that correlation indicates or means 'cause and effect'. It indicates and means only that there is an 'association' between two variables. Be careful when writing about correlational data as it is easy to slip into talking about one variable causing a change in the other variable.

AQA Examiner's tip

You should be able to explain at least two advantages and disadvantages of the different methods. Remember if two marks are available then mere identification of the advantage/disadvantage would only gain you one mark; you need to elaborate to gain the full marks. For example, stating you cannot establish cause and effect would gain one mark; to gain the two you would need to elaborate. For example, 'Correlation does not establish cause and effect, it simply establishes that there is a relationship between the two variables. There may be a hidden third factor that is causing the relationship'.

Research methods

Surveys and interviews

Research methods

- Understand the use of surveys and interviews in psychological research.

- Know the difference between open and closed question types.

- Be able to construct open and closed questions.

- Be able to explain the advantages and disadvantages of questionnaires and interviews.

Surveys

In basic terms, a survey involves asking a large sample of people for information on a specific topic at a particular moment in time. Through asking questions the researcher usually wants to establish what people do and think in relation to the topic. Of all the methods available to psychology researchers, the survey places the greatest emphasis on selecting a representative and large enough sample of participants. This is because the researcher will want to make generalisations about their findings – that the findings obtained from the sample group also apply to the larger research population. Researchers using a survey strategy typically use questionnaires to obtain the data they need. Designing a questionnaire for a survey is a very skilled task. There are a number of key considerations that should be taken into account:

- Type of questions: there are two broad categories of questions that can be used. These are open and closed questions. Consider the table below, which summarises the main features of these two different types of questions.
- Keep the questions and instructions easy to understand.
- Keep the amount of information asked for to a minimum – only ask a question if it is directly related to the research. For example, if you ask for a person's age or gender then there should be a good research reason for it.
- Be mindful of ethics: do not ask invasive or inappropriately personal questions.
- Carry out a pilot study first, making changes if needed.

Table 8 *Types of questions used in surveys*

Type of question	Description	Advantages	Disadvantages	Examples
Open question	Allows the respondent to write their own answer, in words. This produces qualitative data.	Provides rich, detailed data (qualitative). Allows the respondent to express what they say they really think. It is much more realistic.	Because of the qualititative nature of the data collected, this can make analysis difficult.	What do you think about the internet as an educational medium? What are your thoughts on the main causes of stress?
Closed question (fixed choice questions)	The participant chooses their response from a limited number of fixed responses predetermined by the researcher.	Provides quantitative data, which can be statistically analysed.	Artificial: questioning is not realistic. Loses the richness of qualitative responses. We are not clear as to how the respondent has understood the question.	Do you use the internet? Please tick from the list below the sources of stress in your life.

Table 9 *Strengths and weaknesses of questionnaires*

Strengths	Weaknesses
Can be used to question a large sample of people relatively quickly.	**Social desirability:** for example, if you complete a health questionnaire and are asked about the units of alcohol you consume you may underestimate the number to present yourself favourably. If we cannot rely on the authenticity of the response then this is a major threat to the validity of the data.
Used to collect large amounts of data about what people think as well as what they say they do.	People may give untruthful responses particularly in relation to sensitive issues, for example, alcohol abuse, parenting styles.
Efficient in that the researcher does not need to be present while the participant completes the questionnaire.	There may be distortion of the sampling frame, which affects how far the findings can be generalised, i.e. only those who can read and write can take part. Also, postal surveys may have low response rates reducing the representativeness of the sample. This again reduces the validity of the data.
The above point brings with it the advantage that it can reduce investigator effects – there is a reduction in the influence of interpersonal factors.	Difficult to phrase questions clearly; you may obtain different interpretations of questions.

■ Interviews

Interviews are an alternative method for asking questions. They differ from questionnaires in their face-to-face nature. They are particularly useful for gathering more detailed information and enabling a more natural and flexible approach to questioning. An interview generally involves a conversational exchange between the interviewer and one or more other individuals. The interviewer usually has certain topics that they want to explore. The possible structures for interviews can be viewed along a scale from those which are highly structured to those which are very open in nature. Generally, the more the researcher already knows about the topic and range of possible answers, the more structured the interview becomes. Also, if the researcher knows they need to report the results of the interviews in quantitative form then they may prefer a structured format. The clearest example of a highly structured interview is one where there are predetermined questions with fixed responses. The procedure is standardised with exactly the same wording and order of questions being used for every interviewee. An alternative to this form of interviewing is the semi-structured interview. Here the interviewer may use some of the same questions for all interviewees, but the order may vary. In addition, the interviewer may ask follow-up questions to clarify the interviewees' responses or pursue new lines of enquiry.

■ Key term

Social desirability: the tendency of humans to present themselves in the best possible light. Responses to questionnaires may be influenced by this tendency. There is a difference between what people say they do and what in fact they do!

Research methods

Table 10 *Strengths and weaknesses of interviews*

Strengths	Weaknesses
Detailed information can be obtained (qualitative). It allows the interviewer to clarify the meaning and significance of the information being provided.	Statistical analysis can be difficult if the interview is unstructured and the data collected is qualitative in nature.
Allows the participant to freely express themselves.	More time consuming than a questionnaire.
Unstructured interviews may encourage the participant to be honest in their answers and raise new lines of psychological enquiry.	Greater chance of interpersonal variables affecting the responses, i.e. increased risk of investigator effects.

AQA Examiner's tip

You may be asked in the exam to construct a question that will yield qualitative data – an easy way of doing this is to ask an open 'explain' question. A question that allows the respondent to elaborate on their reasons for something will by its nature bring about qualitative data. The worded nature of the response combined with the elaboration will yield a qualitative response, e.g. Explain your reasons... Alternatively if you are asked to construct a question that will yield quantitative data then limit the responses to the question and state that this allows you to calculate the numbers of people who gave a particular response to the questions, enabling quantitative data to be gathered – numerical in form.

Key points:

- Psychologists are interested in asking questions, and questionnaires and interviews allow them to do this.
- The types of questions asked can be categorised as either open or fixed response questions.
- Open questions produce qualitative data that is rich in detail.
- Fixed response questions produce quantitative data that allows for statistical analysis.
- Questionnaires have the advantages of enabling standardised procedure, reducing interpersonal variables and enabling a larger sample to be questioned.
- Interviews have the advantages of producing richer detail (if open questions are used), and allowing new lines of enquiry to be followed up and allowing clarification of how the interviewee has understood the question.

✓ Summary questions

12 Construct two questions that are open in nature.

13 Construct two questions that are closed in nature.

14 In their study of the development of attachments, Schaffer and Emerson (1964) used observations of the babies and interviews with the mothers. The interviews included questions about the baby's reaction to various situations, such as being with a babysitter or being put in their cot. Discuss the strengths and limitations of using interviews in this type of study.

Case study

Learning objectives:

- Describe the key features of the case study method.
- Understand and explain the advantages and disadvantages of case studies.

Key term

Idiographic: relating to individual cases or events.

What is a case study?

A case study is essentially the gathering of detailed information about an individual or group of people. The fact that it focuses on the single case makes it a prime example of research that is **idiographic** in nature. Typically a case study involves the production of a case history. This records relevant details about the individual such as employment history, family relationships, medical history and socioeconomic status. A case study can be longitudinal or retrospective. Additional information may also be gathered using a range of other research methods including interviews, surveys and observations. Case studies are by their nature very individualistic. However you will find that most share the following common features:

- The method is descriptive. The method allows for the collection of qualitative data that is rich in detail.
- The research is often very focused on a particular aspect of behaviour. This is known as a narrow focus in research.

Case studies provide an effective way of gaining insight into the personal experiences of the person under study and for suggesting new avenues of research. Although many 'hard scientists' reject the case study as non-scientific, it is a very rich method that has been known to challenge established thinking in psychology.

Table 11 *Advantages and disadvantages of case studies*

Advantages	Disadvantages
Produces rich, meaningful data (qualitative)	Difficult to replicate therefore difficult to establish the reliability of the data
Offers high levels of ecological validity – realism is high	Because of its idiographic nature it is difficult to generalise the results beyond the individual or group being studied. There is low population validity
Can challenge established thinking and lead to new psychological insights	The possibility of researcher bias is high, which further calls into question its scientific credibility

Key points:

- A case study is an in-depth study of one individual or group of people.
- Case studies are an example of the idiographic approach.
- Case studies can challenge established knowledge and suggest other avenues of research.

✓ Summary questions

15 Review the areas of psychology that you have studied to date and identify and describe as many examples of case studies as you can.

16 Identify what psychology has learned from the different case studies identified.

Chapter summary

Link

Review the research findings relating to the impact of day care on behaviour on p76 and use this to help focus your questions.

- Researchers have a range of methods they can use in their research: the experiment, surveys, interviews, case studies, observations and correlational techniques.

- Experimental methods provide the most rigorous way of testing hypotheses because they seek to establish cause and effect relationships.

- The different types of experiment are: laboratory, field and natural.

- An experiment will employ one of the three following designs: repeated measures design, the matched pairs design or the independent groups design.

- There are different types of observations, with a major distinction being made between natural and controlled observations. In addition observations vary along the dimensions of disclosed–undisclosed, participant–non-participant and structured–unstructured.

- Correlational research concerns itself with establishing the relationships between different variables. The variables to be correlated are known as the co-variables.

- Surveys and interviews involve asking questions. The questions asked can be categorised as either open or closed.

- A case study is the in-depth study of a person or a group of people and is a clear example of the idiographic approach in psychology.

How science works: practical activity

Undertake a survey to investigate parent's beliefs about the impact of day care on children's behaviour, in particular to find out if the beliefs of parents who use day care differ from the beliefs of those who look after pre-school children at home. Working in pairs, construct a suitable questionnaire. Make sure that you gather relevant background information such as whether the parents use day care or care for their children at home. You will need to decide what you want to know and then decide on the most appropriate style of questions to obtain this information. Make sure that the questions are clear and unambiguous. Think about your target population, how you will obtain your sample and the procedure for administering the questionnaire.

Carry out your survey collecting data from at least 10 respondents each.

Keep your results safe as you will use them in a later activity in Chapter 7.

Research methods

7 Data analysis and presentation

Measures of central tendency

Key terms

Qualitative data: analysis that focuses more on words (what people say) rather than numbers.

Quantitative data: analysis that uses numerical data.

Understanding data

In research there are two different types of data that a researcher can collect as a result of their investigation: **qualitative** and **quantitative data**. It is important to understand the difference between these two broad categories and be able to recognise them. The type of data collected will have a significant impact on how you present and analyse your findings.

A researcher who uses the scientific method, e.g. the experimental method, in their investigation will be collecting quantitative data. This is numerical data. Asking 'how many' or 'how often' would be typical research questions that involve seeking numerical, quantitative data. For example, in an investigation into the effect of organisation on memory, the dependent variable (DV) would be the number of words recalled. Once the quantitative data has been obtained, statistical techniques will be used to analyse it. These techniques are used to establish and describe the numerical patterns and relationships that exist in the data, e.g. in the previous example a statistical technique would be to calculate the average number of words recalled by each participant (the mean). The key point to remember about quantitative research is that it will always involve measuring something in some way.

Qualitative data, in contrast to quantitative data, is not numerical. Psychology researchers work with qualitative data when they use case studies, unstructured observations and semi-structured interviews in their investigations. It can provide rich, detailed information that reflects the participant's thoughts or feelings. Qualitative research is based on information that cannot be described meaningfully in a numerical way in its original form but note that it can often be converted into quantitative data, for example through content analysis.

Data tables

Before we actually look at the statistical techniques that you need to be familiar with, let us first consider some basics in relation to the presentation of data. When data is collected as a result of research it is important for the researcher to present their findings in an accessible form. This will allow patterns to be more clearly seen. One of the most basic ways of doing this is to present a summary of the data in a table. Someone reading your research should be able to grasp directly from your tables of results exactly what you are showing.

Table 1 *Results for the effects of organisation on memory*

Condition 1	Condition 2
7.8	6.2
9	7
10	7

This table is difficult to read because the presentation has omitted to tell us exactly what the numbers are showing. By explicitly labelling tables we ensure that if the reader was to go straight to the results section they could understand exactly what the numbers are telling us.

Table 2 *Measures of central tendency for the number of words recalled under organised and unorganised conditions*

Measure of central tendency	Condition 1 (organised condition)	Condition 2 (unorganised condition)
Mean	7.8	6.2
Median	9	7
Mode	10	7

In the example above it is now clear that the numbers are referring to the number of words recalled and the finding that more words are recalled when information is organised is now clearly observed.

■ Measures of central tendency

Identifying the central tendency in a set of data tells a researcher where the average is in a set of data. There are three measures of central tendency: the **mean**, the **median** and the **mode**.

The advantages and disadvantages of the different measures of central tendency can be summarised as follows:

Table 3 *Summary table of measures of central tendency*

Measure of central tendency	What is it?	Advantages	Disadvantages
Mean	Statistical or arithmetic average.	The mean is the most sensitive measure of central tendency, taking all scores into account.	The mean can be distorted by extreme scores with the consequence that it becomes unrepresentative of the data.
Median	The middle score after the data is ordered.	The median is unaffected by extreme scores, thus in a data set where extreme scores exist this would be a more appropriate measure of central tendency than the mean.	Unlike the mean the median only takes one or two scores into account – the middle value(s).
Mode	The most frequently occurring score.	Similar to the median, the mode is unaffected by extreme scores.	Can be affected dramatically by the change in one score , making it an unrepresentative measure.

The advantages and disadvantages of the mean, median and mode as set out in the table above give some indication of when each should be used as a measure of central tendency. Generally the arithmetic mean will give a good indication of central tendency or the typical score unless the data contains extreme scores that distort it. In this situation the mean can be very misleading and shouldn't be used. The median, in contrast, won't be affected by extreme scores and can easily be located as the middle item(s) in a data set. But the median may still not tell us what the typical or most frequently occurring scores or items are in a data set. If we want to know this the mode would be the best measure of central tendency to use.

Key terms

Mean: this is known as the statistical average and is calculated by adding up all the scores in a set of data and then dividing by the number of scores.

Median: the median is a central value of a data set, and is calculated by firstly putting the data in order and then finding the middle score. If there is an even number of scores you should add the two middle scores together and divide by two.

Mode: the mode is the most frequently occurring score and is calculated by a frequency count – quite simply analyse your data and see which score occurs the most.

■ Hint

If you are asked what a mean is don't just say it is the average score, say the statistical average.

AQA Examiner's tip

A common exam question is to ask you to identify and justify an alternative measure of central tendency to the one given in the stimulus material. For example, if the measure used in the stimulus material is the arithmetic mean an alternative would be the median or the mode. The most common mistake made is to explain what it is rather than to say why you would use it instead. Remember justifying is a 'why' question not a 'what is it' question. For example, a good answer would be 'I would use the median as an alternative to the mean as there are some extreme scores in the data, e.g. 26 and 46, which would distort the mean making it unrepresentative. The median has the advantage of being unaffected by these extreme scores'.

Key points:

- The mean, median and mode are all measures of central tendency.

- Measures of central tendency are descriptive statistics that tell us which value is most typical for our data set.

- The mean is the arithmetic average.

- The median is the middle score in our data after the data is ordered.

- The mode is the most frequently occurring score.

✓ Summary questions

1 The following hypothesis was tested: 'There will be more words recalled in the organised condition than in the unorganised condition'. In relation to the data in Table 4, which hypothesis would probably be accepted, the experimental or the null hypothesis?

2 Look at the following data, which was generated by a laboratory-based study of context-dependent learning. Participants were split into groups where they learned a list of words. One week later they were tested for their recall of the words. Participants in one condition recalled the words in the same environment in which they had been learned; in the other condition the students recalled the words in a different environment.

Table 4

	Condition 1: tested in same environment Number of words recalled	Condition 2: tested in a different environment Number of words recalled
Median:	6	2.5

The following hypothesis was tested: there will be a difference in the number of words recalled by participants who were re-tested in the same environment and those participants re-tested in a different environment. Given the above data, which hypothesis would probably be accepted, the null or the experimental?

3 Look at the following data, which was generated by an investigation into the impact of the quality of day care on intellectual development. The IQ of 20 children aged eight was measured. Ten of the children had attended a pre-school nursery rated by Ofsted as outstanding, while the other children had attended a pre-school nursery rated by Ofsted as satisfactory. The results of the IQ test can be found below:

Table 5

Condition 1: attended outstanding pre-school care	Condition 2: attended satisfactory pre-school care
100	98
124	111
123	134
132	98
154	142
109	121
98	100
115	146
105	93
117	102

Calculate the mean, mode and median for the above data. What conclusions would you tentatively draw from the data?

Measures of dispersion

Research methods

Learning objectives:

- Know what is meant by the term 'measures of dispersion'.

- Be able to define the range and standard deviation and know when to use them.

- Understand what the range and the standard deviation indicate about a set of data.

- Know an advantage and disadvantage of each.

In addition to wanting to know where data typically lies in terms of its central tendency, it is sometimes also important to know how much variability there is in a data set. Measures of central tendency do not always paint a true picture of the underlying data. For example, findings from two distinct samples may produce data that have the same mean or median, but completely different levels of variability and vice versa. As a result, a proper description of a set of data should include both a measure of central tendency and a measure of dispersion.

While measures of central tendency are used to estimate 'normal' values of a data set, measures of dispersion describe the spread of the data, or its variation, around a central value. There are various methods that can be used to measure the dispersion of a data set, each with its own set of advantages and disadvantages, including the range and the standard deviation.

Range

The range is simply the difference between the highest and lowest score and is calculated by subtracting the lowest score from the highest score. Very simple!

Standard deviation

The standard deviation is the most common measure of statistical dispersion. It measures how widely spread the values in a data set are around the mean. Unlike the range it takes all the scores into account, making it the most powerful measure of dispersion available to researchers.

If the data points are close to the mean, then the standard deviation is small. If many data points are far from the mean, then the standard deviation is large. If all the data values are equal, then the standard deviation is zero. The standard deviation allows us to see the consistency with which the independent variable (IV) impacted on the DV. Let us illustrate this by looking at Table 6, which shows results for an investigation into the effects of organisation on memory.

Table 6 *Table to show the number of words recalled under organised and unorganised conditions*

	Group 1 (organised condition)	Group 2 (unorganised condition)
	16	11
	13	9
	8	13
	12	26
	17	15
	17	17
	15	16
	11	10
	21	13
	17	13
Mean	14.7	14.3
Standard deviation	3.55	4.58

If we look at the data we can see that the standard deviation was slightly lower in the organised condition, suggesting that the scores (number of words recalled) for this group are more closely clustered around the mean, i.e. there is less variation in the performance of the participants in condition 1. The larger variation in condition 2 (unorganised condition) suggests that there are more individual differences in the performance of the participants, e.g. we might conclude some of the participants have better memories than others.

The table below can be used as a guide to help understand what the standard deviation tells us about data.

AQA **Examiner's tip**

You will not be asked to calculate a standard deviation in the exam. What the examiner wants to know is whether you understand what the standard deviation tells us about the data rather than whether you can calculate a standard deviation.

Table 7 *What standard deviation tells us*

Standard deviation	What it tells us about the data
Large	A large standard deviation tells us that there was much variation around the mean.
Small	A small standard deviation tells us that the data was closely clustered around the mean.
Zero	All the data values were the same.

The advantages and disadvantages of the different measures of central dispersion are summarised as follows:

Table 8 *Summary of measures of dispersion*

Measure of dispersion	What is it?	When should it be used?	Advantages	Disadvantages
Range	The difference between the highest and lowest score in a set of data.	When you wish to make a basic measure of the variation within the data and the data is consistent. If there are extreme scores the range is inappropriate as it will be a distorted measure of variation.	Easy to calculate.	The range can be easily distorted by extreme scores.
Standard deviation	A measure of dispersion that indicates the 'spread' or dispersion of the data around a central value.	When you wish to make a very sensitive measure of dispersion.	Takes account of all scores. It is a sensitive measure of dispersion.	More difficult to calculate compared to the range.

Key points:

■ Measures of dispersion tell us how much variability there is in the data.

■ The range is the most basic measure of dispersion and tells us the difference between the highest score and lowest score in a data set.

■ The standard deviation is a sensitive measure of dispersion. It tells us how the data is spread around the mean.

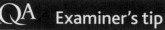

Examiner's tip

A good way of gaining extra marks on the research methods questions is to use the 'compare and contrast approach'. If you are asked for a disadvantage of the range you could say that extreme scores easily distort it. However, to give a detailed answer you could elaborate by contrasting it with the standard deviation. Another way to elaborate is by making reference to the data sets in the stimulus material.

Examiner's tip

In answering question 6, you need to consider what the means and the standard deviation tell you. You might also consider how the limitations of the design might affect confidence in the findings or the conclusions that could be drawn.

✔ **Summary questions**

4 Look at the data listed and calculate the range: 22, 62, 65, 76, 84, 95, 96, 99, 97.

5 Identify one disadvantage of using the range to calculate the dispersion in this data set.

6 A researcher carried out research into the effect of a critical question on recall. The researcher had participants watch a video of a simulated car crash. The participants were then asked questions regarding what they had observed. In one condition the participants were asked the target question 'How fast was the car travelling when it hit the other car?', while in the other condition they were asked 'How fast was the car travelling when it smashed into the other car?' The data was then analysed and a summary table of results can be found below:

Table 9

	Smashed condition	Hit condition
Mean estimated speed of car	65.6 miles per hour	57.2 miles per hour
Standard deviation	5.9	7.8

What do the results in the table suggest about the effects of the initial question?

Graphs

Research methods

✅

Learning objectives:

- Be able to select appropriate graphs to illustrate research data.

- Be able to interpret what a graph is telling us about the data.

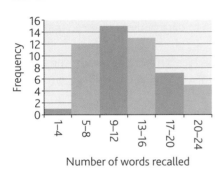

Fig. 1 *A histogram*

Hint

Always remember to label the axes of your graphs clearly and give the graph an explicit title. The rule of thumb is that someone should be able to look at a graph and know exactly what it is telling them without any reference to any additional data.

Statistics such as those discussed in the previous sections provide one way of describing and representing patterns in a quantitative data set. Another is through the use of statistical graphs. These have the advantage of providing a visual representation of the data set that allows us to see the patterns in a data set in an easy-to-understand way. In addition they can show very clearly the distribution of the scores within a data set.

The graphs that we will consider are as follows:

- the histogram
- the bar chart
- the scattergram.

The histogram

A histogram is often used in data analysis to provide a visual illustration of the distribution of data items in a data set. A histogram consists of vertical bars of equal width, which represent the frequencies of the variable placed on the x-axis. According to Coolican (1994) the major features of the histogram can be summarised as follows:

- all categories are represented
- columns are of equal width per equal category
- no intervals are missed because they are empty
- column areas are proportional to the area represented.

Bar chart

Bar charts, like line charts, are useful for comparing classes or groups of data. In the example below you can observe the percentage of students who achieved a particular grade in their A Level Psychology exam. A simple bar chart has one data series, but you can add more data series. The bar chart can represent frequencies or single statistics such as the mean of a sample or the percentage of proportion. There is no need to show all the frequencies on the x-axis, only the ones you are interested in displaying.

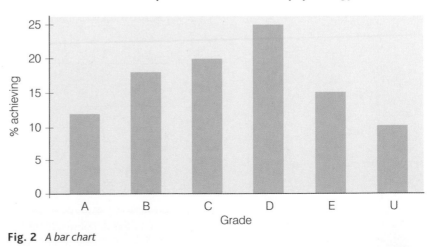

Fig. 2 *A bar chart*

■ Scattergram

A scattergram gives a good visual picture of the relationship between the two variables and aids the interpretation of the correlation coefficient. Each piece of data contributes one point to the scattergram, on which points are plotted but not joined. The resulting pattern indicates the type and strength of the relationship.

Points to note about scattergrams include:

- The more the points tend to cluster around a straight line, the stronger the relationship between the two variables (the stronger the correlation).
- If the line around which the points tends to cluster runs from lower left to upper right, the relationship between the two variables is positive (direct).
- If the line around which the points tends to cluster runs from upper left to lower right, the relationship between the two variables is negative (inverse).

Key points:

- Graphs provide a visual representation of data findings that can make them very accessible to the reader.
- There are different types of graphs used for different purposes. The types of graphs that illustrate descriptive statistics include the histogram, the bar chart and the scattergram.
- Scattergrams are a special type of graph used to represent correlations.

> ■ **Link**
>
> See p116 for visual examples of scattergrams.

✓ Summary questions

7 Revisit Table 6 and plot a histogram to represent the data.

8 Plot a bar chart to compare the means of the data in Table 9 (p128).

9 In a study of the relationship between sociability and child care experience a researcher assessed ten children at the age of eight using a standardised test of sociability (maximum score 200). The other co-variable measured was the number of main caregivers the child had in the first five years of life. Plot a scattergram to represent the data:

Table 10

Participant	Variable 1 Sociability score (age 8)	Variable 2 Number of carers in first five years
1	178	2
2	104	2
3	132	5
4	134	9
5	65	1
6	145	3
7	184	6
8	138	2
9	126	6
10	153	3

What does the scattergram seem to show?

Qualitative analysis

Learning objectives:

- Be able to describe the techniques available to analysis qualitative data.

- Understand what is meant by content analysis.

- Know how to undertake simple qualitative analysis.

Key terms

Content analysis: an analytical approach based on the **coding** and quantification of various elements in any kind of text (including advertisements) in any medium. It involves establishing categories and counting the number of instances when these categories are utilised within a text. At the most basic level, the main purpose of the method is to locate the nature of the relative patterns within and between sets of data.

Coding: the procedure employed to transform raw data into a format that can be used for data analysis purposes. This is necessary to allow the conversion of qualitative data to quantitative data. Coding qualitative data involves identifying recurrent words, concepts or themes.

Link

See p29 for more information about Tuckey and Brewer's bank robbery schema.

Qualitative analysis involves the analysis of non-numerical data. This can include speech, books, magazines, videos, television, pictures and computer games, as well as reflections and accounts of personal experience. If participants complete an interview or questionnaire using open questions then it will produce some qualitative data.

There are many different approaches to analysing qualitative data. We will focus on two of these. The first approach concerns itself with trying to convert qualitative data into quantitative data, such as **content analysis**.

Content analysis

This is where, for example, the researcher would identify a theme and count how many times it occurred. This could be used for a task like creating a schema for a bank robbery. In order to do a content analysis, you need to ask your participants an open-ended question such as 'Imagine you are in a bank and a robbery is taking place. What can you see and hear?' Depending on your research, you can decide what elements of the answers you are going to count before you see any data to prevent your own ideas influencing how you code the data. However, you might have a look at the data first in order to work out appropriate categories.

For this exercise, we are going to see how many people include the points identified by Tuckey and Brewer (2003) as part of the bank robbery schema:

Here are the answers from some of the participants:

- I imagine a crowded room with lots of people in queues in front of the cashiers. Then I imagine two men bursting in wearing balaclavas and brandishing guns. The whole thing is over very quickly – they tell the customers to lie on the floor and keep still; they force the cashiers to hand over bags of money and they run out as you hear police sirens in the distance.

- I think of three or four men with masks on running into a bank with guns, shouting at everybody to get down on the ground. Lots of threatening and scared bystanders. They get into the vault, fill up a bag with money and then make a quick exit in their getaway car.

- I imagine men dressed in stripy shirts with black trousers and black eye masks and black beanie-style hats and black gloves. I imagine that there are 3 of them and that they rush through the door with hand-held pistols and force the cashier to give them money at gun point. There are people screaming in the background and sirens begin to wail. They stuff money into bags and run out into a black Cadillac car.

- Guns, swag bags, masks/balaclavas, murky CCTV footage, shouting, fear, running, speeding getaway car, screaming tyres ...TV news item.

- People queuing, masked men wearing black running in shouting 'everyone get down on the floor' waving guns. Someone going to the cashiers with a briefcase and demanding they fill it with the cash and open the safe. Then all running out and someone behind the cash desks pressing an alarm.

Looking through these answers, if they mention one of the identified points this is counted:

- The bank robbers are male IIII
- The bank robbers wear some kind of disguise ~~IHI~~
- The bank robbers wear dark clothes II
- The bank robbers demand money from the cashiers IIII
- The bank robbers have a getaway car waiting outside the bank II
- The getaway car has a driver sitting in it

The number of times a point is identified gives a total that can be used for quantitative analysis.

One of the main problems with using content analysis is that of validity. It is vital that the classification procedure is reliable in the sense of being consistent. Also, the practice of constructing a category system involves the risk of an investigator imposing his or her meaning-system on the data rather than 'taking' it from the content. In content analysis studies, it is often desirable for multiple coders to set about the task of negotiating categories and quantifying the features present within a given text.

■ Pure qualitative analysis

This approach rejects the conversion of qualitative data to quantitative data and presents the findings of the research in a purely verbal form. Analysis attempts to organise the data not by reducing them to a number but by identifying and categorising recurrent themes. The process of achieving this level of analysis would involve:

- the data collected being transcribed (e.g. write out the answers given in an interview in the exact form in which the interviewee gave them)
- once transcribed the data would be read through repeatedly in an effort to identify recurrent themes
- all data is read and re-read until all emerging themes have been identified that account for all data collected.

Key points:

- Qualitative analysis involves the analysis of non-numerical data items.
- One approach that is adopted is to convert the qualitative data to quantitative data.
- Content analysis is often used to achieve this conversion.
- Pure qualitative analysis rejects the conversion of quantitative data to a quantitative form.

✓ Summary questions

10 Explain in your own words what is meant by qualitative data.

11 Explain two ways in which a psychologist could analyse qualitative data.

12 Identify one advantage of qualitative data and one disadvantage of qualitative data.

13 Identify the type of survey and interview questions that would yield qualitative data.

14 You have been asked to carry out a survey into effective revision techniques. You have constructed a questionnaire and distributed it to an opportunity sample of 10 students. Here are the answers to your open-ended questions:

When revising, at what time of day do you concentrate best?
- I find getting up early and working until mid-morning is most effective.
- I like to arrive home from school and revise before dinner.
- In the middle of the night before the exam.
- If I have a break after school, I can then settle down and work in the evening.
- I like to have a revision period at the beginning of the school day.
- Just after lunch when I'm not hungry or tired is a good time to revise.
- It takes me a while to wake up in the morning, but from about 11 o'clock I'm ready to revise.
- Once everybody else in the house has gone to sleep, I can really concentrate on what I'm learning.
- After school I do swimming training and after that I'm tired physically but mentally ready to work.
- I revise best in the afternoon.

How do you prepare the room you are studying in to help you with your revision?
- I listen to music – it blocks out the noise of my neighbours shouting.
- If there are any sweets in the kitchen, I take them to by bedroom and eat them to keep me awake.
- I get all the notes out that I'll be revising that day so I don't disturb myself trying to find them.
- I make a pot of coffee, and listen to the radio through headphones.
- I sit in front of the television watching my favourite films.
- Lock my bedroom door to keep my sister out, find my multi-coloured highlighters and sheets of paper.
- I switch off my mobile phone, put a 'do not disturb' sign on my door.
- I find all my notes on the subject so if I get stuck I can find the answer.
- I tell my brother that he can't use the computer, and I set a timer to go off when I've worked for a certain amount of time.
- I make myself a drink and take some biscuits.

Analyse the answers using content analysis. What are the emerging themes in relation to the two open questions?

Chapter summary

Further reading and weblinks

For links to useful websites for data analysis:

www.saskschools.ca/curr_content/mathb30

www.southernct.edu

Search for Sixty Minute Statistics

www.mste.uiuc.edu

Search for Descriptive Statistics

- The data collected in your research can be subject to statistical analysis, which will make it easier to detect patterns in your findings.
- It is very important that data is presented in a form that makes it accessible to others, e.g. the use of clear, appropriately labelled tables.
- 'Measures of central tendency' is the collective term for the mean, median and mode. They are all examples of statistical analysis carried out on quantitative data.
- You can also make use of measures of dispersion, which includes the range and the standard deviation. Measures of dispersion tell you about the spread of your data.
- Data can also be presented in visual form. Examples of graphs include the histogram, the bar graph and the scattergram.
- Techniques used to analyse qualitative data include content analysis and pure qualitative analysis.

How science works: practical activity

Part A

Find the data you collected in relation to the task set at the end of Chapter 5.

You are now in a position to analyse and interpret your data using some of the statistical techniques learned in this chapter. You need to analyse the data in the following way:

- present clear tables of results
- analyse the data in terms of an appropriate measure of central tendency
- analyse the data in terms of an appropriate measure of dispersion
- present at least one graph.

Write a paragraph to summarise in words the findings of your study and then discuss your research. You should consider the strengths and weaknesses of the methodology including the design, the effectiveness of control of variables and sampling. You should also relate the findings to relevant theory and studies.

Part B

Find the completed questionnaires from the survey you carried out in Chapter 6.

Analyse the data from each question. In the case of closed questions you should record the frequency of the different responses and summarise this either as percentages or in graphical form. For open questions you could undertake a thematic analysis or a content analysis.

Write a paragraph to summarise in words your findings from the survey.

To find out if those who use day care and those who look after their children at home differ in their beliefs divide the responses into two piles (day care respondents and home care respondents). Analyse and summarise the data as above but this time present the data from the two groups so that it is easy to compare.

Write a paragraph to summarise in words what the survey showed about the two groups of respondents. What could you conclude from your findings?

Biological psychology - stress

Introduction

Key term

Stress: a state of stress is defined as existing when there is an imbalance between perceived demands and perceived coping responses.

We all know what 'stress' is in the sense that we use the term all the time in everyday conversation. There is some sense of pressure from the outside world that leads to anxiety and a feeling of **stress**. Stress is also all around us – relationships, work, money problems, global warming – and is often used as an explanation for illness. In fact it is a common belief that we are more likely to become ill when stressed.

The two chapters that follow review psychological research into various aspects of stress. In any area where a term is in common use and associated with particular beliefs, it is even more important for psychologists to be precise in their use of that term. Chapter 8 therefore begins with a review of how 'stress' has been defined in the past, and how we view it now in terms of demands and coping resources. Our reactions to stressful situations involve brain mechanisms controlling both appraisal processes and the body's response to stress. To illustrate this, an outline description of the brain's functional organisation is followed by a detailed analysis of the major pathways involved in the stress response.

Most people accept a link between stress and illness – it seems common sense that being under pressure for long periods would damage the body in some way. However this is an area where many studies have been done, particularly into stress effects on the immune system, and so we can look at whether research evidence supports the common-sense view. It also allows us to consider different types of research; many studies are controlled laboratory experiments, but others involve real-life stressful situations where for ethical or practical reasons the independent variable cannot be manipulated.

Chapter 9 begins with a review of sources of stress. We all experience the stress of coping with everyday life, while in addition there are major life events such as divorce and bereavement. Do all stressors have similar effects? Does research evidence support links between life events and illness? We focus next on workplace stress, which has become a major issue for workers and employers alike because of its effects on health and productivity.

There are many factors that can influence an individual's response to stress, such as personality. Are some people more vulnerable to stress-related illness? On the other hand, are some people more resistant? Again we can see whether the research evidence supports these views.

Finally we consider coping and stress management. People may have general styles of coping such as emotion-focused or problem-focused styles. In addition they may use specific psychological or physiological methods of coping, each of which has advantages and disadvantages. After reviewing and evaluating several of these methods, this topic closes with a consideration of the important role of social support in helping us cope with stress.

Biological psychology

The body's response to stress

Learning objectives:

- Understand definitions of stress and in particular the role of perception and appraisal.

- Describe the bodily systems activated in stressful situations.

- Understand how these systems might be related to the negative effects of stress.

Key terms

Stressor: a stimulus or situation imposing demands on an individual.

Transactional model: a model of stress that defines 'stress' as an imbalance between perceived demands on an individual and their perceived coping resources.

Primary appraisal: the person appraises or assesses the situation to identify potential threats or demands.

Secondary appraisal: the person appraises their ability to cope with a threatening situation.

AQA Examiner's tip

Nervous system structure and function are not on the specification, and you cannot be asked questions directly on that topic. However, to understand the mechanisms of stress and the effects of drugs used in managing stress, background knowledge of nervous system structure and function is necessary. It also helps understanding of the use of biological therapies in psychopathology, especially drugs.

What is stress?

The first problem we meet in the field of stress research is how to define 'stress'. Although we all have some idea of what we mean by the term, it would be much more difficult for us to write down a concise definition (you could try doing this; it is not as easy as it might seem). But researchers into stress need to be sure that they are all using the term in the same way, so there has to be an agreed definition.

The term 'stress' was introduced into psychology from mechanical engineering, where it referred to the tension placed on metals by heavy loads. It was popularised in the 1930s and 1940s by the work of Selye (reported in his 1956 study). He first noted that rats given repeated daily injections developed gastric (stomach) ulcers. He then wondered whether it was the stress of the injections themselves or what was injected that produced the ulceration.

In a series of careful studies Selye confirmed that it was the stress of the injections themselves. Over the following years he mapped out the body's physiological responses to stressful stimuli, or **stressors**, and eventually concluded that different stressors all produced the same pattern of physiological responses. This is called the stress response.

Selye could then argue that any stimulus producing the physiological stress response was by definition a stressor. This is a response-based definition of stress. Alternatively we can probably agree that certain events, such as physical injury or the death of someone close to you, can be considered as stressful. This is a stimulus-based view of stress, where certain events or stimuli by their very nature are defined as stressful.

Both of these approaches ignore the vital factor of individual differences. Some people with phobias will show the physiological stress response when faced with a tiny house spider, while others will not react to events others would find stressful. Death of a family member is usually stressful, but less so if you have had a long and difficult relationship with them.

So the current approach, developed by Cox and Mackay (1978) and Lazarus (Lazarus and Folkman, 1984), emphasises individual differences. It does this by giving a major role to the individual's cognitive processes. This **transactional model** sees stress as depending upon the person's perception of themselves and the world around them. The key process is appraisal, and this is divided into **primary appraisal** and **secondary appraisal**.

Primary and secondary appraisals are based on our perception of ourselves and the world around us. Putting these two processes together leads to a definition of stress: 'When an imbalance or discrepancy exists between perceived demands and perceived coping resources, then a state of stress exists'.

Although it may sound precise this is still a broad definition. Think of the demands the world makes on people; deadlines for coursework, forming or maintaining relationships, paying the mortgage, driving in the rush hour, loss of a family member, etc. The key point is that they have to be coped with, and if the result of primary and secondary appraisal is that demands outstrip coping resources, then a state of stress exists.

The advantage of the transactional approach is that it takes individual differences into account. Some people appraise spiders as a considerable threat that they cannot cope with. Overestimating the demands of Psychology AS and underestimating your own knowledge and preparation will lead to a stressful time even if final performance is good. The reverse, underestimating the demands of the examination and overestimating your preparation, leads to a stress-free time but a poor performance.

The transactional model shifts the focus from actual demands and coping resources to perceived demands and coping resources. In this way it acknowledges that people see the world in different ways and that research into stress must take these individual differences into account. Although we might criticise Selye for largely ignoring individual differences, we should remember that his early ground-breaking studies used rats and straightforward physical stressors. Individual differences would have been hard to identify.

Also note from Figure 1 that the effects of stress are not limited to the physiological stress response. Reactions to stressful situations include emotions such as anxiety and depression, and also behaviour aimed at coping with the situation. This chapter focuses on the physiological aspects of the stress response, but in the next one we look at some of these other aspects.

■ The body's response to stress: the nervous system

Highly specialised systems are involved in the body's response to stress, involving various glands, hormones and nerve pathways. These systems are coordinated by centres in the brain.

The neuron

The body is made up of billions of cells organised into tissues and systems. Muscle, glands, skin, liver, brain, etc. are all made up of cells specialised to perform particular functions, e.g. contraction, secretion of hormones, fat storage. The cells making up the nervous system are called **neurons.**

Neurons are covered in a complex cell membrane made up of several layers. The biochemical structure of this membrane allows it to conduct or transmit pulses of electrical activity known as **action potentials** or **nerve impulses.** Nerve impulses begin on the **dendrites** and then travel across the cell body and along the **axon.**

These action potentials or nerve impulses are the unit of information processing in the nervous system. All aspects of human behaviour – perception, memory, language, movement, thought, emotion, personality – are coded by patterns of nerve impulses in different parts of the nervous system. However, although this sounds relatively simple, don't forget there are between 15 and 100 billion neurons in the brain, and this is where the complexity comes from.

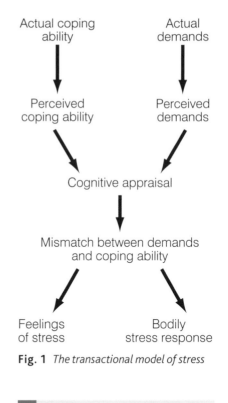

Fig. 1 *The transactional model of stress*

■ Link

For more about drug therapies for stress and psychological disorders, see chapter 9.

■ Key terms

Neuron: the basic unit of the nervous system. Neurons are cells specialised to conduct electrical impulses.

Action potential: technical term for nerve impulses. Pulses of electrical activity conducted along the neuron, action potentials represent coding of information in the nervous system.

Nerve impulses: see action potentials.

Dendrites: part of the neuron, dendrites are short processes connecting to the cell body. Nerve impulses are often triggered on dendrites.

Axon: part of the neuron, the axon is an elongated process running from the cell body. Axons can have up to 1,000 branches connecting via synapses to other neurons.

Biological psychology

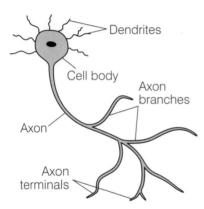

Fig. 2 *The neuron*

Key terms

Axon terminal: the end of a neuronal axon, also known as the presynaptic terminal.

Synapse: tiny gap separating the presynaptic terminal of one neuron and the postsynaptic terminal of the following neuron. Transmission across the synapse is chemical, using neurotransmitters.

Presynaptic terminal: the axon terminal leading into a synapse. Neurotransmitters are released from the presynaptic terminal.

Neurotransmitter: chemical stored in the presynaptic terminal. Nerve impulses stimulate the release of neurotransmitter molecules into the synapse, where they diffuse over to the postsynaptic membrane and combine with receptors.

Postsynaptic membrane: the neuronal cell membrane on which synaptic receptors are located. The neurotransmitter released from the presynaptic terminal combines with these receptors and this combination makes a nerve impulse more likely to occur in the postsynaptic neuron.

Synaptic receptors: molecules located on the postsynaptic terminal that combine with neurotransmitter molecules in a lock-and-key fashion.

All-or-none principle: applied to the nerve impulse. Combination of neurotransmitter with synaptic receptors disturbs the postsynaptic membrane and makes a nerve impulse more likely. If a threshold of disturbance is reached, a nerve impulse is triggered.

The synapse

Looking at Figure 2 you might wonder what happens when the nerve impulse reaches the end of the axon, the **axon terminal**. Neurons are not physically connected to one another. Between the axon terminal and the next neuron is a tiny gap, the **synapse**, visible only under an electron microscope. Although tiny, this gap presents an obstacle to the nerve impulse as it cannot jump across.

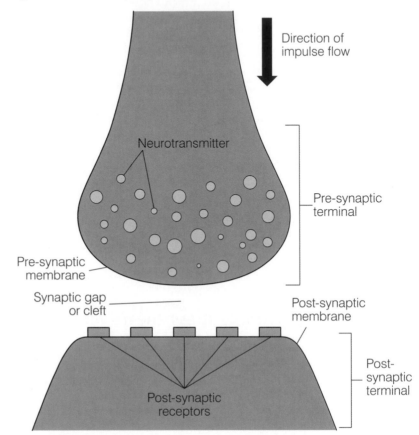

Fig. 3 *The synapse*

Transmission of nerve impulses across the synapse is chemical. Stored within the axon or **presynaptic terminal** are packets of chemicals known as **neurotransmitters.** As nerve impulses travelling down the axon reach the axon terminal they stimulate the release of neurotransmitter molecules into the synapse (Figure 3). The synaptic gap is so small that the molecules can diffuse over to the **postsynaptic membrane** (Figure 3) of the following neuron. Located on this membrane are **synaptic receptors.**

As the neurotransmitter molecule reaches the postsynaptic membrane it binds to the receptor for a brief period of time. This combination of neurotransmitter with receptor alters the biochemical characteristics of the postsynaptic membrane; this makes a nerve impulse more likely to be triggered at that point on the membrane.

It is a feature of the nerve impulse that it is an **all-or-none principle**; either it occurs or it doesn't. For a nerve impulse to be triggered on the postsynaptic membrane sufficient neurotransmitter molecules must be released from the presynaptic terminal. Once triggered, the nerve impulse will be conducted along the postsynaptic neuron, along the axon to the axon terminals, where the process is repeated at the next set of synapses.

The purpose of the synapse is to allow for information processing. To cross the synapse, enough nerve impulses must arrive at the presynaptic terminal in a short space of time to release sufficient neurotransmitter molecules to fire the postsynaptic membrane. If only a few impulses arrive, the amount of neurotransmitter released will not be sufficient, and the postsynaptic membrane will not fire. The information coded by those impulses will be lost. As each neuron in the brain can have axons with up to 1,000 branches they can make up to 1,000 synaptic connections with other neurons; this complexity means that the synapse is a crucial component of information processing in the nervous system.

There are a limited number of neurotransmitters and associated receptors. Synapses can in fact be defined by the neurotransmitter they release, so we have synapses using **GABA**, **dopamine**, **serotonin**, **noradrenaline**, etc. We meet examples of these in the following chapters. Knowing the chemical nature of the synapse enables us to explain the action of drugs on behaviour; many drugs have specific actions at the synapse, increasing or decreasing neurotransmitter activity.

■ Organisation of the nervous system

The billions of neurons making up the nervous system are organised in highly systematic ways. Our main interest is in the brain. This, along with the spinal cord, makes up the **central nervous system (CNS)**. Radiating from the spinal cord are the **spinal nerves**, containing nerve pathways connecting the CNS with the organs of the body. The spinal nerves are referred to as the **peripheral nervous system (PNS)**.

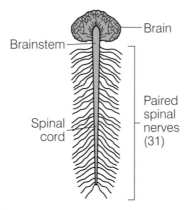

Fig. 4 *Organisation of the nervous system*

The brain is our key information processor. To do its job effectively, it needs to receive sensory input from the body's sensory receptors. Sensory information is carried in **sensory pathways** that run from the sensory receptors to the CNS in the spinal nerves. (One exception to this is the specialised senses, vision and hearing. Visual and auditory sensory pathways do not involve the spinal cord, but are contained within the brain.) The brain also needs to be connected to the muscles of the skeleton, so that it can control movement. It also controls internal organs. Pathways allowing the brain to control movement and responses of internal systems are referred to as **motor pathways**.

The PNS is made up of the spinal nerves. These contain millions of sensory and motor pathways, allowing the brain to be aware of what is going on in the body and outside world, and to control our various response systems. The spinal cord is also packed with thousands of sensory and motor pathways carrying information to and from the brain.

Key terms

GABA: synaptic neurotransmitter involved in the action of anti-anxiety drugs such as Librium and Valium.

Dopamine: synaptic neurotransmitter involved in the action of antipsychotic drugs used in schizophrenia.

Serotonin: synaptic neurotransmitter involved in the action of antidepressant drugs.

Noradrenaline: hormone released from the adrenal medulla, which acts on heart and circulatory system to increase heart rate and blood pressure. Noradrenaline is also a synaptic neurotransmitter in the brain and other parts of the nervous system.

Central nervous system (CNS): major part of the nervous system, made up of the brain and the spinal cord.

Spinal nerves: nerves are bundles of neuronal processes, mainly axons, travelling around the body. The spinal nerves radiate from the spinal cord. They carry sensory information into the central nervous system, and motor commands out to muscles and glands. The spinal nerves make up the peripheral nervous system (PNS).

Peripheral nervous system (PNS): see spinal nerves.

Sensory pathways: pathways in spinal nerves running from sensory receptors into the central nervous system, carrying sensory information.

Motor pathways: pathways in spinal nerves carrying commands from the brain out to muscles and glands.

Key terms

Autonomic nervous system (ANS): part of the peripheral nervous system concerned with the regulation of internal structures and systems. It is vital in maintaining physiological regulation of the body.

Brainstem: collectively, the pons, medulla and midbrain regions of the brain. The brainstem controls vital physiological functions, and contains autonomic nervous system centres.

Homeostasis: regulation of a constant internal environment. The best example is our constant body temperature. Homeostasis is heavily reliant on the autonomic nervous system.

Sympathetic nervous system: one of the two branches of the autonomic nervous system. Sympathetic dominance leads to a pattern of bodily arousal and preparation for energy expenditure.

Parasympathetic nervous system: one of the two branches of the autonomic nervous system. Parasympathetic dominance leads to a pattern of physiological calm.

Hypothalamus: part of the diencephalon in the forebrain. Controls the HPA and SAM (see p146) pathways involved in responses to stress.

The autonomic nervous system (ANS)

The **autonomic nervous system (ANS)** plays a central role in states of bodily arousal associated with stress. ANS centres are located in the **brainstem** (Figure 5). From here ANS pathways run down through the spinal cord and are distributed throughout the body by the spinal nerves; in this way the ANS is classified as a component of the peripheral nervous system. It is concerned with the regulation of our internal environment, controlling such vital functions as body temperature, heart rate and blood pressure. The ANS is central to **homeostasis**. An example of this is the way mammals such as humans keep a constant body temperature. This means that we can be active when it is either very hot or very cold outside. Without homeostasis snakes and other reptiles, for instance, become inactive in the cold; therefore they spend as much time as possible basking in the sunshine to increase their body temperature.

The ANS has two separate divisions, the **sympathetic branch** and the **parasympathetic branch**. Nerve fibres from both branches connect with internal structures such as various glands (e.g. the adrenal medulla, pancreas and salivary glands), the heart and circulatory system, and the digestive system. Usually the two branches are in balance, but under certain circumstances the balance shifts and one branch becomes dominant.

- Sympathetic arousal or dominance leads to a pattern of bodily arousal, with increases in heart rate and blood pressure.
- Parasympathetic dominance leads to the opposite pattern, one of physiological calm.

These shifts are determined by the body's physiological requirements. Physical exercise needs energy, and this is provided by sympathetic arousal. Similarly, if a dangerous or threatening situation is perceived, higher brain centres signal the **hypothalamus** to activate the sympathetic branch of the ANS. So, as we see later, sympathetic arousal is an important part of the body's response to stress.

The brain

The billions of neurons in the brain can be divided into hundreds of separate structures. However an outline of its major components brings this number down to a more manageable level.

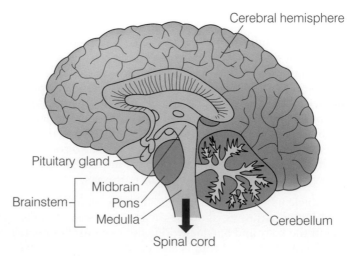

Fig. 5 *Cross-section through the brain*

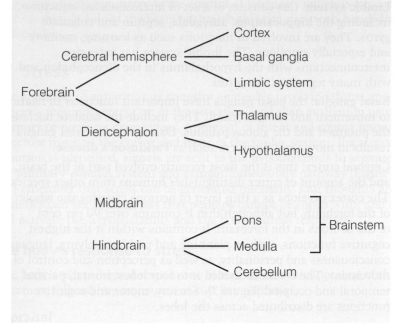

Fig. 6 *Major divisions of the brain*

The brain is initially divided into **hindbrain**, midbrain and **forebrain.** The hindbrain is made up of the medulla, pons and **cerebellum**. The medulla, pons and midbrain (see Figure 6) together are classified as the brainstem. The brainstem is essentially a continuation of the spinal cord within the brain, with sensory and motor pathways carrying information to and from higher brain centres. Also buried within the brainstem is the ascending reticular formation, a network of neurons vital to sleep and arousal functions of the brain. The brainstem also contains the major autonomic centres; autonomic pathways travel down from these centres through the spinal cord and are distributed throughout the body by the spinal nerves. The forebrain is the largest division of the brain, and is subdivided into major components (Figure 6).

The **diencephalon** contains two main structures, the **thalamus** and the hypothalamus. The thalamus is an important sensory structure, relaying sensory information from pathways ascending up through the spinal cord and the brainstem on to the cortex. The hypothalamus lies at the base of the brain (Figure 6). Through its control over the pituitary gland, which lies just below it (Figure 5) and the autonomic centres in the brainstem, the hypothalamus is involved in many of the body's physiological functions. These include stress-related arousal, hunger, thirst, and sexual and reproductive behaviours. The hypothalamus regulates many of these functions automatically. However, when appraisal processes in the cortex and limbic system identify stressful situations of threat and danger, the hypothalamus is stimulated to activate **pituitary-adrenal system** and **sympathomedullary pathway**. It has extensive connections with limbic system structures.

Cerebral hemispheres

The cerebral hemispheres contain the systems and structures of most interest to psychologists. High level cognitive and emotional processes are controlled from these areas, although it must be remembered that all parts of the brain are heavily interconnected, especially the subsystems of the hemispheres. Three major systems make up the cerebral hemispheres:

Key terms

Hindbrain: division of the brain, containing the medulla, pons and cerebellum.

Forebrain: largest division of the brain, containing the systems controlling higher cognitive and emotional functions. Key components are the diencephalon, limbic system, basal ganglia and cortex.

Cerebellum: large structure in the hindbrain, involved in coordination of movement. Damage results in a loss of motor coordination.

Diencephalon: component of the forebrain, containing the thalamus and the hypothalamus.

Thalamus: large structure in the diencephalon of the forebrain. Relays sensory input from sensory pathways on to the cortex.

Pituitary-adrenal system: one of the two key pathways involved in the body's response to stress. The hypothalamus stimulates release of adrenocorticotrophic hormone (ACTH) from the pituitary gland into the bloodstream. ACTH travels to the cortex of the adrenal gland and triggers release of cortisol and other corticosteroids into the bloodstream.

Sympathomedullary pathway: one of the two key components of the body's response to stress. Activated by the hypothalamus, nerve pathways of the sympathetic branch of the ANS stimulate the adrenal medulla to release adrenaline and noradrenaline into the bloodstream.

Biological psychology

143

■ Key terms

Pituitary gland: master gland of the body. Located just below the brain in the cranial cavity, it is controlled by the hypothalamus. The pituitary releases many hormones and controls the activity of many other glands in the body.

Adrenocorticotrophic hormone (ACTH): hormone released from the pituitary gland. ACTH stimulates the adrenal cortex to release corticosteroids as part of the body's response to stress.

Adrenal cortex: part of the adrenal gland, releases corticosteroids into the bloodstream as part of the body's response to stress.

Adrenal gland: the two adrenal glands are located just by the kidneys. The adrenal gland is made up of the cortex and the medulla. The cortex releases corticosteroids and the adrenal medulla releases adrenaline and noradrenaline. These hormones have important roles in the body's response to stress.

Corticosteroids: hormones released from the adrenal cortex as part of the stress response. They include cortisol and corticosterone.

Adrenal medulla: part of the adrenal gland. Under control of the sympathetic nervous system, it releases noradrenaline and adrenaline into the bloodstream as part of the stress response.

Adrenaline: hormone released from the adrenal medulla, acts on heart and circulatory system to increase heart rate and blood pressure.

The pituitary-adrenal system

The **pituitary gland** sits just beneath the brain, connected to the hypothalamus by a short stalk (the infundibulum). The pituitary is the master gland of the body, releasing a number of hormones into the bloodstream. A major function of these hormones is to control other glands spread around the body involved in vital functions such as reproduction and growth. Although released from the pituitary gland, ultimate control of these hormones is located in the hypothalamus and their release depends upon hypothalamic activity.

The key pituitary stress hormone is **adrenocorticotrophic hormone (ACTH)**. The hypothalamus stimulates the release of ACTH from the pituitary into the bloodstream. The hormone travels to the **adrenal cortex**, part of the **adrenal gland**; we have two adrenal glands, located close to the kidney on each side of the body. When ACTH reaches the adrenal cortex it stimulates the release of **corticosteroids** such as cortisol and corticosterone into the bloodstream. These hormones in turn have major effects on the body that we review shortly.

The sympathomedullary pathway

The sympathetic nervous system (SNS) is one part of the autonomic nervous system described above that controls our internal organs, such as various glands, the heart and the circulatory system, and the digestive system. Nerve pathways of the SNS originate in the brainstem (part of the brain just above the spinal cord; Figure 5) and travel via the spinal cord and spinal nerves to the various body organs. One of these pathways runs to the **adrenal medulla**, which along with the adrenal cortex (see above) makes up the adrenal gland. When activated, the SNS stimulates the adrenal medulla to release the hormones **adrenaline** and noradrenaline into the bloodstream.

The ANS functions to control our internal organs automatically without our conscious control, and plays a vital role in stress responses. When appraisal processes in higher brain centres detect a stressful situation (see above), the hypothalamus is instructed to stimulate ACTH release from the pituitary. In addition the hypothalamus also commands the ANS centres in the brainstem to activate the SNS pathways running to the adrenal medulla (sympathomedullary pathway). This results in the increased release of adrenaline and noradrenaline into the bloodstream.

The perception of a stressful situation therefore produces activation of the pituitary-adrenal system and the sympathomedullary pathway, and a number of hormones flood into the bloodstream. These hormones have a number of effects on the body, mainly designed to provide for energy expenditure used in responses to stress, for instance escape or confrontation.

■ The SNS itself has direct connections to the heart and activation speeds up heart rate and raises blood pressure. These effects are increased and sustained by the release of adrenaline and noradrenaline from the adrenal medulla via the sympathomedullary pathway; these act on heart muscle to increase heart rate, and also on blood vessels to constrict them and so raise blood pressure. The end result is that oxygen is rapidly pumped to the muscles of the skeleton allowing for increased physical activity.

■ The body's energy reserves are largely in the form of glycogen stored in the liver and fat reserves in fatty tissue. A major effect of the corticosteroids released in response to pituitary-adrenal system activation is the increased release or mobilisation of these energy reserves; this is in the form of raised blood levels of glucose and fatty acids.

■ Raised levels of corticosteroids, if sustained over a long period, also have the interesting effect of suppressing the body's immune system. This system is the body's defence against infection, and consists of a variety of complex subsystems vital in keeping the person healthy.

■ The body's response to stress involves activation of the pituitary-adrenal system and the sympathomedullary pathway. These systems are extremely old in evolutionary terms, and as you can see their main effects are to allow for energy expenditure in times of stress-related emergencies. This makes sense when stressors, such as predators, required a physical response and a zebra needed to run fast to escape the lion. However the life of modern humans is very different, as fast running isn't usually an effective coping response for the stress of exams or difficult relationships. In these cases it is thought that the body's response to stress can become pathological, i.e. may lead to illness. One of the earliest and most influential models of the body's response to stressors was introduced by Selye, and this remains a useful way of picturing the process.

💡 Selye's general adaptation syndrome

Selye's long career in stress research began in the 1930s, when he noticed that rats given repeated daily injections developed similar stress-related symptoms, such as gastric (stomach) ulcers. On the basis of many studies he developed a three-stage model of how the body responds to stressors:

Stage 1: Alarm

A stressor is perceived and the pituitary-adrenal system and the sympathomedullary pathway are activated. Levels of stress-related hormones surge, heart rate and blood pressure increase, and energy reserves are mobilised.

Stage 2: Resistance

If the stressor persists the body's response systems maintain their activation, with levels of stress-related hormones and bodily arousal remaining high.

Stage 3: Exhaustion

Long periods of stress ('**chronic**' stress) eventually exhaust the body's defence systems and its ability to maintain high levels of circulating stress hormones. This is the stage when stress-related illnesses may develop.

Evaluation

■ Selye's work has been extremely influential in developing the whole area of research into stress. He emphasised the central roles of the pituitary-adrenal system and the sympathomedullary pathway, and the links between chronic stress and illness.

■ Selye emphasised that the **GAS (general adaptation syndrome)** was a common response to all stressors, i.e. he took a response-based approach to stress, which as we have seen ignores individual differences and the cognitive elements of perception and appraisal. Remember that much of Selye's early work was based on rats and a narrow range of physical stressors.

■ It is now thought that stress-related illnesses are not caused by exhaustion of the body's physiological stress responses. Rather, it is the effect of chronic or long-lasting raised levels of stress hormones that can eventually lead to illness.

> ### Key terms
>
> **Chronic:** long lasting.
>
> **General adaptation syndrome (GAS):** Selye's model of the body's response to stress. Consists of three stages: alarm, resistance and exhaustion.

Biological psychology

Key points:

■ The transactional model of stress sees stress as depending on primary and secondary appraisal processes. We identify sources of stress in the environment, and then assess our available coping resources. Stress exists when there is a discrepancy or imbalance between the two.

■ The body's response to stress involves appraisal processes located in higher brain centres and the limbic system, and activation of the pituitary-adrenal system and the sympathomedullary pathway.

■ Pituitary-adrenal system activation involves release of the hormone ACTH from the pituitary gland; this then travels to the cortex of the adrenal gland and stimulates the release of corticosteroids into the bloodstream.

■ Sympathomedullary pathway activation involves nerve impulses travelling along pathways of the sympathetic nervous system from the brainstem out to the medulla of the adrenal gland. This stimulates the release of adrenaline and noradrenaline into the bloodstream.

■ Arousal of the pituitary-adrenal system and sympathomedullary pathway in stressful situations provides the resources for energy expenditure, i.e. muscle activity. Modern stressors do not usually lead to 'fight or flight', and as we do not burn up the energy resources they may contribute to stress-related illness.

■ Selye's general adaptation syndrome was an early and influential attempt to provide a model of the body's responses to stress. It consists of three stages: alarm, resistance, exhaustion.

✓ Summary questions

1 Outline the key elements in activation of the HPA and SAM pathways.

2 Explain the main consequences of HPA and SAM activation.

3 Explain ways in which the body's response to stress might lead to stress-related illness.

Stress-related illness and the immune system

Biological psychology

Learning objectives:

- Understand the major components of the body's immune system.

- Outline and evaluate research findings into the effects of stress on the immune system.

- Show understanding of some of the problems involved in studying the effects of stress on the immune system.

Key terms

Immune system: a complex network of interacting components that provides the body's defences against infection by pathogens such as viruses and bacteria. It is divided into natural and specific immunity.

Acute time-limited stressors: usually studied under laboratory conditions and include experiences such as public speaking or doing mental arithmetic. They usually last for between 5 and 100 minutes.

Brief naturalistic stressors: everyday stressors of limited duration. The situation most often studied is that of students taking examinations.

Chronic stressors: long-lasting stressors. They include caring for dementia patients, coping with long-term illness or disability, or long-term unemployment.

Atherosclerosis: the furring up and narrowing of blood vessels through deposits of fatty material. Can lead to strokes and heart disease.

It is a common view that stress causes a variety of illnesses, and in fact it has become a truism that if you develop a cold, for instance, it must be stress related. Taking effects of stress on the **immune system** as an example we will look at the evidence behind these claims. First, however, some points need to be made:

- Stress is a normal and expected part of life. We are constantly facing challenges and demands, some of which we can cope with easily and others that are more stressful.

- Stress is an essential motivating and arousing factor, energising behaviour and driving us to achieve our goals.

- The hormones released during the bodily arousal associated with stress have a variety of effects on the body. These effects are adaptive in the short term, but long-term or chronic arousal leaves open the possibility that the effects of stress hormones may become pathological and lead to illness.

Types of stress

The following chapter reviews various sources of stress in everyday life, while this chapter on stress and the immune system introduces some of the different types of stressors investigated by psychologists. To understand the findings of some of these studies, however, we need at this stage to review one important way in which stressors can differ. In general stressors can vary substantially in duration, i.e. how long they last, and this can be a critical variable influencing the effects of stress on the individual. Examples identified by Segerstrom and Miller (2004) include **acute time-limited stressors**, **brief naturalistic stressors** and **chronic stressors**.

An alternative approach to studying links between stress and illness is to focus on the individual rather than specific types of stressor. This usually involves participants completing questionnaires on the range of stressful events encountered in the previous months, and correlating this with stress-related illnesses such as heart disease. We review some of this work in the next chapter.

Stress and the immune system

There are many possible pathways linking stress to physical illness. For instance, the increased heart rate and blood pressure can lead to physical damage to the lining of blood vessels or to the muscles of the heart. In cases of prolonged or chronic stress blood levels of glucose and free fatty acids can remain high, and contribute to the 'furring up' of arteries – called **atherosclerosis** – and this can result in heart disease and strokes. However, another major research area has studied the effects of stress on the body's immune system, on the assumption that a weakened immune system leaves the body vulnerable to infection and illness.

The immune system is an immensely complex set of interacting processes that provides the body's defences against infection and illness. It is made up of various cells and circulating proteins and is designed to cope with a variety of hostile viruses, bacteria and infectious

■ Key terms

Immunodeficiency diseases:
illnesses caused by long-term
problems with the body's immune
system. Examples include acquired
immunodeficiency syndrome
(AIDS).

Autoimmune disease: illnesses
caused by the immune system's
failure to recognise host tissues,
and attacking them. Examples
include some forms of cancer,
diabetes and rheumatoid arthritis.

Natural immunity: one component
of the body's immune system.
Natural immunity is a rapid
response in which cells such as
macrophages and phagocytes
absorb invading pathogens.

Pathogens: invading organisms such
as viruses, bacteria and parasites.

Natural killer (NK) cells: part of
the body's natural immunity
system, NK cells destroy invading
pathogens. They are also a popular
dependent variable in studies of
stress and the immune system.

Specific immunity: division of the
body's immune system. Specific
immunity is based on various
types of lymphocyte that learn to
recognise pathogens and destroy
them.

Lymphocytes: cells that are the basis
of specific immunity. Lymphocytes
develop in lymph system
structures such as the spleen and
the thymus gland.

Antibodies: chemicals released from
lymphocytes that recognise and
destroy pathogens such as viruses
and bacteria. A key component of
humoral immunity.

Cellular immunity: division of the
body's immune system. Cellular
immunity involves a variety
of lymphocytes that destroy
intracellular pathogens such as
viruses and bacteria.

processes. In fact we have learnt a great deal about the immune system
from disorders of immune function. **Immunodeficiency diseases** such
as AIDS (acquired immune deficiency syndrome) involve widespread
destruction of the immune system and leave people vulnerable to a
wide range of illnesses and infections. In other conditions the immune
system fails to recognise host body tissues and attacks them. Some
forms of diabetes, cancer and rheumatoid arthritis are **autoimmune
diseases.**

The first and most important subdivision of the immune system is into
natural and specific immunity:

■ **Natural immunity** is a more primitive system and is made up of
cells in the bloodstream (white blood cells or leukocytes). These
non-specifically attack and ingest (absorb) invading **pathogens**
such as viruses and bacteria. These natural immunity cells include
macrophages, phagocytes and **natural killer cells.**

■ **Specific immunity** is based on cells known as **lymphocytes**.
Specific immunity is a more sophisticated system than non-specific
natural immunity, as the cells that make it up have the ability
to recognise invading pathogens and produce specific **antibodies**
to destroy them. Specific immunity is divided into cellular and
humoral immunity.

■ **Cellular immunity** involves a number of different types of cell called
T lymphocytes, as they grow in the **thymus gland**; these include
killer T cells, memory T cells, and helper T cells. In combination
these T cells attack intracellular (within cells) pathogens such as
viruses.

■ **Humoral immunity** is coordinated by another subset of lymphocytes
called B cells, as they grow and mature in the bone marrow. The
end-product of humoral immunity is the secretion of antibodies from
these B lymphocytes that attack and destroy extracellular (outside
cells) pathogens such as bacteria and parasites.

■ Finally, the components of the immune system do not function
independently of each other. Lymphocytes release a variety of
chemicals that can act as signals activating other parts of the immune
system as part of a coordinated response to pathogens.

Although even this basic subdivision can look forbidding, it does lead
to some important general points about research into stress and the
immune system, and it is these you should focus on:

■ Compared to specific immunity, natural immunity processes act
quickly in response to any challenge (within minutes or hours) and
are our first line of immune defence.

■ Specific immunity develops over days as the components recognise
the invading pathogens and mobilise cellular and humoral immune
systems.

■ Stress may have general effects on the immune system, i.e. leading
to overall suppression of immune function. Alternatively it may affect
natural immunity more than specific, or may even alter the balance
between cellular and humoral immunity.

■ We will not be looking in detail at all of these possibilities, but
after outlining some representative studies we will try to draw
out some general conclusions on relationships between stress
and the immune system. But it is important to bear in mind
that interpreting findings is often complicated by these various
possibilities.

Research study: Cohen *et al.* (1993)

Cohen *et al.* investigated the role of general life stress on vulnerability to the common cold virus. Three hundred and ninety-four participants completed questionnaires on the number of stressful life events they had experienced in the previous year. They also rated their degree of stress and their level of negative emotions such as depression. The three scores were combined into what Cohen *et al.* called a stress index.

The participants were then exposed to the common cold virus, leading to 82 per cent becoming infected with the virus. After seven days the number whose infection developed into clinical colds was recorded. The findings were that the chance of developing a cold, i.e. failing to fight off the viral infection, was significantly correlated with stress index scores.

Cohen *et al.* concluded that life stress and negative emotions reduce the effectiveness of our immune system, leaving participants less able to resist viral infections.

Methodological issues

■ This was an indirect study in that there were no direct measures of immune function. However it is supported by Evans and Edgerton (1991) who found that the probability of developing a cold was significantly correlated with negative events in the preceding days.

■ It did measure health outcomes (development of clinical colds), showing a relationship between life stress and illness. This can be compared with studies that use measures of immune function rather than illness outcomes (see below).

■ There was no direct manipulation of the independent variable (the stress index), and so a cause and effect relationship cannot be confirmed.

■ This study does not tell us which element of the stress index is most important.

Ethical issues

■ Clinical studies in psychology and medicine are always covered by rigorous ethical considerations. All applications are reviewed by professional committees, who consider a variety of issues.

■ Participants should be in good health with no illnesses or infections prior to the study.

■ Participants should be able to give fully informed consent, with debriefing afterwards.

■ During the study participants should be constantly monitored to check for any reactions to the viral challenge.

■ The scientific value of the study should be balanced against any psychological or physical distress to participants.

Key terms

Thymus gland: key structure of the immune system. T lymphocytes, the basis of specific immunity, develop in the thymus gland. The thymus gland can also be damaged by chronic high levels of circulating corticosteroids.

Humoral immunity: division of the body's immune system. Humoral immunity involves secretion of antibodies from B lymphocytes that recognise and destroy invading pathogens.

Link

For more information about correlation, see p116. This study uses questionnaires. See p118 for a review of the advantages and disadvantages of using questionnaires.

Hint

The most important division in the immune system is between natural and specific immunity. Make sure you understand this division before moving on to the different types of specific immunity.

Biological psychology

■ **Research study: Kiecolt-Glaser *et al.* (1984)**

Kiecolt-Glaser has been particularly interested in naturalistic life stressors and their impact on measures of immune function. In this study her group used 75 medical students preparing for final examinations. As an index of immune function they used natural killer (NK) cell activity, part of our natural immunity system.

Measures of NK cell activity were recorded from blood samples taken one month before exams (low stress) and during the exam period (high stress). Participants also completed questionnaires on experience of negative life events and social isolation. Findings were that NK cell activity was significantly reduced in the high stress samples, compared to the low stress samples. In addition, the greatest reductions were in students reporting higher levels of social isolation.

Kiecolt-Glaser *et al.* concluded that examination stress (a brief naturalistic stressor in Segerstrom and Miller's approach) reduces immune function, making people potentially more vulnerable to illness and infections. The effects are more noticeable in students experiencing higher levels of isolation.

Methodological issues

■ In contrast with Cohen *et al.*, this study did not assess actual illness outcomes although it did have a direct measure of immune function. Although reductions in immune function should make people more vulnerable to illness, it might be that the significant reductions seen in this study are still too small to increase the chances of stress-related illness.

■ However Kiecolt-Glaser's group (Kiecolt-Glaser *et al.*, 1995) have shown that small wounds take longer to heal in highly stressed groups such as carers for **Alzheimer** patients. As they have also shown that this group have reduced immune function (Kiecolt-Glaser *et al.*, 1991), the link between stress and health outcomes is supported.

■ Although this study used medical students, and you could argue that results should not be generalised, Kiecolt-Glaser and her group have done similar studies on other groups. They have shown that immune function is reduced in long-term carers for Alzheimer patients and women going through divorce proceedings (Kiecolt-Glaser *et al.*, 1987, 1991). Besides these chronic and long-term stressors they have also shown that short-term marital conflict also reduces immune function, with this effect being more noticeable in women than men (Malarkey *et al.*, 1994).

■ Kiecolt-Glaser and her group usually measure natural killer cell activity as the index of immune function. This is only one component of a highly complex and sophisticated system. It was pointed out earlier that stress may alter the pattern of immune responses, such as reducing natural immunity but leaving specific immunity unchanged or increased, or shifting the balance from cellular to humoral immunity. We look at ways of gaining an overall picture of stress and the immune system next.

■ **Key term**

Alzheimer's disease: progressive degeneration of brain tissue leading to memory loss and dementia (confusion, loss of contact with reality). Associated with age, the full name is senile dementia, Alzheimer type (SDAT).

■ **Link**

A study based on a narrow range of participants such as students is said to lack ecological validity. See p92 for a discussion of reliability and validity in psychological research.

■ In this study there was no manipulation of the independent variable (examinations stress) and so a cause and effect relationship cannot be confirmed. However the range of findings from a number of different studies is highly suggestive of a relationship between life stress and reduced immune function.

Ethical issues

■ Kiecolt-Glaser's studies are usually measures of immune function in people experiencing natural life stressors, such as examinations or long-term caring. They are not exposed to any further stressful procedures or conditions apart from giving a blood sample for immune measurement. Participants would need to give fully informed consent, be debriefed and be aware of the mild stress of having their immune function measured.

■ Studies where small wounds are inflicted and healing rates measured have more serious issues. A degree of pain and distress is involved. Full approval by an ethics committee is required, plus full informed consent from participants. Medical supervision would also be essential.

The overall conclusion to these studies, using a variety of methods and participants, is that life stressors such as examinations, negative life events, divorce and social isolation can all reduce immune function and make people more vulnerable to illness and infection. However they do not address some of the issues raised in the outline of the immune system above, e.g. are there different effects of different stressors on different components of immune function? A single study, or even a few, cannot of course address all of these issues.

■ Meta-review of stress research

The effects of stress are influenced by many factors, such as the type of stress, how long it lasts and the individual's personality characteristics such as age, lifestyle and coping style. Any one research study can only look at some of these factors; therefore each study is, unfortunately, different in some way from all the others. However a number of studies may be in the same general area of, for example, effects of stress on immune function. We have looked at some studies on stress and the immune system and results look quite consistent. To confirm this we can use a technique known as a **meta-review**.

Putting all the data together provides a more reliable overall result than any single study, meaning we rely less on a single study, which may have methodological limitations, such as a small sample, but can look for consistent results across many studies.

Segerstrom and Miller (2004) have performed such a meta-review on 293 studies that have looked at the effects of different stressors on measures on immune system functioning. Using their categorisation of stressors outlined on p149, their conclusions are summarised below. It would help if you remind yourself of the subdivisions of the immune system described on p150:

■ Acute time-limited stressors: overall these lead to an **upregulation** of natural immunity, measured for instance as an increase in the numbers of natural killer cells. This is logical as natural immunity is a fast response system that would be activated by the immediate onset of stressors.

Link

In psychological research we can usually only study cause and effect relationships when the independent variable is systematically manipulated.

See p95 for a discussion of this issue.

Biological psychology

Key terms

Meta-review: research technique in which results from all papers studying a similar problem are statistically analysed together to provide a more reliable overview of findings. A meta-review uses both quantitative and qualitative data.

Upregulation: refers to an improvement or increase in immune functioning.

Key terms

Downregulation: refers to an impairment or reduction in immune function.

Global immunosuppression: downregulation (inhibition) of all components of the immune system. Global immunosuppression can be caused by long-term (chronic) stress.

■ Brief naturalistic stressors: the meta-analysis showed no overall effects on immune function, despite some significant findings such as Kiecolt-Glaser *et al.* (1984). However there was evidence for a shift from cellular immunity towards humoral immunity.

■ Chronic stressors: chronic or long-lasting stressors have the most consistent effects on immune function. Virtually all measures of natural and specific immunity showed a significant **downregulation**. These suppressive effects of chronic stress were consistent across gender and age groups.

■ Non-specific life events: in their meta-review, Segerstrom and Miller also analysed studies using a life event questionnaire (see p158). These assess the frequency and intensity of a range of life events over, for instance, the previous year. Overall there were no significant changes in immune function. However, when studies using participants aged over 55 were looked at, there was a significant relationship between life event stress and reductions in natural killer cell activity, i.e. life events produced a reduction in immune function in older participants.

General conclusions from this meta-review would be:

■ The clearest outcomes are that acute time-limited (short-lasting) stressors produce an increase (upregulation) in natural immunity, and that chronic (long-lasting) stressors produce a general reduction (downregulation) in immune function. This is sometimes referred to as **global immunosuppression.**

■ As Segerstrom and Miller point out, acute time-limited stressors are exactly the type to stimulate the fight or flight stress response and Selye's GAS. Rapidly occurring natural immunity responses can be seen as part of our adaptive response to these situations, preparing the body to fight off infection and deal with pathogens. Specific immunity involves processes that take longer to organise and are energy-intensive.

■ Chronic or long-lasting stressors mean that our immune system is activated beyond the 'adaptive' time frame. Changes become less adaptive, and eventually global immunosuppression occurs, leaving the person vulnerable to stress-related illnesses and infections.

■ Immune changes in response to stress are rarely simple. They may involve shifts from natural towards specific immunity, and within specific immunity perhaps a shift in the balance between cellular and humoral immunity.

■ There was no general evidence across all the studies for gender differences in immune reactivity to stress. However Kiecolt-Glaser *et al.* (1998) did show that women showed greater reductions in immune function than men in response to marital conflict.

To further refine the conclusions from work on stress and the immune system, we can also list factors that should be taken into account when evaluating any particular study:

■ What stressor was investigated and how was it measured? Was it acute (short-lasting) or chronic (long-lasting)?

■ What indicator of immune function was measured?

■ Were individual differences such as gender and age taken into account? In the next chapter we look at some other individual differences, such as personality characteristics, that may also influence reactions to stress.

Finally we can briefly consider how chronic stress might lead to global immunosuppression. The simplest explanation is that hormones released

AQA Examiner's tip

Research findings are the lifeblood of any science. Answering questions on stress and the immune system is no different – the key issue is what the findings and conclusions tell us about stress, immunity and illness. Make sure you can quote the findings of at least two studies, and show that you understand the conclusions and implications.

as part of HPA activation directly affect the immune system. There is clear evidence that high levels of corticosteroids in the bloodstream reduce production of T lymphocytes and lead to shrinkage of the thymus gland. This gland is a key component of the immune system. The effect of corticosteroids in suppressing immune function has in fact led to them being used therapeutically. Autoimmune diseases such as some cancers and rheumatoid arthritis occur when specific immunity systems fail to recognise host tissues and attack them. Steroid treatment suppresses immune function and can relieve the condition. A side effect, of course, is that it can leave the patient vulnerable to outside infections.

Key points:

■ An important feature of stressors is how long they last; for instance they may be acute time-limited, brief naturalistic or chronic stressors. Links to illness may depend on how long stressors last.

■ There are many possible pathways linking stress to illness. Two major areas are effects of stress on the cardiovascular (heart and circulatory system), and effects of stress on the immune system.

■ The immune system is extremely complicated, but a basic division is into natural and specific immunity.

■ Specific immunity is further divided into cellular and humoral immunity.

■ Natural immunity acts faster in response to any challenge, while specific immunity is energy-intensive and may take days to develop.

■ Potentially, different types and durations of stressor may affect different parts of the immune system.

■ The studies of Cohen *et al.* (1993) and Kiecolt-Glaser *et al.* (1984), using different methods, both demonstrated that life stress could reduce or impair immune function.

■ In a major meta-review, Segerstrom and Miller (2004) concluded that acute short-lasting stressors lead to an upregulation (activation) of natural immunity, while chronic (long-lasting) stressors lead to general suppression or downregulation of most measures of immune function.

■ One important mechanism linking stress to downregulation of the immune system is the action of corticosteroids in reducing lymphocyte production and shrinking the thymus gland.

■ **Biological psychology**

✓ Summary questions

4 Outline the main components of the immune system.

5 Summarise the findings from the studies of Cohen *et al.* (1993) and Kiecolt-Glaser *et al.* (1984) and explain one conclusion from each study.

6 In their meta-review, what conclusions did Segerstrom and Miller draw concerning the different effects of acute time-limited stressors and chronic stressors on the immune system? What are the implications of these conclusions?

Chapter summary

🎧

Further reading and weblinks

www.psyonline.org.uk

Essential site dedicated to broad coverage of A Level Psychology.

www.bbc.co.uk

The BBC Science and Nature: Human Body and Mind covers many aspects of physiological psychology and psychology in general. Good sections on brain structure and function.

R.M. Sapolsky, *Why Zebras don't get Ulcers*, Freeman (1994)

Excellent and readable review of stress mechanisms and links with illness. Particularly good on the immune system.

F. Jones and J. Bright, *Stress: Myth, Theory and Research*, Prentice Hall (2001)

Comprehensive coverage of all aspects of stress, including stress management and coping.

- The transactional model defines a state of stress as occurring when there is an imbalance between perceived demands on an individual and their perceived coping resources.
- In the body's response to stress, appraisal processes identify an imbalance between demands and coping resources. This leads to activation of HPA and SAM pathways.
- HPA and SAM activation lead to the release of corticosteroids, adrenaline and noradrenaline from the adrenal gland. The body's response to stress is designed to provide for energy expenditure and behavioural responses to situations of threat and danger.
- Modern stressors activate HPA and SAM pathways, but coping responses may not require muscle activity. Raised blood levels of glucose and fatty acids contribute to atherosclerosis and heart disease. In addition, corticosteroids released as part of the body's stress response can suppress the immune system.
- The body's immune system can be divided into fast-reacting natural immunity and slower-reacting specific immunity. Specific immunity is further divided into cellular and humoral immunity. Both types are based on cells called lymphocytes.
- Studies using direct and indirect measures of immune function have shown that life stress can impair the immune system.
- Reviews of the area conclude that acute short-lasting stressors lead to an upregulation of natural immunity; chronic long-lasting stressors can lead to global immunosuppression.

How science works: practical activity

You wish to do a study on the effects of stress on the immune system. Consider carefully how you might identify and measure stress, and what measure of immune system activity you could use. Are there particular ethical issues you should consider?

If you have already completed Unit 1, also consider the following questions:

- What would your hypothesis be?
- How would you select your participants?
- What are the independent and dependent variables?
- Assuming significant findings, what would the implications be and how would they relate to previous research?

Stress in everyday life

Life changes and daily hassles

Learning objectives:

- Understand the strengths and weaknesses of questionnaire measures of life changes.

- Be aware of research findings linking life stress to health and illness, and be able to evaluate studies in terms of methodological and ethical issues.

- Understand the significance of differences between life events and daily hassles as a source of stress.

Key term

Life events: major life events including marriage, death of a partner, redundancy, moving house, etc. According to Holmes and Rahe (1967) events can be rated in terms of life change units and can lead to stress-related illness.

Everyday stress

It is a commonly held view that stress is a major factor in everyday life. Even going to college or work in the morning can involve minor problems – travel hold-ups, boring job or lecture, being with people you don't like. In the medium term there may be issues over relationships, or with imminent exams. There is the future to consider; what career to follow, or if you have started one, is it the right one and is it going well? If you are in work there is a whole range of potential stressors apart from career; the physical environment, getting on with colleagues, balancing work and play or family.

Occasionally what we call major **life events** may happen. Even so-called pleasurable activities such as Christmas and holidays have their stressful side – organisation, being with the same person or people for long periods. Leaving home for the first time, getting married, buying property and having children; all involve major upheaval and are potentially stressful. Bereavement, chronic illness or disability, or having to care in the long term for a partner or family member, can be further sources of stress.

So stress is seen as part of everyday life, and can be either relatively minor or short lasting (acute stress), or more severe and perhaps longer lasting (chronic stress). People often attribute physical illness and psychological problems to the stressful nature of life, but we need to recall some observations from the previous chapter:

- Everyone is under some stress most of the time, but most people do not develop stress-related illness.

- Stress is an unavoidable fact of life; life is always making demands on us that we have to cope with. The stress associated with, for instance, a job or upcoming examinations, is motivating and arousing and not entirely negative.

- Stress exists only when perceived demands outstrip our perceived resources and ability to cope.

Measuring stress

In this section we review some of the work on the relationship between stress and life changes due to major life events, and also between stress and everyday life.

There are many ways of measuring the degree of stress in someone's life. As we noted above, there are a variety of sources of stress in people's lives, which can all, if necessary, be measured. In specialised areas such as the workplace there are carefully designed sets of questionnaires to assess the different sources of stress, and similarly there are questionnaires and other methods for assessing general life stress. These include:

- self-report questionnaires on frequency of life stress, e.g. in relation to major life events, or to minor daily stressors

Biological psychology

■ self-report questionnaires on perceived or subjective stress, i.e. How stressed do you feel?

■ semi-structured interviews, in which the participant talks through their life stressors and the trained interviewer assesses the impact of these stressors. This is a qualitative approach.

💡 Research study: Holmes and Rahe (1967)

From their work in hospitals Holmes and Rahe noticed that many patients, in particular those with heart disease, reported significant life events in the preceding year. They introduced the concept of a life event as a change in life circumstances requiring a degree of adjustment on the part of the individual. To rate the impact of different events they asked 394 people to compare 43 life events with marriage in terms of the degree of adjustment necessary. Marriage was given an arbitrary value of 500 and the other events were scored higher or lower. For the final scale scores were divided by 100 and referred to as **life change units** (LCUs), and the whole scale (see Table 1) called the social readjustment rating scale (SRRS).

Methodological issues

The main issue is that this study was carried out in the US and so the events and how they were rated would have been culturally specific. In addition there was no objective assessment of the degree of adjustment necessary; they relied on participants' opinions.

Ethical issues

As a questionnaire study with no manipulation of variables there are no serious ethical issues with this type of study. Standard procedures such as informed consent and debriefing would need to be followed.

Key term

Life change units: major life events can be rated in terms of life change units (LCU) using Holmes and Rahe's social readjustment rating scale. High LCU scores have been linked to stress-related illness.

Table 1 *Examples of items from the Holmes and Rahe social readjustment rating scale (SRRS)*

Life event	Stress value
Death of a spouse	100
Divorce	73
Jail term	63
Personal injury or illness	53
Marriage	50
Fired at work	47
Retirement	45
Pregnancy	40
Beginning or ending school	26
Vacation	13
Christmas	12

As you can see, death of a spouse (life partner) was rated as the event that requires the most adjustment, and is therefore the most stressful, with divorce and marital separation following but a long way behind. At the bottom we see holidays and Christmas.

The scale is easy to use, as you simply add up the LCUs for life events occurring during the preceding year. A score of over 150 is classified as a life crisis and according to Holmes and Rahe increases the chances of a stress-related illness by 30 per cent. A score over 300 is a major crisis and increases the illness risk by 50 per cent.

Some of the studies of Holmes and Rahe (Holmes and Masuda, 1974; Rahe and Lind, 1971) were **retrospective**. This means that people already undergoing treatment for heart disease and other stress-related illnesses were asked to remember life events from the previous year. These studies found support for a significant relationship between LCU scores and stress-related disease.

A **prospective** study is one in which the participant's LCU units are assessed and then they are followed up to see if illness develops. An example is given below:

Research study: Rahe *et al.* (1970)

Rahe *et al.* (1970) investigated the link between LCUs and illness in a sample of healthy participants. Two thousand five hundred male US navy personnel filled in the SRRS for the previous six months. They were then followed up over the following seven-month tour of duty, and all stress-related illnesses recorded and rated for number and severity, producing an overall illness score.

The findings were that there was a positive correlation of 0.118 between LCU scores and illness scores. Although this is a relatively low correlation (remember that correlation coefficients can vary from +1.0 through 0 to −1.0) it was statistically significant. Rahe *et al.* concluded that there is a relationship between life events and the development of stress-related illness. As the correlation was relatively low, however, other factors must also be involved.

Methodological issues

- The study used male US navy personnel and results are therefore gender and culturally specific and should be generalised to other groups only with caution.
- Below we also review general problems with the use of retrospective questionnaires that would apply to this study.
- All illness outcomes were recorded. There were no specific hypotheses about which illnesses should be related to life event stress.
- This was a correlational study. Correlations do not imply causality, only an association. They are particularly important when for practical or ethical reasons the investigator cannot manipulate the independent variable. It may be that factors other than life events produce the correlation: for example people who experience major life events may also drink and smoke more, and it is this change in lifestyle that leads to illness.

AQA Examiner's tip

Don't spend time memorising all of the events on the SRRS. Know a few examples, but spend more time understanding the purpose of the SRRS and developing your critical thinking.

■ **Key terms**

Retrospective: refers to the past. Participants may be asked to recall events from the previous year in studies of life events and stress.

Prospective: refers to the future. Prospective studies involve following participants over a period of time from the start of the study. An example would be studies of life stress and health.

■ **Link**

For more information about correlation, see p116.

■ **Link**

Hypotheses in psychological research should be carefully operationalised.

See p90 for a review of how hypotheses should be constructed.

Biological psychology

Ethical issues

■ The study would require informed consent and debriefing.

■ There may be some distress in recalling traumatic life events.

Although this study was carried out on American sailors and you might argue that the results are difficult to generalise, it does support other studies using the SRRS that find similar correlations. However some studies find no significant relationship, while even when significant the correlation coefficients are usually low. If there is a strong link between LCUs and illness, why should this be? A key issue that emerged rapidly was the nature of the SRRS scale itself:

■ No account is taken of the emotional impact of the event, i.e. is the impact positive or negative? Taking out a mortgage you can easily afford to move to a more desirable property is very different to overstretching yourself financially simply to get on the property ladder. Holmes and Rahe assumed all events, regardless of their nature, involved readjustment and were therefore stressful.

■ The scale takes no account of individual differences. Each of us could construct a personal life event scale, and each would be different. Divorce, for instance, is often perceived very differently by each of the parties. This relates to the primary and secondary **appraisal** discussed in the previous chapter, processes that are crucial in deciding the severity of stressful conditions.

■ Retrospective self-report of life events over the preceding year can be unreliable. Asking people several times to recall events from the same time period reveals surprising variability in accounts of the same period (Raphael *et al.*, 1991). This can be a particular problem when people are already ill, as they may be looking for explanations for their illness, i.e. they may exaggerate the number of life events.

■ Results are usually in the form of correlations. As you know, correlations do not imply causality, only an association. Divorce may be a factor correlated with depression, but perhaps the depression of one partner led to the marriage break up rather than the other way round.

Subsequently other life event scales have been developed that try to avoid some of these problems. The life events scale (LES; Sarason *et al.*, 1978) allows people to rate 57 life events in terms of severity of impact and whether the impact is positive or negative. This allows for individual differences. In addition specialised sections can be added for particular groups, such as students. The life events scale produces three scores – negative change, positive change and total change (similar to the SRRS). In general negative life change scores correlate more highly with illness outcomes.

For most of us, unless we are very unlucky, major life events are by their very nature rare. The regular sources of stress in people's lives tend to arise from the ongoing problems of day-to-day living. Lazarus, one of the key stress researchers of the last 30 years, felt that these **hassles**, as they became known, were more significant for health than major life events. His research group (Kanner *et al.*, 1981) devised the hassles scale specifically to assess these sources of stress:

■ The original scale had 117 items covering all aspects of daily life. It could be modified for special groups such as students, where items such as study problems and unfriendly tutors were particularly relevant.

■ Key terms

Appraisal: refers to perceiving and evaluating a situation as positive or negative. In models of stress a crucial component involves appraising both the demands of the situation and the person's coping resources.

Hassles: refers to the stresses of everyday life, as opposed to major life events.

■ Lazarus felt that life also contained positive events, known as **uplifts** that could counteract the negative effects of daily hassles. An uplifts scale was created with 135 positive items, such as getting good grades or getting on well with friends.

Scores on the hassles scale correlate with stress-related problems, in particular depression and anxiety (also note the Evans and Edgerton study on p151, which uses a similar approach linking negative daily events to the probability of colds developing). De Longis *et al.* (1982) did a study comparing scores on both the hassles scale and a life event scale and found that correlations with health outcomes were greater for the hassles scores. Uplifts were unrelated to health outcomes. Similarly, Jandorf *et al.* (1986), using a different measure of daily events (the assessment of daily experience scale, ADE; Stone and Neale, 1984), found higher positive correlations between daily events and health outcomes than between major life events and health.

Life changes and daily hassles are important sources of stress in people's lives. Many daily hassles relate to the work that people do, either directly related (e.g. physical environment, relationships with co-workers) or indirectly related (commuting problems, balancing work and home responsibilities). Work has become a subject of major concern in stress research, and it is to this we now turn.

Key points:

■ Holmes and Rahe introduced the social readjustment rating scale (SRRS), the first widely-used questionnaire assessing the impact of life events on the individual. They reported significant correlations between life event scores and subsequent illness.

■ The original SRRS made no allowance for the positive or negative impact of events, and did not take individual differences into account.

■ The hassles scale focuses on everyday stressors rather than life events, and research suggests hassles scores may correlate better with illness outcomes.

✔ Summary questions

1. Explain two advantages and two limitations of the SRRS.

2. The Rahe *et al.* (1970) study on US navy personnel found a correlation of +0.118 between life event scores (LCUs) and illness outcomes. Comment on this correlation value.

Key term

Uplifts: refers to everyday positive events, as opposed to hassles.

Biological psychology

Workplace stress

i

Learning objectives:

- Understand the range of sources of workplace stress.

- Understand the methods, results, and implications of Marmot *et al.*'s (1997) Whitehall II study, including its strengths and weaknesses.

- Understand the principles behind managing stress in the workplace.

Fig. 1 *The workplace is now one of the major sources of stress*

Key terms

Home–work interface: a source of stress in the workplace, in which employees try to balance the competing demands of home and work responsibilities.

Work–life balance: this is the idea that in a civilised society everyone should strive for a healthy balance between work responsibilities and life outside work.

Decision latitude: the sense of control an individual has over their workload and how it is organised. High decision latitude is associated with a lower vulnerability to stress-related illness.

Possible causes of workplace stress

Workplace stress is now considered one of the major sources of stress for many people; every week there are reports of the increasing levels of stress attached to a variety of jobs, such as nursing, police work and teaching. This type of stress is considered even more important because it not only distresses the individual but can lead to poor performance at work, increased absenteeism and stress-related illness. It is therefore important for organisations to identify and minimise sources of stress in the work environment, and to help employees cope with them.

Every workplace is different. However it is possible to identify areas of stress at work that apply to most organisations:

- Environment: heating, lighting and the physical arrangement of the workplace are all potential sources of stress. Many studies have shown that intense noise and increases in temperature can lead to frustration, stress and, in some cases, aggression. The physical layout of the workplace can affect the psychological well-being of the employee in terms of 'personal space' and privacy.

- **Home–work interface:** with many people having to balance the competing demands of home and work, in particular parents with small children, this potentially very stressful area has become the subject of much debate. The concept of **work–life balance** refers to the ideal situation where an individual has time for both work and home responsibilities, leading to less stress and better psychological adjustment.

- Control: this has been a central focus of research into workplace stress (see research study below). The degree of control a person has over their workload (sometimes referred to as **decision latitude**) has been shown to directly affect the level of stress experienced. High levels of control lead to lower levels of stress, while low levels of control, typically experienced by workers lower down the organisation hierarchy, can increase stress levels.

- Workload: this is one of the most obvious factors in workplace stress, but interestingly research shows that it is not just overload that can be stressful (Dewe, 1992), but that having too little to do can have similar effects.

Sometimes these factors do not operate independently. In particular the relationship between workload and control has been extensively studied. Karasek's (1979) model has been a popular way of picturing the relationship between job demand (workload) and levels of control. He suggests that the most stressful jobs involve high demand and low control, and the least stressful involve low demand and high control.

Table 2 *Karasek's model of the relationship between demand (workload), control (decision latitude) and job strain (stress)*

	High demand	Low demand
Low control	High strain job (vulnerable to stress)	Passive job
High control	Active job	Low strain job

Biological psychology

Research supports the idea that a combination of high demand and low control is the most stressful combination, but also shows that these relationships can be modified by other factors, such as social support.

Research study: Marmot et al. (1997)

Since the 1960s a long-term series of studies has been running on the relationships between workplace stress and health. They also include various individual and social risk factors such as smoking, blood pressure and cholesterol levels, obesity and socioeconomic status. Participants are taken from London-based government civil servants, and the studies are therefore referred to as the Whitehall studies. In the first, Whitehall I, clear differences between workers were found with regard to heart problems and mortality rates: workers in lower-paid grades had twice the illness rate of workers in the highest-paid grade. Differences in risk factors (e.g. workers in lower grades tend to smoke more and have higher levels of blood pressure) accounted for about a quarter of this difference.

Marmot et al. (1997) analysed data from over 7,000 participants in the Whitehall II study. Participants were followed up over five years. All were free of heart problems when the study began. The data showed similar differences in heart disease to Whitehall I, with the rate in the lowest grades being 1.5 times the rate in the highest grades. When the researchers analysed the data in detail they found that risk factors such as smoking, obesity and hypertension could account for some of the increase in lower grades. However, the most significant factor was the degree of 'decision latitude' or control that participants felt they had.

Methodological issues

- The study was largely based on self-report questionnaires, which raises issues of biased responding by participants, for instance underestimating risk factors such as smoking.

- Some factors that were not measured may have contributed to the results. For example, workers in lower grades may have in common some characteristic that makes them vulnerable to heart disease but that was not measured in the study.

- The sample was of government civil servants. Although males and females were represented, this is otherwise a biased sample and it would be difficult to automatically generalise the results to other groups of workers. However the findings are supported by many other studies that have demonstrated a clear relationship between stress at work and lack of control. In a very different workplace Johannson et al. (1978) found higher levels of stress hormones and stress-related illness in a group of highly skilled sawmill employees whose work was machine-paced, i.e. giving them little or no control over their work rate.

Ethical issues

There is little risk of psychological harm in this type of questionnaire study of workplace stress, although informed consent and debriefing should be routine. Workers developing illnesses should also be provided with the necessary support.

Link

In psychological research experimenters identify the variables they are interested in, such as workload and illness. However, other variables can influence their results and need to be controlled if possible. See p95 for a discussion on these 'extraneous' variables.

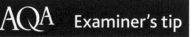

AQA Examiner's tip

The findings from single studies in psychology can be interesting but not very reliable. What is more important is whether a number of studies produce similar results. If possible, you should refer to at least two studies in key areas and be able to assess the consistency of findings.

The findings of Marmot *et al.* (1997) are supported by many other studies. For instance Fox *et al.* (1993) found that a combination of low control and high demands was related to higher blood pressure in nurses. High blood pressure is a major risk factor for heart disease. In a review of this area of research, Van der Doef and Maes (1998) conclude that substantial evidence from a range of studies supports the hypothesis that a combination of high demand and low control increases the risk of heart disease.

Given the consistency of the evidence that workplace stressors can lead to illness, managing workplace stress has become an important issue for society.

Measuring and dealing with workplace stress

In addition to the sources of stress mentioned above there are several others, such as role ambiguity (being unsure of your responsibilities), relationships with other employees and career progression. There are a variety of questionnaire packages available to assess workplace stress and employee characteristics. The occupational stress indicator (Cooper *et al.*, 1998), for instance, uses self-report questionnaires to measure the sources of stress as perceived by the employee. In addition it measures characteristics such as social support, Type A behaviour and coping strategies. The eventual outcome is a profile of the individual and the organisation in terms of sources and degree of stress in its workforce.

These findings are then used to devise strategies to reduce the negative effects of stress on the individual (health problems) and on the organisation (absenteeism, lowered productivity). These can include individually tailored stress management programmes for employees, and changes to the way the organisation is structured and managed. For instance workers at all levels can be given more control over the distribution and organisation of workloads. Psychological methods of stress management (see p172) may also be made available.

So far we have reviewed various sources of stress in people's lives, from major life events through daily hassles to stressors specific to the workplace. One thing that stands out across all these areas is the role of individual differences. People vary in their vulnerability to stress-related problems. This may be because they react to stressors differently, or perhaps they have different methods of coping with stress. In the next chapters we review both of these possibilities.

Key points:

- There are a variety of sources of stress in the workplace, including the environment, home–work interface, workload and control.

- There is substantial evidence that a combination of high demand (workload) and low control (decision latitude) is most stressful and can lead to illnesses including heart disease.

- Workplace stress can be reduced by a combination of individual stress management programmes and changes to the organisation's work practices.

✓ Summary questions

3 Explain Karasek's model of the relationship between job demands and decision latitude (control).

4 Discuss the main findings and conclusions of the Whitehall II study, and whether the findings are supported by other studies.

5 Explain two ways in which organisations could reduce the stress caused by home–work conflict.

6 Explain why daily hassles might be more important than major life events in relation to stress-related illness.

Personality factors

- Describe the Type A behaviour pattern (TAB).

- Understand and evaluate research findings linking TAB to vulnerability to stress-related coronary heart disease (CHD).

- Describe the characteristics of hardiness, and be aware of attempts to describe other personality types that may be vulnerable to stress-related illness.

Key term

Type A behaviour (TAB): a behaviour pattern characterised by time pressure, competitiveness and hostility. It has been suggested that high levels of TAB increase vulnerability to heart disease.

The study of human personality is extremely complicated, with a variety of different approaches leading to a variety of different models. Potentially there are literally hundreds of characteristics that could be studied in relation to stress, but only a few have generated significant amounts of interest and research.

Type A behaviour

Type A behaviour (TAB) refers to a pattern of behaviours and attitudes that has long been linked to a vulnerability to stress-related illness.

The Type A concept evolved from the work of Friedman and Rosenman in the 1950s and 1960s. They studied the characteristics of patients with coronary heart disease (CHD) and decided that a particular pattern of behaviour seemed to be associated with a vulnerability to heart disease. The characteristics are listed in Table 3. They also defined a Type B pattern that was essentially the opposite of Type A, i.e. relaxed, not competitive and not hostile.

Table 3 *Type A behaviour*

Behaviour pattern	Examples
Time pressured	Always working to deadlines Unhappy doing nothing Multi-tasking; doing several jobs at the same time
Competitive	Always oriented towards achievement Plays to win, whether at work or on the sports field
Hostility	Becomes easily irritated and impatient with co-workers Easily angered Anger can be directed inwards

Early studies by their research group suggested that a Type A person was around twice as likely to develop CHD as a Type B. A typical study is described below.

Research study: Rosenman *et al.* (1976)

Rosenman *et al.* (1976) studied 3,154 middle-aged men on the west coast of the US. They were categorised as either Type A or Type B by structured interview. As the participant answers the questions the trained interviewer also notes behavioural signs of the Type A pattern. These could be rapid finger tapping on the table, restlessness and the pace of talking. Answers to the questions and the general behaviour are put together to provide an overall assessment of TAB.

The participants were followed up for 8.5 years. During that time there were 257 heart attacks, 69 per cent of which were in the Type A group. This was a significant effect even when lifestyle risk factors such as obesity and smoking were controlled for. Rosenman *et al.* concluded that the high TAB individual was vulnerable to heart disease.

Biological psychology

Biological psychology

Link

Participants were categorised as Type A or Type B on the basis of a structural interview. On p119 interviews are discussed as a research method.

Methodological issues

■ The study is culturally and gender specific, and findings should be generalised with caution. Note that even the definition of TAB is based on Western cultural concepts.

■ There are many individual and lifestyle variables that can affect vulnerability to heart disease. Although some of these were controlled for, it is possible that some important variable was missed. The study has high ecological validity, but such real-life studies do not have perfect control over all variables.

Ethical issues

The participants were volunteers giving informed consent and were debriefed at the end of the study. They were not manipulated in any way and so there is little chance of psychological harm. Such real-life studies that do not manipulate the independent variable (IV) rarely involve serious ethical issues.

Results like this seem to make intuitive sense, in that the competitive and pressured life makes the Type A person appear highly stressed. However, it soon became apparent that the link between TAB and heart disease was not reliable. For example, Shekelle *et al*. (1985) studied over 12,000 male participants, with TAB assessed by a self-report questionnaire and structured interview. They found over seven years that there was no difference in the incidents of heart disease between the Type A and the Type B groups.

A number of general reviews (e.g. Matthews and Haines, 1986) suggest that only about half of the studies on TAB and CHD find a significant link. The general picture that emerged was that TAB was not a strong predictor of heart disease. TAB is a complex combination of many characteristics and one interesting question is whether particular characteristics are more important than others. Booth-Kewley and Friedman (1987) reviewed a number of studies in this area and concluded that the component of hostility and other negative emotions was a key element in linking TAB and CHD. In fact, Dembroski *et al*. (1989) found that hostility was more strongly linked to CHD than the overall TAB score. This was supported in a meta-review by Miller *et al*. (1996) who identified hostility as a risk factor, independent of TAB.

What can we conclude from research into Type A behaviour?

■ Friedman and Rosenman's introduction of the Type A behaviour pattern has stimulated an enormous amount of interest and research.

■ It focused interest on personality factors and health, and demonstrated that there could be links between personality and heart disease.

■ As early findings failed to be replicated the TAB concept was analysed in more detail, and this led to the identification of the hostility dimension as an important risk factor for heart disease.

■ The fact that high TAB individuals seem in general to cope with stress fairly well may also suggest that some of their characteristics protect them against the negative effects of stress. This brings us to a consideration of **hardiness.**

Key term

Hardiness: a personality type described by Kobasa, consisting of high levels of control, commitment and challenge. Evidence suggests that high levels of hardiness protect against the negative effects of stress.

■ Hardiness

The concept of hardiness was introduced by Kobasa (1979) who was interested in factors that might protect or buffer people against the effects of stress. There are three basic elements to hardiness:

■ control: this is the idea that you can influence events in your life, including stressors

■ commitment: this is the individual's sense of involvement and purpose in life

■ challenge: this refers to the idea that changes in life should be viewed as an opportunity rather than a source of stress.

Kobasa devised questionnaires to assess control, commitment and challenge, and in her early studies found that people with high scores on these dimensions reported fewer stress-related symptoms. This work was mainly on male white-collar workers and you could argue that it lacked ecological validity. However, the findings were supported by later studies (Kobasa *et al.*, 1982) and in particular by Beasley *et al.* (2003) who investigated the effects of life stress in university students. Students who scored more highly on hardiness showed reduced levels of psychological distress.

Although the area of research into personality and stress has a number of controversies and disagreements, there are some obvious connections between the work on TAB and Kobasa's concept of hardiness. According to Kobasa, high levels of control, commitment and challenge protect against the harmful effects of stress. Research into TAB suggests that Type A people are less vulnerable to the effects of stress than was originally thought.

If you look back at the characteristics of people who score highly on TAB you will see that they have high levels of competitiveness and are very achievement oriented. You could argue that people with these characteristics are showing commitment and also see life as a series of challenges to be overcome. Commitment and challenge are key components of hardiness, so a conclusion might be that the Type A behaviour pattern also contains aspects of hardiness. What can we conclude?

■ Some characteristics of TAB such as time pressure and hostility may increase vulnerability to stress.

■ Other characteristics such as commitment and challenge may increase resistance to stress.

■ So, the TAB pattern is made up of factors, some of which increase and some of which decrease resistance to stress.

■ This mixed pattern might explain why the results of studies trying to link Type A behaviour and heart disease are inconsistent.

■ Other personality types

There have been various attempts to identify other personality types vulnerable to illnesses, some of which could be linked to stress. Eysenck (1988) proposed two types of personality; the first was a personality type vulnerable to cancer, and this personality was associated with difficulties in expressing emotions and with social relationships. The second was a personality type vulnerable to CHD. This was similar to the TAB described above. These people were characterised by high levels of anger and hostility.

AQA Examiner's tip

Work on TAB has led to some complicated findings. For the examination, being fully up-to-date with research in this area would not be necessary for high marks. Knowing and, more importantly, understanding the original work of Friedman and assessing the degree of support from other studies would enable you to reach the higher mark bands.

■ Link

See p92 for a discussion of reliability and validity in relation to psychological studies.

Biological psychology

However, as with the work on TAB, there is no consistent evidence linking these personality types to either cancer or coronary heart disease.

More recently, Denollet (2000) has proposed yet another personality type that in his view is vulnerable to heart disease. This is the Type D personality where the D stands for 'distressed'. People with this personality type experience high levels of negative emotions (note that this is similar to the hostility dimension of TAB) and social inhibition, i.e. they tend to avoid social interactions. Denollet and his group have shown in a number of studies (Denollet *et al.*, 1996; Denollet and van Heck, 2001) that high levels of negative emotions combined with social inhibition are associated with increased risk of heart disease.

■ As we can see, there have been numerous attempts to link aspects of personality to stress-related illness. These approaches assume that personality is a factor influencing the relationship between stress and its effects on the individual. However, we have also seen that such relationships are difficult to demonstrate consistently. Looking at the work on TAB, hardiness and other personality types, what we can conclude is that negative emotions such as anger and hostility do seem to increase stress-related vulnerability to heart disease.

■ We should also note at this stage that in any study there are always other factors that could influence the results. For instance high levels of hostility and anger may be associated with smoking and drinking and other dysfunctional lifestyles. They may also lead to social isolation, which Denollet's work suggests is another important factor in the stress/illness relationship. We look at social support in more detail later (see p178).

Key points:

■ Friedman and Rosenman first introduced the concept of Type A behaviour pattern (TAB), a pattern that seemed to be vulnerable to stress-related heart disease. It is characterised by time pressure, competitiveness and hostility.

■ Although early studies suggested a significant relationship between TAB and heart disease, later findings were inconsistent. Hostility alone may be a better predictor than TAB.

■ Kobasa's concept of hardiness, characterised by high scores on challenge, commitment and control, refers to a personality that is resistant to the negative effects of stress.

■ Denollet has described a Type D ('distressed') personality, characterised by high levels of negative emotions and social inhibition, that is also vulnerable to stress-related heart disease.

✔ Summary questions

7 List the key features of the Type A behaviour pattern.

8 Name two key characteristics that TAB might have in common with hardiness, and explain their significance.

9 Outline research findings linking TAB to heart disease, and give reasons for their inconsistency.

Coping with stress

Learning objectives:

- To be aware of the range of coping styles used in stressful situations.

- To understand the differences between emotion-focused and problem-focused coping methods.

- To be able to describe situations where one approach may be more adaptive than the other.

Key terms

COPE scale: questionnaire used to assess an individual's coping strategies. It provides ratings on 15 different strategies.

Approach coping: coping with stress by tackling the situation directly. It is more adaptive with long-term stressors.

Avoidant coping: coping with stress by denying the significance of stressful situations and pretending they don't exist.

Problem-focused coping: a coping style that tries to target the causes of stress in practical ways that directly reduce the impact of the stressor.

Emotion-focused coping: a coping style that targets the emotional impact of stressors. Strategies include denial and seeking support from friends.

Link

P138 describes the transactional model of stress. You should consider how coping styles might relate to this method.

Measuring how we cope with stress

Later in this chapter we review some specific psychological techniques of stress management, often aimed at particular stressors and involving training and practice. Usually, however, we cope with everyday stressors and even major life events on an individual basis using a range of different methods. Some idea of this range is given by the **COPE scale** (Carver *et al.*, 1989), a widely used research questionnaire on coping styles. This has 15 different coping strategies, such as denial, turning to religion, active coping, using emotional support, turning to alcohol, etc. This scale gives a good idea of the range of methods people use, but it is still an unwieldy instrument.

Table 4 *Table of examples from COPE*

Scale	Description
Active coping	Taking direct action to deal with a problem.
Seeking instrumental support	Talking to others about the problem, looking for practical advice and support.
Seeking emotional support	Discussing feelings about a problem with friends and family.
Focus on and venting of emotions	Becoming upset and expressing feelings when distressed.
Denial	Refusing to believe something has happened, or pretending it hasn't.
Humour	Laughing and making fun of the situation.

The distinction between emotion-focused and problem-focused approaches

It has been suggested that people may use a particular style of coping. For instance Roth and Cohen (1986) introduced the idea of **approach** and **avoidant coping**. Avoidant coping might be more adaptive for short-term stressors and approach coping for long-term stressors (Holahan and Moos, 1986), but people tend to adopt one style consistently.

An alternative and more flexible approach is based on the idea that stressful situations can involve practical demands ('what can I do actively to confront this stressor and reduce its impact'), and also an emotional impact ('this situation is alarming and distressing'). The individual may address the practical side of the situation – this is **problem-focused coping** – or they may target the emotional impact – this is **emotion-focused coping**. But a key point is that these are not opposites; the same person may use problem- and emotion-focused coping simultaneously, or switch from one to the other depending on the situation. This would depend upon the person's appraisal of demands and coping resources.

Problem-focused coping can involve:

■ reducing the demands of the stressor by active coping, for instance systematically planning a revision schedule for an important examination

■ improving your coping resources by, for instance, using your social network (see p178) for informational and practical support.

Emotion-focused coping can involve:

■ cognitive emotion-focused coping, such as denial of the severity of an illness (this is a form of avoidant coping), or distraction by thinking about other things

■ behavioural emotion-focused coping, such as becoming angry ('venting emotion'), drinking and smoking more, or seeking emotional support from friends.

■ Which is the more effective strategy?

It might seem obvious that problem-focused coping would always be the more effective strategy, but a moment's thought would show you that this is not always the case. We do not always have control over stressors in our lives. This is particularly the case with diagnoses of life-threatening illnesses such as cancer, where the scope for problem-focused coping is limited. Carver *et al.* (1993) found that the emotion-focused strategy of denial led to better adjustment in women with breast cancer, while emotional social support has also been found to help in coping with cancer (De Boer *et al.*, 1999). Factors that may affect the type of coping response shown therefore include the following:

■ The stressor itself: Vitaliano *et al.* (1990) concluded that problem-focused coping was used more often with work problems. Emotion-focused coping was used when there were problems with personal relationships.

■ A key feature of stressors is whether they are controllable or not: Lazarus and Folkman (1987) suggest that, quite sensibly, people use more problem-focused coping when they see a situation as controllable, and as emotion-focused when they see it as out of their control. Problems at work and examinations could be seen as more controllable than life-threatening illness and relationships.

■ Gender may be a factor, although research is not that consistent: some findings (Stone and Neale, 1984) suggest that women use more emotion-focused strategies and men more problem-focused, but others (Hamilton and Fagot, 1988) found no differences between the genders in coping styles.

An interesting question about coping styles is whether people consistently use the same one. Tennen *et al.* (2000) studied daily coping styles in patients with chronic (long-lasting) pain, in a longitudinal study. Each day, participants completed a coping-style questionnaire and assessed their level of pain. Results were:

■ Individual patients used different strategies simultaneously; emotion-focused strategies were used 4.4 times more on days when problem-focused strategies were also used, than on days when problem-focused strategies were not used. The different styles of coping are not therefore independent, but interact.

■ Success or failure of a given strategy was also important. An increase in pain associated with problem-focused coping would be followed the next day by an increase in emotion-focused coping; i.e. the patient was responsive to the success or failure of a particular strategy on a particular day.

■ **Link**

This is an unusual study, using self-report techniques over many days from the same participants. Different research methods are explained on p106.

This shows that we constantly assess the success of a particular strategy and modify our coping techniques accordingly. This does not mean that we do not have characteristic coping styles; we may tend to try our preferred method at first, whether it is problem-focused ('I can deal with any problem directly') or emotion-focused ('Whatever happens, I would always talk to my friends first'), but we are able to alter our approach on the basis of success or failure.

Key points:

- At least 15 different types of coping strategy can be identified.
- Two major general styles of coping are problem-focused and emotion-focused coping.
- Problem-focused coping uses practical methods to reduce life stress.
- Emotion-focused coping focuses on the emotional impact of stress.
- Style of coping is influenced by type of stressor, controllability and perhaps gender.
- Individuals may have a preferred style, but will use both problem-focused and emotion-focused coping as situations change.

✓ Summary questions

10 Explain the differences between problem-focused and emotion-focused coping.

11 Why should 'controllability' be an important factor in deciding which approach is most appropriate?

12 Explain the conclusions of the Tennen *et al.* (2000) study, and how they relate to everyday life.

Biological psychology

Psychological and physiological methods of stress management

Learning objectives:

- Understand the general principles behind methods of stress management.

- Describe psychological and physiological methods of stress management.

- Explain the strengths and weaknesses of methods of stress management.

Links

The transactional model of stress is discussed on p138.

Stress-induced arousal is described on p146.

Biological psychology

Key terms

Cognitive-behavioural therapy (CBT): a therapeutic approach to stress and psychological disorders that aims to alter irrational thoughts and cognitive biases that are assumed to be the cause of the problem.

Stress inoculation training (SIT): a cognitive-behavioural approach to managing the negative effects of stress.

At the start of the chapter we noted how stress has become something of an epidemic in Western societies. In parallel with the increasing amount of research into the effects of stress, there has been an explosion in the 'coping with stress' industry. Nowadays most newspapers and magazines will have articles on the best ways of coping with or managing the stress of daily life.

However, it was also pointed out earlier in the chapter that stress is an inevitable part of daily life, and for many people is an essential motivating factor. It is unrealistic to expect a stress-free life, or that any methods of stress management will reduce stress to zero. We reviewed in the previous chapter some general approaches to characterising ways in which individuals cope with stress, using problem-focused and emotion-focused strategies. These are not always effective and so in this chapter we look at some specific psychological and physiological methods of stress management that have proved useful in reducing harmful levels of stress.

Psychological methods of stress management

Psychological approaches to managing stress are many and varied. We can only cover a few in these pages, and we will focus on those that can be easily related to the concept of stress. The current concept of stress involves appraisal processes; these are cognitive evaluations of the demands being made on us and our coping resources. High levels of stress may be caused by faulty or mistaken appraisals; for instance, overestimating the difficulty of the examination, combined with underestimating your level of preparation. If high levels of stress are encountered they lead to the bodily arousal described in the previous chapter. Negative effects of stress have been linked to these high levels of physiological arousal.

These broad characteristics of stress can immediately provide ways of tackling harmful levels of stress:

- if stress is caused by faulty appraisal and evaluation, one approach to stress management might be to target those faulty cognitions

- another approach would be to target the symptoms of stress, such as increased levels of physiological arousal.

Approaches that target people's perception and evaluation of stressful situations come from a category of therapies known as **cognitive-behavioural therapy (CBT)**. We cover CBT in detail in chapter 13 on abnormality in relation to treatment of psychological disorders (see p261). However, it is a general approach to understanding and changing behaviour that can be applied in many different areas, including stress management.

Cognitive-behavioural therapy and stress management

Meichenbaum's stress inoculation training (SIT)

One CBT approach to stress management is Meichenbaum's **stress inoculation training (SIT)**. This consists of three stages:

1   Conceptualisation: in this stage the client works with the therapist to identify the sources of stress in their lives. This may involve thinking back to stressful encounters and trying to identify the key

features of these encounters. In addition, they would be encouraged to keep a diary to record stressful experiences during the daytime. The therapist may also challenge some of the client's appraisals of stressful situations if they seem exaggerated.

2 Skills training and rehearsal: for a number of stresses in people's lives it is possible for them to acquire specific skills to address those situations. For instance, a common source of stress is social anxiety, that is, interacting with other people either at work or socially. These types of situation can be addressed by specific training in relevant skills:

■ People with social anxiety often have poor non-verbal communication, for example not making eye contact or appearing unapproachable. They can be shown how to improve their social communication through skills training and practice.

■ A background issue in most stressful situations is physiological arousal. Therefore, regardless of the particular source of stress, training in relaxation is always useful. So whether it is entering a room full of people, or the examination hall, the individual will have a relaxation technique they can use to keep their bodily arousal under control.

3 Application in the real world: after practising specific skills and relaxation techniques in the therapeutic setting the client is then encouraged to apply them in the real world. That is not the end of the story as the client and the therapist continue monitoring the success or failure of the therapy. A key to the approach is that the client should learn from experience, by reflecting on the success or failure of their new skills. If necessary, there would be opportunities for further training and rehearsal.

Evaluation

■ The first stages in managing stress involve identifying the sources of stress in one's life and assessing how well you have dealt with them in the past. SIT is a cognitive-behavioural approach that focuses on exactly these elements.

■ Stress exists where there is a gap between perceived demands and the resources you have to cope with them. The cognitive element of SIT is aimed at producing a realistic appraisal of demands, while the training in relevant skills is aimed at increasing resources to cope with those demands. This training is an example of problem-focused coping.

■ Training in relaxation techniques gives clients some control over any stressful situation. It can be seen as emotion-focused, in that it reduces the emotionally arousing effects of stress.

■ SIT, like most CBT programmes, takes time, commitment and money. It is not, therefore, suitable or available to everyone. However it has been shown to be effective in managing in a variety of situations, including examination stress in students (Berger, 2000) and as a treatment for the stress associated with snake phobia (Meichenbaum, 1985).

Kobasa's hardiness training

We saw earlier in this chapter how Kobasa introduced the concept of hardiness and the hardy personality. This personality type was characterised by high levels of commitment, challenge and control. She proposed that these characteristics were not fixed but could be increased through training. **Hardiness training** is another form of CBT and has similarities with stress inoculation training. There are three stages:

■ Focusing: in this stage the therapist encourages the client to focus on the physiological symptoms associated with stressful situations.

■ **Key term**

Hardiness training: a programme to increase people's level of hardiness (control, commitment, challenge), and so improve their ability to deal with stress.

Biological psychology

This helps them identify sources of stress. The therapist will also help them acquire new skills and strategies for coping with stress.

■ Reconstructing stressful situations: here the client is encouraged to think about recent stressful situations, and in particular how they might have turned out better and how they might have turned out worse. This is a cognitive strategy to encourage the client towards a realistic appraisal of life stress and how they cope with it. Realising that things could have been worse should help them feel more positive and optimistic.

■ Self–improvement: to improve the client's sense of **self-efficacy**: the therapist will suggest taking on manageable sources of stress. This may involve skills training similar to Stage 2 of stress inoculation training. The experience of coping with these will increase the sense of self-efficacy, and even though there will always be stressors around the client should feel more optimistic about dealing with them.

Evaluation

■ As with any CBT approach, hardiness training targets both the appraisal of sources of stress and, through training, the resources available for dealing with them. In this way it theoretically reduces the gap between demands and coping resources.

■ It should provide the client with an increased sense of self-efficacy and this should enable them to deal with future stressful situations more effectively.

■ Hardiness training involves time, commitment and money. It is therefore not appropriate for everybody.

■ Studies have shown the effectiveness of hardiness training in improving health and performance in working adults and in students (Maddi, 1987; Maddi *et al.*, 2002).

■ Physiological methods of stress management

Drugs

Benzodiazepines

Stressful situations are usually associated with feelings of anxiety. Up to the 1960s anxiety was treated with drugs from the barbiturate family. Although these could be effective, barbiturates are lethal in overdose and also produce high levels of physical dependency. In the 1960s a class of drugs called the benzodiazepines (also known as BZs) was introduced, and these rapidly took over from the barbiturates in the treatment of stress and anxiety.

Benzodiazepines have become the most prescribed of the drugs used to treat clinical disorders. The best-known examples of these drugs are Librium, Valium and Mogadon. One reason for the popularity of this group is that some benzodiazepines such as Librium and Valium can be effective anti-anxiety drugs (or **anxiolytics**), while others such as Mogadon are effective sleeping pills.

Benzodiazepines act in the brain. They increase the action of the neurotransmitter GABA (see p141); GABA is an inhibitory neurotransmitter meaning that its role is to reduce the activity of other neurotransmitter pathways throughout the brain. By increasing this inhibitory action of GABA, benzodiazepines therefore produce greater inhibition of neurotransmitter activity in the brain, and there is some evidence that the inhibition of noradrenaline and serotonin is particularly important for the anti-anxiety and antistress effects of benzodiazepines.

Biological psychology

Key terms

Self-efficacy: the sense of personal effectiveness and control over one's life.

Anxiolytics: drugs used in the treatment of anxiety states and stress.

Link

See p140 for a review of neurotransmitters and how they work.

Librium and Valium are successful anti-anxiety drugs and are often prescribed for the stress and anxiety associated with life events such as bereavement. However, as with all drug treatments for psychological conditions, there are weaknesses as well as strengths associated with the use of benzodiazepines.

Evaluation of benzodiazepines:

■ Compared with barbiturates benzodiazepines are relatively safe in overdose.

■ Benzodiazepines do have a range of side effects. They can produce feelings of tiredness and sedation, and impaired motor coordination. There is also evidence for memory impairment, especially during long-term treatment with benzodiazepines.

■ The major problem with benzodiazepines is that they can lead to a state of physical dependence. This means that if the drug is stopped the person goes into a withdrawal syndrome. The symptoms of withdrawal include sleeping problems, sweating, tremors and raised heart rate. This has led to the recommendation that they are prescribed only for short periods.

■ Benzodiazepines do not target the sources of stress or help the individual develop more effective coping strategies. They may help people recover from specific life events such as marriage break-up or bereavement, but even then a psychological grieving or mourning process has to be gone through.

■ Effective stress management should specifically target sources of stress in one's life and/or one's available coping resources. This reduces the gap between perceived demands and perceived resources. The use of benzodiazepines is most effective if combined with psychological and alternative methods that address the causes of stress.

■ There are ethical issues associated with the use of benzodiazepines. Because they can lead to dependence and may also have a range of distressing side effects, fully informed consent should be obtained before they are prescribed. It is possible that some people with severe stress-related anxiety would not be fully competent to give informed consent.

Beta-blockers

This group includes drugs such as Propranolol and Alprenolol. These drugs act directly on the heart and circulatory system of the body. They reduce activation of the **cardiovascular system** by sympathetic fibres of the autonomic nervous system (see p142). In this way they directly reduce increases in heart rate and blood pressure that are associated with stressful situations, and are also used in the management of chronic hypertension (raised blood pressure).

In this way **beta-blockers** are useful in controlling bodily arousal. It is interesting to note that they are sometimes prescribed for musicians and snooker players whose smooth motor-control can be upset by high levels of arousal.

Evaluation of beta-blockers:

■ Beta-blockers act directly to reduce heart rate and blood pressure. They can act rapidly and have a life-saving function in people with life-threatening hypertension (note that hypertension is not always related to stress; there may be genetic or lifestyle factors that are equally or even more important).

■ **Link**

See p142 for an outline of the autonomic nervous system.

■ **Key terms**

Cardiovascular system: the heart and blood vessels.

Beta-blockers: drugs used in the treatment of the bodily arousal associated with stress. They act directly on the cardiovascular system of the body rather than in the brain.

Biological psychology

AQA Examiner's tip

It is easy to become confused by the physiological aspects of drug action, especially when it involves neurotransmitters. Try to understand the key differences in the mechanism of action of benzodiazepines and beta-blockers. Also, though, make sure you understand their effects on the physiological and psychological responses to stress.

■ Although they can interact with other drug treatments, especially those for asthma, beta-blockers do not have severe side effects, partly because their main action is in the body and they do not penetrate the brain easily.

■ Beta-blockers are clearly targeting the physiological stress response. They can reduce this response in stressed individuals and lower stress-related bodily arousal. They are not targeting the sources of stress but only the physical symptoms. Therefore they are inappropriate for the long-term management of stress-related arousal, which is more effectively treated with psychological methods.

■ Alternative methods of stress management

Methods such as stress inoculation training are clearly psychological, while the use of drugs is clearly physiological. There are a number of other methods established as useful in stress management that are not so easily classified, usually because they combine elements of both psychology and physiology.

Biofeedback

Biofeedback is a technique that combines both physiological and psychological techniques. The individual is wired up to machines that provide feedback on their physiological processes. For instance, heart rate might be recorded and displayed on a monitor. Or perhaps a buzzer might sound if heart rate goes above a certain level. The person is then helped to develop techniques for reducing physiological arousal, such as the progressive muscle relaxation described next, or perhaps visualisation of calm scenes and meditation. The aim is for the individual to develop their own psychological techniques to lower heart rate and blood pressure, using the biofeedback as a guide as to when they are successful.

After training they should then be able to apply these techniques in real life, and be confident that even without immediate biofeedback they are reducing their physiological arousal.

Evaluation of biofeedback:

■ There is evidence that biofeedback is effective for controlling heart rate and in the treatment of headaches caused by muscle tension (Attanasio *et al.*, 1985). Biofeedback on breathing patterns has been found to be effective in people with panic disorder (Meuret *et al.*, 2004). The biofeedback helps them maintain a regular breathing pattern.

■ Attanasio *et al.* (1985) showed that biofeedback for tension headaches was especially effective in children, probably because of the exciting machinery involved.

■ Biofeedback is harmless and has no side effects but it does require motivation and commitment for the training programme to be successful.

■ As biofeedback involves relaxation, a stress management technique in itself, it is possible that biofeedback may be no more effective than relaxation techniques used on their own (Masters *et al.*, 1987).

Progressive muscle relaxation and meditation

Muscle relaxation is not seen as a stress management technique in its own right, but is a common component of, for instance, CBT approaches. One of the main features of the body's stress response, as outlined in the previous chapter, is an increase in general physiological arousal. One way to exert some control over this is to have available a reliable technique for relaxing body muscles and reducing general arousal.

The most common procedure taught is based on Jacobson (1938). Muscles are alternately tensed and relaxed in a systematic fashion, i.e. beginning with toes and feet and working up to the arms and hands, shoulders and muscles of the lips and forehead. As the person becomes more practised they should be able to achieve a state of relaxation without going through the full tense/relax procedure.

Once acquired, this fairly rapid method of achieving bodily relaxation can be used in times of stress. Along with, perhaps, cognitive reappraisal taught through CBT, this gives the individual an increased sense of control over stressful situations.

Meditation has similarities with muscle relaxation, in that it has the immediate effect of reducing bodily arousal. There are a number of different approaches, but they all essentially involve focusing away from the immediate situation and instead dwelling on neutral or relaxing stimuli. This may be helped by having a mantra – a single word or sound repeated over and over – and concentrating on steady and deep breathing. As with muscle relaxation, meditation works against the bodily arousal associated with stress. Studies have shown (Murphy, 1996) that meditation can be an effective stress management technique in the workplace, leading to reductions in blood pressure and anxiety.

Evaluation of progressive muscle relaxation and meditation:

- Both of these techniques reduce the arousal associated with stress, and give the individual an increased sense of control over stressful situations.
- Neither technique targets the sources of stress, or provides specific skills for dealing with stress.
- They can be extremely useful in combination with more systematic and focused methods.

Physical exercise

In the last chapter we saw how the fight or flight response to stressors results in physiological arousal and the mobilisation of energy reserves for use in physical activity. One of the issues in modern society is that physical activity is rarely an appropriate response to modern day stressors. However, anxieties about examinations, relationships or paying the mortgage, still arouse these systems.

As a result long-term or chronic stress can result in high levels of energy reserves such as glucose and free fatty acids in the bloodstream. This contributes to the development of circulatory problems such as atherosclerosis. It would seem logical that physical exercise would help burn up these energy reserves and prevent these stress-related conditions developing. In fact the evidence is quite mixed and it is not clear that regular exercise does reduce physiological reactivity to stressors. However there is evidence that regular exercise reduces resting levels of heart rate and blood pressure, so that while stress-related increases may occur, they are starting from a lower level and should not be so harmful.

In contrast to research on physiological reactivity, there is clear evidence that exercise can lower levels of stress and have very positive effects on mood (Biddle, 2000).Throne *et al.* (2000) found that regular exercise reduced levels of stress in fire fighters. Besides reducing stress levels,

Biological psychology

Key term

Enkephalins: neurotransmitters in the brain involved in emotion circuits. Their release may be associated with improvements in mood.

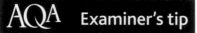

Examiner's tip

Techniques such as relaxation and exercise can be discussed by anybody even without a psychology background. To earn marks in the AS exam you must make sure your answer is 'psychologically informed'. This means you must analyse and evaluate the techniques in relation to models of stress, and/or be able to quote research findings.

exercise makes people feel better and can lead to reductions in clinical states such as depression (Mutrie, 2000). As we have seen in relation to personality and stress, negative mood states are associated with vulnerability to stress-related illness, and so the positive effects of exercise on mood may indirectly help in coping with stress.

Finally, there is no clear explanation for the effects of exercise on mood. It may be the effect of taking positive action and exerting some control over this area of life, so increasing self-efficacy. Alternatively it has been proposed that chemicals called **enkephalins** are released during exercise and act in the brain to directly improve mood. However there is very little direct evidence for this idea.

Evaluation of physical exercise:

■ Physical exercise lowers resting heart rate and blood pressure, but may not affect physiological reactivity to stress.

■ It has positive effects in raising mood, possibly through the actions of enkephalins in the brain.

■ It can also reduce reported levels of stress and depression.

■ There is some risk of injury, especially if exercising too vigorously or when starting an exercise programme.

Social support

Social support is not technically a method of stress management. However many studies over the last 40 years have shown that the level of social support can be a critical factor in reactions to the stress. These studies cover a variety of different situations, ranging from physiological reactions to stress, to patients coping with life-threatening illnesses such as cancer and heart disease.

On a commonsense level, social support simply refers to the network of family, friends and co-workers on whom you rely in times of stress.

The functions of social support can be divided into four major categories:

■ Emotional support: this is where your social network shows concern for your situation and provides reassurance.

■ Practical or instrumental support: this is where your support group may provide practical advice or help, for instance lending you money.

■ Informational support: your support group may be a source of valuable advice on how to deal with particular stressors. Some of the group may have been through the same situation previously and you can benefit from their experience.

■ General network support: being part of a network of people provides a sense of belonging and social identity, and improves self-esteem.

Research has consistently shown that social support reduces vulnerability to stress-related arousal. Mortality from heart disease has been shown to be closely related to social support (as rated by size of network and number of categories covered; Vogt *et al.*, 1992), while social support in the workplace reduces job-related stress (Constable and Russell, 1996).

We have already referred to the value of meta-reviews in psychology (p153). Uchino, Cacioppro and Kiecolt-Glaser (1996) reviewed studies of social support and the body's physiological processes. They concluded that:

■ across 28 different studies degrees of social support showed a consistent relationship with reduced blood pressure

■ across 19 studies there was a significant association between level of social support and immune function, for instance carers for dementia patients showed reduced immune function (see p149), and this was particularly marked in those reporting the lowest levels of social support.

The conclusions of Uchino *et al.* are supported by a variety of other studies. In a laboratory experiment heart rate and blood pressure during a difficult arithmetic task were lower in women with a companion than those who did the task alone (Kamarck *et al.*, 1998). Using the procedure described on p151, Cohen *et al.* (1997) found that vulnerability to the common cold was greatest in participants who reported having the fewest social roles (i.e. friend, brother, parent, etc.) and hence the smallest social networks.

Overall it is clear that social support is a key factor in dealing with stressful situations. One study (Allen *et al.*, 2002) even found that the presence of a pet lowered heart rates during the performance of stressful tests! We also know that social isolation in monkeys leads to increases in heart rate and blood pressure and eventually to heart disease (Watson *et al.*, 1998), so it appears that the importance of social support is not limited to humans.

Key points:

- An example of cognitive-behavioural therapy (CBT) for stress is Meichenbaum's stress inoculation training (SIT), where sources of stress are identified and training given in specific and general skills for coping with stressful situations.

- CBT techniques such as SIT and Kobasa's hardiness training target both the sources of stress and the coping resources available to the person. However CBT involves time, commitment and money, and may not be appropriate for everyone.

- Physiological methods of stress management include the use of benzodiazepine drugs and beta-blockers. Drugs can target the psychological and physical symptoms associated with stress, but do not affect the causes. They are also associated with problems of side effects and dependence.

- Biofeedback uses a combination of physiological and psychological techniques. The person is trained to use psychological methods of relaxation and meditation to reduce physiological measures of arousal. There is some doubt as to whether biofeedback is more effective than relaxation techniques alone.

- Progressive muscle relaxation and meditation are useful general techniques for reducing bodily arousal in stressful situations. They provide some control in these situations but do not directly target the sources of stress or provide specific coping skills.

- Physical exercise is a valuable technique for reducing baseline arousal and improving mood.

- Research has demonstrated that social support is a significant factor in reducing the physical effects of stress. Social networks can provide emotional, practical, informational and self-esteem support.

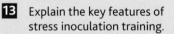

Summary questions

13 Explain the key features of stress inoculation training.

14 Outline the strengths and weaknesses of managing stress with drugs.

15 What characteristics should an effective method of stress management possess?

Biological psychology

Chapter summary

Further reading and weblinks

www.psyonline.org.uk

Essential site dedicated to broad coverage of AS and A2 Psychology.

www.psychlotron.org.uk

Resource sharing site dedicated to AS and A2 Psychology. Some exceptionally fine materials on physiological psychology and stress.

F. Jones and J. Bright, *Stress: Myth, Theory and Research*, Prentice Hall (2001)

Comprehensive coverage of all aspects of stress, including stress management and coping.

J. Ogden, *Health Psychology*, 4th edn, Open University Press (2007)

Broad coverage of issues including stress, coping and individual differences.

Links

For more information about gender and the strategy used to cope with stress, see Vitaliano *et al.* (p170) and Stone and Neale (p170).

For more information on content analysis, see p131.

- Holmes and Rahe's social readjustment rating scale (SRRS) was the first attempt to assess life event stress. Early studies also suggested that life event stress was linked to stress-related illnesses such as heart disease.
- The hassles scale focuses on everyday stressors, and research suggests hassles scores may correlate better with illness outcomes.
- Many factors can contribute to workplace stress, but research suggests that a combination of high workload and low control is particularly stressful.
- Type A behaviour (TAB) pattern is characterised by time pressure, competitiveness and hostility. Early research suggested a link between high TAB and heart disease, but later results were inconsistent. Since then hostility has emerged as a key personality factor in vulnerability to heart disease.
- Hardiness is characterised by high levels of control, commitment and challenge. Research suggests that this personality is more resistant to the negative effects of stress.
- Problem-focused and emotion-focused coping are general styles of coping. Individuals may however switch from one to the other depending on the specific situation.
- Psychological methods of stress management include techniques based on cognitive-behavioural therapy. Stress inoculation training and hardiness training focus on accurately identifying sources of stress and then acquiring specific coping skills.
- Drugs are a physiological method of stress management. They can provide rapid relief from the symptoms of stress but do not target the sources of stress. They may also have problems of dependence and side effects.
- Alternative methods of stress management include muscle relaxation, meditation and exercise. These can provide effective general coping resources but again do not target the sources of stress.
- Research has shown that social support is a significant factor in protecting against the negative effects of stress. It can provide both practical and emotional help, reducing demands and improving coping resources.

How science works: practical activity

Research into emotion-focused and problem-focused coping strategies has suggested that factors such as the source of stress (e.g. work v personal relationships) and the gender of the individual can affect the strategy used to cope with stress.

Investigate one of these factors by undertaking a content analysis of stories from magazines that recount how men and women have coped with stress e.g. *Chat*, *Pick Me Up* and *Woman*. Use the features of emotion- and problem-focused coping listed on p169 to help in coding/categorising the coping behaviours described in the stories. If you are looking at the source of stress make sure you can distinguish consistently between elements of coping that are work related and those that focus on relationships. You will need to consider the magazine(s) you will use, how you will select the articles and how you will decide if the situation being described constitutes 'stress'. You will need to make sure that categorisation is reliable and valid.

Record the frequency of emotion-focused and problem-focused strategies for *either* male and female characters *or* for work and personal relationships as sources of stress.

Draw up a bar chart to depict your results. Consider what the results suggest about coping strategies.

Question 1

1 Use the phrases below to complete the diagram, so that it shows the role of the hypothalamus in the body's response to stress.

- Gets body ready for 'fight or flight'
- Stimulates the adrenal medulla
- Stimulates the adrenal cortex
- Releases adrenalin
- Releases corticosteroids
- Stimulates the pituitary gland to release ACTH   *(6 marks)*

AQA specimen question

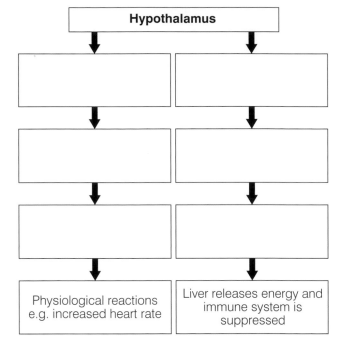

Fig. 1

2 In a study of stress, the stress and blood pressure of participants were measured. Data from the study were plotted on the graph below.

Outline what the graph seems to show about stress and blood pressure, and explain difficulties in drawing conclusions from this data.   *(4 marks)*

AQA specimen question

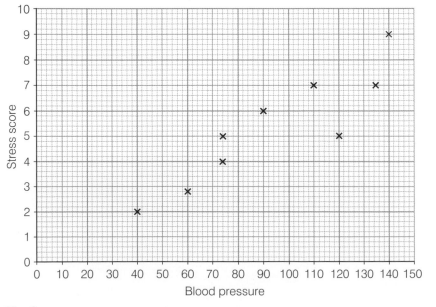

Fig. 2

3   Jake and Sarah are finding revising for their A Levels quite stressful.

Jake has planned a detailed revision schedule with regular time for breaks. He also compares notes with his friends as to the best methods of revision.

Sarah has left her revision to the last minute. She tends to snap at her parents when asked about the exams and spends long periods of time on the phone to her friends looking for support.

With reference to the scenario above, outline the distinctions between emotion-focused and problem-focused approaches to coping with stress.   *(6 marks)*

AQA Examiner's tip   To help with Question 1, part 3 you may find it useful to identify the particular features of emotion-focused and problem-focused approaches to coping with stress in the scenario.

4   Using your knowledge and understanding of research into workplace stress, suggest possible strategies for reducing stress in the workplace.

(8 marks)

Question 2

1   Outline the pituitary-adrenal system's response to stress.   *(4 marks)*

2   Discuss the use of questionnaires in investigating stress.   *(4 marks)*

AQA Examiner's tip   For Question 2, part 2, discussing questionnaires in general will not gain you marks. You must relate your answer directly to how questionnaires have been used to investigate stress.

3   (a)   Identify two factors that have been shown to affect stress levels in the workplace.   *(2 marks)*

       (b)   Explain how one of these factors affects stress levels in the workplace.   *(2 marks)*

4   Outline and evaluate psychological methods of stress management.   *(12 marks)*

Social psychology – social influence

Introduction

This section of the course is concerned with social psychology. Social psychologists are interested in the social world. Rather than focusing on the cognitive processes that take place within the individual, social psychologists are interested in what takes place between people. We live our lives surrounded by other people and interact with them on a daily basis. Some of these interactions are with strangers as we get on the train to go to school, some are with casual acquaintances at college or work and others are with our close friends and partners. For this reason, social psychologists choose to study interactions, how people form friendships and sexual relationships and the processes that take place when people are in groups or large crowds.

One area that social psychologists are interested in is social influence. Much of the time we tend to think that we act as we choose to, for example in the music we listen to, the clothes we wear and our choices of A Level subjects. Often we do not think about or appreciate the strong and often hidden influence other people may have upon us. While most people can identify situations in which others such as parents, teachers or bosses have influenced or forced them into acting in certain ways, most people like to believe that their behaviour is freely chosen and that they think and act as they want to most of the time. The study of influence examines how much actions and thoughts can be influenced by people around us and the social roles in which people are placed. In this section of the course we will consider the study of conformity and of obedience – two ways in which others may influence us.

Social psychology

What is conformity?

Learning objectives:

- Distinguish between conformity, compliance and internalisation.

- Explain how psychologists have investigated different types of conformity.

- The differences in conformity shown in different times and places.

- Design a short experiment to test conformity.

Key term

Conformity: the tendency to change what we do (behaviour) or think and say (attitudes) in response to the influence of others or social pressure. This pressure can be real or imagined.

How we conform

Conformity can be seen in many everyday situations. From the group of people who conform to a dress code at work, to those who choose a huge hat for Ascot, social pressures and the behaviour of others are clearly influential. When you update your wardrobe to follow this season's fashion or to reflect your new music tastes, it is likely you will be influenced by others around you. This chapter is going to explore different types of conformity and to introduce you to some of the important research studies that have investigated them.

Fig. 1 *City traders dressed identically on floor of stock exchange*

One of the earliest studies into conformity was carried out by Sherif in 1936. Sherif argued that people use the behaviour of others to decide what to do, especially when they are unsure or lacking in confidence about how to act. Sherif used an ingenious method to test his ideas, making use of the autokinetic effect, an optical illusion in which a stationary spot of light in a dark room appears to move.

Fig. 2 *Conforming to the dress code at the races*

In Sherif's study, each participant was taken individually to a dark room and asked to focus on a single spot of light. In a totally dark room with no visible objects there are no points of reference and the light will appear to move, due to the movement of the eyes, generally in a circular movement (you can try this for yourself if you are able to create a totally dark room). Sherif asked each participant to estimate how far the light moved and in what direction. This is an example of an ambiguous task – as the light does not actually move there is no correct answer. In fact, Sherif found that participants' estimates of distance and direction varied quite dramatically, as would be expected. In the second condition of his experiment, Sherif asked each participant to return to the laboratory several days later to repeat the perceptual task. This time they were placed in groups of three, comprising individuals with quite different estimates. Again Sherif asked each participant to estimate the distance and direction of the 'moving light' many times.

Sherif found that individuals changed their individual views and converged or agreed on similar answers. Those with high estimates lowered them and those with low estimates increased their judgements, so by the third trial each individual group member produced a very similar answer. Sherif noted that a 'group **norm**' was formed by members.

In later studies carried out by Rohrer *et al.* (1954) using Sherif's method, it was found that group norms formed in this experiment persisted, so that when participants were re-tested up to one year after, they continued to use the group answer rather than reverting to their own individual views. This shows the power of the group to influence behaviour even when the group no longer exists! This is something we shall return to later when considering explanations of conformity.

> ### Key term
>
> **Norm:** an unwritten rule about how to behave in a social group or situation that members accept as correct.

☑ Are there different types of conformity?

Kelman (1958) argued that we can distinguish between three different types or levels of conformity:

- Compliance is the most superficial type of conformity. Here, the person conforms publicly (out loud) with the views or behaviours expressed by others in the group but continues privately to disagree. For example, they may laugh at a joke that others are laughing at while privately not finding it very funny, or they might give a positive view of a film they found rather mediocre just because others are raving about it. Their personal views on the subject do not change. Compliance is also used to describe the process of going along with the requests of another person while disagreeing with them.

- Identification is a deeper type of conformity, which takes place when the individual is exposed to the views of others and changes their view publicly and privately to fit in with them. In order to do this, the person identifies with the group and feels a sense of group membership. The person identifies to be like the person or group they admire. An example of this is a recruit joining the police or armed forces who may change their views and beliefs in order to fit in with the views held by others in the group and the overall group culture. However, when identification takes place, the change of belief or behaviour may be temporary.

- Internalisation is the deepest level of conformity. When the views of the group are internalised, they are taken on at a deep and permanent level, and they become part of the person's own way of viewing the world or their cognitive system. For example, a student who becomes a vegetarian while sharing a flat with animal rights activists at university may retain those views and continue to be a vegetarian for the rest of their life. People can internalise the views of a larger group (majority influence) or of a small group or individual (minority influence). Internalisation is also known as 'conversion'.

These different types of conformity reflect the amount of change that has taken place to the person's views or actions, with some affecting the person's beliefs more deeply than others. They also reflect the reasons or motives for the change, from superficial group acceptance to a sense of 'belongingness' and permanence of change.

This chapter is going to explore these different types of conformity by considering research studies that demonstrate them. Asch's study of majority influence shows the importance of compliance, in which individuals may go along with group views outwardly while privately

Social psychology

Key terms

Majority influence: takes place when a person changes their attitudes, beliefs or actions in order to fit in with a larger group. An everyday example of this would be following a fashion trend you don't like or saying that you had enjoyed a film that everyone else had when in reality you didn't.

Confederates: 'non participants' working for the experimenter who have been briefed to answer in a particular way. The real participant believes the confederate is simply another naïve participant.

disagreeing. Clark's (1989) research examines the processes of conversion, which can take place when a minority influences others to change to their viewpoint, in the context of a jury. Finally we shall consider identification by examining Zimbardo's research in a mock prison. When asked to play the role of prisoner or warder, students rapidly identified with their roles and behaved in ways that were surprising and shocking to them.

Compliance

We have said that compliance takes place when individuals conform publicly but continue to disagree underneath. One of the earliest studies to demonstrate this type of conformity was carried out by Solomon Asch, an American researcher, in 1951. Asch had noted the research carried out earlier by Sherif and wanted to set up a situation in which there was a clear, right answer to a simple task – the judgement of line length. Asch wished to see if people would conform when a clearly wrong answer was systematically given by other group members. This experiment examined conformity by looking at **majority influence**.

Research study: Asch (1951)

Solomon Asch believed that conformity was a rational process in which people work out how to behave from other people's actions. Sherif had found that people will change their views in an ambiguous situation when they are unsure of the 'correct' response. However, Asch wished to assess what would happen when people were confronted with a majority who were plainly wrong in their judgements, to see if they would change their own views to conform to the majority.

For this reason, he created an experimental paradigm or method to study responses to group pressure, which allowed him to manipulate a variety of variables. In the original study, he recruited 123 male students and asked them to take part in a 'task of visual perception'. They were placed in groups of between seven and nine, and seated around a large table. The experimenter showed them two cards, one of a standard line and the other showing three comparison lines. Participants were asked to call out in turn which of the three comparison lines, A, B or C matched the standard line in length – to which there was an easy and obvious answer. There were a total of 18 trials for each group. However, Asch used **confederates** who were instructed to give the same wrong answer in 12 out of the 18 trials (called critical trials). In six trials they gave the incorrect answer of a longer line and, in six, a shorter line was incorrectly identified. The real participant was seated second to last or last around the table so they were exposed to the same wrong answer repeatedly before giving their own view.

Fig. 3 *Asch's experiment*

Asch measured a variety of results in this experiment including the following:

■ The overall conformity rate (i.e. the number of trials in which naïve participants gave the same wrong answer as the confederates on the critical trials). This was 37 per cent or just over one in three.

■ The large individual differences in the extent to which the participants conformed. Five per cent (1/20) of the participants conformed on every critical trial. These could be seen as the most conformist.

■ Twenty-five per cent (one-quarter) remained completely independent. They gave the correct answer on all 12 critical trials and chose to remain strongly independent despite considerable group pressure.

After the study, Asch asked the participants why they had answered as they did. The participants referred to a range of explanations for their conformity. Some felt that their perceptions may have been inaccurate and doubted their eyes, whereas others knew that the rest of the group were wrong but conformed because they did not wish to stand out from the group. As the trials progressed, participants became increasingly anxious and self-conscious regarding their answers and some reported feelings of stress.

Methodological issues

■ Asch's and Sherif's research studies are classic examples of the traditional, 'cognitive' approach to social psychology. In experiments, a complex social situation is reduced to its elements in a laboratory – the elements being an individual faced with group pressure and asked for an individual decision. The situation is highly controlled in terms of the number of people present and, in Asch's case, the use of confederates to ensure that social pressure can be manipulated. The research can therefore establish cause and effect – for example, if a larger majority causes more people to conform.

■ Since artificial groups are created for the purpose of the experiment, Asch's research lacks validity because people are among strangers. In real-life situations conformity usually takes place when people are in groups with whom they have long-lasting ties; groups of friends, colleagues or family members rather than artificial groups of strangers.

■ Others have argued that Asch's research is situated within a particular historical and cultural context – 1950s America. We will examine this criticism later in the chapter.

Ethical issues

■ One principle of psychological research is that those who take part should be given the opportunity to provide their fully informed consent, that is, they should know what they are letting themselves in for at the start and should be free to choose whether they wish to participate. This principle of informed consent did not take place in Asch's (or indeed Sherif's) study. This is because it would be extremely difficult, if not virtually impossible, to study conformity if participants were fully

■ **Links**

You can read more about the advantages and limitations of laboratory experiments on p107.

Ethical issues including deception are covered on p100.

■ **Key term**

Minority influence: takes place when an individual or small group of people influence the majority or larger group to change their attitudes or behaviour towards an issue.

informed of the nature of the study. Participants might behave differently if they were made aware that conformity and not perception was being considered.

■ The participants in Asch's study experienced stress and temporary discomfort, although it is unlikely that they suffered lasting damage.

Asch's research demonstrates the importance of compliance. In this experiment, three-quarters of the participants conformed with others outwardly, but most inwardly disagreed. People are most likely to comply when the views and approval of the group are important to them.

Internalisation

A different type of conformity is internalisation. Internalisation takes place when the individual changes both their public view and their own private view. They internalise the views of the influencing group and adopt the new ideas at a deep level. This change is also likely to be permanent. The process of internalisation can be seen in research into both majority and **minority influence**. Here we shall consider the internalisation of a minority viewpoint.

There are many examples of minority influence taking place throughout history. Galileo was one of the first to suggest that the earth travelled round the sun rather than the other way round and this idea was seen as highly controversial at the time! At the start of the twentieth century, a group of women who became known as suffragettes challenged the British law that women could not vote, and through consistent protest, changed the laws to enable equal voting rights for men and women. More recently, gay rights campaigners have argued for and have won the right to civil partnerships for gay couples.

An early experiment into minority influence was carried out by Serge Moscovici (1969), a French psychologist. Groups of six people were brought together, with four real (naïve) participants and two confederates. They were shown a series of 36 slides of different shades of blue and asked to name aloud the colour of the slide. In one condition (the consistent condition) the confederates called all 36 slides green. Under this condition just over 8 per cent of the real participants moved to the minority position and called the slides green. In the second (inconsistent) condition, the confederates called 24 out of 36 of the slides green and the move to the minority position was around 1.25 per cent. This study strongly suggests that minorities should be consistent in order to exert an influence.

Experiments of this nature have been criticised for lacking ecological validity as the task is unlike a real task and participants are aware they are being studied. For this reason, more recent research has considered the processes of minority influence in relation to those taking part in jury service. Juries consist of 12 randomly selected adults who must make a group decision regarding the innocence or guilt of a defendant. Due to the ethical difficulties in studying real-life juries, psychologists including Tanford and Penrod (1986) and Clark (1999) have chosen to use mock juries constructed for the purpose of the research.

Fig. 4 *Still from* 12 Angry Men

Research study: Clark 1998/99

Clark carried out a series of studies using the 1954 film *12 Angry Men* in which a single juror (the actor Henry Fonda) believes that a defendant is innocent of killing his father and sets out to convince the rest of the jury that the young man is innocent. Participants were asked to play the role of jurors and to make up their minds about the guilt or innocence of the young man.

Clark wanted to test two different predictions in these studies:

■ that the minority could exert its influence through the information presented and the persuasive nature of the minority's arguments

■ that the minority could influence the majority through changes in behaviour or 'defections'. Seeing other people change their view can have a powerful effect on the individual's own beliefs.

In the first study, Clark used 220 psychology students, 129 women and 91 men. The participants were given a four-page booklet with a summary of the plot of *12 Angry Men*. This booklet contained evidence *for* the defendant's guilt:

■ that he had purchased and used a rare knife from a local store

■ that he had been seen by two eyewitnesses, one an old man who claimed he had heard the defendant say 'I am going to kill you', and the other a woman who had been in the apartment opposite, who identified the defendant as the murderer.

Clark varied whether or not the students were given information about Henry Fonda's defence and the counter-arguments. He found that a minority juror only led people to change their minds when they could provide counter-evidence to the charge. If they did not provide evidence, people did not move from the majority position. This supports his claim that the information given by the minority is important.

In another study, Clark focused on the impact of behaviour, or people defecting to the minority position. Student participants were given a three-page summary of the jury's discussion in the

Hint

You might want to watch this film!

Social psychology

film. This contained the main counter-arguments presented by the minority juror played by Henry Fonda. These were:

- that he (Henry Fonda) had been able to produce in court an identical 'rare' knife, which he had bought from a nearby junk shop
- that the man could not have seen or heard the murder as his old age and disabilities meant it took him too long to get to the window in the apartment
- that the old woman could not have seen the defendant as she had very bad eyesight and was not wearing glasses.

Clark presented different scenarios to the students in which he showed varying numbers of defectors (people changing their behaviour to adopt the 'not guilty' position) from one to six. Clark asked the students to use a nine-point scale to give their opinion of whether or not the man was guilty. He found that participants were influenced by the number of defectors to the 'not guilty' position. When they heard that four or seven jurors had changed their mind to agree with Henry Fonda they were more likely to adopt the 'not guilty' position themselves. Seven defectors had no more influence than four. Clark argued that after four people have changed their minds, a 'ceiling of influence' is reached, meaning that more defectors do not produce more influence. The findings of this study support Clark's view that minorities can influence people to change their views through changing their own behaviour.

Methodological issues

- Clark's study provides a very good example of how research into social psychology has changed over the last 30 years. In contrast to Asch and Moscovici, who used laboratory experiments to investigate conformity, Clark's participants were asked to play the role of jurors. The task was a simulation of a realistic situation in which social influence takes place – that of jury decision making.
- The costs of making an error for participants in this research study were much lower than in real-life jury service, where it is likely that decisions would be accompanied by much more soul searching. It is questionable how far the results of this role-play can be generalised to real-life jury service.

Ethical issues

In this study, participants were not misled as to the nature of the task and were subjected to little by way of stress or discomfort during the role play. This means that the role play is much more ethically acceptable than previous experimental studies, which have involved stress and deception.

Link

You can read more about *Ethical Principles for Conducting Research* on p100.

Identification

The changing face of social psychology – identification with social roles, then and now

A third type of conformity is identification. This happens when the individual takes on the views of a group they join or admire. Identification was shown in a famous study by Philip Zimbardo in 1971, which changed the face of social psychology. Working at Stanford University in America, Zimbardo set up a mock prison in the basement of the university over the summer vacation. Zimbardo wished to see if the brutality found in many American prisons at the time was a consequence of the personality of the guards or identification with the social roles in which they were placed.

Zimbardo recruited 24 male students from volunteers, using a variety of psychological tests to select those who were the most stable, with no violent or anti-social tendencies. He randomly allocated each student to the role of prisoner or guard. Prisoners were arrested at their homes early on Sunday morning, taken to the prison, searched, de-loused and dressed in smock uniforms. They were referred to by number. The guards were given uniforms, a 'night stick' or truncheon and dark glasses. They were instructed to keep the prisoners under control but to use no physical violence.

Within a day the prisoners rebelled and ripped off their numbers. The guards responded by locking them in their cells and confiscating their blankets. As the experiment continued, the punishments imposed by the guards escalated. Prisoners were humiliated, deprived of sleep and made to carry out roll-call in the night. One, who went on hunger strike in protest at the treatment, was force fed by the guards and locked in a dark cupboard measuring only around 4 feet in size. The prisoners rapidly became depressed and passive with some showing serious stress-related reactions to the experience. The role play, which had been intended to run for two weeks, was called off after six days. The findings were interpreted as showing the power of the situation to influence conformity. The implication from these findings was that ordinary, stable individuals can abuse power and behave in violent and anti-social ways if placed in a situation that facilitates this.

Zimbardo's research has become notorious in social psychology due to the implications of the findings and the ethical debates it provokes. Critics have argued that although Zimbardo asked for consent from his participants, he became too involved to see clearly what was happening and should have called off the study even earlier. Critics have called the prison a 'living hell'.

In 2006, a study based on Zimbardo's research was carried out in the UK by Stephen Reicher, a psychologist working at St Andrew's University and Alex Haslam from Exeter University, and broadcast on UK television by the BBC, in a series called *The Experiment* (although it was not technically an experiment). Volunteers responded to an advert in the national papers asking 'How well do you really know yourself?', and 15 males aged between 22 and 44 were selected from 500 applicants, following a battery of psychological tests. They were randomly allocated to roles of nine prisoners and six guards and placed in a purpose-built prison at Elstree film studios. The guards were unwilling to impose authority over the prisoners who rapidly took charge of the prison. Following the breakdown of authority in the prison, both groups attempted to establish a fair and equal social system. When this failed, a small group of prisoners took power in the prison and the experiment was called off. Reicher and Haslam have suggested that the findings of their study indicate that tyranny may become acceptable when law and order established by the group breaks down and groups experience feelings of powerlessness.

These findings are very different from those of Zimbardo 30 years earlier. Zimbardo (2006) himself has argued that there are substantial differences between the two studies, notably that most of the prisoners in Reicher and Haslam's study were much tougher and more streetwise in comparison to his own prisoners. In this 'prison' all participants wore microphones and were constantly aware that they were being filmed, rather than being observed through hidden cameras as in Zimbardo's study. However, the findings indicate that research can only really be understood within the social and cultural context that it takes place. Social roles in the twenty-first century are less clearly defined and authority is seen in a different light from in the 1970s.

Social psychology

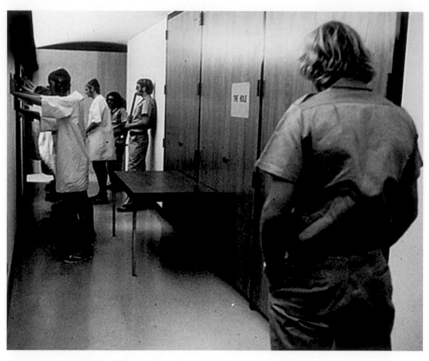

Fig. 5 *The Zimbardo prison experiment*

Fig. 6 *Still from* The Experiment

■ Factors affecting conformity

The size of the majority

Asch's experimental method allowed him to manipulate a variety of factors to see which influenced conformity rates. In one set of variations, Asch manipulated the size of the group of confederates carrying out the conformity trial by using 1, 2, 3, 4, 8, 10 and 15 in the group.

- Asch found that conformity was very low when there was one confederate and one real participant with only 3 per cent of the real participants changing their view to that of the confederates. (Note that this condition does not fit the criteria for majority influence as there was no majority in a one-to-one situation.)

- When the group was increased to include three confederates and one real participant, conformity climbed to 33 per cent. It did not increase much beyond this regardless of group size.

- In some conditions, a greater majority of 15 led to slightly lower levels of conformity, perhaps because participants became increasingly suspicious when confronted with a majority of 15 apparently mad people.

- Many replications of Asch's study have shown these findings to be robust. Conformity seems to be at its maximum with a three-to-five person majority (Stang, 1976).

In a final version of Asch's experiment, he arranged for one confederate to agree with the real participant and give the correct answer. In this condition, conformity dropped dramatically, implying that people are able to remain independent in a group situation when they have a small amount of support, even from just one other person.

The importance of time

The extent to which people conform varies in different times and places as well as between different people. One of the criticisms made of Asch's work was that it was carried out in America in the 1950s when conformity was high. This is not surprising as Asch lived and worked in 1950s America. However, there is a serious issue at stake here. Research always takes place within a social, historical and cultural context, within a specific time and place. It does not occur in a social vacuum. Therefore what is researched, the questions asked and the way in which the research is carried out can be seen to reflect the time and place in which the researcher is working.

The question remains as to how much conformity varies in different places and at different historical periods. Perrin and Spencer (1981) argued that Asch's classic studies of conformity reflected the social and historical aspects of 1950s America where pressures to conform were very strong. For this reason they carried out an experiment to assess the differences in conformity 25 years after Asch's original research, comparing different groups of young men. They replicated Asch's study using the same line task with different groups. In one condition, 33 male students were used. In another, 20 male students who were on probation were used. Probation is given as an alternative sentence to prison to young people who have broken the law. In this condition, the confederates used were probation officers who supervised the young people and carried out the sentence. Perrin and Spencer also studied 16 young, unemployed West Indian men with a mean age of 19 years. They found striking differences in conformity to Asch's original study and between the different groups involved.

- In male students not on probation, conformity was almost non-existent with only 1 in 396 trials producing a conforming response. This suggests that conformity in 1981 was much lower than Asch had originally found in the 1950s.

- The young men who were on probation showed very similar rates of conformity to those found by Asch in the 1950s studies, implying that conformity still takes place when people are placed with those who have power or authority over them.

■ High rates of conformity were found when young West Indian participants were placed in groups with a majority of confederates who were white. Note that this study was carried out in 1981 when racial equality was much less well established in the UK.

These findings strongly support the claim that we cannot generalise regarding rates of conformity. Whether or not people conform depends on many factors including the time and place research is carried out, as well as the specific characteristics of the people studied and the possible power relationships within the group. Others have assessed conformity more recently using a modified version of Asch's task, which is more ambiguous and has a less obvious answer. Lalancette (1990) used 40 students. Like Perrin and Spencer, he found no evidence of conformity and concluded from this that the conformity effect shown in Asch's study was an 'unpredictable phenomenon, not a stable tendency of human behaviour' (1990, p7). Together, the findings of these studies suggest that conformity is much lower in the Western world today than it was in the middle of the last century.

The importance of place and culture

Some psychologists have considered whether there are differences in the tendency to conform, which can be seen across different cultures. Smith and Bond (1993) carried out a meta-analysis of research, using Asch's method for studying conformity in a number of different cultures. They found significant variations in the level of conformity in different places. Conformity was highest in Fiji, an island in the Pacific, at 58 per cent on critical trials. The lowest rate of conformity was found in Belgium, an EU country, at 14 per cent. One explanation for this refers to the differences between **individualistic** and **collectivist cultures**. Individualist cultures such as those of the US and UK value characteristics such as autonomy, independence and individuality, so it is not surprising that people are encouraged to make and stand by their own decisions rather than being influenced by others. In contrast, collectivist cultures attach importance to the social group and interdependence is stressed (Markus and Kitayama, 1991). This makes it more likely that people will try to fit in with the views of other people wherever possible. Belgium is an example of an individualistic culture, whereas Fiji is highly collectivist. Smith and Bond also compared the average conformity rates for individualistic and collectivist cultures. They found that the rate was just over 25.3 per cent conforming in individualistic cultures compared with 37.1 per cent in collectivist cultures. These findings suggest that the characteristics of the culture and the qualities that are valued and encouraged as children are brought up may be a significant influence on how much people are prepared to conform with others.

The importance of modern technologies

More recently, cross-cultural differences in conformity have been investigated in computer mediated communication where people interact without seeing each other. Much social interaction today takes place through this medium in the form of chat rooms and social networking sites such as Facebook and MySpace. Early research into conformity by Crutchfield suggested that people who were unable to see each other were less prone to conforming with the (invisible) majority. In order to look at conformity in computer mediated communication, Cinirella and Green (2005) investigated cross-cultural differences in conformity comparing face-to-face (f2f) communication and computer meditated communication. They found the expected cultural differences in f2f

Key terms

Individualistic cultures: those where personal independence and achievement are valued. Examples of individualistic cultures are North America and Germany.

Collectivist cultures: those where there is a high degree of interdependence between people. Examples of collectivist cultures are Japan, China and Israel.

communication, with conformity being higher in collectivist than individualistic cultures. However, in computer mediated communication there were no cultural differences implying that conformity is less likely when people are unable to see each other.

Key points:

■ There are three types of conformity: compliance, internalisation and identification.

■ Compliance can be seen in Asch's study of majority influence where three-quarters of participants complied publicly with a wrong answer given by the majority, despite privately disagreeing.

■ Internalisation takes place when the individual changes their private viewpoint. This can be seen in studies on both majority and minority influence.

■ Identification to social roles was shown in Zimbardo's prison study.

■ Rates of conformity differ across time and cultures. They are generally lower now than in the mid-twentieth century and lower in individualistic than collectivist cultures. Conformity may be less when people communicate using technologies rather than face-to-face.

✔ Summary questions

1 Explain one difference between compliance and internalisation.

2 Describe one study that has investigated conformity.

3 a Give one example of how conformity rates differ across time or place.
b Give an explanation of why this difference might exist.

4 Explain one criticism that has been made of research into conformity.

5 Compare the methods used by Moscovici and Clark to investigate minority influence. Which do you consider to be better and why?

Why do people conform?

Social psychology

☑

Learning objectives:

■ Understand explanations
that have been given for
why people conform to both
majorities and minorities.

■ The evidence that supports
these explanations.

■ Explaining majority influence

A range of explanations has been given for why people conform.
Following Asch's study of conformity, a two-part framework was put
forward by Deutsch and Gerard (1955) and developed into the 'dual-
process dependency model'. More recently, a 'social identity' approach,
based on the importance of group membership, has been put forward by
Hogg and Abrahams (1988).

The dual-process dependency model (Deutsch and Gerard, 1955)

Following Asch's research, Deutsch and Gerard (1955) suggested two
reasons for conformity:

■ Normative social influence: the person conforms because of their
need to be accepted by and belong to the group. This may be because
belonging to the group is rewarding (think of the need to belong and
be accepted by various groups at school) and the group has the power
to punish or even exclude those who do not fit in and toe the line.
They may personally and privately continue to disagree but conform
on the surface. This is known as compliance, and was the type of
conformity seen in Asch's experiment when participants knew that
the answers given by the confederates were wrong but continued to
conform with them.

■ Informational social influence: different motives and needs drive
this type of social influence. In many social situations, people may
be unsure of how to behave, or unclear as to what they think or feel
about an issue. In this case they may conform with others and copy
their actions because they do not know what to say. In this case, the
drive for conformity is the need to be right. If the majority are acting
in a particular way then conformity may be a sensible decision. If they
are right, then the conformer will be too. If they are not, at least they
will not stand out from others and appear conspicuous. This was the
type of conformity seen in Sherif's experiment.

This approach has become known as the dual-process dependency
model (Turner, 1991) as it suggests that people conform for two
reasons (dual) because of their dependency on other people. The two
types of dependency are social approval (acceptance) and information.
This explanation has been criticised as it does not acknowledge the
importance of a sense of belonging to a group. Many studies have
shown how conformity to group norms can persist long after the group
no longer exists. As participants in an experiment cannot fear group
exclusion, this implies that factors other than dependency on the group
may be important. The dual-process model of conformity sees the choice
to conform as a rational process in which the person weighs up the
information given to them and their need for group approval.

Social identity explanations (Hogg, 2003; Hogg and Abrahams, 1988)

In contrast to the dual-process model, theories based on **referent
informational influence** point to the need to consider the importance

■ Key term

Referent informational influence:
the pressure to conform with the
norms set by a group because
we have defined ourselves as a
member of that group.

198

of relationships and emotional ties with other group members to help in understanding why we conform with them. These include social identity approaches (Hogg, 2003; Hogg and Abrahams, 1988), which are based on Tajfel and Turner's social identity theory.

Tajfel's minimal group experiments (1971) were the first to show the importance of group membership and belonging. Teenage boys aged 14–15 living in Bristol were randomly allocated to one of two groups on the basis of their preference for one artist or another. They then played a game in which they were able to allocate points that could be exchanged for money, to their own and the other group. The boys consistently chose to allocate more points to their own group (for example, giving their group three points and the other group one point), even when they could gain more points and rewards by allocating equal amounts (i.e. five points each). Tajfel argued that there was a tendency to favour one's own group (the in-group) and discriminate against other 'out-groups'.

From these findings, Tajfel suggested that as well as personal identity, we each have a social identity. People define themselves by the social groups they belong to, such as female or Asian. These groups serve as reference groups to us and have powerful influences on our behaviour.

Why do people conform according to social identity explanation?

According to social identity theory, people classify themselves as belonging to particular social groups, such as Liverpool supporters. This process of self-categorisation leads members to feel part of that group and to see strong differences between themselves and other groups, for example Everton supporters. This tendency to maximise perceived differences from other groups is known as the **meta-contrast principle**. According to this approach, groups provide norms or rules to regulate the behaviour of members. These norms are internalised or taken in as ideas or standards about ways of behaving by members. Group members use the norms of their group to regulate their behaviour when they are with the group, but can also refer to group norms and abide by them when other group members are not there. People conform to group norms according to this approach because they are group members; conformity isn't simply to gain the approval of other group members or because of the fear of rejection. Upholding group norms can also continue in the absence of other group members. Once a Liverpool supporter, always a Liverpool supporter!

This approach helps to explain why people may often conform to group norms in the absence of anyone from the group being present. This would explain the findings of Rohrer's study using Sherif's autokinetic effect. Here, participants conformed to group norms up to one year after they had been exposed to them. Any adequate explanation for conformity must be able to account for the persistence of conformity in the absence of the group.

The social identity explanation has received considerable support from four conformity experiments carried out by Hogg and Turner in 1987. These studies asked for participants' private responses to a conformity task similar to that of Asch. Private responses remove the need for participants to conform for normative reasons as others cannot show disapproval or rejection when they do not see the response. Under these conditions, Hogg and Turner found that people only conformed when the majority consisted of members of their 'in-group' rather than an 'out-group' supporting the idea that we conform with members of our own reference group.

Key term

Meta-contrast principle: the tendency for group members to see strong similarities between themselves and other members of their group and to see large differences with other social groups.

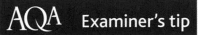

Examiner's tip

Make sure that you can explain the differences between normative, informational and referent social influence.

Social psychology

■ Explaining minority influence

Other psychologists have attempted to explain conformity to a minority group. Moscovici's study showed that minorities exert most influence when they are consistent. Clark (1989) has argued that a minority can exert an influence in two ways:

■ By providing persuasive arguments: people listen to what is said and change their views if they are convinced by the evidence presented. In Clark's 1989 study, majority members were likely to adopt the minority verdict when the sole dissenter could produce evidence to change their minds, but unlikely when they could not. This shows clearly that information is an important part of minority influence.

■ By showing defecting behaviour: minorities can produce change through their behaviour. When people see others changing their views and adopting a minority viewpoint, they are more likely to follow, perhaps without examining the arguments themselves.

As well as this framework, we shall consider here two explanations that have been put forward for minority influence; Latane and Wolfe's (1981) social impact theory and Tanford and Penrod's (1986) social influence model.

Latane and Wolf's (1981) social impact theory

Social impact theory starts from the premise that both minority and majority influence involve a number of people that they divide into sources (people who provide the influence) and targets (people who may be influenced). Latane refers to social influence as a 'series of forces operating in a social field'.

According to this approach, the impact, or amount of influence, depends on three factors that interact. These are:

■ strength, namely the importance, power or status of the person/people providing the influence

■ immediacy, namely the psychological, physical or social distance of the person providing the influence

■ the number of people providing the influence. Latane and Wolf argue that as the influence increases in numbers it gathers progressively more influence, thus three people have more impact than two, who have more impact than one.

As the number of people increases, the impact made by each person gets less and less, which Latane and Wolf call a 'negatively accelerating positive function'. A single individual taking a minority position will produce lots of impact and influence. When they are joined by a second person arguing the same, their personal impact is slightly less and each one after that has a lesser effect. Hogg and Vaughan (2003) give a good example to explain this. Switching on a single light in a dark room has a dramatic effect. Switching on a second light has slightly less impact although it may still have an effect. By the time the tenth light bulb is switched on the effect is minimal!

Social impact theory has been tested in a number of experiments. In one, Hart, Stasson and Karau (1999) measured the impact of strength and immediacy on social influence. They placed participants in groups of three, consisting of two naïve participants and one confederate who argued for a minority position. Their task was to rate 40 university applicants for places. Immediacy was manipulated by having the confederate 4 feet away (high immediacy) or 10 feet away (low immediacy) and strength was manipulated by having the confederate acting as a student (low strength) or as an expert (high strength). They found the expert confederate had more impact than the student confederate, but only in the low impact setting when they were physically further away. There was no difference in the importance of strength in the high impact setting when the confederate was close by, implying that immediacy may be the most important factor in minority influence.

Tanford and Penrod's (1986) social influence model

Social influence theory agrees with social impact theory that minority influence increases as the size of the minority increases and that each additional member or defector to the minority adds less to the cumulative impact. Three defectors have more influence than two who have more influence than one. However, where Tanford and Penrod differ from Latane and Wolf is in their claim that a ceiling of influence is said to be reached when there are three or four defectors. According to Tanford and Penrod, four people in a minority will have an equal amount of influence to five or even ten. It may even be that further defectors weaken rather than strengthen the minority position.

Key points:

■ According to the dual-process dependency model, conformity can be explained in terms of informational social influence and normative social influence.

■ Social identity explanations focus on the importance of group membership and referent social influence.

■ Social impact theory argues that immediacy, numbers and strength interact to create influence.

■ Both theories agree that each additional defector creates less impact on the majority. However, the social influence model argues that a ceiling of influence is reached after four defectors.

■ Research into conformity illustrates the changes in methods and approaches to social psychology that have taken place over the last 30 years.

✔️ Summary questions

6 Explain what is meant by normative social influence, informational social influence and referent social influence.

7 Explain one criticism of the dual-process dependency model of majority influence.

8 Outline the main features of social impact theory.

9 'Jenny has been to see a horror film with five of her new friends from college. After the film, the group are discussing how great it was. Jenny thought the film was pretty ordinary but joins in praising it with the rest of the group.' Identify the type of conformity shown here and give one reason why Jenny conforms in this situation.

10 'People conform because they want to fit in and be accepted by a group'. How far does research support this claim?

Obedience to authority

Learning objectives:

- How psychologists have investigated obedience in the laboratory and in field experiments.

- Understand ethical and other criticisms of research into obedience.

- Explanations of why people obey including situational and personality factors.

Key term

Obedience: complying with an order from another person to carry out an action. The person who gives the instruction usually has power or authority.

■ Research into obedience

Here we are going to look at how psychologists have investigated **obedience** in both laboratory and in field settings. You will notice as you work through this section that much of the research included here was carried out in the middle to late twentieth century. This is because psychologists have become much more aware of the need to treat research participants with respect and to ask for their fully informed consent to take part in research. Experiments involving obedience to authority can be difficult to carry out in an ethical framework as they often involve deception of research participants.

Every day there are occasions when we are told to do things by other people. At school, then at work, we operate within a hierarchy in which teachers, supervisors and bosses have power over us. Most of the instructions we are given are legitimate, although we may resent or disobey them if we do not want to carry them out. It is unlikely, however, that we will be given an instruction to do something that goes against our conscience or involves us inflicting serious harm on another person. We have noted earlier in the chapter that psychological interest in topics often relates to the social context, time and events that are taking place. This is true of research into obedience that thrived after the 1939–45 war. Much of this interest came from the reports of extreme obedience that had taken place in Nazi Germany and in the Vietnam War in the 1950s and 1960s. When Stanley Milgram, a psychologist working at Yale University in the US in the early 1960s, set out to study obedience, the trial of Adolf Eichmann, a prominent Nazi, was taking place in Nuremberg in West Germany. What was most noticeable in this trial was the ordinariness of Eichmann, who presented his defence as an ordinary man, simply obeying orders given to him by those in authority. Hannah Arendt was later to refer to this as 'The Banality of Evil' in her 1965 book portraying the trial of Eichmann. It was within this context that Milgram set out to investigate obedience to authority in an infamous series of experiments at Yale University.

☐ Research study: Milgram (1963)

In Stanley Milgram's original obedience to authority study in 1963 he wanted to set up a situation in which single individuals were ordered to act against a stranger in an inhumane way and to see at what point they would refuse to obey the order. Milgram had noted the reports of extreme obedience carried out during the 1939–45 war and wondered to what extent ordinary decent people could do extraordinary things.

Milgram advertised for male volunteers by placing an advert in a local paper, which offered $4.50 as payment for taking part in a study of 'memory and learning'. Forty respondents from a range of occupations and backgrounds were selected and individual appointments were made to attend the laboratory at Yale University. When they arrived, they were greeted by the 'experimenter', a 31-year-old teacher in a white coat, and introduced to a middle-aged man whom they believed to be another participant, Mr Wallace, in reality a confederate of the experimenter. The experimenter explained to both men that one participant was to be the teacher and the other the learner, then they drew lots to allocate roles. These were rigged so that the real participant was always the teacher. Both teacher and learner were taken to a room, which contained a shock generator. This had a series of switches ranging from 15V to 450V increasing in 15V increments. There were written labels on the generator including slight shock (15– 60V), moderate shock (75–120V), strong shock (135–180V), intense shock (255–300V), danger of severe shock (375–420V) and finally XXX (435–450V).

Fig. 7 *Milgram's electric shock generator*

The experimenter explained to the 'teacher' that it was his job to teach the 'learner' a series of word pairs and then test their recall. The learner was to indicate, by means of a switch, which words had originally been paired. If he answered correctly they would proceed to the next pair but if he made an error, the teacher was instructed to administer an electric shock starting at 15V and increasing by one increment each time. Both teacher and learner were taken to an adjacent room containing an electric chair. The teacher was given a sample electric shock to convince them the procedure was real, then the learner was strapped into the chair and electrodes were attached to his wrists and electrode paste applied to prevent burns. In response to an anxious enquiry from the learner about the danger of the shocks, the experimenter replied that 'The shocks may be painful but they are not dangerous'. Teacher and learner were then placed in separate rooms so the teacher was able to hear but not see the learner.

When the experiment started, the learner gave a predetermined set of responses to the test, with roughly three incorrect answers for every correct answer. As the shocks became higher, the learner's screams (which were pre-recorded) became more dramatic. At 180V he complained of a weak heart and at 300V he banged on the wall and demanded to be allowed to leave. At 315V he refused to answer and became silent. When the teacher objected to the procedure, the experimenter responded with a series of 'prods', which were standardised. These included 'Please continue' or 'Please go on' and 'The experiment requires that you continue, teacher'. As the teacher protested, they were told 'It is absolutely essential you continue, teacher' and 'You have no other choice. You must go on'. During the experiment, many of the participants showed sign of extreme tension. They shook, sweated and stuttered, with 14 out of the 40 showing nervous laughing fits. Many of the participants repeatedly argued with the experimenter but continued to obey.

Milgram found that all 40 participants went to 300V on the shock generator and 65 per cent administered the maximum shock of 450V. This finding was as shocking to Milgram as it was to other psychologists. Before Milgram carried out the study, he had asked a variety of groups including psychiatrists and students how many people they thought would obey completely. Psychiatrists had predicted that only 2.6 per cent of participants would continue to administer a very strong shock of up to 240V.

However, it is also important to note the issue of disobedience in Milgram's study. Despite the pressure put on his participants and the prestigious nature of the university, a full 35 per cent of participants managed to defy the considerable pressure of the experiment.

Methodological issues

■ The use of the experimental method and the laboratory setting allowed Milgram to investigate obedience in a systematic and controlled way. Standardised procedures were used (for example the recorded screams and the scripted 'prods') to ensure that participants were exposed to similar conditions.

■ Milgram's research has been criticised for lacking both internal and external validity. Some have claimed that his participants could not have been fooled by the experimental set-up into thinking that the shocks were real whereas others have argued that the situation in Milgram's lab was unlike any situation experienced in real life. Again we shall examine these criticisms in detail later.

Ethical issues

Milgram's study has been criticised for its ethics. Milgram failed to ask his participants for informed consent, he deceived them and made it difficult for them to withdraw. They experienced considerable stress and potential psychological harm. We shall be considering these criticisms in detail later in this chapter.

Links

You can read more about the advantages and limitations of laboratory experiments on p107.

Ethical issues including deception, debriefing and the protection of research participants are covered on p100.

Factors affecting obedience

In order to further explore the factors that influenced obedience, Milgram replicated his experiment carrying out 18 studies in total with over 1,000 participants. In these variations he systematically varied the setting of the experiment, the power of the experimenter and the closeness of the learner to the teacher. Each of these factors gave increased understanding of when and why people obey or disobey orders.

■ The setting of the experiment: one factor that Milgram thought may have contributed to the high levels of obedience was the setting of the experiment, the prestigious Yale University. In order to see if obedience was caused by the prestige of the setting, Milgram packed up his shock generator and moved his experiment into a seedy office above a shop. Calling himself Research Associates Ltd he advertised for participants in the paper and replicated the study exactly. Under this condition he found a significant drop in obedience. Forty-eight per cent of his participants in this setting continued to 450V on the shock generator. This led Milgram to conclude that the prestige of Yale University was one factor that contributed to high levels of obedience.

■ Reducing the power of the experimenter: in another version of the experiment Milgram reduced the power of the experimenter by removing him from the room and instructing him to give the teacher orders over the phone. In this variation many more teachers were able to resist the authority of the experimenter with only 20 per cent going to the full 450V. He also reduced the authority of the experimenter by asking the teachers to work in pairs to administer the shocks. The second teacher was again a confederate of the researcher who refused to continue to administer the shocks. Under these conditions, Milgram found that 90 per cent of those he studied were able to resist the orders to shock the learner at some point and only 10 per cent went to the full 450V.

■ Increasing awareness of the plight of the victim: Milgram also noticed that obedience may be easier when the victim is relatively remote. In the original version of the experiment, the teacher was unable to see the learner (as they were in separate rooms) but could hear his screams. In a series of variations Milgram altered the proximity of teacher and learner in several ways. In one variation, the learner was brought into the same room so he could be seen and heard. Obedience dropped. In another variation, the teacher and learner were again in the same room and in order for the learner to receive the shocks he had to place his hand voluntarily on a shock plate. When he refused to do this, the teacher was instructed to force his hand down onto the shock plate. Under this condition, a staggering 30 per cent of participants still continued to 450V.

As with conformity, others have replicated Milgram's method to investigate obedience in different places. High rates of obedience have been found across Europe, with 90 per cent going to 450V in Spain and the Netherlands. Lower rates of obedience have been found in Australia where 40 per cent of men and a mere 16 per cent of women administered the highest level shocks. Again it is apparent that while obedience does take place in different cultures, the extent to which people are prepared to obey varies and relates to the values and norms of the culture at the time.

Obedience in the field

As well as investigating obedience in laboratory settings, psychologists have carried out research using field experiments. This has a range of advantages in that people are usually unaware they are taking part in a psychology experiment that minimises the likelihood of **demand characteristics** and produces research that has generally higher ecological validity. However, research in the field can pose serious ethical dilemmas for psychologists as it is often impossible to ask participants for their consent and it may be difficult to debrief them afterwards. For this reason, more recent field experiments such as those carried out by Bickman (1974), Bushman (1988) and Sedikides and Jackson (1990) tend to involve compliance with fairly trivial requests.

In one field study set in a hospital, Hofling *et al.* (1966) looked at nurses' responses to an order from a 'bogus' doctor. An experimenter phoned 22 nurses who were working alone on wards at different hospitals and introduced himself as 'Dr Smith'. There was no real Dr Smith working at the hospital. The researcher instructed each nurse to check the drug cupboard for a drug called 'Astroten'. When they had done this, he ordered them to administer 20 milligrams of the drug to a patient on the ward. This order broke several hospital rules:

■ Nurses should not take orders over the phone but should wait for the doctor to visit the ward and sign the prescription.

■ Nurses should not take orders from an unknown doctor.

Key term

Demand characteristics: cues in the environment that help the participant work out what the research hypothesis is. This can lead to social desirability effects where the participant behaves in a way that the hypothesis will be supported or the 'screw you' effect where the participant purposefully disrupts the research.

Link

You can refresh your memory about demand characteristics by looking at p96 and ecological validity by looking at p107.

Social psychology

■ The dosage instructed was twice the maximum dosage on the bottle.

■ The drug (being fictional) was not on the ward list.

Hofling was interested to see if the nurses would obey an order given by an authority figure when it went against hospital rules. Despite the clear contradiction of rules, 21 out of the 22 nurses studied were prepared to obey and went to collect the drug to administer it to the patient. They were stopped on the way to administer the drug by a confederate, and debriefed. Afterwards, when debriefed, many nurses argued that an order of that nature was not unusual and that obedience was expected.

The power of a uniform

Bickman (1974) carried out a field experiment in New York in which he asked passers-by to carry out an unusual order – to pick up rubbish, stand on the other side of a bus-stop sign or lend money to a stranger for a parking meter. Half of the time the experimenter was dressed in a security guard's uniform and the rest of the time in street clothes. This formed the two conditions of the independent variable. Bickman measured the number who obeyed the request (the dependent variable) and found that 92 per cent of participants would comply with the request to lend money when he was uniformed, compared with 49 per cent when he was wearing street clothing. Bushman (1988) used Bickman's method of studying obedience, this time using a female confederate dressed in one of two ways – a uniform or smart clothes. This time, the confederate ordered passers-by to give a small amount of change to a motorist who was searching for money at a parking meter. Bushman found that 70 per cent complied when she was uniformed, compared with 58 per cent when dressed in smart clothing. This difference is rather less than that found by Bickman.

A more recent study has attempted to test the predictions of social impact theory in relation to compliance to an order. Sedikides and Jackson (1990) examined the effects of strength and immediacy on obedience to a simple request at a zoo. One hundred and fifty-three adults and 55 children attending the zoo were approached by an experimenter dressed either as a zoo keeper (high strength) or as an ordinary visitor to the zoo (low strength). The experimenter asked them not to lean on a railing next to an exhibit. The behaviour of participants was observed immediately after the request (high immediacy condition) when the experimenter was still present and after they had left the scene (low immediacy condition). Sedikides and Jackson found that the high strength/high immediacy condition produced more compliance to the request than the low strength/low immediacy condition, providing further support for social impact theory. Together these three studies indicate that a uniform can be a powerful social symbol of authority.

Evaluation of research into obedience

Research into obedience has been criticised in a number of ways:

■ The ethics of the research (Baumrind, 1964).

■ The validity of the research (Orne and Holland, 1968; Aronson and Carlsmith, 1988).

■ The creation of an obedience alibi (Mandel, 1998).

■ The consequences of a situationalist perspective (Berkowitz, 1999).

The ethics of obedience research

Milgram's research into obedience has been criticised for the ethical issues it raised. Two critics of Milgram were Baumrind (1964) and Rosnow (1981), who levelled a number of charges at Milgram's research.

Link

You can refresh your memory about social impact theory by returning to the previous topic on explanations of conformity – see p200.

For more information about independent variables, see p95.

Social psychology

Milgram responded to some of these charges with his own 'defence' although his death in 1983 meant that he was later unable to contribute to the continuing debate regarding the ethics of his research.

The charges against Milgram

It has been argued that the participants were not fully informed about the nature of the study and thus were unable to give their fully informed consent. They were deceived as to the nature of the study and it was made very difficult – if not impossible – for them to withdraw due to the pressure placed upon them. They were put in an extremely stressful situation in which they believed that they may have seriously injured or killed another person. This may have resulted in temporary or permanent psychological damage.

The defence

Milgram responded to these charges by a number of defences. With reference to the issue of consent, Milgram had attempted to gain presumptive consent before the study by asking the psychological community to predict the findings of the study. Most suggested that only one or two in a hundred would go as far as 450V. Milgram has argued that critics of his research would not have given such strong opposition if this had been the actual result. In effect what people object to is not what Milgram did, but what he found.

In response to the issue of coercion, Milgram argued that each person who took part in his experiment was able to accept authority or to reject it and that although it was difficult to withdraw, it was possible. In fact, 35 per cent of the participants were able to stop the experiment and refuse to continue to give the shocks.

With reference to the issue of psychological harm, Milgram argued that his participants were provided with a thorough debriefing at the end of the experiment. They were told that the shocks were not real and were reintroduced to the unharmed 'learner'. Milgram also took steps in the immediate debriefing to ensure that participants' feelings about their behaviour were minimised. Obedient participants were told that their behaviour was normal and that many others had also obeyed. Disobedient participants were told that their behaviour was desirable. In this way Milgram attempted to make all participants feel better about their actions.

In the aftermath of the experiment, Milgram sent out a questionnaire to over 1,000 people who had taken part in his studies. Ninety-two per cent of his participants responded. Of these:

- 84 per cent were either glad or very glad to have taken part
- 15 per cent were neither glad nor sorry to have taken part
- 1.3 per cent were either 'sorry' or 'very sorry' to have taken part
- 74 per cent had learned something of personal importance.

Milgram also argued that he had shown concern for his participants in the longer term. In order to assess potential psychological damage, they were visited and interviewed by an independent psychiatrist one year after the experiment who found no evidence of psychological harm.

However, it could be argued that this was good luck on Milgram's part rather than good management. A series of studies were carried out between 1959 and 1962 by a psychologist called Dr Henry Murray at Harvard University. Some of these attempted to find out which types of people were best able to withstand or resist brainwashing. They involved

> ### Link
>
> You can look at the *Ethical Principles for Conducting Research* from the British Psychological Society on p100. You may wish to consider how research by Milgram, Hofling and others has contradicted some of these ethical principles.

Social psychology

subjecting participants to 'stress tests' in which they were strapped in chairs with electrodes attached to them. One of these participants was a student called Theodore Kaczynski who was later to come to notoriety, nicknamed the 'Unabomber' by the press. Starting in 1978 and continuing for almost 20 years, Kaczynski carried out a series of parcel bomb attacks directed at universities and airlines in the US, killing three and injuring 23 in total. His lawyers argued that his emotional instability resulted in part from his participation in Murray's research. While his later actions may not be attributable to his participation in Murray's experiments, it may be difficult to predict or assess what, if any, damage has been sustained by those who take part in research of this nature.

The validity of obedience research

Others have criticised research into obedience on the grounds of its validity. Aronson and Carlsmith (1988) have argued that the most important problem for social psychology is that of balancing the need for control in experiments against the need for realistic settings. Aronson and Carlsmith distinguished between two types of realism: **experimental** and **mundane realism**.

Aronson and Carlsmith argued that Milgram's research is high in experimental realism but lower in mundane realism. This criticism was made earlier by Orne and Holland (1968) who have argued that Milgram's research lacked both internal and external validity. Orne and Holland argued that the participants in Milgram's study simply did not believe the shocks were real. They also pointed out that participants should have questioned why there was a need for the 'teacher' at all and why the experimenter himself did not administer the shocks if the study was really about punishment and learning.

Milgram responded to these criticisms by referring to the behaviour shown by participants in the film footage of the experiment. This shows clearly the intense signs of stress experienced by the participant as they are shown to tremble, sweat, burst into laughter and stutter. Orne and Holland counter-argued that the participants behaved this way to please the experimenter.

Others such as Rank and Jacobson (1977) have extended these criticisms regarding validity to cover Hofling's research into obedience in nurses. As this was a field experiment, the nurses studied were unlikely to respond with demand characteristics due to their naïvety that the experiment was taking place. However, Rank and Jacobson argued that there were a number of threats to ecological validity in the study.

■ The use of the drug 'Astroten'. This drug was fictional and it was unlikely that experienced nurses would come across a drug they had not heard of.

■ The order coming from the unknown 'Doctor Smith'. Even in a large hospital, nurses would be very likely to work regularly on a specific ward and be familiar by name and in person with the consultants covering the ward.

■ The nurses were phoned when they were alone on the ward. Again this would be unlikely to happen. In a real situation, nurses would be working with at least one other colleague and would be able to discuss an order with their workmates.

Taking this into account, Rank and Jacobson replicated Hofling's study in 1978 making three changes. The fictional drug was replaced with a real drug, Valium, which the nurses were familiar with. A real, named doctor

AQA Examiner's tip

Make sure that you can explain the main ethical criticisms that have been made of Milgram's research.

■ Key terms

Experimental realism: where the participants are fooled into believing that the set-up in the experiment is real and they take the situation seriously. This is also known as internal validity.

Mundane realism: refers to the similarity of the set-up in the experiment to situations that take place outside the laboratory in real life. This is also known as external or ecological validity.

who worked on the ward gave the order by phone and nurses were able to consult with colleagues working on the ward. Under these conditions, those prepared to obey the order fell to a minimal 1/18. These findings imply that there is a need to be cautious when interpreting the results of Hofling's original research.

The obedience alibi

David Mandel (1998) has argued that Milgram's research provides an alibi for those charged with war crimes as it implies that any ordinary person could commit terrible acts under social pressure. This can be seen as providing a justification for their behaviour – that they were just obeying orders. David Mandel has argued that Milgram's research is offensive to people who survived the Holocaust and to those who lost many family members as it underestimates and justifies the brutality to which they were subjected.

Adolf Eichmann was tried for crimes against humanity carried out in Nazi Germany in the Nuremberg trials in 1961. Eichmann insisted throughout his trial that he was simply obeying orders and that he had abdicated his own conscience to follow the *Führerprinzip* (Fuhrer's principles). Eichmann was convicted in December 1961 and sentenced to death. The same 'obedience to orders' defence was used by Lieutenant William Calley who was tried for his part in the My Lai massacre of South Vietnamese villagers in March 1968. Below, you can read an extract from the trial of Lt Calley:

Q. Did you learn anything in those classes of what actually the Geneva Convention covered as far as rules and regulations of warfare are concerned?

A. No, sir. Laws and roles of warfare, sir.

Q. Did you receive any training in any of those places which had to do with obedience to orders?

A. Yes, sir.

Q. What were the nature of the – what were you informed were the principles involved in that field?

A. That all orders were to be assumed legal, that the soldier's job was to carry out any order given to him to the best of his ability.

Q. Did you tell your doctor or inform him anything about what might occur if you disobeyed an order by a senior officer?

A. You could be court-martialled for refusing an order and refusing an order in the face of the enemy, you could be sent to death, sir.

Q. Well, let me ask you this: what I am talking and asking is whether or not you were given any instructions on the necessity for – or whether you were required in any way, shape or form to make a determination of the legality or illegality of an order?

A. No, sir. I was never told that I had the choice, sir.

Q. If you had a doubt about the order, what were you supposed to do?

A. If I had – questioned an order, I was supposed to carry the order out and then come back and make my complaint.

The consequence of a situationalist perspective

A related point has been made by Berkowitz (1999). Both Milgram's and Zimbardo's studies have been interpreted as showing that ordinary people can do extraordinary things to others when placed in a situation where they are under pressure to act in a certain way. Berkowitz has argued that this presents a 'situationalist view of evil' in which vile acts are largely seen as a consequence of the situation in which people are placed, rather than acts of personal choice and responsibility. Berkowitz argues that such accounts simply fail to acknowledge the sadism and horrific acts of torture that took place in concentration camps. He cites extracts taken from Arendt's (1966) book about the trial of 22 SS officers in which it was noted that babies had been used as shooting targets by throwing them in the air. Berkowitz argues that the evil in these acts is not 'banal' but is extreme and bears little resemblance to the shocks given in Milgram's study.

💡 Why do people obey?

We have seen that people may choose to obey or disobey orders given by others. Some psychologists have considered the situational factors that lead people to obey – these are the features of the setting or the environment that influence obedience. For example if someone was to give you an instruction to carry out an action and pointed a gun towards you, it is likely that you (and indeed most people) would obey. Other psychologists have considered whether some types of people (or personalities) are more likely to exhibit higher levels of obedience than others. Personality factors are those characteristics of individuals that make some individuals consistently more obedient than others in a range of different situations. Later in the section we shall consider the factors that lead people to be more likely to defy orders or to disobey (independent behaviour).

Situational factors in obedience

Legitimate authority

An important factor in obedience is legitimate authority. This refers to the amount of social power held by the person who gives the instruction. Most human (and, indeed, many other animal) societies are ordered in a hierarchical way, with some members of the group having legitimate social power to issue instructions to those beneath them in the hierarchy. From early childhood, socialisation in the family and at school teaches us that we are more acceptable if we obey those who have authority over us. We may obey people with legitimate authority because we trust them. Alternatively, we may obey them because they have power to punish us.

The importance of legitimate authority can be seen in three research studies we have considered so far. We have seen in Milgram's experiments how obedience was much higher when the setting was Yale University, a prestigious academic establishment. Participants who carried out the experiment at an office in a district of New York were less likely to be obedient, as the power and authority of the experimenter was diminished by setting the experiment outside the academic context. It is reasonable to assume that the setting influenced the degree of trust participants felt in the experimenter.

In Hofling *et al.*'s 1966 field study, 21 out of 22 nurses were willing to carry out an instruction given by the unknown 'Doctor Smith'. This can be explained by the degree of power and trust invested at that time in hospital doctors. Lesar *et al.* (1997) go so far as to suggest that many drug errors in hospitals can be explained by the tendency of nurses to obey doctors, even when the orders given are extremely dubious. In Bickman's 1974 field experiment in New York, 92 per cent of pedestrians obeyed an order to give a stranger money for a parking meter when the researcher was dressed as a guard, compared to only 49 per cent when the same man was dressed in civilian clothing. In the last two examples, authority figures are immediately recognisable by their uniforms, and these symbols of authority are often enough to produce unquestioning obedience. Those who hold legitimate authority generally have the power to punish, which is another reason why people are more likely to obey them.

The authority figure takes responsibility

In order for an authority figure to be obeyed it is important that they are prepared to take the responsibility for their order and for their subordinates' actions. The importance of this is shown in film evidence and transcripts of Milgram's experiment. Many of his participants had serious reservations about continuing to administer shocks and asked the experimenter if they were personally responsible. When participants were told that the full responsibility was the experimenter's, they continued to obey. If the experimenter had replied that the participant were personally responsible, it is likely that the outcome of this experiment would have been very different.

Milgram explained the importance of responsibility through agency theory. He argued that people operate in two different ways in social situations:

- When they act as autonomous individuals they are aware of the consequences of their actions and choose voluntarily to behave in particular ways.
- In an **agentic state**, the person sees themselves as the agent or subordinate of others. They carry out their orders but do not feel personally responsible for the actions they take.
- The change from an autonomous to an agentic state is known as the agentic shift.

The importance of the agentic state can also be seen in Hofling *et al.*'s 1966 experiment with nurses. In this study the nurses acted in their agentic state as employees of the hospital carrying out orders from 'Dr Smith' rather than as autonomous individuals. Brief, Dukerich and Doran (1991) have argued that organisational obedience – the tendency to obey authority in bureaucratic organisations – may be even greater than Milgram suggested.

Graduated commitment

An important reason why people obeyed in Milgram's original experiment is graduated commitment. This means that in the experiment participants became locked into obedience in small stages. At the start of the experiment participants were asked to give the learner a small shock of 15V. This was increased in 15V increments each time the learner made a mistake. Each action for the participant was a small step beyond the previous action, making it difficult to back out at any time. It is likely that few would have obeyed if Milgram had started the experiment by instructing the participants to give 300V shocks. However, by committing them in small stages, Milgram established a basis for obedience, which made it very difficult for his participants to disobey. The method of

■ **Key term**

Agentic state: a state in which an individual carries out orders of another person acting as their agent with little personal responsibility.

Social psychology

AQA Examiner's tip

Make sure that you can explain the situational reasons why people obey orders.

■ Key terms

Authoritarian personality: a type of person who has extreme respect for authority and who is very obedient to those who have power over them. They may also be hostile to those of lower rank.

Projective tests: involves presenting people with neutral stimuli such as a picture and asking them to describe what is going on. A famous projective test is Rorschach's ink blot test.

■ Hint

You may wish to find out more about the scales developed by Adorno. You can do this by going to www. anesi.com/fscale, where there is a complete copy of the original F scale.

starting with small requests and gradually increasing them is known as the 'foot in the door technique' and is often used as a sales technique. Smith and Mackie (2003) have argued that similar processes take place in real-life crimes of obedience in which people are led in gradual stages from the acceptable into the unthinkable.

Personality factors in obedience

The authoritarian personality

Other psychologists have attempted to establish whether certain types of people are more likely to be obedient than others. Theodore Adorno was a psychologist working in America in the late 1940s and early 1950s along with a group of European psychologists who had fled Nazi persecution in Europe. Adorno argued that the key to understanding extreme obedience and racial prejudice lay in early childhood experiences where personality is formed. He argued that people with an '**authoritarian personality**' have a tendency to be extremely obedient.

Adorno studied over 2000 American students from mainly white, middle-class backgrounds. He interviewed them about their political views and their early childhood experiences. He also used **projective tests** to assess whether or not they were racially prejudiced. Adorno found that people who had been brought up by strict parents who used harsh, physical punishments when they were children often grew up to be very obedient. Under these conditions, children quickly learn to obey and develop a strong respect for authority. Adorno drew on psychodynamic concepts to build his explanation, arguing that harsh and physical punishment led to the child feeling hostile and angry towards their parents. This hostility was uncomfortable for the child and created feelings of conflict, so it might be repressed or locked away into the unconscious mind. The child then displaces these hostile feelings on to others, often of a different racial group, which then become an alternative target for their hostility.

From his research, Adorno developed a number of scales to measure aspects of behaviour and attitudes, including ethnocentricism (the preference for one's own racial group), anti-Semitism (prejudice against Jewish people) and most famously, potential for fascism, which has become known as the 'F scale'. The F scale measures the 'authoritarian personality'.

Although the role of personality and individual differences was played down in Milgram's experiment, Elms and Milgram (cited in Miller, 1986) carried out interviews with a sub-sample of those who had taken part in Milgram's first four experiments. They found that those who were fully obedient and went to 450V scored higher on tests of authoritarianism and lower on scales of social responsibility than those who defied the experimenter, supporting Adorno's claims. We shall be returning to consider personality differences in disobedience in the next chapter.

Table 1 *Sample items from Adorno's F scale adapted from Gross (2001, p369)*

Conventionalism	Obedience and respect for authority are the most important virtues children should learn
Authoritarian aggression	Sex crimes such as rape and attacks on children deserve more than imprisonment: such criminals ought to be publicly whipped or worse
Power and toughness	People can be divided into two distinct classes: the strong and the weak

Fig. 8 *The Rorschach test*

Can these explanations help us to understand real-life obedience atrocities?

Many examples of extreme obedience have taken place throughout history. Some of the most notable include the massacres in My Lai in Vietnam (1968) and at Tiananmen Square in China (1988), in which protesting students were gunned down by tanks. Other reported cases of extreme obedience to military orders have been reported in Bosnia, Kosovo and Rwanda. In this section of the chapter we are going to consider how far the research into obedience can help us to illuminate extreme and sometimes incomprehensible actions.

A study of extreme obedience – the massacre at My Lai (1968)

The massacre of My Lai took place in March 1968 in a village in South Vietnam during the Vietnam War. Unarmed Vietnamese civilians, mostly women and children, were rounded up, herded into a ditch and executed. The US Military were informed that members of the Viet Cong, a resistance group, were hiding in the village of My Lai and that genuine civilians would have left to go to market. When the soldiers searched the village on 16 March they found no insurgents. However, the platoon led by Lt William Calley killed hundreds of civilians by herding them into a ditch. The actual number killed remains unclear with estimates put at between 347 and 504. The memorial at the site of the massacre contains 504 names. In the trial which followed, Calley claimed that he was simply following orders.

> ### ■ Hint
>
> You can find out more about these historical events by using web sources such as Wikipedia.

> ### ■ Link
>
> You can read more about social identity theory in the chapter on explanations of conformity (see p199).

It is unlikely that destructive obedience, such as that seen in the ethnic cleansing policies in Bosnia and Kosovo, the extermination of the Jews in Nazi Germany and the massacre at My Lai in Vietnam can be explained in simple terms. Smith and Mackie (2000) and Cardwell (2001) have argued that we need to consider other important factors if we are to understand and explain cases of extreme obedience in real life:

Social psychology

■ The context of inter-group hostility: we have noted that social identity theory argues that people classify themselves as members of certain social groups (the in-group) and accentuate differences from other 'out-groups' using the meta-contrast principle. Many crimes of obedience have taken place in a history and climate of strong inter-group hostility and conflict such as that between Hutus and Tutsis in Rwanda.

■ The importance of self-justification and blaming the victim: in order for people to carry out acts of extreme violence against others, there is need for the individual to explain and justify their actions to themselves. This is often done by blaming the victim and convincing oneself that they have deserved what has happened to them. Blaming the victim serves important psychological functions, as it allows people to continue to view themselves as decent, responsible people while carrying out their actions. Blaming the victim was evident in Milgram's study where those who administered high levels of shocks would often justify their actions by claiming that the victim 'deserved' such treatment for their stupidity (Milgram, 1974). It has also been evident in Nazi Germany, where the prevailing view was that Jews were responsible for their plight, and more recently in Kosovo.

■ The role of motivational factors: Cardwell (2001) has argued that Milgram's research tells us very little about the extreme obedience seen in Nazi Germany because it ignores the important motivational factors involved. One of these was clearly personal gain. Those who worked in the gas chambers used the opportunity to plunder corpses, removing jewellery and gold fillings from teeth and even cutting the hair of female victims to sell later for wigs.

Key points:

■ Milgram's experiments have shown that obedience is highest when the setting of the experiment is prestigious and the teacher cannot see the learner.

■ Obedience is lowered when teacher and learner are brought into closer proximity or when the power of the teacher is reduced.

■ Field studies have shown that many people will obey an order if given by an authoritative figure in a uniform.

■ Experiments into obedience have been criticised for their ethical issues. Participants have not been asked for informed consent and they have sometimes been subjected to high levels of stress. It is difficult to assess the long-term effects of participation.

■ People are more likely to obey orders when acting in an agentic state than as autonomous individuals.

■ People may become seduced into obedience by small requests that gradually escalate.

■ Those with an authoritarian personality (Adorno) may be particularly susceptible to being obedient.

✔ **Summary questions**

11 Explain what is meant by the terms 'obedience' and 'validity'.

12 Discuss one ethical criticism of research into obedience.

13 How has legitimate power been shown to be important in two experiments into obedience?

14 What kinds of experiences lead to the development of an 'authoritarian personality'?

15 Are field experiments always high in ecological validity? Explain your answer.

Chapter summary

Further reading and weblinks

K. Deaux, F. Dane and L. Wrightsman, *Social Psychology in the 90s*, Brooks/Cole (1993)

M.A. Hogg and G. Vaughan, *Social Psychology*, Pearson Prentice-Hall (2005)

E.R. Smith and D.M. Mackie, *Social Psychology*, Psychology Press (2000)

You may also be interested in the following films, which are relevant to conformity and obedience:

Rebel without a Cause (1955, Nicholas Ray): a classic film starring James Dean, which examines anti-conformity and teenage rebellion

12 Angry Men (1954): Henry Fonda plays a lone juror who convinces other jury members that a young man is innocent in a murder trial

Links

For more information about experimental design, see p109.

For information about summarising data, see pp123–130.

Social psychologists are interested in the reasons why people conform:

- People may comply with a group because they need to belong and to feel accepted.
- Groups also provide norms to regulate the behaviour of those who belong to them.
- Groups can persuade people to accept or internalise their viewpoint when they present consistent arguments and show defecting behaviour.
- Situational factors including legitimate power and graduated commitment are important in producing obedience.
- Early childhood experiences may lead to the development of the authoritarian personality who is extremely obedient.
- The claim of an agentic state has led to the obedience alibi.
- Research into obedience has been criticised for lacking validity and for the ethical issues it presents.
- There is some debate as to how far research into obedience can explain real-life crimes of obedience.

How science works: practical activity

You can investigate conformity yourself using a method similar to that devised by Jenness (1932). Jenness asked people to estimate the number of beans in a bottle when alone and then after a discussion in a group, finding greater consensus in individual estimates after the group discussion.

You could show participants a large transparent jar of beans and ask them to estimate how many there are in the jar. Approach participants individually. Ask half the participants (group 1) to write their estimates on a sheet, which shows written estimates given by other people, providing them with an idea of the possible answer. Ask the other half to write their estimates on a blank sheet. Before collecting your data you should consider ethical issues around consent and debriefing.

Compare the mean estimates of the two groups to see if group one has been influenced by the views of other people. Discuss what your findings show about conformity. Consider the type of conformity shown and relate the findings to other studies.

Things you will need to think about are: what the estimates you will put on the sheets for group 1 as they will have to present reasonable consensus and represent an incorrect answer. What instructions will you give participants? What controls do you need to put in place? How many participants do you need?

If you have already studied research methods for Unit 1 you could use the materials suggested above but design a study to investigate one of the factors that has been shown to affect levels of conformity. Complete an investigation planning form (p104) for the experiment giving detail and justification of the design decisions and the procedure. Think carefully about the hypothesis, how to operationalise the variables, the investigation design, sampling and control of extraneous variables.

When you have collected the data summarise your findings and discuss the findings of your investigation. In your discussion you should consider the methodology and how far the findings support memory theory and studies.

Explanations of independent behaviour

Learning objectives:

- Understand what is meant by the terms 'independent behaviour' and 'counter-conformity'.

- Describe research studies into disobedience.

- Discuss the importance of situational factors in helping people to resist pressures to obey authority.

Key term

Independent behaviour: takes place when the individual does not respond to group norms. Although they can see how others are behaving, they do not pay attention to this and are not influenced by it.

How people resist pressures to conform and to obey authority

The studies by Asch, Milgram and Hofling that we have considered have indicated that many people will conform or obey when put under pressure. However, in each of these studies there have been examples of individuals who have resisted the degree of pressure put upon them to conform or defied orders from authority.

- In Asch's original study of conformity, 24 per cent of people did not conform to the confederates' estimates at any point.

- In Milgram's original experiment, 35 per cent of the 40 male participants disobeyed the experimenter and refused to give the full 450V shocks.

- In Hofling's study, 1/22 nurses resisted the order from Dr Smith to administer 'Astroten' to a patient.

This chapter will examine how and why people are able to resist the pressures to conform or to obey. We shall consider the role of situational factors in disobedience as well as the influence of individual differences on **independent behaviour**, including cognitive factors such as locus of control.

We can distinguish between different types of non-conformity. An important distinction can be made between anti-conformity (also known as counter-conformity) and independent behaviour. Anti- or counter-conformity takes place when the person acts in opposition to rules or group norms. For example, if most male students are wearing their hair short, the anti-conformist will grow theirs long in reaction against this. This behaviour can still be seen as group dependent as the individual's actions are determined by those of the group although they do the opposite to others in the group. In contrast, the truly independent person notices what others are doing but is not influenced by their actions or decisions.

The role of situational factors in disobedience and non-conformity

Many researchers have pointed to the importance of situational factors in disobedience and non-conformity. Milgram's study showed that disobedience could be encouraged when the authority of the experimenter was challenged, for example by carrying out the study in a less prestigious venue. Alternatively, increasing the proximity of the victim by bringing them into the same room or forcing the experimenter to have physical contact with the victim (the 'touch proximity' condition) led to higher disobedience. These findings imply that situational factors may be very important in enabling people to challenge the dictates of authority and the power of groups. In 1982, Gamson and colleagues set out to explore the factors that led to rebellion and disobedience in an ingenious study.

Research study: Gamson, Fireman and Rytina (1982)

Gamson *et al*. wished to set up a situation in which participants were encouraged to rebel against an unjust authority. The researchers placed an advert in the local papers in a town in Michigan, US, asking for volunteers to take part in a paid group discussion on 'standards of behaviour in the community'. Those who responded were asked to attend a group discussion at a local Holiday Inn. When they arrived they were put into groups of nine and met by a consultant from a fictional human relations company called Manufacturers Human Relations Consultants (MHRC). The young man explained that MHRC was conducting research for an oil company, which was taking legal action against a petrol station manager. They argued that the manager had been sacked because his lifestyle was offensive to the local community. In contrast, the manager argued that he had been sacked for speaking out on local television against high petrol prices.

Participants were asked to take part in a group dicussion about the sacking, and this was filmed. As the discussion unfolded, it became apparent that the participants' own views were irrelevant and that the HR company wanted them to argue in favour of the sacking. At a number of points during the discussion, the cameraman stopped filming and instructed different members of the group to argue in favour of the oil company's decision to sack the manager. Finally, the participants were asked to sign a consent form allowing the film to be shown in a court case.

Of the 33 groups tested by Gamson, 32 rebelled in some way during the group discussion. In 25 out of the 33 groups the majority of group members refused to sign the consent form allowing the film to be used in court. Nine groups even threatened legal action against MHRC. Rebellion against authority in this context involved challenging two well-established social norms in the situation, the norm of obedience and the norm of commitment, both of which participants had engaged in by agreeing to take part in the study.

Methodological issues

■ Gamson's research had a high level of realism. While the situation itself was rather unusual, participants' behaviour was likely to be free from demand characteristics as they were unaware they were participating in a research study.

■ It was difficult to separate the many factors that may have led to disobedience in this study. Rebellion could have been influenced by a number of factors including the high costs involved of being seen to lie on film in court as well as the group nature of the decision. Both of these are likely to have contributed to the high levels of disobedience shown.

Ethical issues

A number of ethical issues were involved in this study. Participants were deceived as to the nature of the exercise and did not give their fully informed consent. In addition, the experience was exceedingly stressful for those who took part.

Link

You can read more about the ethical principles governing psychological research on p100.

Why did people disobey in Gamson's study?

Smith and Mackie (2000) have identified three key factors, which may have led to disobedience in Gamson's study.

■ The importance of a group: a group of people who share a similar view can be used against an authority figure to present an alternative consensus of the correct way to behave. In Gamson's study, the participants established a strong group identity in which the members agreed that the demands of authority were unreasonable. This could be seen by the way in which they addressed the HR coordinator saying that 'we don't want to go on record, even pretending that we agree with what we're saying. We don't. All three of us feel the same way' (cited in Smith and Mackie, 2000, p409). It is unlikely that the same participants would have felt able to deny authority if they had been alone.

■ Reactance: this is the response of individuals to attempts to limit their freedom of choice. Many people will react against unjust attempts to make them do something by doing the opposite. In Gamson's study participants rebelled against attempts to control their behaviour.

■ Systematic processing: rebellion is more likely when people are able to take time to think carefully about what they are being asked to do. In Gamson's study, participants had sufficient time to consider their actions.

Key points:

■ Psychologists have investigated situational factors in conformity, obedience and disobedience.

■ Disobedience is easier when people are in a group and construct alternative group norms to resist authority.

■ Reactance may take place when people feel their freedom of choice is restricted.

✓ Summary questions

1 Explain one difference between counter-conformity and independent behaviour.

2 Outline two situational factors that can produce disobedience.

3 Explain how psychologists have investigated disobedience. How far does research in this area help us to understand real-life disobedience?

Individual differences in independent behaviour

Learning objectives:

- Understand the influence of individual differences on independent behaviour.

- Explain the importance of cognitive style including locus of control.

- Design a correlational study to test the relationship between locus of control and conformity.

Hint

You might like to watch the film *Schindler's List* (Spielberg, 1993) or read Thomas Keneally's Booker Prize-winning novel *Schindler's Ark* on which the film is based. This story is based on the real life of Oskar Schindler, a member of the Nazi party who saved the lives of more than 1,100 Jews during the Holocaust.

Key term

Locus of control: refers to the sense of control people have over the successes, failures and events in their lives. Locus of control is measured on a scale. Those with a high internal locus of control largely feel that their actions are their own choice and responsibility. Those with a high external locus of control see their actions as resulting largely from factors outside their control such as luck or fate.

Personality characteristics

Early psychological research set out to compare the personality characteristics of those who conformed, with the characteristics of those who chose to remain independent in studies of conformity. Crutchfield (1955) argued that conformers tended to have lower self esteem in comparison to non-conformers. In addition they tended to be less intelligent and had a higher need for social approval whereas non-conformers generally tended to be more self-confident with leadership abilities.

Other researchers set out to investigate the personality characteristics of those individuals who have been found to be disobedient to authority. Oliner and Oliner (1988, cited in Blass, 1991) used an interview method to study two groups of non-Jewish people who had lived through the Holocaust in Nazi Germany. They compared 406 people who had protected and rescued Jews from the Nazis with 126 who had not done this. Oliner and Oliner found that the 'rescuers' scored higher on measures of social responsibility and had scores demonstrating an internal **locus of control**. Elms and Milgram (1974, cited in Miller, 1986) set out to investigate the background of disobedient participants by following up and interviewing a sub-sample of those involved in the first four of Milgram's experiments. In agreement with Oliner and Oliner, they also found that disobedient participants scored higher on a social responsibility scale and had a high internal locus of control. From these studies, it appears that these two characteristics – social responsibility and locus of control – may be important factors in an individual's ability to disobey orders or to defy social norms.

Locus of control

The concept of the locus of control was put forward by Julian Rotter in 1966. Rotter argued that we can measure an individual's sense of personal control over events in their life using a scale. At one end of the scale are those with a strong internal locus of control who largely believe that they can influence events in their life. In contrast, those with an external locus of control believe that outside factors such as luck, fate or 'the stars' strongly influence what happens in their life. The individual with an internal locus of control who receives promotion at work is likely to feel this is due to hard work whereas the person with an external locus of control may think their boss was simply in a good mood that day or that their luck is in as Venus has moved into Mercury!

Studies into locus of control and conformity have yielded some interesting results. In an early experiment, Williams and Warchal (1981) studied 30 university students who were given a range of conformity tasks based on Asch's experimental paradigm. Each student was also assessed using Rotter's locus of control scale. Williams found that those who conformed the most were significantly less assertive but did not score differently on the locus of control scale, implying that assertion may be more important than locus of control to conformity. More recently, Avtgis (1998) carried out a meta-analysis of studies, which considered locus of control and conformity, and found that those who scored higher on external locus of control were more easily persuaded

Social psychology

Table 1 *Sample items from Rotter's (1966) locus of control scale (adapted from BPS Manual of Psychology Practicals)*

Item	Agree very much	Agree somewhat	Agree slightly	Disagree slightly	Disagree somewhat	Disagree very much
By taking an active part in political or social affairs people can control world events.						
Who gets to be the boss depends on who was lucky enough to be in the right place.						
The world is run by a few people in power and there is not much the little guy can do about it.						
What happens to me is my own doing.						
Most people don't realise the extent to which their lives are controlled by accidental happenings.						

and likely to conform that than those with a low score. The average correlation between the locus of control and conformity was 0.37 which was statistically significant. This suggests that there are genuinely higher rates of conformity in 'externals' than 'internals'.

■ Developing independent behaviour

Other researchers have asked the question 'Can independent behaviour be fostered or encouraged?' Nemeth and Chiles (1988), two American researchers, have carried out a series of intriguing studies to see if participants can be influenced to become more independent. Using a similar method to Moscovici's blue–green slide experiment, 48 male participants were exposed to two attempts to alter their views. In the first part of this experiment, participants were placed in groups of five (made up of four naïve participants and a confederate) and asked to judge the colour of a series of blue slides. Nemeth and Chiles created four conditions using consistent and inconsistent confederates who called either all or some of the blue slides 'green' as Moscovici had used.

In the second part of the experiment, the same participants returned to the laboratory and carried out another 'colour perception task' using red slides. In this condition they were exposed to four confederates forming a majority of the group of five, who called all the red slides 'orange'. What did Nemeth and Chiles find? Those who had been exposed to a minority in the first part of the experiment and who gave a different answer were significantly more likely to stand their ground in the second part and call the slides 'red' defying the power of the majority group. While this study suffers from many of the criticisms that can be made of laboratory experiments, it strongly implies that exposure to a model of independent behaviour can influence the individual's ability to stand firm against the majority and resist group pressure.

Key points:

- Psychologists have investigated personality factors in conformity, obedience and disobedience.

- Those who defied the Nazi regime tended to have higher levels of social responsibility.

- Those who score highly on an internal locus of control scale (ILC) are less likely to conform or obey than those with an external locus of control (ELC).

✓ Summary questions

4 Explain what is meant by locus of control.

5 Outline findings of research into locus of control and conformity.

6 'Some people are naturally disobedient.' How far does research support the view that disobedience results from personality characteristics rather than situational factors?

Using and abusing social psychology

Learning objectives:

- Explain how research into social influence has been used in both positive and negative ways.

- Understand the processes by which minority groups can increase their status through social change.

- Know about the misuse of social influence research including false confessions, indoctrination and 'thought reform' in China.

Key term

Social change: the term given to the range of strategies used by groups to improve their social status.

Social psychology has told us a great deal about the processes involved in social influence. Every day attempts are made by others to influence us using education, persuasion and occasionally brute force. Social influence can operate on a personal level when friends try to influence us into behaving in certain ways. Social forces can also operate on a wider level when companies try to persuade us to buy products through TV and magazine advertising or when governments try to channel our behaviour, for example towards safe drinking or safe sex. In this chapter we shall consider the ways in which psychological knowledge has been used for both positive and negative social outcomes. We will start off by examining ways in which groups can improve their status via social change and finally we shall consider how social psychological knowledge can be misapplied for social control.

Improving group status through the process of social change

Protest marches, campaigns, strikes, legal battles ... these are all familiar tactics that can be used by minority groups in order to address inequalities and discrimination. The previous chapter discussed the processes by which minorities come to influence and change the views of those belonging to majority groups. In this chapter we shall examine the ways in which minority groups exert pressure and produce **social change**.

We have seen earlier (see p199) that Tajfel wished to understand the processes that led people to conform to groups they belonged to, which acted as 'reference groups'. As well as his interest in the relationships between groups and their members, Tajfel was also interested in the relationships between social groups, especially those that may lead groups into conflict.

Fig. 1 *The power of peaceful protest*

Fig. 2 *The Countryside Alliance march attracted large numbers of protesters*

In social identity theory (SIT) Tajfel argued that people identify themselves as belonging to particular social categories (such as male and Asian) and they differentiate their own group from others in an 'us and them' way. For example, Celtic fans may accentuate the differences between themselves and Rangers supporters, maximising differences between them. Tajfel argued that people wish to achieve or maintain a positive social identity and that this is largely based on their membership of specific social groups. If the social identity or status of the group they belong to is unsatisfactory and is seen by others in a generally negative light (for example, the often negative portrayal of asylum seekers in the British press in the first decade of the twenty-first century), then they can attempt to increase their status using **social change.** Hogg and Vaughan (2000, p411) define social change as the idea that 'a lower status individual can improve their social identity by challenging the legitimacy of the higher status group's position'.

The individual who belongs to a lower status social group has two main choices: social mobility and social action. Social mobility involves the individual attempting to leave their own social group and join a group that has higher social status. This is often seen as the most legitimate strategy in the Western democratic world where group boundaries are relatively permeable. For example, a young asylum seeker may seek to achieve positive social status by training for a professional job and becoming a lawyer or doctor. By migrating to a higher status group, a more positive social identity can be achieved.

An alternative strategy involves trying to improve the status of the existing group to which the individual belongs through the process of social action. This is often the only available strategy in cultures where group boundaries are inflexible, for example in India where the caste system makes it difficult to move to a different social group. It is also the strategy used by group members who have a strong emotional attachment to their group. The status of the group can be improved in a number of ways including the following:

■ Social creativity: this takes place when the group attempts to redefine their attributes in a way that makes them have a positive value.

A study by Lemaine (1974) involved young French boys attending a summer camp. Divided into teams, the boys took part in a hut building competition. One group who were provided with inferior materials and were unable to compete on equal terms used social creativity and created a beautiful garden around their hut, thus allowing themselves to 'win' on their terms. Real-life examples of social creativity include the 'black is beautiful' campaign, which took place during the 1960s and 1970s and led to a positive redefinition of black characteristics including skin colour, language and cultural heritage. A more recent example can be seen in the change of status of indigenous peoples such as Maoris in New Zealand.

■ Social competition: this takes place when a minority group enters into direct competition with the powerful majority group and takes **social action** to improve the power, status and position of their own group and challenge the social conditions that disadvantage them. Examples of this can be seen in radical feminist and gay and lesbian organisations that have systematically campaigned for equal rights in the workplace and in civil law, for example campaigning for civil marriages and for an end to discrimination. Groups representing disabled people such as the Coalition of Disabled People have systematically campaigned for a redefinition of disability, for example through events such as the Paralympics. Social competition may produce conflict between groups, which is an inevitable part of how societies develop.

Key term

Social action: takes place when a minority group campaigns for equal rights and challenges the existing power base in society.

Interrogation and false confessions

Social psychological knowledge can be used for social control as well as social change. As we have seen in studies of conformity, uncertainty leads to people being particularly vulnerable to the influence of others around them. These findings have been used by those who interview suspects and to encourage confessions. In an ingenious experiment to examine the process of false confession, Kassin and Kiechel (1996) carried out a study using college students who were asked to compete in pairs in a 'reaction time' test. Their task was to type letters on a keyboard at a fast speed and they were warned not to touch the ALT key at any time as the computer would crash and important data would be lost. The computers were set to crash after a time interval and participants were accused of pressing the ALT key. Under these highly pressured conditions, a massive 69 per cent were prepared to sign a confession document even though they had not touched the key. In subsequent interviews, 28 per cent had convinced themselves that they had actually done the deed.

If false confessions can be produced in such artificial conditions, then it is very likely that under real pressure of interview, many innocent suspects may end up confessing to crimes they have not carried out. Smith and Mackie (2000) have argued that police use a range of techniques on suspects in order to present them with a version of events and reality that they may eventually come to accept.

Thought reform

The term 'thought reform' has been used to refer to the techniques that were used in China from the 1920s onwards to change people's political views and beliefs to accept the new communist regime. These techniques have been written of by many of those who were subjected to them. One such writer is Jung Chang whose novel *Wild Swans* considered the experience of three generations of a family in China during this period.

Social psychology

Another writer on this subject was Lifton (1957) who wrote about the processes used by the 'revolutionary colleges', which were set up in China in the 1940s. Students who attended these colleges took part in a three-stage indoctrination programme to change their beliefs and views and become positive towards the new communist regime.

■ During the first stage, students would join a small discussion group of about ten people in which they would be encouraged to discuss their own views and hear others talking of their hatred of the old regime in China. They would also be given lectures on the new ideologies. This would target their ideas at the intellectual level.

■ In the second stage, the techniques used became personal and emotional. Considerable pressure was put on students to adopt and show the 'correct' views. Those who did not comply were singled out, threatened and publicly humiliated.

■ In the third stage the student was made to prepare a 'confession' of between 5,000 and 25,000 words, which was read out to the study group renouncing their old beliefs and embracing the new communist ideologies.

Social influence techniques have also been applied to the indoctrination of prisoners of war. Indoctrination attempts were carried out on around 21,000 United Nations soldiers captured by the Chinese during the Korean War in the 1950s. A range of techniques was used to 'convert' their political views to embrace communism (Brown, 1996). When men entered the camps they were surprised to find that they were viewed by the guards as 'political students' with the guards seeing themselves as 'tutors'. Prisoners were isolated from the outside world, contact with families and news was cut off, and their treatment by guards and their physical survival depended on how well they could convince the guards that they had embraced the ideals of communism. Despite their conversions, few prisoners actually chose to stay and embrace the communist regime at the end of the war. Some of these soldiers were interviewed on release to assess their condition and the extent of their brainwashing. There were wide individual differences in the ability to resist the attempts to brainwash them. Those who were most resistant to persuasion were the 'bloody-minded' and those who had strong beliefs or religious convictions (Brown, 1996).

Key points:

■ Attempts to influence and persuade are made every day.

■ Social change takes place when minority groups use social creativity and competition to improve their status.

■ Social control takes place when pressure is applied through interrogation and brainwashing techniques to coerce people into changing their views.

✓ **Summary questions**

7 Explain what is meant by social action and social change.

8 Outline two strategies that can be used by minority groups to improve their social status.

9 When are minority groups more likely to use social action rather than social mobility to improve their social position?

10 Discuss the view that social psychological research can be used and abused.

Social psychology

Chapter summary

Further reading and weblinks

The film *Schindler's List* (1993, Spielberg) tells the story of Oskar Schindler, a member of the Nazi party who saved the lives of over 1,100 Jews during the Holocaust.

The film *In the Name of the Father* (1993) examines the case of the Guildford Four, incorrectly charged with the bombing of a pub in Guildford during the IRA campaign of the 1970s. Interrogation techniques are portrayed at length in this film.

J. Chang, *Wild Swans*, HarperCollins (1991)

If you are interested in the (mis)applications of social influence research you might like to read *War on the Mind: the military uses and abuses of psychology* (Watson, 1980)

Links

For information about pilot studies, see p106.

For information about scattergrams, see p130.

For information about correlation, see p116.

- There are individual differences between people in their tendency to conform and obey.
- Those with an internal locus of control may be more likely to challenge authority.
- Social change can be used by groups to improve their status via social creativity and social competition.
- Social psychology can also be used to influence and control individuals.

How science works: practical activity

This correlational activity focuses on the relationship between locus of control and obedience. Previous research has suggested that individuals with a strong internal locus of control are less likely to obey than those with an external locus of control. In order to assess the possible relationship, you will need to devise some way of measuring these two variables. Use the internet or your library to find and print a locus of control scale. To measure obedience, devise a list of between five and ten situations in which people are given orders that they can obey or disobey – for example, being asked to turn an MP3 player down by fellow passengers on the train or to pick up a cola can in the school playground. Ask a sample of people to complete both scales and record their scores. Before collecting your data you should consider ethical issues around consent and debriefing. You will need to think about constructing your scales, devising standardised instructions and deciding which scale should be given to participants first. It would be a good idea to pilot your scales and if necessary amend them. When you have collected the data, plot your results using a scattergram to assess the relationship. Discuss your findings and outline your conclusions.

In your discussion you should consider the methodology and how far the findings support or challenge the findings of published research and consider the implications of these findings.

If you have already studied research methods in Unit 1, you should complete an investigation planning form for the experiment giving detail and justification of the design decisions and the procedure. Think carefully about: the hypothesis, how to operationalise the variables remembering that for a correlational study we do not distinguish the independent and dependent variable, sampling, control of extraneous variables.

Social psychology

Question 1

1   Individual differences have been shown to exert an influence on independent behaviour.

(a)   Explain what is meant by locus of control.   *(4 marks)*

(b)   Explain how locus of control can influence independent behaviour.   *(4 marks)*

2   Stanley Milgram performed various experiments into obedience. Data from some of these experiments are plotted on the graph below.

Outline two things that the data in the graph seems to indicate about why people obey.   *(4 marks)*

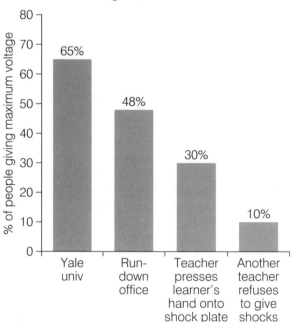

Fig. 1

3   Discuss explanations of why people conform.   *(12 marks)*

Question 2

1   Two of the following are descriptions of types of conformity.

[A] Publicly conforming to views of others, but maintaining one's own private views.

[B] Movement neither away from nor towards a group norm.

[C] True conversion of public and private views to match those of a group. These views are not dependent on group membership.

(a)   In the table below, write down which example A, B or C matches each type of conformity listed in the table.   *(2 marks)*

Type of conformity	Example
Internalisation	
Compliance	

(b)   Outline a real-life example of:

(i)   internalisation   *(2 marks)*

(ii) compliance   *(2 marks)*

AQA
Examiner's tip   Question 2, part 1(b) asks for real-life examples. Ensure your examples are relevant, concise and clearly expressed.

2   Many investigations into conformity have raised the ethical issue of deception.

(a)   Explain why deception is an ethical issue.   *(2 marks)*

(b)   Outline a strategy for dealing with this ethical issue.   *(2 marks)*

3   Lachlan, a manager in a large company, has a problem managing employees in the storage department. Although most employees obey his instructions those in the storage department frequently do not. When he gives orders face to face they generally obey, but when he sends instructions via e-mail employees in the storage department often don't follow his orders. He has also noticed that when he moves employees from other departments into the storage department they quickly fall into the pattern of not obeying instructions.

(a)   Explain one factor that may be contributing to employees not obeying Lachlan's orders.   *(2 marks)*

(b)   Outline ways in which Lachlan could increase obedience levels among employees in the storage department.   *(6 marks)*

4   (a)   What is meant by social influence?   *(2 marks)*

(b)   Explain what social influence research can tell us about social change.   *(4 marks)*

AQA
Examiner's tip   For Question 2, part 4, you need to use the knowledge you have gained from social influence research and apply it to a wide range of examples of social change.

Individual differences – psychopathology (abnormality)

Introduction

Besides studying normal behaviour, psychologists have always been interested in psychopathology, also commonly referred to as 'abnormality'. The field of abnormal psychology has expanded rapidly over the last 40 years for a variety of reasons. The first is that scientific research is helping us understand the biological aspects of many psychopathologies. Secondly, society has become more aware of psychopathologies; disorders such as anxiety and depression are becoming more common, while others, such as eating disorders feature prominently in the media.

This growing public awareness is reinforced by various bodies such as drug companies and alternative therapists claiming to be able to 'cure' these conditions. There is therefore a great deal of potential confusion in the public's awareness of psychopathology. One of the aims of psychology in relation to psychopathology is to provide a systematic and objective approach to this complex area.

▇ Problems in the study of psychopathology

Whatever approach we take to psychopathology there are central problems that need to be solved, the first and most obvious one being how to define 'abnormal behaviour'? This may seem obvious for some of the more severe conditions such as schizophrenia where people may hear voices and behave in a bizarre fashion but even with schizophrenia there can be disagreements over the diagnosis. Other conditions such as depression and anxiety are experienced to some extent by everybody, so we then have to decide when the condition becomes serious enough to be classified as an abnormality. So we begin this chapter with a review of some different definitions of abnormality. We will refer to the diagnostic systems used by psychiatrists to show how they have incorporated different ways of looking at abnormality.

The next problem is how to explain abnormal behaviour. We will be highlighting the differences between the biological, psychodynamic, behavioural and cognitive approaches used to explain behaviour.

Finally, we have to decide how to treat it. There is a very close relationship between approaches used to explain abnormality and the therapies that we use. Chapter 13 reviews the different therapies associated with each approach.

In theory a wide variety of therapies is available. Which one is most appropriate? A sensible approach would be to use the one that works best, so the last section of Chapter 13 reviews the effectiveness of different types of therapy.

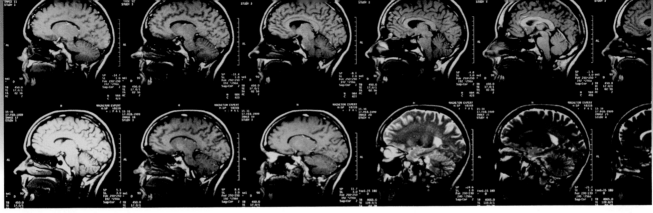

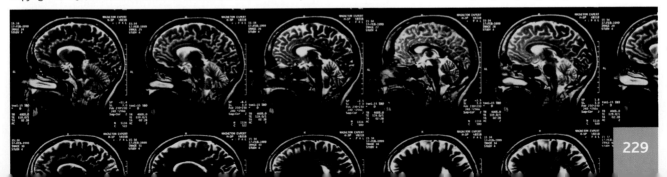

Individual differences

Defining and explaining psychological abnormality

Definitions of abnormality

⚡ ✓

Learning objectives:

- To develop knowledge and understanding of three definitions of abnormality.

- To be able to outline at least two limitations associated with each of these definitions.

- To understand in outline approaches to modern psychiatric diagnosis.

Key terms

Anti-psychiatry: this was a movement associated with Szasz and Laing that rejected the medical model of psychopathology. Instead they proposed that people had 'problems with living' rather than psychological disorders.

Psychosis: this refers to a state when the individual appears to have lost contact with reality. It occurs in disorders such as schizophrenia and bipolar depression. The individual does not have insight into their condition.

■ Introduction

Psychopathology, also referred to as psychological abnormalities or disorders, has fascinated people since recorded history began. Behaviours resembling contemporary conditions such as schizophrenia, severe depression and phobias can be identified in the earliest stories recorded. The history of psychiatry (the study and treatment of psychological disorders) is beyond the scope of this text, but we should note that the modern era emerged from the nineteenth-century technological and scientific revolution. This began a more objective assessment of disorders and how they might be treated, although some of the ideas and therapies that first emerged seem to us today bizarre and highly unethical.

Through the twentieth century a variety of different approaches attempted to explain and treat disorders. Although the aim was theoretically to help the individual, some so-called scientific treatments, such as psychosurgery and electroconvulsive therapy (see pp250–251), still have major ethical drawbacks.

The starting point for any model of abnormality was to establish that abnormality existed. An extreme position, championed by **anti-psychiatrists** such as Thomas Szasz (1972) and Ronald Laing (Laing and Esterson, 1964), was that there is no such thing as 'abnormality', only 'problems with living'. Abnormal behaviour was seen in some cases to be a sane reaction to an insane world, and psychiatry was seen as a political tool to label and control 'difficult' people. Their alternative suggestion was that the legal system should be used to control violent or antisocial behaviour, but that otherwise people should not be forced to undergo psychiatric diagnosis and treatment.

Most people would see this position as too extreme. Where people suffer complete detachment from reality, as in **psychosis**, or become a danger to themselves or others, or are themselves utterly distressed by their condition, it seems a key part of a civilised society to offer what help is available.

Before looking at some of the main issues we must first be clear on the role of psychology in relation to people with psychological disorders. In the UK drug treatment of conditions can only be authorised by medically trained doctors and psychiatrists. A psychiatrist is a person who has completed their medical training and then specialised in psychopathology. They tend to deal with the more severe conditions such as schizophrenia, major depression and personality disorders. However if you go to your GP with mild anxiety or depression, they may prescribe drug therapy if they feel it is appropriate.

Psychologists who work with psychological disorders may only use psychological therapies. These clinical psychologists have completed a psychology degree and then specialised in the study of psychological disorders. The sorts of therapies they might use range from relatively simple behavioural techniques to psychoanalytic methods based on the ideas of Freud and his successors.

There is no doubt that there are still major issues in the diagnosis and treatment of abnormality (see further reading at the end of this chapter), but equally many people have been helped through application of the approaches and therapies outlined in this topic. Before looking at these, we need to consider some general definitions of how we might identify abnormal behaviour.

Case study

Jenny is 23. After doing well at school she went to university to study law, hoping eventually to become a solicitor. When she first went to university she was a sociable and outgoing personality. In her first year, however, her older brother, who had always suffered from periods of severe depression, tried to commit suicide after a marriage break-up, and her favourite grandmother died after a long illness. Jenny gradually became more withdrawn. She had difficulty sleeping and would take long walks across the university campus at night. She lost weight and stopped seeing her friends, eventually not leaving her room for days at a time. She watched daytime TV for hours without any apparent interest or pleasure. Her work inevitably suffered. Coursework was never completed, and she missed her first year examinations. Alerted by her friends and her tutor at university, Jenny's parents, greatly distressed by her condition, eventually overcame her resistance and persuaded her to contact the university's counselling service.

As we review some definitions of abnormality, try to apply them to the case study above.

■ Deviation from social norms (DSN)

Every society has commonly accepted standards of behaviour. Sometimes these are written and form the set of laws that govern behaviour. Sometimes these norms of behaviour are unwritten but generally accepted; examples might include the British habit of queuing in shops and at ticket offices or not standing too close to people when you are talking to them. You can immediately see that these social norms of behaviour vary between different cultures. In some countries queuing is uncommon, while in conversation people may stand closer than someone from the UK would find comfortable. We will return to the cultural aspect later.

Whether written into the legal system or what we call implicit, i.e. generally accepted but not legally binding, social norms allow for the regulation of normal social behaviour. One approach to defining abnormality, therefore, is to consider deviations from social norms as an indication of abnormality. In many cases this can be clear cut, such as the patient with **schizophrenia** who reports hearing voices, or the person with **obsessive-compulsive disorder** who washes their hands 50 times a day. So this definition can provide an indication of disordered behaviour. However there are clear limitations with this approach:

■ Behaviour that deviates from social norms is not always a sign of psychopathology. Eccentricity for instance might involve avoiding the cracks in the pavements, but this is a mild superstition and not in itself a form of psychopathology. Or you may see someone in a full diving suit staggering along the pavement; this looks like a deviation from social norms, but then you realise they are taking part in a charity walk. This also emphasises the importance of taking the context of behaviour into account.

■ As social norms reflect the beliefs of a society they also have a political dimension. For instance in some countries dissidents, that

■ Key terms

Schizophrenia: this is a complex disorder. Some people with schizophrenia will have hallucinations (such as hearing voices) and delusions (e.g. paranoid delusions, where they feel persecuted by others). These are referred to as positive symptoms. Others become inactive and show little in the way of behaviour or emotional responsiveness. These are referred to as negative symptoms. People can show a mix of positive and negative symptoms.

Obsessive-compulsive disorder: this is a disorder where people have obsessive thoughts that constantly run through their minds (an example would be ruminations, where this same thought repeats over and over again). Along with obsessive thoughts they will also have compulsive behaviours, such as frequent hand washing or checking that the gas has been turned off.

Individual differences

231

is people who disagree with the ruling party, might be classified as schizophrenic and locked up in psychiatric hospitals. In terms of deviation from social norms, this looks justified, but of course only in a society that does not accept a range of different political opinions as part of their social norms. In these cases this definition is being used as a means of political control.

■ Social norms vary over time. Homosexuality was included in the American classification system for psychiatric disorders up until the 1960s. Since then attitudes have changed and homosexuality is no longer seen as a psychopathology. This means that the DSN does not provide an absolute definition of abnormality, but is era-dependent.

■ The legal system assumes that people have control over their own behaviour, therefore those convicted of crimes are not usually considered mentally ill. So deviating from social norms by committing illegal acts need not always involve psychopathology. However an interesting development in this area is the idea that some violent offenders may have brain abnormalities that mean they are not responsible for their actions. In this case you might argue that they are showing a genuine form of psychopathology.

■ **Cultural relativity** is a key issue in relation to the DSN definition. Social norms by their very definition are specific to a particular culture or society, so a behaviour seen as a deviation in one society may appear quite acceptable in another and vice versa. Walking around Nottingham city centre naked would be seen as a deviation from our social norms, but walking around the Amazonian rainforest in a three-piece suit would be a deviation from the social norms of Amazonian Indians.

■ Failure to function adequately (FFA)

This definition of abnormality focuses on the everyday behaviour of an individual. Conventionally we wake up in the morning, get dressed, go to work. As adults we may have a family to support and relationships to maintain. When someone deviates from this normal pattern of behaviour we might argue that they are failing to function adequately. Common examples would be severe depression, which leads to apathy and inertia, meaning that the depressed person may fail even to get up in the morning, let alone hold down a job. The condition may well affect their relationships and family life. Such a change from their normal pattern of behaviour would be a clear sign of psychopathology. We should note however that failing to function adequately is a general sign of disorder, and not itself specific to any condition. The **agoraphobic**, afraid to leave their house, or the schizophrenic patient with **paranoid delusions** that make them avoid their family are both failing to function adequately.

Rosenhan and Seligman (1989) have suggested some characteristics of abnormal behaviour that are related to the FFA definition. Examples include the following:

■ Observer discomfort, where another's behaviour causes discomfort and distress to the observer.

■ Unpredictability; we rely on the behaviour of people around us being predictable. FFA can involve behaviour that is unpredictable and sometimes uncontrolled.

■ Irrationality; we can usually interpret the behaviour of others as being entirely rational. FFA can involve behaviours that look irrational and hard to understand.

■ Key term

Cultural relativity: the idea that some aspects of psychology vary from culture to culture. So patterns of infant attachment might vary across different cultures, and definitions of abnormality such as DSN are certainly culture-specific.

AQA Examiner's tip

To cover DSN well, don't forget to be clear on what is meant by social norms; have an example or two to quote to demonstrate your understanding.

■ Key terms

Agoraphobia: a disorder where the person is fearful of open spaces to the extent that it interferes with everyday life.

Paranoid delusions: a thought disorder that is sometimes seen in schizophrenia and personality disorders, where the individual feels persecuted by those around them.

Individual differences

- Maladaptiveness; this characteristic is central to the FFA definition of abnormality. It refers to behaviour that interferes with a person's usual daily routine.

However, the FFA approach in general has limitations:

- In similar fashion to the DSN definition, behaviour that looks like FFA may instead represent normal behaviour, depending on the context. Some political prisoners go on hunger strike as part of their political protest. Although starving yourself is technically unpredictable, irrational and maladaptive, this example of failing to function adequately is understandable in this particular context.
- Failing to function adequately may simply not be linked to psychological disorder. Holding down a job and supporting a family may be impossible due to economic conditions. This may be particularly the case in subcultures such as immigrant communities. Prejudice and discrimination may prevent such people finding jobs and developing careers.
- The opposite also applies, in that psychological disorders may not prevent a person from functioning adequately. People often maintain adequate function in the face of clinical levels of anxiety and depression, and others with personality disorders related to **psychopathy** can appear perfectly normal most of the time.
- There is a cultural dimension to FFA. Standard patterns of behaviour will vary from culture to culture, so failing to function adequately may look very different depending upon which culture you are in. However there may be aspects in common although details may vary; in any culture people need to earn their livelihood and raise children and failing to carry out these functions would satisfy the FFA definition.

■ Deviation from ideal mental health (DIMH)

This definition stands out by not defining abnormality directly, but instead attempting to define a state of ideal mental health. Deviation from these ideals would then be defined as abnormality. Jahoda introduced the first systematic approach in 1958, listing a number of characteristics she felt indicated ideal mental health. These are listed below (Vaillant, 2003):

- an individual should be in touch with their own identity and feelings
- they should be resistant to stress
- they should be focused on the future and **self-actualisation**
- they should function as **autonomous** individuals, recognising their own needs and with an accurate perception of reality
- they should show **empathy** and understanding towards others.

As we shall see there are clear limitations to this approach. However it has one important characteristic in that it emphasises a positive attitude to human behaviour and experience. Using the DIMH we should not simply aim for an absence of psychopathology but instead try to improve ourselves. The DIMH therefore has value as a general and positive approach to defining normality. However as a means of defining abnormality it has severe limitations:

- The characteristics listed by Jahoda are rooted in Western societies and a Western view of personal growth and achievement. In non-Western collectivist cultures concepts such as autonomy and self-actualisation would not be recognised, and the individual would instead follow collectivist goals. This cultural relativity severely limits the scope of DIMH.

■ Key terms

Psychopathy: a term used to refer to an apparent lack of empathy and understanding of others. People with high levels of psychopathy exploit others with no guilt or remorse.

Self-actualisation: this refers to our motivation to achieve our full potential as individuals.

Autonomy: the ability to function as an independent person, taking responsibility for one's own actions.

Empathy: the ability to put yourself in another's shoes and seeing the world from their point of view. It is thought to be a basic requirement for social communication.

■ Hint

The best way to demonstrate understanding for any of the definitions of abnormality is to use examples effectively, linked to a particular definition. For instance, schizophrenia can be used to illustrate all these definitions.

AQA Examiner's tip

If you cover DIMH in an examination, outlining and showing your understanding of two or three of Jahoda's criteria will earn more marks than simply listing all of them.

Individual differences

■ As its name implies, DIMH represents deviation from an ideal state. Very few people would match the criteria laid down by Jahoda and so by definition the majority of the population would be classified as abnormal. It is also unclear how far a person could deviate before being defined as abnormal.

■ Defining and classifying psychopathology – DSM-IVR and ICD-10

Defining behaviour as abnormal is only the first stage in classifying psychopathology. The three definitions we have looked at can give some indication that abnormality exists, but each has limitations and none is entirely satisfactory. Looking back at the case study on p231 we can see that Jenny's behaviour represents a deviation from social norms, that she is failing to function adequately and that she is deviating from ideal mental health. Where do we go from there?

The dominant approach to psychopathology is the biological or medical model. We look at this in detail later, but the important point in relation to defining abnormality is that it uses the model of physical illness (the **disease model**) and applies it to psychological disorders. This approach has several elements:

■ Abnormality is associated with certain signs or symptoms. These may be reported by the person concerned (always referred to as the 'patient' in the disease model) or observed by family, friends or the doctor/psychiatrist.

■ Signs and symptoms that regularly occur together are referred to as **syndromes**. So depression, for instance, is a syndrome characterised by a depressed mood, apathy, sleeping problems, etc. Schizophrenia is another syndrome, in this case associated with hallucinations and delusions.

■ The disease model assumes that the various syndromes represent distinctive disorders that can be considered independently of one another. It then tries to develop explanations and treatments for each separate disorder.

There are two widely used systems in psychiatry for defining and classifying psychopathology into separate syndromes. The International Statistical Classification of Diseases (ICD) is used mainly in Europe, while the American-based Diagnostic and Statistical Manual of Mental Disorders (DSM) has a more international usage. Both follow the approach of categorising different disorders, but differ in some particulars. They have also evolved over the years with changes in approaches to defining and classifying psychopathology. At present we have the tenth version of ICD (ICD-10) and the revised fourth version of DSM (DSM-IVR). Both systems categorise disorders on the basis of signs and symptoms, with over 150 currently recognised.

The DSM-IVR system also uses elements of the definitions we reviewed earlier. After using signs and symptoms to identify the particular syndrome, DSM-IVR also takes into account social and environmental problems that might influence the disorder. Finally it uses a **global assessment of functioning scale** to rate the impact of the disorder on the patient's daily life; this is closely related to the deviation from social norms and failure to function adequately approaches discussed earlier. However it is important to note that this global rating is secondary to the main aim of identifying the disorder through signs and symptoms.

■ Key terms

Disease model: this is the idea that psychological disorders can be seen as similar to physical illnesses and diseases. Each disorder has its own distinct symptoms and is separate from all others. However, it is likely that psychological disorders will often overlap with each other.

Syndrome: a cluster of physical or psychological symptoms that regularly occur together is referred to as a specific syndrome.

DSM-IVR: the *Diagnostic and Statistical Manual of Mental Disorders*. A system used by psychiatrists to diagnose and classify psychological disorders.

Global assessment of functioning scale: one of the scales used in the DSM-IVR system. It assesses the impact of the disorder on the individual's everyday life. In this sense it has elements of the FFA definition of abnormality.

There are a variety of issues with this medical disease model of psychopathology, both practical and ethical:

■ Although identifying specific syndromes sounds objective and straightforward, in fact there can be significant disagreements between psychiatrists. Hallucinations and delusions can indicate schizophrenia, but they sometimes occur in association with bipolar disorder and can also be caused by infections of the brain. Anxiety and depression often occur together and can be hard to disentangle.

■ The medical model of psychopathology emphasises the biological aspects of disorders. Although DSM-IVR takes some account of social and economic factors, the possible role of psychological factors in causing psychopathology is minimised.

■ One ethical issue is that treating the individual as a patient in the medical sense has the advantage of taking away any blame for their condition; they are not responsible for their disorder.

■ However, labelling a person as schizophrenic, for instance, is likely to **stigmatise** them. Society on the whole has little understanding of mental illness and people tend to avoid those with serious disorders. Labelling patients is a serious ethical issue for the medical model.

Key points:

■ DSN, FFA and DIMH definitions of abnormality each represent different views of abnormality, focusing on social norms, ability to function in society and an ideal state of mental health respectively.

■ Each definition emphasises important criteria for assessing normal and abnormal behaviour.

■ Each in turn has limitations, and all are culturally specific.

■ These definitions do not allow specific syndromes to be identified. This is done using psychiatric classification systems such as DSM-IVR. In DSM-IVR the global assessment of functioning scale includes elements of DSN and FFA.

✔ Summary questions

1 Outline key features of the three definitions of abnormality and explain one strength and one weakness of each.

2 With reference to the case study on p231, identify aspects of each definition in Jenny's behaviour.

3 Discuss the purpose of defining abnormality.

■ **Key term**

Stigmatise: to identify and treat people in a more negative way because of particular characteristics, illnesses or psychological disorders.

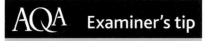 **Examiner's tip**

DSM-IVR and ICD-10 are not listed in the specification and you cannot be asked direct questions about them. However they are closely linked to definitions and discussion of abnormality. Broader knowledge and wider reading in any area will always lead to higher marks when used effectively, as it demonstrates clear understanding.

Individual differences

235

Biological and psychological approaches to psychopathology

Learning objectives:

- To develop knowledge and understanding of four major approaches to psychopathology.

- To understand key differences in the assumptions made by the four approaches.

- To be able to evaluate each approach in terms of strengths and weaknesses.

Key terms

Cognitions: this term refers to the cognitive processes underlying behaviour. It can include attention, perception and memory, and more complex thought processes such as reflection and problem solving.

Cognitive neuroscience: this is an area of research that investigates the brain mechanisms underlying cognitive processes such as perception, language and memory.

Introduction

As outlined in the introduction to this chapter, psychology uses a variety of very different approaches, each of which makes certain assumptions about the causes of normal and abnormal behaviour (psychopathology). Other subjects such as physics and biology reflect a single, general approach that all physicists and biologists would follow. Psychology is very different in that different approaches each have their supporters, and you can even find considerable tension between the followers of different approaches.

One reason for this complexity is that human behaviour itself is very complicated. This seems obvious from everyday experience – just think about all your thoughts and emotions and how the person you are now has developed, not just during your childhood but right from the start of embryonic development. Consider for a moment all the possible influences on development. There could be a genetic component inherited from your parents. Development in the uterus would depend on the supply of nutrients from your mother. From birth onwards there will be a range of experiences and environmental influences that could affect the child's physical and psychological development.

The problem for psychology is trying to disentangle all of these potential influences. Naturally, different types of psychologist will focus on different aspects of behaviour or influences. Those who follow the biological approach will concentrate on biological factors such as genetics and neurotransmitters in the brain. A cognitive psychologist is more interested in the thought processes (**cognitions**) underlying behaviour; they follow an information processing approach based very much on computer models. The behavioural approach assumes that learning experiences are critical in understanding normal and disordered behaviour. Finally the psychodynamic approach is based on the belief that early experience and unconscious processes are the key influences on behaviour.

Of course the different approaches need not be mutually exclusive. For instance, one of the most rapidly developing areas in psychology is **cognitive neuroscience**. Cognitive behavioural therapy, which we will look at later, represents a combination of the cognitive and behavioural approaches.

Finally an obvious question would be: which approach is the right one? Frankly, even after 100 years of psychology we still cannot say which approach is 'right'. However the application of these different approaches to an understanding of psychopathology does provide one way of comparing them. Do they provide convincing accounts of disorders such as schizophrenia and depression, and do they lead to effective treatments?

The biological approach

The biological approach in psychology studies the relationship between behaviour and the body's various physiological systems. The most important of these is the nervous system, especially the brain. The outline structure and functioning of the brain was discussed in Chapter 8, p142. The brain is the focus for most biological psychologists as it is the processing centre controlling all complex behaviour. This means that in theory all behaviour, normal and disordered, can be related to changes in brain activity.

In addition, over the last 20 years the study of brain and behaviour has been revolutionised by the increasing use of brain scanners; these enable us to study brain structure and function in living people, including those with conditions such as schizophrenia, depression and obsessive-compulsive disorder.

Assumptions of the biological approach

- As all behaviour is associated with changes in brain function, psychopathology will be caused by changes in either the structure or function of the brain. This might involve changes, for example, in the relative size of brain structures, or in the activity of brain neurotransmitters and hormones.

- The development of the body, including the brain, is heavily influenced by genetics, and biological psychologists tend to assume that most behaviours, normal and disordered, involve a component inherited from the biological parents. So they are very much on the nature side of the **nature–nurture debate.**

However there is a most important distinction to be drawn between biological and genetic. Many people assume that they are pretty well equivalent, so that if you find that depression, for instance, is linked to low levels of the brain neurotransmitter serotonin then depression is likely to be a genetic or inherited condition. But this is not necessarily so. Brain activity is affected by all sorts of factors, including our environment and our experiences. For instance, isolating monkeys from their social group leads to reduced activity of brain serotonin (Watson *et al.*, 1998) and also to a state that looks very much like depression. Life stress is also strongly linked to depression, showing clearly that depression is associated with low levels of serotonin but can simultaneously be caused by non-genetic factors.

To spell this out, as it is a crucial point, everyday experiences can affect brain chemistry, and this in turn can lead to psychopathologies such as depression. So, while depression is associated with reduced brain serotonin activity and therefore a biological cause, the reduction can be caused by environmental factors and is not necessarily genetic. Similar arguments can be applied to all normal and disordered behaviour.

Evaluation of the biological approach

The biological approach is currently the dominant approach in studying and treating psychopathology. Diagnosing and treating psychopathology is dominated by psychiatrists, who qualify as medical doctors before specialising in psychiatry. They try to apply the medical model of physical illness to psychological disorders, identifying biological aspects of a disorder and using physical treatments, usually drugs, to treat it. This approach has both strengths and weaknesses:

- Use of brain scanning and other modern techniques has identified biological aspects of many psychopathologies. Depression, for instance, seems to be associated with lowered levels of brain serotonin, while schizophrenia has been linked to overactivity of the neurotransmitter dopamine. In addition, scans have revealed that some patients with schizophrenia appear to have brain pathology, i.e. loss of tissue in some areas of the brain.

Link

To find out more about the organisation of the brain, see pp142-144.

Neurotransmitters and their action at the synapse are discussed on p140.

Key term

Nature–nurture debate: for at least the last century psychologists have argued over whether behaviour is influenced more by our genetic inheritance (nature) or by environmental factors such as upbringing and socialization (nurture).

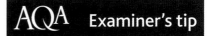

AQA Examiner's tip

If you are uneasy about biology, there is no need to go into great detail on the brain and nervous system. Just be clear on the outline assumptions of the biological approach: the nature–nurture debate and the possible role of genetics; changes in brain structure; and neurotransmitter activity. Remember at this level understanding the principles is the first step, followed by clear understanding of one or two examples of how the approach has been used.

Individual differences

■ Key terms

Bipolar disorder: formally known as manic depression, this is a psychological disorder characterised by swings between episodes of depression and episodes of mania (overactivity).

Reductionism: this is the attempt to explain behaviour by reducing it to the smallest possible elements. There are many types of reductionism but biological reductionism is the most common. This involves the assumption that biological changes in the brain can provide a complete explanation for behaviour.

Diathesis-stress: this refers to a model that explains behaviour through an interaction between nature and nurture. For example, a vulnerability to depression is inherited, but the condition is only triggered if severe life stress is encountered.

Psychodynamic: approaches to understanding behaviour that emphasise the balance between conscious and unconscious processes, and the significance of early development.

Repression: one of Freud's most important defence mechanisms. Material that is too threatening to be dealt with consciously is repressed into the unconscious.

■ Research into behavioural genetics has identified a genetic, or inherited, component in many psychopathologies, such as schizophrenia, **bipolar disorder** and some phobias.

■ Drug treatment, based on the biological or medical model, targets the biological bases of disorders and can be very effective in conditions such as depression, schizophrenia and anxiety disorders.

So a wealth of scientific evidence has been produced to support the biological approach, and this is its greatest strength. There are also some problems:

■ The approach is heavily **reductionist**. This means that it assumes that the most important aspect of any behavioural disorder is the biological changes in the brain, rather than looking more generally at the behaviour, symptoms and environmental influences. For instance we know that depression is linked to low serotonin levels, but we also know that these can be caused by environmental stresses. A full picture requires a study of both biology and environmental influences.

■ Although a genetic component has been identified in many disorders, in no case does this component provide a complete explanation. So even where there is evidence for a genetic influence, it is assumed that this must interact with non-genetic environmental factors. A popular choice for the environmental factor is stress, and the hypothesis that some disorders involve a genetic vulnerability triggered by stress is known as **diathesis-stress**.

■ Although drug treatments can provide support for the biological approach, they are never effective for all people with a particular condition. In fact for some conditions, such as phobias and eating disorders, drugs are largely ineffective.

■ The psychodynamic approach

The **psychodynamic** approach assumes that adult behaviour reflects complex dynamic interactions between conscious and unconscious processes, many of which have their origins in development from birth onwards. There are a number of different psychodynamic approaches, but all have their origins in the pioneering work of Sigmund Freud.

Freud was born in 1856 and spent virtually all of his working life in Vienna. He left Vienna after the Nazi take-over in 1938 and died a year later in London. Freud originally trained in medicine focusing on clinical neurology, but he was then heavily influenced by the work of Joseph Breuer, who was using hypnosis to treat 'hysterical reactions' in female patients. Struck by the emergence of apparently **repressed** material during hypnosis, Freud then devoted his career to the investigation of the human mind and its development. In particular he was interested in the interaction between conscious and unconscious processes.

Freud referred to his approach as psychoanalytic, and it has formed the basis of most subsequent psychodynamic approaches to understanding behaviour. The two key elements in Freud's work on abnormality were his model of human personality and his detailed theory of psychosexual development in childhood.

The structure of personality

Freud proposed that personality is made up of three interacting elements:

■ The id: this is the reservoir of unconscious and instinctual psychic energy that we are born with. The most important aspect of this psychic energy is the **libido** or life instincts, but this energy may also be directed into aggression. The id operates on the pleasure principle and constantly tries to gratify these instincts through sex and other forms of pleasurable activity, but may also lead to aggression and violence.

■ The ego: this represents our conscious self. It develops during early childhood and regulates interactions with our immediate environment. It also tries to balance the demands of the id for self-gratification with the moral rules imposed by the superego or conscience. The ego operates on the **reality principle**, in that it constantly balances the demands of the real world against the instinctive drives of the id.

■ The superego: this is our personal moral authority, or conscience. It develops later in childhood through identification with one or other parent, at which point the child **internalises** the moral rules and social norms of society.

If the ego fails to balance the demands of the id and superego, conflicts may arise and psychological disorders may result. Dominance of id impulses may lead to destructive tendencies, pleasurable acts and uninhibited sexual behaviour. If the morality of the superego dominates, the individual may be unable to experience any form of pleasurable gratification.

As the id is present from birth while the ego and superego develop through the early childhood years, such conflicts are particularly likely at this time when the ego is undeveloped, hence Freud's focus on the early years as the source of adult disorders. It is also important to remember that we are not conscious of these underlying dynamics and conflicts.

One important consequence of **intra-psychic** conflict between id, ego and superego is anxiety. In order to protect itself against this, the ego tries to maintain its balancing act in relation to id and superego. To do this an important role is played by what Freud called **ego defence mechanisms**. Some examples are given in Table 1.

> ### Key terms
>
> **Libido:** sexual energy, a major component of the instinctual energy of the id.
>
> **Reality principle:** the ego operates on the reality principle, trying to balance id and superego in the face of the demands of the real world.
>
> **Internalisation:** a process by which the child takes in the moral attitudes of the parent, which then make up his or her superego.
>
> **Intra-psychic:** in Freud's model, the psyche, or mind, is made up of id, ego and superego. Conflict between these components (i.e. intra-psychic) can lead to anxiety.
>
> **Ego defence mechanisms:** these protect our conscious self from the anxiety produced by intra-psychic conflict.

Table 1 *Defence mechanisms*

Defence mechanism	Description
Repression	This is the most significant of the defence mechanisms. Threatening impulses are repressed into the unconscious. They do not disappear but the individual is unaware of them. However such repressed conflicts can eventually emerge as symptoms of anxiety or other emotional disorders.
Displacement	Displacement occurs when an unacceptable drive such as hatred is displaced from its primary target to a more acceptable target. For instance, hatred towards your mother is socially unacceptable so the child displaces it, for instance, on to a brother or sister.
Denial	Denial occurs when an individual, child or adult, refuses to accept that a particular event has happened. For instance the surviving partner of a long and happy marriage may continue to act as though their husband or wife was still alive.

Erogenous zones: in Freud's theory the instinctual energy of the id is focused on different parts of the body (the erogenous zones) at different psychosexual stages.

Fixated: in Freud's theory of psychosexual stages, failure to resolve one of the stages may lead to fixation at that stage. The characteristics of, e.g. the oral stage, may then show themselves in adult behaviour such as smoking.

Oedipus complex: during the phallic stage of psychosexual development boys develop love for their mother, leading to fear of the father. To resolve this fear the boy identifies with the father, leading to development of the superego or conscience. Its name is derived from the mythical Greek character Oedipus, who ended up killing his father and marrying his mother.

Electra complex: the equivalent in girls to the Oedipus complex in boys. It is less detailed in Freud's theory than the Oedipus complex, leading to criticism of the phallocentric nature of Freud's work. It was named after the mythological Greek character Electra, who encouraged her brother to murder their mother.

There are a number of other ego defence mechanisms and one of the aims of psychodynamic therapy is to break through these defences to reveal the underlying conflicts. Defence mechanisms protect our conscious self from the anxiety produced by unconscious intra-psychic conflict. If they are unsuccessful this anxiety may reveal itself through clinical disorders such as phobias and generalised anxiety.

Psychosexual development

The other key element in Freud's psychoanalytic theory of normal and abnormal behaviour is psychosexual development. According to the theory the child goes through a series of stages where the instinctive energy of the id looks for gratification in different bodily areas: the so-called **erogenous zones**. If the developing child is either deprived or over-gratified at a particular stage they may become **fixated** at this stage and this will have effects on their adult behaviour. The stages are outlined below:

Oral stage

This lasts from birth to about 18 months. Id impulses are satisfied by feeding, and so the mouth is the focus of this stage. Activities include sucking initially, and then, as teeth develop, biting. Fixation at this stage may produce an adult gaining pleasure from oral gratification through activities such as smoking, drinking or eating. As this stage also involves complete dependency of the infant, the fixated adult may also show overdependence in their relationships.

Anal stage

From 18 months to about three years of age, gratification focuses on the anus. Key activities revolve around retaining and expelling faeces. This is a significant stage in Freudian theory as for the first time the child can exert some control over its environment. He or she can show obedience or disobedience by expelling or retaining faeces. Fixation at this stage may lead to an obsession with hygiene and cleanliness, and perhaps obsessive-compulsive disorder.

Phallic stage

After the anal stage comes the phallic stage, which lasts until age four or five, where the focus is on the genitals and gratification comes through genital stimulation. This is a key stage in sexual development as gender differences are noticed and psychosexual development differs between the sexes. The most important feature of this stage is the **Oedipus complex.** Freud developed this concept in relation to boys, proposing that their sexual curiosity and close physical contact with the mother leads to intense affection and desire for the mother. This leads the boy to see his father as a rival, and this in turn produces a fear of losing his father's love and even of castration. To cope with these conflicting feelings the boy identifies with the father, and in the process absorbs or internalises his father's moral attitudes; this is the foundation of the superego.

A justified criticism of Freud is that his theory is heavily phallocentric, i.e. focused very much on the male, and this is particularly evident in his treatment of the Oedipus conflict. The equivalent in girls, the **Electra complex**, lacks detail and is almost an afterthought. Freud proposed that in the phallic stage the girl realises she has no penis. This produces a state of penis envy, and although up to that time she has been closer to the mother penis envy leads her to develop more affection for the father.

Latency period

During the period from four or five up to puberty psychosexual development enters a latent period, to re-emerge at puberty. At puberty, sexual feelings become less focused on the self and instead are directed at potential partners.

Evaluation of the psychodynamic approach

■ Freud's psychoanalytic theory was the first to emphasise the significance of unconscious processes and repressed material influencing our behaviour. This is now widely accepted, with many studies on the effects of, for instance, childhood sexual abuse on adult psychopathology. Repression of such traumatic experiences may reveal itself in adult anxiety and depression. Eating disorders have also been linked to childhood sexual abuse.

■ He was also the first to suggest how our adult behaviour could be influenced by early childhood experiences. This approach is supported by the work of Ainsworth, for instance, on early attachment styles and later adult relationships (see p58).

■ Freud overemphasised infantile sexuality to the exclusion of other aspects of development. He assumed that later psychological disorders could be caused by problems with early psychosexual development. Later psychodynamic approaches placed less emphasis on this aspect.

■ Freud did not study children directly, but developed his theory largely on the basis of case studies with adults who came to him with **neurotic disorders**. Freud then linked these disorders to their early experiences.

■ The fundamental concepts of Freudian psychoanalytic theory, such as the id, and defence mechanisms such as repression, are almost impossible to test using conventional scientific methodology. This does not mean that they are wrong, but does leave a great deal of room for speculation and differing opinions. Freud himself constantly refined and developed his ideas, and even today some of his classic case studies of psychological disorders are subject to reinterpretation (Tolpin, 1993).

■ Freud's theory of normal and abnormal behaviour was developed in the late nineteenth and early twentieth centuries in Vienna. Aspects of it are clearly related to this historical and cultural period, for instance its phallocentric nature. However it has heavily influenced other major psychodynamic figures such as Jung and Adler, and contemporary psychodynamic approaches. Many of his ideas and concepts, such as repression, fixation, denial, etc. have passed into everyday language, and have been used in relation to adult psychopathology. Regardless of whether you believe in the detail of his approach, he remains one of the most influential psychologists of all time.

■ The behavioural approach

This approach to psychopathology emphasises the role of learning and experience in causing psychological disorders. Behavourists deal with three main forms of learning: classical conditioning, operant conditioning and social learning.

Classical conditioning

This is one of the simplest forms of learning studied originally by Pavlov (1927) using dogs and the natural salivation response to the presence of food. By pairing the sound of a bell with the presentation of food he

---

AQA Examiner's tip

Freud's theory is extremely complicated and it is easy to become lost in all the ideas. Try to understand the outline of the theory of personality and the role of unconscious processes, and the stages of psychosexual development. Don't forget that this section focuses on abnormality, so you need some examples of how Freud's theory can be related to examples of psychological disorders. Evaluation of Freud's theory should also be set in the context of abnormality.

■ Key term

Neurotic disorders: now largely discarded, this term refers to disorders such as anxiety and depression where the person has insight into their condition. It is contrasted with psychotic disorders such as schizophrenia, where insight is lost.

■ Link

See the introduction to the research methods chapters (p86) for an outline of the scientific method.

■ Key terms

Classical conditioning: the association of conditioned and unconditioned stimuli through repeated paired presentations. It was first demonstrated by Pavlov using the salivation response in dogs, and pairing food (unconditioned stimulus) with a bell (conditioned stimulus). Classical conditioning involves automatic reflexive responses.

Stimulus generalisation: a phenomenon in which a response to one stimulus can be elicited by a similar stimulus. Little Albert's fear response to the rat generalised to other furry objects.

Preparedness: Seligman introduced the idea that our evolutionary history has 'prepared' us to be more fearful of biologically significant stimuli such as spiders and heights.

Operant conditioning: the work of Thorndike and Skinner originally demonstrated how voluntary responses could be controlled through positive reinforcement (rewards), negative reinforcement and punishment.

■ Link

See p121 for a discussion of the strengths and weaknesses of case studies.

eventually could stimulate salivation merely by sounding the bell. He had associated or conditioned the stimulus of the bell to the response of salivation.

Classical conditioning involves unconditioned (natural) responses or reflexes. Although it seems a long way from complex human behaviour it does appear to have a role in some forms of psychopathology.

■ Research study: Watson and Rayner (1920)

In one of the most celebrated if unethical studies in psychology, Watson and Rayner (1920) classically conditioned an 11-month-old child, since known as Little Albert, to fear fluffy animals. They did this by pairing presentation of a tame white rat with a sudden loud noise. The noise caused fear, an unconditioned reflex equivalent to salivation in Pavlov's experiment, while the rat was the equivalent of the bell. Eventually Albert was conditioned to associate the rat with fear. Little Albert also became afraid of other fluffy objects similar to the white rat such as a rabbit and white dog; this is known as **stimulus generalisation.**

Methodological issues

We should also note that this was a single case study and there was no systematic and objective measure of any signs of 'fear'; instead Watson and Rayner relied on general verbal descriptions.

Ethical issues

Besides the serious ethical issue of scaring a young child and causing psychological harm, Watson and Rayner did not de-condition Little Albert as his mother, with Watson and Rayner's knowledge, removed him from the research programme.

In this way classical conditioning has been used to account for the development of phobias. Phobias are characterised by extreme fear of certain objects or situations. Examples include fear of heights and enclosed spaces, or of spiders and snakes. One simple explanation of phobias is that a traumatic experience, especially early in life, leads to the conditioning of fear to that particular object or situation. This fear then generalises to similar objects or situations. This leads to the adult having a general phobia of, say, all spiders or all enclosed spaces.

Although classical conditioning provided an explanation for the development of phobias it soon became clear that many people with phobias had not actually experienced traumatic encounters with, for instance, spiders or enclosed spaces. This led Seligman (1971) to propose the concept of **preparedness**. Preparedness is the idea that our evolutionary history has prepared humans to be sensitive to biologically-relevant stimuli such as dangerous animals and situations. So even today we are more likely to be phobic of spiders than, for example, tulips. In fact Ohman *et al.* (2000) have shown experimentally that fear in human participants can be conditioned to pictures of spiders but not to pictures of flowers.

Operant conditioning

Skinner (1974) was the major figure in the development of the theory of **operant conditioning**. He demonstrated in rats and pigeons that voluntary or controlled responses such as pressing bars and pecking coloured discs could be learned if the behaviour was rewarded. Although it sounds simple Skinner was able to show how quite complex patterns of behaviour could be learned or modified by suitable patterns or **schedules of reinforcement.**

Skinner proposed that operant conditioning through rewards and punishment (punishment leads to inhibition or reduction of behaviour) was fundamental in human development. As adults, normal and disordered behaviour are shaped by years of conditioning.

Before evaluating the role of operant conditioning in psychopathology we must first look at an extension of Skinner's approach: social learning theory.

Social learning theory

Social learning theory was developed by Albert Bandura and others in the 1960s; they extended the idea of operant conditioning by demonstrating that human participants could learn by watching human models who were rewarded for particular behaviours. This learning by observing another's actions and their consequences is known as **vicarious learning**. People will tend to imitate models that are rewarded but will not imitate models that are punished.

The combination of operant conditioning and social learning through vicarious reward can explain much of normal human behaviour. However the application of these processes to explaining psychopathology is less obvious. Disorders such as schizophrenia, for instance, do not appear to have an obvious learning component. However, social learning explanations can be applied in areas such as eating disorders; these are found mainly in young women, and one popular hypothesis is that observation and imitation of slim models and film stars plays an important role.

Although it can be difficult to explain the causes of many disorders, it is easier to see how operant conditioning can contribute to their persistence. One effect of disorders such as depression or anorexia nervosa is that they attract attention from family and friends. If this attention and concern is rewarding then the behaviour itself is reinforced and more likely to continue.

Evaluation of the behavioural approach

- The behavioural approach can provide convincing explanations of some psychological disorders, including the role of classical conditioning in phobias and social learning in eating disorders. However for many people with phobias of, for instance, spiders, there is little evidence for early fearful encounters that might lead to classical conditioning of fear to the spider. Seligman's concept of 'preparedness' suggests that, through evolution, we are more likely to develop phobias to biologically significant stimuli.
- As we shall see later, treatments based on the behavioural approach can be effective in some disorders, such as simple phobias.
- The behavioural approach is reductionist in that it explains behaviour in terms of relatively simple learning principles. It ignores cognitive and emotional contributions to the development of psychopathology.
- The pure behavioural approach explains all behaviour through learning experiences (nurture) and has no role for any genetic contribution (nature).

■ Key terms

Schedules of reinforcement: in operant conditioning the pattern of rewards and punishments can be used to 'shape' behaviour. Continuous reinforcement is when every response is rewarded and leads to rapid learning. However the response rapidly fades or extinguishes when reinforcement is withdrawn. Occasional rewards (intermittent schedules) lead to slower learning, but the behaviour persists for longer when reinforcement is withdrawn. Gambling is an example of the power of intermittent reward schedules.

Social learning theory: based largely on Bandura's work, this is an extension of conditioning theory that focuses on learning through observation and imitation of others. Vicarious learning and reinforcement are key components of social learning theory.

Vicarious learning: this is an important part of social learning theory, and refers to learning through observing the consequences of behaviour in others. Observed behaviour that is reinforced is more likely to be imitated.

AQA Examiner's tip

A consistent problem students can have with the behavioural approach is to demonstrate their understanding by distinguishing between classical and operant conditioning. Remember that classical conditioning involves automatic reflexive responses such as salivation and fear, while operant refers to voluntary controlled behaviour.

■ Key terms

Cognitive approach: in relation to abnormality, the cognitive approach emphasises the role of cognitive processes (beliefs, thoughts, perceptions) in causing psychological disorders.

Schemata: organised systems of knowledge that we use to understand and interpret the world.

Negative automatic thoughts (NATs): in the cognitive approach to depression negative schemata lead to NATs. Examples of NATs include cognitive biases such as minimisation and selective abstraction.

Cognitive biases: in the cognitive approach to abnormality biases are irrational and maladaptive thoughts that can lead to depression. They include the tendencies to maximise failures and minimise successes.

■ The behavioural approach is heavily deterministic, viewing human behaviour as simply a product of stimuli, rewards and punishments. There is no role for conscious choice.

■ The cognitive approach

Over the last 20 years the **cognitive approach** (often referred to as the cognitive-behavioural approach) has become perhaps the most popular of the psychological approaches to understanding and treating behavioural disorders. It is unusual in that it uses elements derived from other approaches.

Pioneers of the cognitive approach, such as Aaron Beck (1963) and Albert Ellis (1962), were heavily influenced by their backgrounds as therapists. Disappointed in what they saw as the ineffectiveness of psychodynamic and humanistic approaches, they were also influenced by the behavioural approach (see above) and the cognitive revolution in psychology that occurred in the 1960s.

Up to about 1960 psychology was dominated by the behavioural approach of Skinner, with an emphasis on observed behaviour. Cognitive processes such as attention, perception and thought were largely ignored by experimental psychologists. Then during the 1960s the pendulum swung towards these critical cognitive processes. It was fuelled by the development of computers as information processors, providing a model of how the human brain might work.

While acknowledging the success of therapies based on the behavioural approach in treating some psychological disorders, Beck and Ellis were concerned that little attention was paid to underlying cognitive processes. Therefore they developed the cognitive approach to abnormality as a combination of behaviourism (e.g. the role of conditioning principles in changing behaviour) and cognitive models of psychopathology. The approach makes several basic assumptions:

■ Human behaviour is heavily influenced by **schemata**. Many of these schemata relate to how we see ourselves, for instance, 'I am confident and self-assertive', 'I am good at relationships', 'I am generally a happy person'.

■ Schemata develop on the basis of early experience. Traumatic or unhappy experiences early in life may lead to the development of negative schemata, e.g. insecure attachment may lead to the schemata of 'I am not loved and will always be alone', while early failure at school may produce the schemata of 'I will always be unsuccessful'.

■ Negative schemata, or core beliefs as they are sometimes called, when activated lead to **negative automatic thoughts** (or NATs). In the cognitive approach negative automatic thoughts are misplaced and dysfunctional; no one need always be alone, no one is unsuccessful at everything.

Negative automatic thoughts are unconscious and rapid responses to certain situations. They can be identified in the **cognitive biases** that depressed people apply when they interpret situations. These biases prevent the person focusing on the positive side of life and so reinforce their negative views. Some examples of these biases can be seen in Table 2.

Table 2 *Examples of cognitive biases that may be used by depressed people*

Cognitive bias	Explanation
Minimisation	The bias towards minimising success in life. For instance attributing an excellent exam result to luck on the day.
Maximisation	The bias towards maximising the importance of even trivial failures. For instance failing to complete a difficult sudoku puzzle as a sign of general stupidity.
Selective abstraction	A bias towards focusing on only the negative aspects of life and ignoring the wider picture.
All or nothing thinking	A tendency to see life in terms of black and white and ignoring the middle ground; you are a success or a failure, rather than not good at some things but OK at others.

One of the clearest examples of the cognitive approach to psychopathology is Beck's (1979) model of depression. This involves three negative schemata:

■ Negative view of the self, i.e. I am incompetent and undeserving.

■ Negative view of the world, i.e. it is a hostile place.

■ Negative view of the future, i.e. problems will not disappear; there will always be emotional pain.

Beck refers to these as the **negative triad**, and they can also be seen in the attributions that depressed people make. Attributions refer to our interpretations of why things happen. There are three dimensions:

■ Attributions can be internal or external, i.e. the cause is seen as internal to the person ('it's my fault') or due to external circumstances.

■ Attributions can be specific or global, i.e. the cause may be specific to a particular event or apply to all events.

■ Finally attributions can be stable or unstable, i.e. the individual consistently makes the same types of attribution, or they can vary over time and situation.

In the cognitive model of depression attributions or interpretations of negative events are internal, global and stable. In contrast attributions in depression for positive events tend to be external, specific and unstable.

> ■ **Key term**
>
> **Negative triad:** in Beck's model of depression, the negative triad of cognitive biases are pessimistic thoughts about the self, the world and the future.

Ellis's ABC model

This model is similar to Beck's approach. Ellis considers that activating events (A) in an individual's life have consequences (C) such as feelings and actions. However these consequences are affected by beliefs (B) about these events. Rational beliefs are likely to be confirmed by events, and even negative events will lead to appropriate negative emotions such as mild regret, sadness or irritation. Irrational beliefs, such as 'I must always be excellent at everything', can lead to inappropriate negative emotions such as guilt, anxiety and depression when things go wrong.

Beliefs are an important cognitive component in how we see the world, and can be affected by the same cognitive biases that are central to Beck's model.

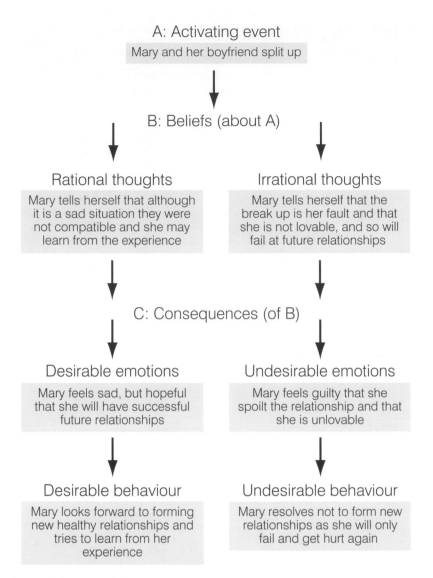

Fig. 1 *Ellis's ABC model*

Evaluation of the cognitive model

- There is clear evidence for cognitive biases and dysfunctional thinking and beliefs in depression and anxiety disorders. For instance, in panic disorder the individual may exaggerate the significance of anxiety symptoms such as raised heart rate (Clark, 1986).

- Therapy based on the cognitive model can be very effective for anxiety disorders and depression.

- The idea of schemata and how they develop is rather vague and lacking detail. Similarly it is not always clear how irrational thoughts should be defined and measured.

- The cognitive approach takes no account of biological or genetic factors in psychopathology. However it does emphasise the important role of cognitive factors in psychological disorders.

- In some cases disorders such as depression may lead to dysfunctional thinking rather than the other way round; i.e. depression may encourage a focus on the negative aspects of life and the future.

AQA Examiner's tip

The cognitive approach can seem complicated, but if you concentrate initially on Beck's model and understand the role of cognitive biases in maintaining depression then you have the basic elements. Make sure you understand and are able to outline examples of cognitive biases.

■ Negative thoughts sometimes reflect an accurate view of the world; this is referred to as **depressive realism**. In these instances it is life circumstances that need to be targeted rather than any cognitive biases.

Key points:

■ The biological approach links psychopathology to changes in the structure and functioning of the brain, especially the activity of neurotransmitters. It also emphasises the role of genetics in psychological disorders.

■ The biological approach is supported by a wealth of scientific evidence. However it is heavily reductionist and minimises the influence of psychological and environmental factors.

■ The psychodynamic approach focuses on unconscious processes in abnormality and the important role of early childhood development.

■ Concepts and ideas in psychodynamic approaches are impossible to test scientifically, while Freud's pioneering work was limited by his failure to study children directly and his focus on infantile sexuality.

■ The behavioural approach sees abnormal behaviour as caused by maladaptive learning experiences. It emphasises the processes of classical and operant conditioning, and social learning.

■ It is a reductionist approach based on relatively simple learning principles. It does not take into account emotional and cognitive aspects of disorders, and neither does it consider any genetic contributions.

■ The cognitive approach links psychological disorders to dysfunctional thoughts and perceptions, especially negative views of the self, the world and the future.

■ The cognitive approach takes no account of biological or genetic factors in psychopathology.

Key term

Depressive realism: this refers to the fact that the beliefs and thoughts of the depressed person can be a rational reflection of reality rather than irrational and maladaptive.

✔ Summary questions

4 Outline two key assumptions of each of the four approaches to explaining abnormality.

5 Consider reasons why psychology has at least four distinct approaches to explaining psychopathology.

6 What is reductionism? Evaluate the approaches in terms of reductionism.

Individual differences

Chapter summary

🎧

Further reading and weblinks

R.J. Comer, *Abnormal Psychology*, 5th edn, Worth (2004)

Thorough coverage of all aspects of abnormal psychology. Very good on classification and diagnosis.

G. Davison, J.M. Neale and A.M. Kring, *Abnormal Psychology*, 9th edn, Wiley (2004)

N. Frude, *Understanding Abnormal Psychology*, Blackwell (1998)

Readable and concise introduction to abnormal psychology.

www.psyonline.org.uk

Site dedicated to AQA Psychology with broad coverage of the specification.

www.bbc.co.uk

Besides their excellent Science site the BBC site has a range of relevant programmes on aspects of abnormality. They are not all on at the same time, but programmes such as *All in the Mind* provide coverage of contemporary issues in psychology and psychopathology.

■ Psychopathology, also known as abnormal psychology, is the study of psychological disorders. Treatment of psychopathology is dominated by medically trained psychiatrists and doctors. Psychologists who have specialised in the study of psychological disorders are known as clinical psychologists. They may only use psychological therapies.

■ There are many aspects to the study of psychopathology. Key issues include the problems of defining abnormality, diagnosing specific psychological disorders, explaining the origins of psychopathology and finding effective therapies.

■ Three different approaches to defining abnormality each emphasise different aspects of behaviour.

■ Deviation from social norms (DSN) focuses on the generally accepted rules of social behaviour and how abnormality can be defined as behaviour that deviates from these rules or norms. However social norms vary over time and also differ between different cultures.

■ Failure to function adequately (FFA) can identify individuals whose disorder affects their everyday behaviour. However people may show FFA for reasons other than psychopathology. In addition, some disorders may not prevent people living relatively normal lives.

■ Deviation from ideal mental health (DIMH) tries to define abnormality as the opposite of ideal mental health. This definition is subjective and based very much on Western values. This makes it highly culturally specific.

■ For diagnosing specific disorders psychiatrists use a detailed classification system such as the widely used DSM-IVR.

■ The biological approach to explaining psychopathology focuses on genetics and brain neurotransmitters. It is supported by extensive research evidence for genetic factors and changes in brain activity associated with psychological disorders. It is also supported by the effectiveness of drug treatments.

■ The biological approach is heavily reductionist, and largely ignores psychological and environmental factors.

■ The psychodynamic approach explains psychopathology through the influence of unconscious processes and early experience. The leading figure is Freud, whose psychoanalytic model influenced later psychodynamic approaches.

■ The key concepts in the psychodynamic approach, such as repression and fixation, are impossible to test objectively and scientifically. However Freud's ideas have been very influential and the psychodynamic approach in general treats people as complex.

■ The behavioural approach assumes that all behaviour, including psychopathology, has been learnt through processes of classical and operant conditioning, and social learning.

■ It provides convincing explanations of some disorders, but is essentially a reductionist and deterministic approach. There is no role for genetic factors.

■ The cognitive approach has a central role for dysfunctional and maladaptive thoughts. Negative schemata lead to cognitive biases that serve to maintain conditions such as depression.

■ There is evidence for the existence of cognitive biases in depression and anxiety states. However the concept of schemata is poorly defined, and there is no place for genetic and biological factors. Therapies based on the cognitive approach have proved effective in a variety of disorders.

■ How science works: practical activity

Psychology as science

Science involves a process of observation, hypothesis generation and empirical testing to develop theories that allow us to explain and predict behaviour. In psychology different approaches have generated different explanations of the causes of abnormality.

Working in groups review each of the four approaches to abnormality covered in this chapter: biological, psychodynamic, behavioural and cognitive. For each approach make sure you have details of the assumptions that underpin its explanation of abnormality, the key features of the approach and the methods that would be used to investigate the causes of abnormality.

For each approach:

■ Generate two predictions about abnormal behaviour based on the assumptions or features of the approach. If you have already studied research methods in depth you might devise an operationalised hypothesis.

■ Outline how someone adhering to this approach might test these predictions.

Therapies based on the biological approach

Individual differences

Learning objectives:

- To develop knowledge and understanding of therapies associated with the biological approach.

- To understand links between therapies and the assumptions of the biological approach.

- To understand practical and ethical issues associated with these therapies.

Key terms

Electroconvulsive therapy (ECT): a treatment for severely depressed patients who have proved resistant to other forms of psychological and biological therapies. It involves passing a small current through the brain to cause epileptic-like electrical discharges.

Psychosurgery: a now extremely rare biological treatment for psychological disorders that involves systematically damaging the brain. The most extreme form, the frontal lobotomy, was a popular treatment for schizophrenia in the 1940s and early 1950s.

Lesion: to damage deliberately and systematically parts of the brain, as in psychosurgery.

Introduction

There are many issues to be considered in the treatment of psychological disorders. Each of the approaches discussed previously has associated with it a number of therapeutic techniques. This might suggest that for any particular disorder there needs to be a careful choice of the most appropriate treatment. However, certainly up until recent years, any given therapist would suggest only a limited range of therapies.

For instance, therapists following the psychodynamic approach would use only the techniques associated with that approach. Similarly a cognitive therapist would use cognitive-behavioural therapy, and a therapist committed to the biological/medical model would prescribe drugs or **electroconvulsive therapy (ECT)**.

An obvious question that could be asked is what therapies work best with particular psychological disorders. If one type of therapy was consistently more effective then you would expect this therapy to be the treatment of choice. As we shall see, this is nearly always the case with some disorders but by and large there is no consistent evidence that the therapies derived from one approach are always more effective than those derived from another.

A difficulty in this area is that studies comparing different therapies for the same condition are relatively rare. For a number of reasons they are difficult to set up, as we shall see on p265. In addition, besides effectiveness there are other issues that need to be considered in deciding on a form of treatment. These can be practical, for instance the availability and cost of treatment. Ethical issues are also an important factor; for instance is there fully informed consent from the client? Or does the treatment have unpleasant side effects? In this section we review some of the most popular treatments derived from the approaches described earlier, and consider them in the light of these issues.

Biological therapies

As mentioned in the previous chapter, the biological/medical approach dominates the diagnosis and treatment of psychopathology. Medically trained psychiatrists and doctors are responsible for treating the majority of people with psychological disorders and therefore the treatments based on this model are by far the most common. They divide into three categories: **psychosurgery**, ECT and drugs.

Psychosurgery

The term psychosurgery refers to systematically damaging the brain in order to change behaviour. For instance in the 1950s the amygdala was **lesioned** in over-aggressive people to reduce levels of violence. In relation to psychopathology the most dramatic use of psychosurgery was the **frontal**

lobotomy used throughout the 1940s and early 1950s as a treatment for schizophrenia. The operation involved cutting pathways between higher and lower centres in the brain. In the standard procedure developed by Freeman and Watts (Freeman, 1971) this was done by inserting a scalpel through a hole drilled through the skull and waggling it up and down.

There was no evidence that psychosurgery improved the specific symptoms of schizophrenia, but it could make patients more manageable. As a treatment for schizophrenia it was rapidly replaced by the drugs introduced in the early 1950s.

Nowadays psychosurgery is extremely rare. It is occasionally used for conditions such as severe depression and obsessive-compulsive disorder that have proved resistant to all other treatments. Areas to be damaged are precisely localised using brain scans, and limited amounts of tissue destroyed using electrical current or small radioactive pellets.

Evaluation of psychosurgery

■ Psychosurgery is so rare now that it is hard to judge its effectiveness. When it was a common treatment for schizophrenia it did not target the specific symptoms but at best made patients more manageable.

■ Psychosurgery has major ethical issues; damage to the brain is irreversible and the consequences unpredictable. In addition people with severe disorders are unlikely to fully understand the procedure and be able to give informed consent.

Electroconvulsive therapy (ECT)

ECT involves passing a small electric current through the brain. This causes the equivalent of a seizure as seen in **epilepsy**, with violent electrical discharges in the brain and behavioural **convulsions**. It was introduced in the 1930s and originally tested as a treatment for schizophrenia. It then became apparent that ECT could be an effective therapy for some forms of severe depression and it became a popular antidepressant treatment by the 1950s. We do not know how ECT works, but it is likely that the electrical discharge will have an effect on the activity of a number of brain neurotransmitters.

The introduction of antidepressant drugs, described in the next section, reduced the use of ECT but it still remained an option. Through the 1960s and 1970s doubts grew as to the effectiveness of ECT in comparison with drugs, and there were also increasing concerns over ethical issues. Although full body convulsions are now prevented by the use of muscle relaxant drugs, it is still a violent assault on the brain and its mode of action is unknown. Nowadays its use in the UK is recommended only for the most severe forms of depression that have proved resistant to alternative psychological and drug therapies. In around 50 per cent of these cases it can be effective when all other treatments have failed.

Evaluation of ECT

■ ECT is a violent electrical assault on the brain. It is never given once only, but in a series of sessions, perhaps a dozen over a few weeks. Research suggests that this can lead in some cases to long-term memory impairment.

■ ECT is now recommended only for severely depressed people resistant to other therapies. Individuals with severe depression may not fully grasp the nature and consequences of ECT and so cannot give fully informed consent.

Key terms

Frontal lobotomy: a psychosurgical operation used as a treatment for schizophrenia in the 1940s and early 1950s. It was of doubtful effectiveness and disappeared with the introduction of drug therapy.

Epilepsy: a neurological condition characterised by violent and uncontrolled electrical discharges in the brain. Electroconvulsive therapy (ECT) for depression involves causing epileptic-like discharges by passing a small current through the brain.

Convulsions: whole body convulsions were associated with electroconvulsive therapy (ECT) for depression. Nowadays these are controlled using muscle relaxant drugs given before ECT.

Links

Ethical procedures and informed consent are discussed on p100.

See p140 for background on neurotransmitter function in the brain.

■ ECT can be an effective antidepressant treatment for patients unresponsive to other therapies.

Drugs

If you are diagnosed with a psychological disorder the most likely outcome today is that you will be treated with one of the many available drugs. In the last 50 years there has been an explosion in the range of drugs targeted at psychological disorders. We will briefly consider two psychological disorders, schizophrenia and depression, to illustrate how drug therapy has developed.

Schizophrenia

Schizophrenia was first diagnosed in the early years of the twentieth century when it was recognised as a severe psychological disorder that required treatment. The key symptoms are hallucinations and delusions and a loss of insight and contact with reality. Drugs were not available at that time and effective treatments for schizophrenia were lacking. In the 1930s Moniz (1936) introduced the frontal lobotomy for schizophrenia, discussed on p250. Although widely used the frontal lobotomy did not target the symptoms of schizophrenia but at best tranquillised the patient and made them more manageable.

In 1952 Laborit, a French doctor, decided to try out a drug, **chlorpromazine,** which had just been introduced as a sedative given before operations on his surgical patients. He found that chlorpromazine significantly reduced post-operative stress, and imaginatively suggested to psychiatrist colleagues that they try the drug on their patients with schizophrenia. Chlorpromazine significantly reduced symptoms such as hallucinations, delusions and thought disorder. The drug rapidly took over from the frontal lobotomy as the treatment of choice for schizophrenia, and the age of mass drug therapy for psychological disorders had begun.

We now know that effective drugs for any disorder act on brain neurotransmitters (see p174). At the time chlorpromazine was introduced, little was known about brain chemistry, and it wasn't until the early 1970s that the relationship between chlorpromazine and the neurotransmitter dopamine was discovered. Chlorpromazine and other **antipsychotics** act by reducing dopamine activity in the brain, and this led to the long-lasting model that linked schizophrenia to raised levels of dopamine activity.

Although chlorpromazine is still used in the treatment of schizophrenia newer compounds have been introduced over the last 15 years, and these have been shown to be as effective as chlorpromazine with fewer side effects. They have also been shown to act in some patients resistant to chlorpromazine. Interestingly these new drugs, such as **clozapine,** seem to act on a wide range of neurotransmitters in the brain, such as dopamine and serotonin, and this may account for their different pattern of actions.

However, when we look at drug treatment of schizophrenia, even with the new compounds we can identify some key strengths and weaknesses:

■ Drugs can be effective in suppressing the symptoms of schizophrenia, and many people are able to live normal lives because of drug therapy. However the drugs are only effective in 50–60 per cent of patients, and so do not work in 40–50 per cent of patients.

■ Drugs can effectively suppress the symptoms, but they do not cure the disorder, and symptoms will return in about 80 per cent of patients who come off the drugs. Drug treatment for schizophrenia is for life.

■ Key terms

Chlorpromazine: the first antipsychotic drug used as a treatment for schizophrenia. Introduced in 1952 it rapidly became the treatment of choice for the disorder.

Antipsychotics: name given to drugs used in the treatment of schizophrenia. Examples include chlorpromazine and clozapine.

Clozapine: recently introduced antipsychotic drug used in the treatment of schizophrenia. Clozapine has fewer side effects than older drugs such as chlorpromazine.

■ Link

Drug action at the synapse is discussed on p140.

Individual differences

- All drugs used in treating schizophrenia have unpleasant side effects. For instance, long-term treatment with classic drugs such as chlorpromazine often led to movement disorders resembling Parkinson's disease. Clozapine lowers the number of white blood cells, part of our immune defence system, and levels have to be carefully monitored during treatment.

- There are ethical issues involving **informed consent** and the extent to which a person with hallucinations and delusions can give this. On the other hand a small minority of such patients can be a danger to themselves or others, so it might be argued that the drugs should be prescribed anyway.

- As knowledge of the action of these drugs in the brain has increased, it has contributed to biological models of schizophrenia and our understanding of the disorder.

Depression

Depression, along with anxiety, is the most common of the psychological disorders, characterised by sad, depressed mood and symptoms such as sleeplessness and loss of appetite. Effective drug treatment for depression developed rapidly in the 1960s with the introduction of two groups of drugs:

- **monoamine-oxidase inhibitors** (MAOIs)
- **tricyclic antidepressants**.

As with chlorpromazine little was known about the action of these drugs in the brain but by the 1970s it had been established that both groups of drugs raised levels of the neurotransmitters serotonin and noradrenaline. These discoveries led to the **monoamine theory of depression**, a strictly biological explanation that related depression to low levels of brain serotonin and noradrenalin.

Although used successfully for many years, both MAOIs and tricyclics could have serious side effects. MAOIs interact badly with various food groups and other medications while long-term use of tricyclics was associated with heart problems. In the 1990s a new class of antidepressants was introduced. These were the selective serotonin reuptake inhibitors (**SSRIs**) of which the most famous is **Prozac**. As their name implies, these drugs selectively raise levels of serotonin in the brain and were considered to be more effective and also safer than MAOIs and tricyclics in the treatment of depression.

Subsequent research suggests that SSRIs are sometimes no more effective than the earlier drugs, and have also been associated with outbursts of violence and suicides. While some of these reports are anecdotal, there are concerns over the increasing prescribing of Prozac and other SSRIs to young people. Overall there are strengths and weaknesses of drug treatment for depression:

- Drug therapy can be effective in the treatment of depression but even the highest estimates suggest that only 60–70 per cent of depressed people respond. This is even less impressive when we consider that up to 30 per cent of depressed people respond to **placebo** treatment.

- Drugs do not cure depression. They target the biological changes associated with depression but do not change any life circumstances, daily stressors or cognitive biases that may also be involved.

- There can be problems of **psychological and physical dependence** with prolonged use of antidepressants. People become convinced that they need to keep taking them or the depression will return, or the

Key terms

Physical dependence: when people become physically dependent on a drug, meaning that when the drug is withdrawn they go into a withdrawal syndrome with unpleasant physical symptoms. It implies that the body, especially the brain, has adapted to the presence of the drug.

Anti-anxiety drugs: also known as anxiolytics. Librium and Valium are drugs used in the treatment of anxiety conditions. They come from a group of drugs called the benzodiazepines (BZs).

Benzodiazepines (BZs): a group of drugs including the anti-anxiety agents Librium and Valium, and the sleeping drug Mogadon. Benzodiazepines are also called 'minor tranquillisers'.

Lithium: a drug used specifically for the treatment of bipolar depression.

■ Hint

When evaluating drug therapy, make sure your material has breadth, i.e. that you understand the importance of effectiveness, ethical aspects, and relation to the biological approach.

brain becomes so adjusted to the chemical presence of the drug that it cannot cope without it.

- As mentioned above, prolonged treatment with antidepressants is associated with a range of unpleasant side effects.
- There are ethical issues, in particular informed consent. The severely depressed individual may be unable to make a clear judgement on the benefits of drug treatment.
- Our increasing knowledge of the action of antidepressants on neurotransmitters has contributed to the development of biological models of depression, in particular the roles of serotonin and noradrenaline.

Other drug groups

We have had a detailed look at antipsychotics and antidepressants. Other classes of drugs used in the treatment of psychological disorders include the following:

- **Anti-anxiety drugs:** also known as anxiolytics or minor tranquillisers, they include the most prescribed drugs over the last 40 years, Librium and Valium. These come from a group called the **benzodiazepines** (also known as BZs) and are used in the treatment of general anxiety, stress and for sleep disorders. Prolonged use of benzodiazepines is associated with psychological and physical dependence, and also with side effects such as drowsiness and memory impairment.
- **Lithium:** this is an unusual drug in that it is used for one specific condition, bipolar depression (previously called manic depression). This is a disorder where the person has periods of clinical depression followed by periods of mania or hyperactivity. Lithium can stabilise the condition, but can also have severe side effects. These can include heart and digestive problems.

Evaluation of drug therapy

- Drugs can be effective in a range of psychological disorders and many people are able to live normal lives through drug therapy. However, there are some disorders such as phobias, panic and eating disorders for which there is no consistently effective drug therapy.
- Even when effective, drugs only treat the symptoms of a disorder, via their effect on the biological changes in the brain. They are therefore a highly reductionist treatment that ignores any cognitive, emotional or environmental influences.
- Most drugs used to treat psychological disorders have problems of side effects and dependence, which need to be carefully managed.
- Drug therapy is a fundamental part of the biological/medical approach. Its use confirms the view of the person as a patient. As mentioned earlier, while taking away individual responsibility for the disorder it can also lead to stigmatising the person as a schizophrenic or depressive, etc. However the increasing use of antidepressants and anti-anxiety drugs in particular has generally lessened the stigma associated with drug therapy.

Key points:

■ Therapies based on the biological approach target the brain. Drugs affect the activity of neurotransmitters, electroconvulsive therapy produces electrical seizures, while psychosurgery physically damages or removes brain tissue.

■ Psychosurgery involves systematically damaging parts of the brain. Today psychosurgery is extremely rare. It is ethically highly controversial as it is a highly stressful procedure that involves irreversible damage to the brain. There is the common problem of whether people with severe psychological disorders can fully understand the procedure and give informed consent.

■ ECT can be an effective form of antidepressant treatment, but nowadays is recommended only for severe depression resistant to other forms of therapy. There are concerns that it can lead to memory problems, and also doubts that severely depressed people can fully grasp the nature and consequences of ECT.

■ Drugs were introduced for the treatment of schizophrenia in 1953. These antipsychotic drugs reduce the activity of the neurotransmitter dopamine in the brain and can suppress symptoms of schizophrenia in up to 60 per cent of patients. They do not 'cure' the disorder, and also have serious side effects, especially affecting movement.

■ Antidepressant drugs work by raising levels of the neurotransmitters noradrenalin and serotonin in the brain. The selective serotonin reuptake inhibitors (SSRIs) such as Prozac act specifically on serotonin.

■ Up to 70 per cent of depressed people respond to drug therapy, but drugs only target the biological changes and do not alter any environmental or personal factors that can lead to depression.

■ However our understanding of the way in which drugs work in the brain has contributed to the development of biological models of schizophrenia and depression.

■ Ethical issues in drug therapy include the problem of side effects and the ability (or not) of people with serious conditions such as severe depression or schizophrenia to give fully informed consent to treatment.

■ Overall drugs can be effective, but some conditions such as eating disorders and simple phobias do not respond to drug therapy. Drug therapy is highly reductionist, ignoring any cognitive, emotional or environmental influences on psychopathology.

✔ Summary questions

1 The biological approach to psychological disorders assumes that psychopathology may be associated with changes in brain neurotransmitters or in brain structure. Explain how each of the three biological therapies links in with these assumptions.

2 Discuss ethical issues in relation to each of the biological therapies.

3 There are serious ethical concerns in relation to ECT. However, it can be an effective treatment in some cases of severe depression that are not helped by other therapies. Discuss whether the use of ECT is justified.

Therapies based on psychological approaches

Learning objectives:

- To be able to outline and evaluate a range of therapies associated with psychological approaches to abnormality, including psychoanalysis, systematic desensitisation and cognitive-behavioural therapy (CBT).

- To understand links between therapies and the assumptions of the different approaches to explaining abnormality.

- To understand ethical issues associated with the various therapies.

- To be able to use studies of the effectiveness of different therapies to evaluate their usefulness.

Key terms

Neuroses: relatively mild mental illnesses that do not have a biological cause.

Free association: technique used in Freudian psychoanalysis. The client is encouraged to express anything that comes into their mind and follow any associations that occur to them. The free association technique is also referred to as the talking cure.

Dream analysis: technique used in Freudian psychoanalysis. The therapist uses the dream work to interpret the manifest content of the dream and uncover the latent content. Processes such as displacement and symbolisation distort the latent content into the manifest content.

Therapies associated with the psychodynamic approach

The example we have used of the psychodynamic approach to psychopathology is Freud's psychoanalytical model. This makes several assumptions about the origins of psychological disorders, for instance, that adult **neuroses** such as anxiety and depression are rooted in early childhood experience. The adult is protected from the conflicts that lie at the root of these problems by ego defence mechanisms such as those mentioned earlier (p239); therefore they are not consciously accessible to the individual concerned.

The aim of psychoanalytic therapy is to uncover this repressed material and help the client come to an understanding of the origins of their problems. There are traditionally several techniques available to the therapist: **free association**, **dream analysis** and projective tests.

Free association

The client is encouraged to express anything that comes into their mind. This could begin, for instance, with an account of what had happened to them on the way to the therapist's consulting room. Each incident may then, through free association of ideas, lead to other thoughts and memories perhaps extending back into childhood. The client must not censor the material at all, and in this freewheeling way ego defences may be lowered and repressed material accessed. The role of the therapist is to intervene occasionally, perhaps to encourage some reflection on a particular experience. In addition, during the free association, the therapist will be identifying key themes and ideas that can be analysed further during the therapeutic process.

Freud introduced free association to try and get around the defences put up by the ego and so bring to the surface material from the unconscious. It is one of the most valuable techniques used in psychoanalytic therapy and can also be used in combination with other techniques such as dream analysis. It is also why Freud's approach was referred to as the 'talking cure'.

Dream analysis

Freud referred to dreams as the 'royal road to the unconscious'. He felt that during dreams the normal barriers to unconscious material were lifted and the symbolic imagery of dreams was a reflection of this unconscious material. Therefore by analysing the content of dreams the therapist might be able to identify significant conflicts repressed into the unconscious.

For Freud dreams were essentially wish fulfilment, but the wishes, often sexual or aggressive from the id, were too threatening to be consciously acknowledged. They were therefore distorted and reflected in the imagery of the dream. In order to understand the underlying meaning of the dream Freud made various assumptions:

- Dreams have an obvious content that the client can recall. Freud referred to this as the **manifest content.**

■ Beneath the manifest content lies the actual meaning of the dream that could only be revealed through the therapist's interpretation. Freud referred to this as the latent content.

■ The **dream work** was the process by which the latent content was distorted into the manifest content. This can happen through various processes, two of which are outlined in Table 1.

The therapist's role is to use their understanding of how the dream work operates to interpret the symbolism of the dream. Putting together the themes that gradually emerge through the continuing processes of free association and dream analysis regular anxieties and conflicts emerge. The client can then work through these issues with the therapist, identifying and hopefully resolving the source of their current anxieties.

Key terms

Manifest content: dream imagery as reported by the dreamer. To uncover the meaningful, latent, content, the therapist uses the dream work.

Dream work: the processes that distort the underlying meaning of a dream (the latent content) into the manifest content reported by the dreamer. It includes processes such as displacement and symbolisation.

Table 1 *Processes involved in converting latent to manifest content*

Process	Description
Displacement	Freud refers to a dream where the client was strangling a white dog. Free association had revealed tensions between this client and her sister-in-law and Freud concluded that in the dream the client had substituted the dog for her sister-in- law. To dream of actually strangling her sister-in-law would have been too threatening and so the wish was displaced onto the dog.
Symbolisation	Freud was impressed by the way that some objects and images found in a particular culture come to represent significant ideas. When these objects and images appeared in dreams he concluded that they could be acting as symbols for these ideas. The most well known example is that penis-shaped objects such as snakes, swords and trains often appear in dreams and may therefore symbolically represent the penis. Similarly cupboards, tunnels and ships could be symbolic of the vagina. We should note that Freud's theory of development heavily emphasised psychosexual aspects of early childhood.

Projective tests

Although not a part of Freud's original therapeutic techniques, projective tests are used in a variety of psychodynamic approaches. In these tests the client is required to project or impose their own thoughts and associations on some particular stimulus material. The most famous is the Rorschach ink blot test, in which the client is presented with a series of ink blot shapes. They are asked what the shape means to them, and by repeating this with a sequence of different blots particular themes and anxieties may emerge.

Evaluation of therapies based on the psychodynamic approach

■ These therapies accept that human beings are complicated and that many adult disorders may have their roots in childhood and in repressed material. This is almost certainly true.

■ Because of the need to identify the roots of psychopathology, psychodynamic therapy can be very long lasting (months or even years) and therefore expensive. More recently brief psychodynamic therapy has been introduced in which both the therapist and client agree that there will only be a fixed number of sessions.

Link

See p213 for an example of the Rorschach ink blot test.

Individual differences

■ Psychodynamic therapies depend upon the client developing insights into their condition. It is not therefore suitable for those people who might be unable or unwilling to analyse their lives in this way.

■ As they require insight psychodynamic therapies are not suitable for all disorders. In particular they are unlikely to be effective with psychoses such as schizophrenia, where the individual often does not have insight into their condition.

■ There are ethical issues in confronting clients with perhaps distressing material during the course of analysis. It is important that such issues are worked through with the client to a satisfactory conclusion, but as some childhood sexual abuse cases have shown the effects can be traumatic for the whole family.

Opinions on the effectiveness of psychodynamic therapies are many and varied. In 1952 Eysenck concluded that not only did these therapies not work, but they were actually worse than no treatment at all! However Eysenck's work itself has been heavily criticised and over the last 50 years a number of more controlled studies have looked at the effectiveness of psychodynamic therapies. We review some of these later in the chapter, but in brief, evidence suggests that such therapies can be effective for depression and for anxiety disorders.

It is important to note that Freud himself spoke more in terms of reducing unhappiness rather than 'curing' it. To paraphrase Freud himself, the aim was to convert misery into everyday unhappiness. Giving clients an understanding of their condition may itself be beneficial without actually providing them with a complete cure.

■ Therapies based on the behavioural approach

The behavioural approach assumes that disordered behaviour is learnt through classical and operant conditioning (including social learning). Therefore the approach to therapy is to try and alter behaviour using the principles of conditioning. The three main processes in the behavioural approach, classical conditioning, operant conditioning and social learning, are related to particular therapies. **Behaviour therapy** refers to techniques based on classical conditioning, while **behaviour modification** refers to therapies based on operant conditioning and social learning. The specification refers to systematic desensitisation, one of the key therapies based on the behavioural approach, but we need to put this particular form of treatment in the context of the overall behavioural approach.

Behaviour therapy

Therapies based on classical conditioning include **systematic desensitisation**, **flooding** and **aversion therapy**. Before looking at these in detail it is useful to recall that classical conditioning involves automatic reflexive responses or feelings. One of the most common automatic responses to situations of danger is fear or anxiety. These responses can be seen as equivalent to salivation in Pavlov's dogs (see p51). The behavioural approach assumes that fear can be associated through classical conditioning with certain objects or situations. When this fear becomes extreme and inappropriate, it can lead to a variety of anxiety-related disorders, such as phobias and panic.

Therefore the aim of behaviour therapy is to remove or extinguish the conditioned association between fear and the situation or object, and there are various techniques for achieving this.

■ Link

Effectiveness of therapies is discussed on p263.

AQA Examiner's tip

The aim of psychoanalytic therapy is to uncover material repressed into the unconscious. When you outline one of the techniques be prepared to show your understanding of how it relates to psychoanalytic theory if the question requires it.

■ Key terms

Behaviour therapy: behavioural therapeutic techniques based on the principles of classical conditioning. They include systematic desensitisation and aversion therapy.

Behaviour modification: behavioural therapeutic techniques based on the principles of operant conditioning. Examples include token economies.

Systematic desensitisation: behaviour therapy technique where people with phobias are gradually desensitised to the phobic object or situation. This is done by using gradual exposure from the least up to the most feared situation.

Flooding: behaviour therapy technique where people with phobias are exposed to the feared object or situation, without the possibility of escape, until the fear response extinguishes.

Aversion therapy: behaviour therapy technique where undesirable behaviour is paired with an unpleasant stimulus.

Systematic desensitisation

This is the most popular form of behaviour therapy. Introduced by Wolpe (1958) it is a form of **counter-conditioning**, where the therapist attempts to replace the fear response by an alternative and harmless response. This involves using a hierarchy of increasingly fearful situations:

■ For spider phobics the therapist would ask the person to list situations from the least to the most fearful; the lowest might be seeing a picture of a small spider while the highest might be finding a tarantula in their bed.

■ The therapist trains the client in deep relaxation techniques. Relaxation is the alternative harmless response to the feared situation and the aim of the procedure is to replace the fear response with relaxation.

■ The therapist asks the client to visualise the least feared situation. Simultaneously they perform their deep relaxation procedure.

■ Once the client feels comfortable at that level, they are asked to imagine the next situation in the hierarchy. The same procedure is repeated, with visualisation of the feared situation associated with the alternative response of relaxation.

■ Over a series of sessions the client will cope with every level of the hierarchy, although they can of course stop at any time and restart at a lower level. Eventually they can cope with the most feared situation at the top of the hierarchy.

An alternative to visualising fearful situations is to use real examples, for instance pictures of small spiders, through life-like models, up to handling real spiders. It is unclear whether this more realistic approach is actually more effective than visualisation.

Flooding

The aim of behaviour therapy is to extinguish or remove the learned association between the stimulus and the response. In systematic desensitisation this is done in a gradual or graded fashion. An alternative approach is flooding, which involves inescapable exposure to the feared object or situation that lasts until the fear response disappears. For example, someone who has claustrophobia (fear of enclosed spaces) might be shut in a small room for at least an hour or until their initial high levels of anxiety reduce. The procedure assumes that very high levels of fear and anxiety cannot be sustained and will eventually fall.

If the flooding session ends too soon, when anxiety levels are still high, it may have the opposite of the desired effect, in that the phobia will be reinforced rather than extinguished.

An issue specific to flooding is that it is clearly a highly threatening and stressful procedure. Ideally it should only be carried out by trained therapists and with medical supervision available. Its advantage, of course, assuming it works, is that it is very quick.

Aversion therapy

As opposed to the previous techniques, which aim to replace or extinguish an undesirable association, aversion therapy aims to associate undesirable behaviour with an unpleasant stimulus. It has a controversial history in that it was used in the 1950s to try and 'cure' homosexuality by pairing electric shocks with pictures of naked men. It was assumed that homosexuals would learn the association between

> ### Key term
>
> **Counter-conditioning:** a process underlying systematic desensitisation in which the conditioned response of fear to an object or situation is replaced through counter-conditioning by relaxation.

the fear of the electric shock and the pictures. However, besides being ethically and scientifically unsound, there was never any evidence that it worked.

Nowadays aversion therapy is sometimes used as a therapy for addictive states. The idea behind the procedure is to pair an unpleasant or punishing stimulus with, for instance, smoking or drinking. One way to do this is to make the person feel sick using pills, simultaneously with their smoking. Through classical conditioning the feeling of sickness is associated with smoking and should act to prevent smoking in the future.

Evaluation of behavioural therapies

- The assumptions of the behavioural approach, that all behaviour is learned through relatively simple conditioning principles, means that therapy targets these learnt associations. There is no attempt to address any deeper psychological or emotional issues related to the disorder, i.e. these therapies focus on symptoms rather than any deeper underlying causes.

- However, systematic desensitisation in particular can be extremely effective in the treatment of simple phobias. Success rates of between 60 and 90 per cent have been reported for spider phobics and blood injection phobics (Barlow *et al.*, 2002). Despite the emphasis on symptoms, there is no evidence that improvement is temporary.

- There are significant ethical issues in relation to flooding and aversion therapy, in that clients are subjected to intense fear and anxiety. Even systematic desensitisation requires the client to visualise or experience feared situations. There should be careful monitoring to ensure there are no long-term negative consequences for the client.

Behaviour modification

Techniques of behaviour modification are based on the principles of operant conditioning. They attempt to change a person's voluntary controlled behaviour rather than the reflexive behaviours involved in classical conditioning. The two main techniques in this area are the token economy and social learning theory.

Token economy

A token economy is a straightforward version of increasing desirable behaviours by reward or positive reinforcement. It is used mainly in institutions such as psychiatric hospitals, where tokens are given as rewards for improved behaviour. Tokens can then be exchanged for sweets, cigarettes, etc. The aim is to reduce levels of antisocial behaviour by substituting desirable responses such as good hygiene and cleanliness.

- Note that when used in this way the token economy is modifying behaviour but not directly addressing symptoms. In a ward of patients with schizophrenia general behaviour might improve and they would be easier to manage, but their specific psychotic symptoms are not being targeted.

The simple use of reward to change behaviour can have some clinical relevance. An example would be eating disorders. To increase body weight in hospitalised individuals with life-threatening anorexia nervosa, rewards such as having visitors or being allowed to leave hospital can be an effective means of encouraging weight gain. The problem of course is that once outside the hospital they may revert to weight loss.

Individual differences

Social learning theory

Social learning theory adds a cognitive element to operant conditioning techniques, in that observation and imitation of models is an important feature. When a model is rewarded for certain behaviour the observer is more likely to imitate. Bandura (1969) has demonstrated the importance of social learning theory in normal development. It has also been established that phobic people can benefit from observing a model coping effectively with the phobic situation. It has also proved useful in helping people deal with social anxiety (Bandura, 1969).

Evaluation of behaviour modification

- Rewards are an effective way of changing behaviour, and the token economies are a useful way of improving antisocial behaviour. They do not target specific symptoms or conditions but may help the patient become more receptive to psychological therapies.

- Token economies are usually set in highly structured institutions. A key problem is whether the behavioural improvement generalises to the outside world when the patient returns to the community, and rewards are less consistent.

- There is an ethical aspect to token economies in that they follow the very mechanistic approach of treating patients as stimulus-response machines; this is a highly reductionist approach to complex behaviours.

- Social learning theory includes cognitive processes such as observation and imitation, and emphasises the role of models in changing behaviour. Although based on conditioning principles it takes a more complex view of human behaviour than either classical conditioning or simple operant conditioning.

Both behaviour modification and behaviour therapy are based on learning principles and ignore any genetic and biological factors in psychological disorders.

> ■ Link
>
> For more information about cognitive behavioural therapy see p172.

■ Therapies based on the cognitive approach

We noted in the previous chapter that the cognitive approach links psychological disorders to irrational and dysfunctional thoughts. You fail an examination and make the all-or-none assumption that you are hopeless at that subject and probably at all subjects. Failing the examination has triggered the negative schemata that you may have acquired in childhood that you will never succeed at anything; this leads to the negative automatic thoughts that you are indeed a failure at everything.

The aim of cognitive therapy, more usually referred to as cognitive-behavioural therapy (CBT), is to challenge these irrational and dysfunctional thought processes. Two examples of the cognitive approach are Beck's cognitive therapy for depression, and Ellis's rational-emotive therapy (RET). Although developed independently they follow the same assumptions and share many similarities.

Beck's cognitive therapy

Beck (1976) believed that negative schemata lead to pessimistic thoughts about the self, the world and the future. These in turn lead to the sort of cognitive biases outlined on p245, which in turn maintain the negative thoughts. The aim of Beck's approach is to challenge these irrational cognitions and replace them with more realistic appraisals.

Individual differences

■ The therapist helps the client identify particular negative thoughts such as 'I have never had a successful relationship and I never will'. To do this the client is encouraged to keep a record of their thoughts and anxieties and perhaps a diary. These can then be reviewed with the therapist and negative automatic thoughts recognised.

■ Using this material the therapist challenges the dysfunctional cognitions by drawing attention to positive incidents or examples, however trivial, which contradict the client's negative assumptions.

■ This is a form of **reality testing**, a key component in cognitive therapy.

■ Along with challenging the client's negative thoughts and showing them to be irrational and unrealistic, Beck also uses behavioural techniques to encourage more positive behaviour.

■ For instance in severe depression the person may find it difficult to do anything at all. Beck would encourage them to set a list of small goals to be achieved. These could be as trivial as actually getting out of bed and making a cup of tea. However in theory these small achievements should help the depressed person develop a sense of personal effectiveness.

■ Another aspect of cognitive therapy can be training in problem solving skills, if there are particular situations that trigger negative thoughts. For instance if social situations are a major issue social skills training can be given. More generally clients can be taught relaxation techniques to reduce anxiety in stressful situations.

■ However the focus of the therapy is very much on cognitive restructuring, and behavioural change without cognitive change is unlikely to alter the depressed state.

Ellis and rational-emotive behavioural therapy (REBT)

Ellis's (1962, 1991) REBT approach is very similar to Beck's. Ellis's ABC model was reviewed in the previous chapter (see p246, Figure 1) and summarises the approach that underlies all cognitive behaviour therapy. A specific event activates irrational thoughts and these in turn lead to negative emotions and maladaptive behaviour. These irrational thoughts need to be challenged and rationalised. Ellis believes that people maintain negative and self-defeating beliefs by constantly telling themselves how inadequate they are, and constantly looking for confirming evidence that they are inadequate.

The therapy is similar to Beck's in that the therapist and client work together to identify situations and the negative reactions they produce. The therapist then helps the client rationalise the situation, giving the client a more realistic perspective. Ellis developed a more confrontational approach to therapy than Beck, challenging the client's self-defeating beliefs in intense debates.

However a key issue for both approaches to cognitive therapy is that some negative thoughts are based on a rational and accurate perception of reality; and that dealing with this depressive realism was as important as correcting dysfunctional thoughts.

Key term

Reality testing: a technique used in cognitive-behavioural therapy. The therapist encourages the client to compare their irrational cognitions against the real world.

Evaluation of CBT

- As a combination of behavioural and cognitive elements, CBT is a structured approach to therapy but acknowledges that complex cognitive processes are important in psychological disorders.

- Depression may sometimes be based on a perfectly rational and accurate perception of reality. It is important that the therapist acknowledges this and does not give the impression that depression is always unjustified.

- It is effective as a treatment for depression and social anxiety. There is evidence that the beneficial effects of CBT in depression may last longer than those of antidepressant drugs.

- There are some conditions where CBT seems less effective. Behavioural therapies are more effective in treating phobias, while more severe conditions such as schizophrenia are not obviously suited to CBT. However, some therapists believe that where the person with schizophrenia has some insight into their condition CBT can have beneficial effects in coping with the disorder, and research in this area is rapidly increasing.

- The cognitive approach ignores genetic and biological factors in states such as depression.

- The idea of schemata lacks detail and in particular there is no clearly described mechanism for how negative schemata develop in the first place.

- Courses of CBT are generally limited to a number of sessions over a few weeks. It is therefore less time consuming and more cost effective than psychoanalytic therapies.

- Although it requires a degree of insight on the part of the client, it avoids the in-depth probing associated with psychoanalysis and which might be unpleasant or even damaging for some clients. However, it should be acknowledged that some people might still find the self-monitoring and analysis associated with CBT threatening.

> **Hint**
>
> CBT can seem quite complex, but in fact represents a logical approach to psychopathology once you accept the underlying assumption that thoughts are important. Focus on Beck's triad or Ellis's ABC model (pp245–246) and these will provide a straightforward background to CBT.

■ Effectiveness of therapies

The most important feature of therapies is whether they work or not. Besides being the whole aim of treatment, comparative effectiveness of different techniques can also be used to evaluate the underlying approaches. If one type of therapy is consistently more effective than any others, then this would suggest that the underlying approach, whether biological, cognitive, behavioural or psychodynamic, is perhaps the most valid.

We have already drawn some general conclusions concerning the effectiveness of therapies, e.g. systematic desensitisation works well with specific phobias, schizophrenia responds best to antipsychotic drugs, CBT can be effective in depression and anxiety states. However the most reliable method of comparing therapies is to do so in the same study, although these studies face considerable practical difficulties:

- Large numbers of participants are required, who have to be diagnosed with the same psychological disorder at the same level of severity across all the different therapy groups.

- There needs to be careful assessment of patients before and after treatment, and some agreement on how long the study should last.

Individual differences

Should improvement last for two months, six months or a year before being considered significant?

■ When drug therapy is one of the comparisons, there should be a placebo control group. A placebo is an inactive or harmless substance that the patient thinks is the active drug. Studies of depression and anxiety show that up to 30 per cent of people will improve with just the placebo treatment; this placebo effect shows the influence of psychological factors in responding to therapies. An effective therapy should show an improvement over and above the placebo effect.

Research study: Elkin *et al.*, 1989

This was a study across several treatment centres. In all 240 patients with depression were treated with either CBT, psychotherapy or antidepressant drugs. There was also a placebo control group. Treatment lasted for 16 weeks.

The findings were:

■ There was a large placebo effect of 35–40 per cent.

■ All therapies were significantly more effective than placebo, and overall had similar levels of effectiveness.

■ Drugs tended to be the most effective therapy for severe depression.

■ The individual therapist was a significant factor in the effectiveness of psychotherapy.

■ Across all treatment groups, 30–40 per cent of patients did not respond to therapy. It is a common finding in studies of effectiveness that no treatment is ever 100 per cent effective.

The conclusions were that drugs, CBT and psychotherapy are all more effective than placebo in treating depression. Also note that the follow-up was only 16 weeks. Ideally patients should be followed up for 6–12 months, as there is evidence that the therapeutic effect of CBT in anxiety conditions is longer lasting than the effect of drugs (Bechdolf *et al.*, 2006).

Research study: Davidson *et al.*, 2004

Two hundred and ninety-five patients with generalised social anxiety (fear of social situations) were treated either with CBT, with the SSRI antidepressant fluoxetine, or with combined CBT + fluoxetine.

The findings were:

■ The overall placebo effect was 19 per cent.

■ All therapies were effective over and above the placebo effect, and after 14 weeks there were no differences between the therapy groups. The combined therapy was not superior to either therapy alone.

■ 40–50 per cent of patients did not respond to therapy.

The conclusions were that drugs and CBT are equally effective in treating social anxiety, and combining them does not improve their effectiveness. However many patients do not respond to either treatment.

Link

See p95 for a discussion of extraneous variables.

Studies comparing treatments – methodological issues

Studies such as those above are not conventional experiments such as those we come across in psychology. They do have independent variables (the different treatments) and a dependent variable (the effect of the treament measured by improvement in patients). Key methodological points to be considered include the following:

■ The separate patient groups to be given the different treatments should be matched in terms of the severity of the disorder. It would also be desirable if they were matched on other characteristics, such as age, gender, socioeconomic status. This is rarely possible, but these factors have been shown to influence, for instance, depression.

■ The length of the study should be sufficient for treatment effects to be observable. Even with drugs effects can take weeks to develop. Ideally observation should continue for at least a year to check that any improvement is sustained and not temporary.

■ There should be a non-treated group to control for the specific effects of treatment. With drugs this is a placebo group given a non-active substance they think is the drug. For psychological therapies it is more difficult. Often an 'interaction' condition is used where participants talk to the therapist but there is no attempt to apply specific techniques such as CBT or free association. This controls for the effects of being given attention by a therapist.

■ Measurement of improvement should be consistent and thorough across the groups. Questionnaires can be given to participants, and there should also be ratings of clinical improvement by qualified staff; these staff should not know what treatment group the participant is in to prevent bias and investigator effects.

Studies comparing treatments – ethical issues

These studies should be subject to the same ethical criteria as psychological experiments. For instance a major issue in the study of psychological disorders is informed consent; people with disorders may be less able to understand the full consequences of a treatment. Avoidance of psychological harm is also important, and debriefing should be carried out.

An issue specific to studies evaluating treatments is that a non-treated control group is used. If treatments are effective, the control group is being denied help. As a control group is essential to measure improvement this is unavoidable, and is justified by the hope of identifying the most effective treatment.

■ The picture that emerges is that in terms of general effectiveness no one therapy is consistently the best, and this is particularly the case for depression and general anxiety. However there are other considerations that can help decide the most appropriate treatment.

■ For accessibility and speed of action, i.e. how easy is it to provide treatment and how quickly it works, drug therapy stands out. Drugs are readily available for most disorders, and although it usually takes a few days for the therapeutic effect to appear, this is faster than for CBT, behavioural and psychodynamic therapies.

■ Links

P95 describes independent and dependent variables.

On p96 there is a discussion of investigator effects.

Individual differences

Drugs are the first line of treatment for doctors and psychiatrists and therefore the most common form of therapy. There are, however, encouraging signs of a growing awareness among doctors of psychological therapies, in particular CBT.

■ Duration of action: there is some research evidence (Otto *et al.*, 2000) that the benefits of CBT last longer than those of drugs and that overall therefore treatment with CBT is more cost effective. For some conditions, though, notably schizophrenia, drug therapy has to be life-long in order to suppress symptoms and there is no reliable alternative.

■ Ethical issues: all therapeutic drugs used to treat psychological disorders have side effects to a greater or lesser degree. These may be cognitive, for instance memory loss or confusion, or physical, ranging from dry mouth to the severe movement problems found with classical antipsychotics. Patient compliance – the extent to which patients stay on the treatment programme – can be seriously affected by these side effects. We have previously referred to the potentially traumatic effect of deep psychoanalysis revealing repressed material, and the stressful effects of behavioural therapies.

Key points:

■ Freud's psychoanalytical therapy is an example of the psychodynamic approach. The aim of this therapy is to uncover material repressed into the unconscious.

■ Therapeutic techniques include free association, dream analysis and projective tests. They are designed to evade the ego defence mechanisms and uncover repressed conflicts.

■ Systematic desensitisation is an example of a therapy derived from the behavioural approach. These therapies are divided into behaviour therapy (such as systematic desensitisation and aversion therapy, based on classical conditioning) and behaviour modification (such as token economies and social learning, based on operant conditioning).

■ Systematic desensitisation is particularly effective for phobias, where the technique tries to replace the conditioned response of fear with a state of relaxation and calm. This is known as counter-conditioning.

■ Therapies based on the behavioural approach address symptoms and not underlying causes, and have no role for genetic or wider psychological factors that may be involved in a particular disorder.

■ Cognitive behavioural therapy (CBT) is based on the cognitive approach, which emphasises the role of dysfunctional schemata and thinking in psychopathology.

■ The aim of CBT is to work with the client in challenging dysfunctional and unrealistic thoughts and so modifying the underlying negative schemata. The behavioural aspect may include training in specific problem-solving skills.

■ CBT does not consider genetic or other biological factors that may be involved in psychopathology.

✓ Summary questions

4 Explain assumptions behind the use of
   a psychoanalysis
   b systematic desensitisation
   c cognitive-behavioural therapy.

5 Discuss ethical issues in relation to psychological therapies.

6 What are the implications of the finding that people with depression can be helped by either psychoanalytic or cognitive-behavioural therapies?

Chapter summary

☑ 🎧

Further reading and weblinks

G. Davison, J.M. Neale and A.M. Kring, *Abnormal Psychology*, 9th edn, Wiley (2004)

N. Frude, *Understanding Abnormal Psychology*, Blackwell (1998)

A.M. Kring, G.C. Davison, J.M. Neale and S.L. Johnson, *Abnormal Psychology*, 10th edn, Wiley (2006)

Comprehensive text with excellent resource websites

T.F. Oltmanns, J.M. Neale and G.C. Davison, *Case Studies in Abnormal Psychology*, 4th edn, Wiley (1995)

Gives an excellent insight into individual disorders.

www.mentalhealth.com

Excellent coverage of issues in abnormality, and specific coverage of a variety of disorders.

www.rcpsych.ac.uk

Royal College of Psychiatry website. A great deal of useful information on current approaches to abnormality.

- Each of the approaches to abnormality described in the previous chapter leads to particular forms of therapy. Issues such as effectiveness, cost, availability, side effects and ethical aspects need to be considered in relation to therapies.

- Treatments based on the biological approach include electroconvulsive therapy (ECT), psychosurgery and drugs.

- Drugs include the antipsychotics, antidepressants and anti-anxiety drugs. Drugs often work through changes in the activity of brain neurotransmitters such as dopamine, noradrenaline and serotonin.

- Drug therapy is never effective for all patients. It is also associated with problems of side effects and dependence. However many people have been helped by drug treatment.

- ECT causes electrical seizures in the brain. It can be effective in patients with severe depression resistant to other forms of treatment, but has considerable ethical issues attached to it.

- Psychosurgery involves irreversible damage to parts of the brain. It is now used only rarely for severe conditions that have not responded to any other sort of therapy.

- The best-known therapies associated with the psychodynamic approach are those derived from Freud's psychoanalytic model. Psychoanalytic therapies aim to reveal material repressed into the unconscious that is the cause of psychological disorder. They include free association, dream analysis and projective tests.

- Psychoanalytic therapies treat the patient as complex, and emphasise the role of unconscious processes and early experience in the development of later problems. However clients may have to confront distressing issues from their past.

- Systematic desensitisation is an example of a therapy derived from the behavioural approach. Along with flooding and aversion therapy it is based on the principles of classical conditioning.

- Systematic desensitisation for phobias involves counter-conditioning, where the association between fear and a particular object, animal or situation is replaced by relaxation. The client works through a hierarchy of feared situations, either through visualisation or through use of real stimuli.

- Techniques based on operant conditioning are known as behaviour modification. The token economy is a form of positive reinforcement and can be effective in shaping more acceptable behaviour. Social learning through imitation of models may be an important factor in the development of conditions such as eating disorders.

- Therapies based on the behavioural model can be effective in conditions such as phobias and social anxiety. Overall they are reductionist in seeing all behaviour as based on conditioned (learned) associations, and have no role for genetic or other biological factors that may be involved in a particular psychopathology.

- The aim of therapies based on the cognitive approach, in particular cognitive-behavioural therapy (CBT), is to challenge the dysfunctional and irrational thoughts that can lead to depression and anxiety.

■ In Beck's CBT the client is helped to identify negative automatic thoughts and schemata. The therapist then challenges these thoughts by pointing out positive incidents and experiences; this is known as reality testing.

■ There is evidence for negative cognitive biases in depression and anxiety disorders, and CBT can be very effective for these disorders.

■ Although there are practical problems in setting up studies comparing different therapies, some have been done. They indicate that for conditions such as depression, therapies derived from biological, psychodynamic, behavioural and cognitive approaches are equally effective.

■ There are indications that some psychological disorders are more effectively treated using one form of therapy. Examples include the use of systematic desensitisation in phobias, and the use of antipsychotic drugs in schizophrenia.

■ Where alternative therapies exist, choice should be made on the basis of other factors. These include accessibility and cost, speed and duration of action, and ethical issues.

■ How science works: practical activity

In the context of psychopathology the different explanations of atypical behaviour give rise to different therapies, each with its particular merits, limitations and risks.

Divide into groups. Each group should select one category or type of therapy – biological, psychoanalytical, behavioural or cognitive-behavioural. Each group should then research arguments for and against the use of their category. Factors to be taken into account should include whether the assumptions on which the therapy is based are sound, effectiveness, availability, cost, duration, ethical issues and side effects.

The class should then come together, and each group should briefly present their findings and conclusions. The class as a whole can then debate the issues.

Question 1

1   The following are examples of different definitions of abnormality:

A   The behaviour is very different from the behaviour shown by most people in the population.

B   The behaviour prevents the person from achieving self-actualisation or personal autonomy.

C   The behaviour means that the person cannot cope with everyday activities.

D   The behaviour is very different from behaviour that is generally regarded as acceptable.

(a)   In the table below, write down which example, A, B, C or D, matches each of the definitions in the table. *(3 marks)*

Definition of abnormality	Example of the definition
Failure to function adequately	
Deviation from ideal mental health	
Deviation from social norms	

(b)   Select two of the definitions given in the table and explain one limitation of each definition. *(2 + 2 marks)*

2   One assumption of the biological approach to psychopathology is that abnormality is inherited. Explain one way in which psychologists have investigated the genetic basis of abnormality. *(4 marks)*

AQA specimen question

3   Outline key features of the cognitive approach to psychopathology. *(6 marks)*

4   James is afraid of flying. Just thinking about flying causes him distress and even going to the airport is a problem. In order to overcome this fear, he consults a behavioural psychologist who feels that he may benefit from systematic desensitisation.

(a)   Which approach to psychopathology would be most likely to advocate the use of systematic desensitisation? *(1 mark)*

(b)   Explain how systematic desensitisation might be carried out to overcome James's fear of flying. *(6 marks)*

AQA specimen question

Question 2

1   (a)   Outline key features of the biological approach to psychopathology.   *(6 marks)*

      (b)   Explain one limitation of the biological approach to psychopathology.   *(4 marks)*

2   A psychologist conducted an experiment to assess the effectiveness of antipsychotic drugs. He gave an experimental group of patients a course of phenothiazines and a completely different group of patients, who acted as a control group, a harmless placebo. It was found that 60 per cent of the patients given phenothiazines were able to lead a relatively normal life in the community, while the patients given a placebo showed no noticeable improvements.

      Discuss what the investigator might conclude from this study.   *(4 marks)*

3   Discuss the use of one psychological therapy in the treatment of abnormal behaviour.   *(6 marks)*

4   The 'failure to function adequately' definition of abnormality sees an inability to cope with everyday activities as a symptom of a psychological disorder.

      Explain two weaknesses of the 'failure to function adequately' definition of abnormality.   *(4 marks)*

AQA Examiner's tip   **This question is an example of how the examination might assess your understanding of How science works.**

Examination skills

Introduction

Now that the subject content is complete, your next psychological experience is the preparation and sitting of the AQA Psychology A AS exam. In this section we examine the skills and knowledge needed to pass your AS in Psychology A. Remember, knowing your subject is one thing, but being able to revise well for it, being able to identify what the questions require and being able to write concisely to the questions set are all skills that need to be developed – often through repeated experience. Preparation is the key to your success. The more opportunities you can give yourself to become familiar with the course content and the structure of the exam, the more confident you will feel on the day; after all, as the old saying goes, 'it is better the devil you know than the devil you don't'!

Examinations of any kind come to be seen as a necessary evil. They are looked upon as a kind of hurdle you have 'just got to cross'. If you think about it though, examinations are rarely discussed positively. This might be because they are often associated (classically conditioned) with the fear of the unknown question or – more commonly – previous failing experiences within them. There is therefore a form of 'psychology' surrounding examinations and exam performance; if you like, a range of factors that could work for or against you in the examination. Bailey (2007) stresses the need for the correct mind set for revision in addition to the techniques that can be used to help you effectively achieve it. Examination skills don't just 'happen', they are a collective – a mixture of mental, physical and socio-environmental factors that combine to create an ethos that embraces learning. Exam success is built upon a realisation of your own weaknesses and a determination to better them. As US President Theodore Roosevelt once said:

> It's not the critic that counts, not the one who points out where the strong man stumbled, or where the doer of great deeds could have done them better. No, the credit belongs to the man who is actually in the arena, whose face is marred by dust and sweat and blood, who errs and comes up short again and again and who, whilst striving valiantly, spends himself in a worthy cause so that his place may not be among those cold and timid souls who have never known a victory or a defeat

Quoted in Bailey (2007)

■ Organising your knowledge: let's take a 'Spec check'

Unit 1 – Cognitive psychology, Developmental psychology and Research methods			
Unit 1 – Cognitive psychology – Memory			
		Have I got notes on	Revised? Yes/ no/revise again
Models of memory	• The multi-store model of memory, including the concepts of encoding, capacity and duration. Strengths and weaknesses of the model • The working model of memory including strengths and weaknesses		
Memory in everyday life	• Eyewitness testimony (EWT) and factors affecting the accuracy of EWT, including anxiety and age of witness • Misleading information, and the use of the cognitive interview • Strategies for memory improvement		
Unit 1 – Developmental psychology – Early social development			
Attachment	• Explanations of attachment, including learning theory and evolutionary perspective, including Bowlby • Types of attachment, including insecure and secure and studies by Ainsworth • Cultural variations in attachment • Disruption of attachment, failure to form attachment (privation) and the effects of institutionalisation		
Attachment in everyday life	• The impact of different forms of day care on children's social development, including the effects on aggression and peer relations. • Implications of research into attachment and day care for childcare practices		
Unit 1 – Research methods			
Methods and techniques	Candidates will be expected to show knowledge and understanding of the following research methods, their advantages and their weaknesses: • Experimental method – including laboratory, field and natural experiments • Studies using a correlational analysis • Observational techniques • Self report techniques, including questionnaire and interview • Case studies		
Investigation design	Candidates should be familiar with the following features of investigation design: • Aims • Hypotheses, including directional and non-directional • Experimental design (independent groups, repeated measures, matched pairs) • Design of naturalistic observations including the development and use of behavioural categories • Design of questionnaires and interviews • Operationalisation of variables including independent and dependent variables • Pilot studies • Control of extraneous variables • Reliability and validity • Awareness of the British Psychological Society (BPS) Code of Ethics • Ethical issues and ways in which psychologists deal with them		

	• Selection of participants, and sampling techniques, including random, opportunity, and volunteer sampling • Demand characteristics and investigator effects
Data analysis and presentation	Candidates should be familiar with the following features of data analysis, presentation and interpretation: • Presentation and interpretation of quantitative data including graphs, scattergrams and tables • Analysis and interpretation of quantitative data. Measures of central tendency, including median, mean and mode. Measures of dispersion including ranges and standard deviation • Analysis and interpretation of correlational data. Positive and negative correlations and the interpretation of correlation coefficients • Presentation of qualitative data • Processes involved in content analysis

Unit 2 – Biological psychology, Social psychology and Individual differences

Unit 2 – Biological psychology – Stress

Stress as a bodily response	• The body's response to stress, including the pituitary-adrenal system and the sympathomedullary pathway in outline • Stress-related illness and the immune system
Stress in everyday life	• Life changes and daily hassles • Workplace stress • Personality factors, including Type A behaviour • Distinction between emotion-focused and problem-focused approaches to coping with stress • Psychological and physiological methods of stress management, including Cognitive Behavioural Therapy and drugs

Unit 2 – Social psychology – Social influence

Social influence	• Types of conformity, including internalisation and compliance • Explanations of why people conform, including informational social influence and normative social influence • Obedience, including Milgram's work and explanations of why people obey
Social influence in everyday life	• Explanations of independent behaviour, including how people resist pressures to conform and pressures to obey authority • The influence of individual differences on independent behaviour, including locus of control • Implications for social change of research into social influence

Unit 2 – Individual differences – Psychopathology (Abnormality)

Defining and explaining psychological abnormality	• Definitions of abnormality, including deviation from social norms, failure to function adequately and deviation from ideal mental health, and limitations associated with these definitions of psychological abnormality • Key features of the biological approach to psychopathology • Key features of psychological approaches to psychopathology including the psychodynamic, behavioural and cognitive approaches
Treating abnormality	• Biological therapies, including drugs and ECT • Psychological therapies, including psychoanalysis, systematic de-sensitisation and Cognitive Behavioural Therapy

■ Revising and preparing for exams

I am sure by now your teacher has probably said those dreaded words 'the exams are soon, so come on, you'd better start revising – the earlier the better…' Or maybe the more direct line 'time is fast running out – so make sure you plan in time for your revision…' So the teacher says this, but reflect for two minutes. Do YOU actually know how to revise? Do you know the range of techniques that can be used, or for that matter the range of techniques that makes your revision more effective, purposeful and productive? It could be a fatal mistake to assume that what worked for your GCSEs might also work now. The exams are different, with very different skills being assessed. The AS (like the A) Level is far more searching – so don't fall into the trap of assuming that 'winging your GCSEs' means that you can 'wing' these examinations, because you can't.

How do I know how I best revise?

A logical question, answered with another logical question – do you know how you best learn? In order to find this out, you need to use one of many types of 'Learning Styles Questionnaires'. Below you will find a simple example:

Instructions: Read the word in the left hand column and then answer the questions in the successive three columns to show how you would respond to each situation. If the answer is yes, write yes by that answer. The column with the most yes answers will identify your most dominant learning style.

When you..	Visual	Auditory	Kinesthetic & Tactile
Spell	Do you try to see the word?	Do you sound out the word or use a phonetic approach?	Do you write the word down to find if it feels right?
Talk	Do you talk sparingly but dislike listening for too long? Do you favour words such as see, picture, and imagine?	Do you enjoy listening but are impatient to talk? Do you use words such as hear, tune, and think?	Do you gesture and use expressive movements? Do you use words such as feel, touch, and hold?
Concentrate	Do you become distracted by untidiness or movement?	Do you become distracted by sounds or noises?	Do you become distracted by activity around you?
Meet someone again	Do you forget names but remember faces or remember where you met?	Do you forget faces but remember names or remember what you talked about?	Do you remember best what you did together?
Contact people on business	Do you prefer direct, face-to-face, personal meetings?	Do you prefer the telephone?	Do you talk with them while walking or participating in an activity?
Read	Do you like descriptive scenes or pause to imagine the actions?	Do you enjoy dialogue and conversation or hear the characters talk?	Do you prefer action stories or are not a keen reader?
Do something new at work	Do you like to see demonstrations, diagrams, slides or posters?	Do you prefer verbal instructions or talking about it with someone else?	Do you prefer to jump right in and try it?
Put something together	Do you look at the directions and the picture?		Do you ignore the directions and figure it out as you go along?
Need help with a computer application	Do you seek out pictures or diagrams?	Do you call the help desk, ask a neighbour, or growl at the computer?	Do you keep trying to do it or try it on another computer?

Source: http://www.chaminade.org/inspire/learnstl.htm Adapted from Colin Rose (1987). Accelerated Learning.

Such a questionnaire is a good example of VAK (Visual, Auditory, Kinaesthetic) assessment of self learning styles. The outcome will decide whether you best learn through visual, auditory or kinaesthetic means. Why not have a go at the test? See which style is your preferred one.

Visual learning strategies: seeing is believing

If you are a visual learner, your revision strategy needs to reflect this. Activities you could use to revise include the creation of illustrations, e.g. tables, graphs, diagrams, pictures, even video. There are IT-based applications that can be used to produce visual-rich material, e.g. you can use professional software such as Inspiration to make mind maps, but you can also make use of freeware on the internet. It is commonly reported that visual learners revise most effectively in a quiet environment.

Auditory learning strategies: learning by listening

Since learning is most effective by sound, why not record your notes onto tape, CD or MP3 player and then listen to them? Test yourself on small sections that you've just heard. You could also try to repeat out loud facts from your notes with your eyes closed. Word association works well when trying to remember key facts or lines from notes. Since sound is central to your system of learning and auditory learners are good at explaining things, why not hear the information from others? You could arrange a revision forum with friends. Hearing the ideas and discussing them strengthens your knowledge. Does your school/college organise psychology revision conferences? You could also download the podcasts from the Nelson Thornes learning space; these summarise the key points from each chapter. Listening to the information from a reliable source will help you to organise and store the information ready for your examinations.

Kinaesthetic learning strategies: activated by action

The kinaesthetic learner likes a 'hands on' approach, and if this is you then you should consider this when planning your revision. It is of utmost importance that your revision activities get you involved in the work, perhaps by working through a student workbook or a 'companion guide' that encourages you to read and then interact with the material. Why not create little tasks, such as a mix and match activity where the details for a topic have to be matched with its broader explanatory details? Since you learn best from participating in the learning, why not revise by carrying out studies that might have been done to support the principles of the points you are trying to learn. Kinaesthetic learners need variety, so don't just make use of one technique but do different activities during each revision session. Computer technology can also help you, e.g. by using well-established learning-by-doing websites such as S-cool or learning environments such as Moodle. In Moodle, you can see straight away the marks you earn in particular assignments. However you revise, remember that you need to interact with the material in order to learn it.

To prepare effectively for the examination, look back at your practice essays and answers and revise the techniques of analysis, application and evaluation.

■ **Hint**

Freemind

http://freemind.sourceforge.net

Freemind is a novel piece of software that allows you to create mind maps. The software allows you to put ideas or concepts in the centre, and then branch out from this the relevant issues and details. Links can be made between points and the whole diagram can be colour-coded accordingly, tools that are particularly useful to the visual learner. Using the enhanced learning characteristics that most visual learners find very conducive to study, entries can be colour-coded, and links between terms stated can be effectively shown. Not only are these easy to produce, but the finished article is printable, and provides a clear and easily accessible means of summarising notes.

Your calendar of action for effective exam preparation and completion

One month (plus) before the exam	• Success is built upon preparation. So ensure that you have all your notes. • Make use of the 'spec check' earlier to ensure your notes cover the whole specification. If not, speak to your teacher about getting additional notes for it. • Complete the Learning Styles Questionnaire. Identify your preferred learning style, and develop activities that complement this. • Bearing in mind your preferred method of learning, plan out times for revision that allow for the specification to be covered, and more than just superficially. • Develop a set of goals that are achievable as you go through your revision. Maybe reward yourself with certain numbers of rest periods that can be used how you like, e.g. shopping, PS2 gaming etc.
Two weeks before	• Revision is well under way. Make sure that you complement your learning of the theory with good practice of the examination questions. • Theory is not everything – being aware of the question type, style and layout is just as important. • Make use of the questions in the next part of this chapter to get you started. Why not also try to use your own imagination – you can use the specification check and some of the specimen questions to create your own questions. By taking the words of the specification you are doing exactly what the Principal Examiners would do when they set the questions. • Remember, practice makes perfect. • Ask your teacher/tutor to look at your attempts. Note down any issues that seem to recur and ask for help in rectifying these. • Now is the time for refining your skills, and clearing up last-minute anomalies in understanding.
One week before	• In this week, focus on the issues that you might find most difficult. There is still time, but be more efficient with it! • You mind will rest easier if you know the material well. So in a self-rewarding way, tick off on the spec check the areas that you have covered and know well. Identify the areas that need to be revisited in order to clarify understanding. • The use of highlighters is a good idea, colour coding the areas of the specification that might be well learnt (green); in need of a little more (orange); really don't understand (red).
The night before	• Should you cram until the last minute, or rest? Most teachers would say that what you don't know by the night before, you will never know. • As a general guide, however, ensure that you have plenty of rest the evening before. Go to sleep early – next morning you will need all the extra energy your body can generate. Remember, your body requires sleep, and a late night of revising may reduce your effectiveness.
The day of the exam	• If it is a morning examination, make sure you have a good breakfast. The examination will require a lot of mental energy, so slow release energy foods are often the best – for example, porridge. Why not also have a couple of bananas as these are high in potassium – another source of 'brain energy'. • If your exam is in the afternoon, you have some more time to gently fine tune your revision. Don't do this excessively. • Get to your examination location with plenty of time to spare. Try to reduce all avoidable sources of stress. • Once in the exam location, make sure you complete the necessary administration. • Start the exam – remember to enjoy it – you have worked hard and prepared for it well, now simply show the examiner what you can do. • After the exam – avoid too much unnecessary dissection of what you have done. This will worry you, and may affect future exam performance.

■ In the exam room

Suitable preparation for the exam is only half the battle. Knowing what to write, how to write it and in what way is the next step. In this section we take a closer look at the AS examinations you will be undertaking, illustrating the skills needed to be successful.

Your AQA Psychology A AS will certify your competence at this level, but the examination searches for three main skills. These are called Assessment Objectives. They are:

AO1: Knowledge and understanding of science and of how science works

For this you should:

■ Recognise, recall and show understanding of scientific knowledge

■ Select, organise and communicate relevant information in a variety of forms.

AO2: Application of knowledge and understanding of science and how science works

For this you should:

■ Analyse and evaluate scientific knowledge and processes

■ Apply scientific knowledge and processes to unfamiliar situations including those related to issues

■ Assess the validity, reliability and credibility of scientific information.

AO3: How science works – psychology

For this you should:

■ Be able to describe ethical, safe and skilful practice techniques and processes, selecting appropriate qualitative and quantitative methods

■ Know how to make, record and communicate reliable and valid observations and measurements with appropriate precision and accuracy, through using primary and secondary sources

■ Analyse, interpret, explain and evaluate the methodology, results and impact of their own and others' experimental and investigative activities in a variety of ways.

Exam technique

1 Knowing your exam

It is important first of all to know what papers you are sitting. Your school/college will choose your likely route of assessment; this might mean sitting PSYA1 first, maybe in January, then PSYA2 in the following summer series of exams.

The two AS papers you will be sitting are:

PSYA1 – Cognitive psychology, Developmental psychology and Research methods (note here that Research methods will be assessed within the context of Cognitive psychology and Developmental psychology)

PSYA2 – Biological psychology, Social psychology and Individual differences

You should organise your folder according to the two different examinations.

2 Knowing the question requirements and answering skills

The new specification has a very different form of assessment. The question styles are a radical shift from those seen in past years. This is not such a bad point, and in many ways actually provides you with a more logical progression from your level 2 studies to your level 3, more applied, work.

In order to know how to answer questions correctly, it is important to understand clearly what it is the examiner is looking for in your examination responses. The examiner is looking to assess 3 main skills:

■ the ability to demonstrate your knowledge and understanding

■ your ability to use, evaluate and apply your knowledge to analyse and evaluate your material

■ your understanding of How science works.

Each of these will be assessed in a variety of different ways in the exam. Question formats can take a number of different forms. For example, 'completing a table', e.g.:

1(a). Using the list below, complete the table to distinguish between long-term memory and short-term memory.
- Unlimited
- Up to a lifetime
- 7 +/- 2 items
- Mainly acoustic
- Seconds
- Mainly semantic *(3 marks)*

	Short-Term Memory (STM)	Long-Term Memory (LTM)
Capacity		
Duration		
Encoding		

AQA specimen question

AQA Examiner's tip

This question assesses your knowledge of key terminology. So here the examiner will be awarding one mark for duration, one mark for capacity and one mark for encoding. In each case both terms need to be correct to gain the mark.

Your understanding of the factual material you have learnt might also be assessed through other styles of questions such as:

1(b). Using the multi-store model of memory, outline how information is transferred from short-term memory to long-term memory.
(2 marks)
AQA specimen question

AQA Examiner's tip

This particular question seeks your knowledge of the model. Look at the mark awarded, the two marks suggests that a single word answer will not suffice. Here one mark could be given for the identification of rehearsal being central to the transfer of information to LTM. The further mark would be given for the elaboration of this process, e.g. the process of rehearsal ensures that information can be maintained in STM, since it is a limited capacity and duration store – until it has been put into LTM store.

It is possible that your knowledge and understanding (AO1) could be assessed in a more extended format. For example:

2(a). Outline the key features of the working model of memory.
(6 marks)
AQA specimen question

AQA Examiner's tip

To achieve high marks what is written must be factually correct. But simple identification of parts of the model is not enough. If you just do this, the mark scheme clearly states that this will limit your marks. In particular there is the expectation that you will be able to outline both structure (the names of the different parts of the model) and function (what these different parts do).

For this particular question, you will notice that you are asked to outline the important features. Again here, look at the marks awarded and the wording of the question – there is the expectation that the response will provide detail, if only briefly, of the main constituent features of the model.

In marking such questions the examiner will use 'mark bands' to accurately assess the quality of the response.

6–5 marks Accurate and reasonably detailed

Accurate and reasonably detailed outline of the working memory model referring to both structure and function.

4–3 marks Less detailed but generally accurate

Less detailed but generally accurate outline of the working memory model referring to structure and/or function.

2–1 marks Basic

Basic outline of the working memory that correctly identifies the three main components but further detail may be muddled or flawed.

0 marks No creditworthy information

The space allowed in the answer booklet will give you an indication of how much to write. To ensure you do this effectively and efficiently, plan and organise your answer to include both structure and function.

Of course, not all questions will focus on the factual knowledge required for AO1. Other aspects of your psychological understanding can be assessed through your knowledge of strengths and limitations, or though the application of your knowledge to a particular situation/scenario. For example:

3. Kate is revising for her driving theory test. She needs to re-member a variety of information such as rules relating to speed limits, stopping distances, etc.

    Outline two strategies Kate might use to improve her recall and explain why each of the strategies you suggest should improve recall.

    (6 marks)

    AQA specimen question

AQA Examiner's tip

In this particular case, the examiner is looking for two different types of information. Firstly, the knowledge of the appropriate strategy, and secondly your ability to justify its use linking it to the example given.

It is useful to underline key points in the scenario to ensure you respond to them.

Remember of course that How science works and in particular your research methods knowledge is being assessed. There is no separate examination section on research methods, rather such questions will be contextualised within the topics. Most of this assessment will be in cognitive and developmental sections. So some questions might get you to analyse or apply research methods knowledge to a given situation:

5. In order to investigate encoding in memory, an experimenter gave participants two lists of words. List A contained 10 acoustically similar words and List B contained 10 semantically similar words.

    Each participant read aloud List A and then recalled the words in the list.

    Then each participant read aloud List B and recalled the words in this list.

    The number of words correctly recalled in each condition was recorded and compared to see whether participants remem-bered more words from List A or from List B.

5 (a). What factors, other than the acoustic and semantic encoding, would the experimenter have to consider when selecting words for the lists?

AQA Examiner's tip

With the above example question you will note how there is often a requirement for knowledge of specific terms. To prepare yourself well for this exam, why not create a glossary list in your revision notes of all key research methods terms from the specification, with meanings by them? Also, revise these terms gradually. Research terminology is a language unto itself, and requires continual use for correct use of knowledge to the situations given in the exam.

_____

_____

_____

_____

_____

(3 marks)

AQA Examiner's tip

Draw on your experience of designing your own experiments in answering this question.

5 (b).   Which type of design was used in this investigation? Tick the correct box.

☐ Repeated measures

☐ Independent groups

☐ Matched participants   *(1 mark)*

5 (c).   Identify one flaw in the design of this investigation and explain how the experimenter could have overcome this flaw.

(3 marks)

AQA specimen question

In both PSYA1 and PSYA2 papers there are questions that require extended writing. This is marked out of 12, 6 marks being awarded for knowledge and understanding and 6 marks for analysis, application and evaluation. For the 12 mark question, there will be a box on the examination paper in which you can plan your answer. Consider the following example taken from a PSYA1 specimen paper:

9.   Outline and evaluate research into the effects of day care on social development (e.g. aggression, peer relations)

(12 marks)

AQA specimen question

AQA Examiner's tip

You will need to show knowledge of research into the effects of day care and be able to evaluate this.

Marks will be awarded on: accuracy, detail and relevance of description; breadth, depth and effectiveness of analysis and evaluation.

Look back at the examiner's tips in the rest of the book. Look carefully at those relating to analysis and application, and evaluation of understanding.

You can get more tips/resources from the Nelson Thornes learning space. Practicing answering examination questions will help you to develop your skills.

For up-to-date information about the AQA specification and mark scheme, see the A Level section on www.aqa.org.uk.

Using the information in this chapter you can have the confidence to identify your areas of misunderstanding, and the methods to provide you with a clear, personalised revision program. Good luck!

References

Abrahamson, L., Seligman, M.P and Teasdale, J.D. (1978) Learned helplessness in humans – critique and reformulation. *Journal of Abnormal Psychology*, **87**, 49–74.

Adorno, T.W., Frenkel-Brunswik, G., Levinson, D.J. and Sanford, R.N. (1950) *The Authoritarian Personality*. New York: Harper.

Allen, K., Blasovich, J. and Mendes, W.B. (2002) Cardiovascular reactivity and the presence of pets, friends, and spouses: the truth about cats and dogs. *Psychosomatic Medicine*, **64**, 727–39.

Andersson, B.E. (1989) Effects of public day care: a longitudinal study. *Child Development*, **60**.

Andersson, B.E. (1992) Effects of day care on cognitive and socioemotional development of thirteen-year-old Swedish children. *Child Development*, **63**.

Asch, S.E. (1951) Effects of group pressure upon the modification and distortion of judgements. In H. Guetzkpw (ed.), *Groups, Leadership and Men*. Pittsburgh, PA: Carnegie Press.

Asch, S.E. (1956) Studies of independence and conformity: a minority of one against a unanimous majority. *Psychological Monographs*, **70**.

Attanasio, V., Andrasik, F., Burke, E.J., Blake, D.D., Kabela, E. and McCarran, M.S. (1985) Clinical issues in utilizing biofeedback with children. *Clinical Biofeedback and Health*, **8**, 134–41.

Aviezer, *et al.* (1994) Perspectives on infant mental health from Israel: the case of changes in collective sleeping on the Kibbutz. *Infant Mental Health Journal*, **19**, 1, 76–86.

Avtgis, T.A. (1998) Locus of control and persuasion, social influence and conformity: a meta-analytic review. *Psychology Reports*, **83**(3), 899–903.

Baddeley, A. and Hitch, G. (1974) Working memory. In G. Bower (ed.), *The Psychology of Learning and Motivation*. Oxford: Elsevier.

Baddeley, A. D. (1996) Exploring the central executive. *Quarterly Journal of Experimental Psychology*, **51A**, 819–52.

Baddeley, A.D. (1999) *Essentials of Human Memory*. Hove: Psychology Press.

Baddeley, A.D. and Logie, R.H. (1999) Working memory: the multiple component model. In A. Miyake and P. Shah (eds), *Models of Working Memory: mechanisms of active maintenance and executive control*. Cambridge: Cambridge University Press.

Baddeley, A.D. and Wilson, B. (2002) Prose recall and amnesia: implications for the structure of working memory. *Neuropsychologia*, **40**, 1737–43.

Baddeley, A.D., Grant, S., Wight, E. and Thomson, N. (1973) Imagery and visual working memory. In P.M.A. Rabbitt and S. Dornic (eds), *Attention and Performance V* (pp205–17). London: Academic Press.

Baddeley, A.D., Thomson, N. and Buchanan, M. (1975) Word length and the structure of short-term memory. *Journal of Verbal Learning and Verbal Behaviour*, **14**, 575–89.

Bahrick, H.P. and Hall, L.K. (2005) The importance of retrieval failures to long-term retention: a metacognitive explanation of the spacing effect. *Journal of Memory and Language*, **52**, 4, 566–77 (special issue on metamemory).

Bahrick, H.P. Phelps, E. (1987) Retention of Spanish vocabulary over eight years. *Journal of Experimental Psychology: learning, memory and cognition*, **13**, 2.

Bailey, R.E. and Denstaedt, L. (2007) *Destinations: an integrated approach to writing paragraphs and essays*. McGraw-Hill.

Bandura, A. (1969) *Principles of Behavior Modification*. New York: Holt, Reinhart & Winston.

Bandura, A. (1977) *Social Learning Theory* (2nd ed). Englewood Cliffs, NJ: Prentice Hall.

Barlow, D.H., Raffa, S.D. and Cohen, E.M. (2002) Psychosocial treatments for panic disorders, phobias, and generalized anxiety disorder. In P.E. Nathan and J. M. Gorman (eds), *A Guide to Treatments that Work* (2nd edn, pp301–35). London: Oxford University Press.

Barrett, H. (1997) How young children cope with separation: toward a new conceptualization. *British Journal of Medical Psychology*, **70**, 339–58.

Baumrind, D. (1964) Some thoughts on ethics of research: after reading Milgram's 'Behavioural study of obedience'. *American Psychologist*, **19**, 421–43.

Beasley, M., Thompson, T. and Davidson, J. (2003) Resilience in response to life stress: the effects of coping style and cognitive hardiness. *Personality and Individual Differences*, **34**, 77–95.

Beck, A.T. (1963) Thinking and depression. *Archives of General Psychiatry*, **9**, 324–33.

Beck, A.T. (1976) *Cognitive Therapy and the Emotional Disorders*. New York: International Universities Press.

Belsky, J. (2006) Early child care and early child development: major findings from the NICHO study of early child care. *European Journal of Developmental Psychology*, **3**, 95–110.

Belsky, J. and Rovine, M. (1987) Temperament and attachment security in the strange situation: a rapprochement. *Child Development*, **58**, 787–95.

Berger, J.A. (2000) The effect of a cognitive-behavioral stress management intervention on salivary IgA, self-reported levels of stress, and physical health complaints in an undergraduate population. *Dissertations Abstracts International*. Section B: The Sciences and Engineering, **60**, 5762.

Berk, L. (1997) *Child Development* (4th edn). Boston: Allyn and Bacon.

Berkowitz, L. (1999) Evil is more than banal. Situationalism and the concept of evil. *Personality and*

Social Psychology Review, **3**, Special Issue – Perspectives on evil and violence, 246–53.

Berz, W.L. (1995) Working memory in music: a theoretical model. *Music Perception*, **12**, 353–64.

Bickman, L. (1974a) The social power of a uniform. *Journal of Applied Social Psychology*, **4**, 47–61.

Bickman, L. (1974b) Clothes make the person. *Psychology Today*, **8**(4), 48–51.

Biddle, S. (2000) Emotion, mood and physical activity. In S.J.H. Biddle, K.R. Fox and S.H. Boutcher (eds), *Physical Activity and Psychological Well-being*. London: Routledge.

Black, K.A. and Schutte, E.D. (2006) Recollections of being loved: implications of childhood experiences with parents for young adults romantic relationships. *Journal of Family Issues*, **27**, 1459–80.

Blass, T. (1991) The Milgram paradigm after 35 years: some things we now know about obedience to authority. In T. Blass (ed. 2000) *Obedience to Authority: current perspectives on the Milgram paradigm*. New Jersey: Lawrence Erlbaum Associates.

Booth-Kewley, S. and Friedman, H.S. (1987) Psychological predictors of heart disease: a quantitative review. *Psychological Bulletin*, **101**, 343–62.

Borge, A., Rutter, M., Cote, S. and Tremblay, R. (2004) Early childcare and physical aggression: differentiating social selection and social causation. *Journal of Child Psychology and Psychiatry*, **45**(2), 367–76.

Bower, G.H. and Winzenz, D. (1969) Groups, structure, coding and memory for digit series. *Journal of Experimental Psychology*, Monograph 80 (No. 3, Pt 2), pp1–17.

Bowlby, J. (1944) 44 juvenile thieves: their characters and their home life. *International Journal of Psychoanalysis*, **25**, 1–57.

Bransford, J.D. and Johnson, M.K. (1972) Contextual prerequisites for understanding some investigators of comprehension and recall. *Journal of Verbal Learning and Verbal Behaviour*.

Brief, A.P, Dukerich, J.M. and Doran, L.I. (1991) Resolving ethical dilemmas in management: experimental investigation of values, accountability and choice. *Journal of Applied Social Psychology*, **21**, 380–96.

Brown, S.D. (2007) Intergroup processes: social identity theory. In D. Langdridge and S. Taylor, *Critical Readings in Social Psychology*. Maidenhead: Open University Press.

Browning, C.R. (1992) *Ordinary Men; Reserve Police Battalion 101 and the Final Solution*. London: HarperCollins.

Bunge, S.A., Klingberg, T., Jacobsen, R.B. and Gabrieli, J.D.E. (2000) A resource model of the neural basis of executive working memory. *Proceedings of the National Academy of Science USA*, **97**, 3573–8.

Bushman, B.J. (1988) The effects of apparel on compliance: a field experiment with a female authority figure. *Personality and Social Psychology Bulletin*, **14**, 459–67.

Campbell, Lamb and Hwang (2000) Early child care experiences and children's social competence between 11/2 and 15 years of age. *Applied Developmental Science*, **4**, 3, 166–76.

Cardwell, M. (2001) Obedience to authority. The legacy of Milgram's research. *Psychology Review*, April 2001, 14–17.

Carver, C.S., Pozo, C., Harris, S.D., Noriega, V., Scheier, M.F., Robinson, D.S., Ketchan, A.S., Moffat, F.L., Jr and Clark, K.C. (1993) How coping mediates the effect of optimism on distress: a study of women with early stage breast cancer. *Journal of Personality and Social Psychology*, **65**, 375–90.

Carver, C.S., Scheier, M.F. and Weintraub, J.K. (1989) Assessing coping styles: a theoretically-based approach. *Journal of Personality and Social Psychology*, **56**, 267–83.

Chase, A. (2000) A lesson in hate. The *Guardian*, 22 June, pp2–3.

Chisholm, K., Ames, E., Fisher, L. and Morison, S. (1999) Some recommendations of a study of Romanian orphans adopted to British Columbia in Tepper, T., Hannon, L. and Sandstrom, D. (eds), *International Adoption: Challenges and Opportunities*. Meadowlands, Pennsylvania: Parents Network for the Post Institutionalized Child.

Detailed explanation of Christianson and Hubinette (1993) in Kapardis, A. (2002) *Psychology and Law – a Critical Introduction (*2nd edn). Cambridge: Cambridge University Press, 42–4.

Cinirella, M. and Green, B. (2005) Does 'cyber-conformity' vary cross culturally? Exploring the effect of culture and communication medium on social conformity. *Computers in Human Behaviour*, **23**(4), 2011–25.

Clark, D.M. (1986) A cognitive approach to panic. *Behavior Research and Therapy*, **24**, 461–70.

Clark, R.D. (1989) Effect of number of majority defectors on minority influence. *Group Dynamics: Theory, Research and Practice*, **3**(4), 303–12

Cohen, S., Doyle, W.J., Skoner, D.P., Rabin, B.S. and Gwaltney, J.M. (1997) Social ties and susceptibility to the common cold. *Journal of the American Medical Association*, **277**, 1940–4.

Cohen, S., Tyrell, D.A.J. and Smith, A.P. (1993) Negative life events, perceived stress, negative affect and susceptibility to the common cold. *Journal of Personality and Social Psychology*, **64**, 131–40.

Constable, J.F. and Russell, D.W. (1986) The effect of social support and the work environment upon burnout in nurses. *Journal of Human Stress*, **12**, 20–6.

Coolican, H. (1994) *Research Methods and Statistics in Psychology*. London: Hodder & Stoughton.

Cooper, C.L., Sloan, S.J. and Williams, S. (1988) *The Occupational Stress Indicator*. Windsor: NFER-Nelson.

Cowan, N. (1998) Visual and auditory working memory capacity. *Trends in Cognitive Sciences*, **2**, 77–87.

Cowan, N. (2000) The magical number 4 in short-term-memory: a reconsideration of mental storage capacity. *Behavioural and Brain Sciences*, **24**, 87–185.

Cox, T. (1978) *Stress*. London: Macmillan.

References

Craik and Lockhart (1972) Levels of processing: a framework for memory research. *Journal of Verbal Learning and Verbal Behaviour*, **11**, 671–84.

Crutchfield, R.S. (1955) Conformity and character. *American Psychology*, **10**, 191–8.

Cumberbatch, G. (1990) Television Advertising and Sex Role Stereotyping: A Content Analysis (working paper IV for the British Broadcasting Standards Council), Communication Research Group, Aston University.

Davidson, J.R.T., Foa, E.B. and Huppert, J.D. (2004) Fluoxetine, comprehensive cognitive behavioural therapy, and placebo in generalised social phobia. *Archives of General Psychiatry*, **61**, 1005–13.

Davies, G.M. (1993) Witnessing events. In G.M. Davies and R.H. Logie (eds), *Memory in Everyday Life*. Amsterdam: Elsevier.

Davies, G.M. (1994) Children's testimony – research findings and policy implications. *Psychology, Crime and Law*, **1**, 175–80.

De Bene, R. and Moe, A. (2003) Presentation modality effects in studying passages: are mental images always effective? *Applied Cognitive Psychology*, **17**, 309–24.

De Boer, M.F., Ryckman, R.M., Pruyn, J.F.A. and Van den Borne, H.W. (1999) Psychosocial correlates of cancer relapse and survival: a literature review. *Patient Education and Counselling*, **37**, 215–30.

De Wolff, M.S. and Van Ijzendoorn, M.H. (1997) Sensitivity and attachment: a meta-analysis on parental anecdotes on infant attachment. *Child Development*, **68**, 604–9.

Deaux, K. Dane, F. C. and Wrightsman, L.S. (1993) *Social Psychology in the 90's*. California: Brooks Cole.

Dekle. D.J., Beal, C.R., Elliott, R. and Huneycutt, D. (1996) Children as witnesses: a comparison of lineup versus showup identification methods. *Applied Cognitive Psychology*, **10**, 1–12.

DeLongis, A., Coyne, J.C., Dakof, G., Folkman, S. and Lazarus, R.S. (1982) Relationships of daily hassles, uplifts, and major life events to health status. *Health Psychology*, **1**, 119–36.

Dembroski, T.M., MacDougall, J.M., Costa, P.T. and Grandits, G.A. (1989) Components of hostility as predictors of sudden death and myocardial infarction in the Multiple Risk Factor Intervention Trial. *Psychosomatic Medicine*, **51**, 514–22.

Denollet, J. (2000) Type D personality: a potential risk factor refined. *Journal of Psychosomatic Medicine*, **49**, 255–66.

Denollet, J. and Van Heck, G.L. (2001) Psychological risk factors in heart disease: what Type D personality is (not) about. *Journal of Psychosomatic Research*, **51**, 465–68.

Denollet, J., Sys, S.U., Stroobant, N., Rombouts, H., Gillebert, T.C. and Brutsaert, D.L. (1996) Personality as an independent predictor of long-term mortality in patients with coronary heart disease. *The Lancet*, **347**, 417–21.

Deutsch, M. and Gerard, H.B. (1955) A study of normative and informational social influences upon individual judgement. *Journal of Abnormal and Social Psychology*, **51**, 629–36.

Dewe, P.J. (1992) Applying the concept of appraisal to work stressors: some exploratory analysis. *Human Relations*, **45**, 143–64.

Dollard, J. and Miller, N.E. (1951) Personality and psychotherapy: an analysis in terms of learning, thinking, culture. *American Sociological Review*, **16**, 3, 414–16.

Dontas, *et al.* (1985) Early social development in institutionally reared Greek infants: attachment and peer interaction. *Monographs of the Society for Research in Child Development*, **50**, 136–46.

Drachman, D.A. and Sahakian, B.J. (1979) Effects of cholinergic agents on human learning and memory. In R. Barbeau (ed.), *Nutrition and the Brain* (vol. 5, pp351–66). New York: Raven Press.

Elkin, I., Shea, M.T. and Watkins, J.T. (1989) National Institutes of Mental Health Treatment of Depression Collaborative Research Program: general effectiveness of treatments. *Archives of General Psychiatry*, **46**, 971–82.

Ellis, A. (1962) *Reason and Emotion in Psychotherapy*. New York: Lyle Stuart.

Ellis, A. (1991) The revised ABC's of rational emotive therapy (RET). *Journal of Rational-Emotive and Cognitive Behavior Therapy*, **9**, 139–72.

Engle, R.W., Kane, M.J. and Tuholski, S.W. (1999) Individual differences in working memory capacity and what they tell us about controlled attention, general fluid intelligence and functions of the pre-frontal cortex. In A. Miyake and P. Shah (eds), *Models of Working Memory: mechanisms of active maintenance and executive control*. Cambridge: Cambridge University Press.

Evans, P.D. and Edgerton, N. (1991) Life-events and mood as predictors of the common cold. *British Journal of Medical Psychology*, **64**, 35–44.

Eysenck, H.J. (1952) The effects of psychotherapy: an evaluation. *Journal of Consulting Psychology*, **16**, 319–24.

Eysenck, H.J. (1988) Personality, stress and cancer: prediction and prophylaxis. *British Journal of Medical Psychology*, **61**, 57–75.

Eysenck, H.J. and Grossarth-Maticek, R. (1989) Prevention of cancer and coronary heart disease and the reduction in the cost of the National Health Service. *Journal of Social, Political and Economic Studies*, **14**, 25–47.

Field, T., Masi, W., Goldstein, D., Perry, S. and Parl, S. (1988) Infant daycare facilitates preschool behavior. *Early Childhood Research Quarterly*, **3**, 341–59.

Fisher, R. P. *et al.* (1987) Critical analysis of police interview techniques. *Journal of Police Science and Administration*, **15**.

Flin, R., Boon, J., Knox, A. and Bull, R. (1992) The effect of a five-month delay on children's and adults' eyewitness memory. *British Journal of Psychology*, **83**, 323–36.

Fox, H.L., Dwyer, D.J. and Ganster, D.C. (1993) Effects of stressful job demands and control on physiological and attitudinal outcomes in a hospital setting. *Academy of Management Journal*, **36**, 289–318.

Fox, N. (1977) Attachment of kibbutz infants to mother and matapelet. *Child Development*, **48**, 1,288–39

Fox, N., Kimmerley, N.L. and Schafer, W.D. (1991) Attachment to mother/attachment to father: a meta analysis. *Child Development*, **62**, 210–25.

Freeman, W. (1971) Frontal lobotomy in early schizophrenia: long follow-up in 415 cases. *British Journal of Psychiatry*, **119**, 621–4.

Freud, S. (1909) Analysis of a phobia in a five year old boy. In J. Strachey (ed. and trans.) (1976) *The Complete Psychological Works: the standard edition*, **10**. New York: Norton.

Fruzzetti, A.E., Toland, K., Teller, S.A. and Loftus, E.F. (1992) Memory and eyewitness testimony. In M. Gruneberg and P. Morris (eds), *Aspects of Memory: The Practical Aspects*. London: Routledge.

Gamson, W.A , Fireman, B. and Rytina, S. (1982) *Encounters with Unjust Authority*. Homewood IL: Dorsey Press.

Geiselman, R.E., Fisher, R., MacKinnon, D. and Holland, H. (1985) Eyewitness memory enhancement in the police interview: cognitive retrieval mnemonics versus hypnosis. *Journal of Applied Psychology*, **70**, 401–12.

Geiselman, R.E., Fisher, R., MacKinnon, D. and Holland, H. (1986) Enhancement of eyewitness memory with the cognitive interview. *American Journal of Psychology*, **99**, 385–401.

Glanzer, M. (1972) Storage mechanisms in recall. In G.H. Bower (ed.), *The Psychology of Learning and Motivation: advances in research and theory*, **V**. New York: Academic Press.

Glanzer, M. and Cunitz, A.R. (1966) Two storage mechanisms in free recall. *Journal of Verbal Learning and Verbal Behaviour*, **5**, 351–60.

Glanzer, M. and Razel, M. (1974) The size of the unit in short-term storage. *Journal of Verbal Learning and Behaviour*, **13**, 114–31.

Goldschmied, E. and Jackson, S. (1994) People under three – young children in day-care. In L. Dryden, R. Forbes, P. Mukherji and L. Pound (eds), (2005) *Early Years*. London: Hodder and Stoughton.

Gross, R.D. (1994) *Key Studies in Psychology* (2nd edn). London: Hodder & Stoughton.

Gruneberg, M.M. and Jacobs, G.C. (1991) In defence of Linkword. *The Language Learning Journal*, **3**, 25–9.

Hamilton, S. and Fagot, B.I. (1988) Chronic stress and coping style: a comparison of male and female undergraduates. *Journal of Personality and Social Psychology*, **55**, 819–23.

Haney, C., Banks, C. and Zimbardo, P.G. (1973) Interpersonal dynamics in a simulated prison. *International Journal of Criminology and Penology*, **1**, 69–97.

Harlow, H. F. and Zimmerman, R. (1959) Affectional responses in the infant monkey. *Science*, **130**, 421–32.

Hart, J.W., Stasson, M.F. and Karau, S.J. (1999) Effects of source expertise an physical distance on minority influence. *Group Dynamics: theory, research and practice*, **3**(1), 81–92.

Hay and Vespo (1988) The different faces of motherhood. In B. Birns and D. Hay (eds), *Social Learning Perspectives on the Development of the Mother–Child Relationship*. New York: Plenum Press.

Hazan, C. and Shaver, P. (1987) Romantic Love Conceptualized as an Attachment Process. *Journal of Personality and Social Psychology*, **52**, 511–24.

Hodges, J. and Tizard, B. (1989) Social and family relationships of ex-institutional adolescents. *Journal of Child Psychology and Psychiatry*, **30**, 77–97.

Hofling, C.K., Brotzman, E., Dalrymple, S., Graves, N. and Pierce, C.N. (1966) An experimental study in nurse–physician relationships. *Journal of Nervous and Mental Disease*, **143**, 171–80.

Hogg, M.A. (2003) Social identity. In M.R. Leary and J.P. Tangney (eds) *Handbook of Self and Identity* (pp479–501). New York: Guilford.

Hogg, M.A. and Abrahams, D. (1988) *Social Identifications: a social psychology of inter-group relations and group processes*. London: Routledge.

Hogg, M.A. and Turner, J.C. (1987) Social identity and conformity: a theory of referent informational influence. In W. Doise and S. Moscovici (eds), *Current Issues in European Social Psychology* (vol. 2 , pp138–82). Cambridge: Cambridge University Press.

Hogg, M.A. and Vaughan, G.M. (2005) *Social Psychology* (4th edn). Harlow: Pearson Education.

Holahan, C.J. and Moos, R.H. (1986) Personality, coping, and family resources in stress resistance: a longitudinal analysis. *Journal of Personality and Social Psychology*, **51**, 389–95.

Holmes, T.H. and Rahe, R.H. (1967) The social readjustment rating scale. *Journal of Psychosomatic Research*, **11**, 213–18.

Jacobs, J. (1887) Experiments in 'prehension'. *Mind*, **12**, 75–9.

Jacobson, E. (1938) *Progressive Relaxation: a physiological and clinical investigation of muscle states and their significance in psychology and medical practice* (2nd edn). Chicago: University of Chicago Press.

Jahoda, M. (1958) *Current Concepts of Positive Mental Health*. New York: Basic Books.

Jandorf, L., Deblinger, E., Neale, J.M. and Stone, A.A. (1986) Daily versus major life events as predictors of symptom frequency. *Journal of General Psychology*, **113**(3), 205–18.

Jenness, A. (1932) The role of discussion in changing opinion regarding matter of fact. *Journal of Abnormal and Social Psychology*, **27**, 279–96.

Jerabek, I. and Standing, L. (1992) Imagined test situations produce contextual memory enhancement. *Perceptual and Motor Skills*, **75**, 400.

Johansson, G., Aronsson, G. and Linstrom, B.O. (1978) Social psychological and neuroendocrine stress reactions in highly mechanised work. *Ergonomics*, **21**, 583–99.

Kamarck, T.W., Peterman, A.H. and Raynor, D.A. (1998) The effects of the social environment on stress-related cardiovascular activation: current findings, prospects, and implications. *Annals of Behavioral Medicine*, **20**, 242–56.

Kanner, A.D., Coyne, J.C., Schaefer, C. and Lazarus, R.S. (1981) Comparison of two modes of stress measurement: Daily hassles and uplifts versus major life events. *Journal of Behavioral Medicine*, **4**, 1–39.

Karasek, R.A. (1979) Job demands, job decision latitude and mental strain: implications for job design. *Administrative Science Quarterly*, **24**, 285–308.

Kassin and Kiechel (1996) The social psychology of false confessions: Compliance, internalization, and confabulation. *Psychological Science*, **7**, 3, 125–8.

Kebbell, M.R. and Milne, R. (1998) Police officers' perceptions of eyewitness performance in forensic investigations. *Journal of Social Psychology*, **138**, 323–30.

Kelman, H.C. (1958) Compliance, identification and internalisation. *Journal of Conflict Resolution*, **2**, 51–60.

Kielcolt-Glaser, J.K., Garner, W., Speicher, G.M., Penn, G.M., Holliday, J. and Glaser, R. (1984) Psychological modifiers of immunocompetence in medical students. *Psychosomatic Medicine*, **46**, 7–14.

Kiecolt-Glaser, J.K., Dura, J.R., Speicher, C.E., Trask, O.J. and Glaser, R.S.O. (1991) Spousal caregivers of dementia victims: longitudinal changes in immunity and health. *Psychosomatic Medicine*, **53**, 345–62.

Kiecolt-Glaser, J.K., Glaser, R., Cacioppo, J.T. and Malarkey, W.B. (1998) Marital stress: immunologic, neuroendocrine, and autonomic correlates. *Annals of the New York Academy of Sciences*, **840**, 656–63.

Kiecolt-Glaser, J.K., Ogrocki, P., Stout, J.C., Speicher, C.E. and Glaser, R. (1987) Marital quality, marital disruption and immune function. *Psychosomatic Medicine*, **49**, 13–34.

Klaus, M.H. and Kennell, J.H. (1976) *Maternal-Infant Bonding*. St. Louis: Mosby.

Kobasa, S.C. (1979) Stressful life events, personality and health: an inquiry into hardiness. *Journal of Personality and Social Psychology*, **37**, 1–11.

Kobasa, S.C., Maddi, S.R. and Kahn, S. (1982) Hardiness and health: a prospective study. *Journal of Personality and Social Psychology*, **42**, 168–77.

Kobasa, S.C., Maddi, S.R., Puccetti, M.C. and Zola, M.A. (1985) Effectiveness of hardiness, exercise and social support as resources against illness. *Journal of Psychosomatic Research*, **29**, 525–33.

Koehnken, G., Milne, R., Memon, A. and Bull, R. (1999) The cognitive interview: a meta-analysis. *Psychology, Crime and Law*, **5**, 3–27.

Koluchova, J. (1976) The further development of twins after severe and prolonged separation: a second report. *Journal of Child Psychology and Psychiatry*, **17**, 181–8.

Koluchova, J. (1991) Severely deprived twins after 22 years of observation. *Studia Pschologica*, **33**, 23–8.

Kounin, J. and Gump, P. (1961) The comparative influence of punitive and non-punitive teachers upon children's concepts of school misconduct. *Journal of Educational Psychology*, **52**, 44–9.

Kyllonen, P.C. and Christal, R.E. (1990) Reasoning ability is (little more than) working-memory capacity. *Intelligence*, **14**, 389–433.

Laing, R.D. and Esterson, A. (1964) *Sanity, Madness and the Family*. Middlesex: Penguin.

Lalancette, M.F. (1990) Asch fails again. *Social Behaviour and Personality*, **18**(1), 7–12.

Lamb, M.E. (1983) Fathers: forgotten contributors to child development. *Human Development*, **18**, 245–66.

Latane, B. and Wolf, S. (1981). The social impact of majorities and minorities. *Psychological Review*, **88**, 438–53.

Lazarus, R.S. and Folkman, S. (1984) *Stress, Appraisal and Coping*. New York: Springer.

Lazarus, R.S. and Folkman, S. (1987) Transactional theory and research on emotions and coping. *European Journal of Personality*, **1**, 141–70.

Lemaine, G. (1974) Social differentiation and social originality. *European Journal of Social Psychology*, **4**, 17–52.

Lesar, T.S., Briceland, L. and Stein, D.S. (1997) Factors related to errors in medication prescribing. *Journal of the American Medical Association*, **277**, 312–17.

Lifton, R.J. (1957) Thought reform of Chinese intellectuals. *Journal of Social Issues*, **13**, 5–20.

Lifton, R.J. (1957) Thought reform of western civilians in Chinese Communist prisons. *Psychiatry – Journal for the Study of Interpersonal* Processes, 19, 2, 178–95.

Lindsay, D.S., Allen, B.P., Chan, J.C.K. and Dahl, L.C. (2004) Eyewitness suggestibility and source similarity: Intrusions of details from one event into memory reports of another event. *Journal of Memory and Language*, **50**, 96–111.

List, J.A.G. (1986). Age and schematic differences in the reliability of eyewitness testimony. *Developmental Psychology*, **22**, 50-57.

Loftus, E.F. (1992) When a lie becomes memory's truth: memory distortion after exposure to misinformation. *Current Directions in Psychology*, **1**, 121–3.

Loftus, E.F. and Burns, T.E. (1982) Mental shock can produce retrograde amnesia. *Memory and Cognition*, **10**, 318–23.

Maccoby, E.E. (1980) *Social Development: Psychological Growth and the Parent Child Relationship*. New York: Harcourt Brace Jovanovich.

MacLeod, C.M. and Donnellan, A.M. (1993) Individual differences in anxiety and the restriction of working memory capacity. *Personality and Individual Differences*, **15**, 163–73.

Maddi, S.R. (1987) Hardiness training at Illinois Bell Telephone. In J. P. Opatz (ed.), Health Promotion Evaluation. Wisconsin: National Wellness Institute.

Maddi, S.R., Khoshaba, D.M., Jensen, K., Carter, E., Lu, J.L. and Harvey, R.H. (2002) Hardiness training for high-risk undergraduates. *NACADA Journal*, **22**, 45–55.

Main, M. and Goldwyn, R. (1984) Predicting rejection of her infant from mother's representation of her own experience: implications for the abused–abusing intergenerational cycle. *Child abuse and Neglect*, **8**.

Malarkey, W.B., Kiecolt-Glaser, J.K. and Pearl, D. (1994) Hostile behaviour during marital conflict alters pituitary and adrenal hormones. *Psychosomatic Medicine*, **56**, 41–51.

Mandel, D.R. (1998) The obedience alibi: Milgram's account of the holocaust reconsidered. *Analyse Und Kritik: Zeitschrift für Sozialwissenschaften*, **20**, 74–94.

Manstead, A.S. R. and McCulloch, C. (1981) Sex-role stereotyping in British television advertisements. *British Journal of Social Psychology*, **20**, 171–80.

Markus, H. and Kitayama, S. (1991) Culture and the self: implications for cognition, emotion and motivation. *Psychological Review*, **98**, 224–53.

Marmot, M., Bosma, H., Hemingway, H., Brunner, E. and Stasfield, S. (1997) Contribution of job control and other factors to social variation in heart disease incidence. *The Lancet*, **350**, 235–9.

Masters, J.C., Burish, T.G., Hollon, S.D. and Rimm, D.C. (1987) *Behavior Therapy: techniques and empirical findings* (3rd edn). San Diego: Harcourt Brace Jovanovich.

Matthews, K.A. and Haynes, S.G. (1986) Type A behaviour pattern and coronary risk: update and critical evaluation. *American Journal of Epidemiology*, **6**, 923–60.

Meichenbaum, D. (1985) *Stress Inoculation Training*. New York: Pergamon.

Meichenbaum, D.H. (1972) Cognitive modification of test anxious college students. *Journal of Consulting and Clinical Psychology*, **39**, 370–80.

Melhuish, E.C. (1990) Research on day care for young children in the UK. In E.C. Melhuish and P. Moss (eds), *Day Care for Young Children: International Perspectives*. London: Routledge.

Melhuish, E.C. (1991) International perspectives on day care for young children. *Journal of Reproductive and Infant Psychology*, 9, 181–9

Memon, A., Wark. L., Bull, R. and Koehnken, G. (1997) Isolating the effects of the cognitive interview techniques. *British Journal of Psychology*, **88**, 179–97.

Menges, R.J. (1973) Openness and honesty versus coercion and deception in psychological research. *American Psychologist*, **28**, 1030–4.

Meuret, A.E., Wilhelm, F.H. and Roth, W.T. (1997) Respiratory feedback for treating panic disorder. *Journal of Clinical Psychology*, **60**, 197–207.

Milgram, S. (1963) Behavioural study of obedience. *Journal of Abnormal and Social Psychology*, **67**, 371–8, 467–72.

Milgram, S. (1974) *Obedience to Authority, an Experimental View*. London: Harper Collins.

Milgram, S. (1974) *Obedience to Authority: an experimental view*. New York: Harper & Row.

Milgram, S. (1974) The perils of obedience. *Harpers magazine*.

Miller, A.G. (1986) *The Obedience Experiments. A case study of controversy in social science*. New York: Praeger.

Miller, G.A. (1956) The magical number seven, plus or minus two: Some limits on our capacity for processing information. *Psychological Review*, **63**, 81–97.

Miller, T.Q., Smith, T.W., Turner, C.W., Guijarro, M.L. and Hallet, A.J. (1996) A meta-analytic review of research on hostility and physical health. *Psychological Bulletin*, **119**, 322–48.

Milner, B. (1966) Amnesia following operation on the temporal lobes. In C.W.M. Whitty and O.L. Zangwill (eds), *Amnesia Following Operation on the Temporal Lobes* (pp109–33). London: Butterworth.

Moniz, E. (1936) *Tentative Operatoires dans le Traitement de Certaines Psychoses*. Paris: Mason.

Moscovici , S., Lage, E. and Naffrenchoux, M. (1969) Influence of a consistent minority on the responses of a majority in a colour perception task. *Sociometry*, **32**, 365–80.

Murphy, L.R. (1996) Stress management techniques: secondary prevention of stress. In M.J. Schabracq, J.A.M. Winnubst and C.L. Cooper (eds), *Handbook of Work and Health Psychology*. Chichester: Wiley.

Mutrie, N. (2000) Physical activity and clinically-defined depression. In S.J.H. Biddle, K.R. Fox and S.H. Boutcher (eds), *Physical Activity and Psychological Well-Being*. Routledge: London.

Naveh-Benjamin, M. and Ayres, T.J. (1986) Digit span, reading rate, and linguistic relativity. *Quarterly Journal of Experimental Psychology*, **38**, 739–52.

Nemeth, C. (1986) Differential contributions of majority and minority influence. *Psychological Review*, **93**, 23–32.

Nemeth, C. and Chiles, C. (1988) Modelling courage: the role of dissent in fostering independence. *European Journal of Social Psychology*, **18**, 275–80.

Ohman, A., Flykt, A. and Lundqvist, D. (2000) Unconscious emotion: evolutionary perspectives, psychophysiological data, and neuropsychological mechanisms. In R.D. Lane and L. Nadel (eds) *Cognitive Neuroscience of Emotion*. Oxford: Oxford University Press.

Oliner, S.P. and Oliner, P.M. (1988) *The Altruistic Personality*. New York: Free Press.

Orne, M.T. and Holland, C.C. (1968) On the ecological validity of laboratory deceptions. *International Journal of Psychology*, **6**, 282–93.

Otto, M.W., Pollack, M.H. and Maki, K.M. (2000) Empirically supported treatments for panic disorder: costs, benefits, and stepped care. *Journal of Consulting and Clinical Psychology*, **68**, 556–63.

Paivio, A. (1965) Abstractness, imagery and meaningfulness in paired-associate learning. *Journal of Verbal Learning and Verbal Behaviour*, **4**, 32–8.

Pavlov, I.P. (1927) *Conditioned Reflexes*. Oxford: Oxford University Press.

Pennington, D. (1996) *Essential Social Psychology*. London: Edward Arnold.

Perrin, S. and Spencer, C.P. (1981) Independence or conformity in the Asch experiment as a reflection of cultural and situational factors. *British Journal of Social Psychology*, **20**(3), 205–9.

Peterson, L.R. and Peterson, M.J. (1959) Short-term retention of individual verbal items. *Journal of Experimental Psychology*, **58**, 193–8.

Poole, D.A. and Lindsay, D.S (2001) Children's eyewitness reports after exposure to misinformation from parents. *Journal of Experimental Psychology: Applied*, **7**, 27-50.

Posner, M.I. and Keele, S.W. (1967) Decay of visual information from a single letter. *Science*, **158**, 137–9.

Rahe, R.H. and Lind, E. (1971) Psychosocial factors and sudden cardiac death. *Journal of Psychosomatic Research*, **8**, 487–91.

Rahe, R.H., Mahan, J. and Arthur, R. (1970) Prediction of near-future health-change from subjects' preceding life changes. *Journal of Psychosomatic Research*, **14**, 401–6.

Rank, S.G. and Jacobson, C.K. (1977) Hospital nurses' compliance with medication overdose orders: A failure to replicate. *Journal of Health and Social Behavior*, **18**, 188–93.

Raphael, K.G., Cloitre, M. and Dohrenwend, B.P. (1991) Problems of recall and misclassification with checklist methods of measuring stressful life events. *Health Psychology*, **10**, 62–74.

Reicher, S. and Haslam, A. (2006) Rethinking the psychology of tyranny: the BBC prison study. *British Journal of Social Psychology*, **45**(1), 1–40.

Rohrer, J.H., Baron, S.H., Hoffman, E.L. and Schwander, D.V. (1954) The stability of auto-kinetic judgements. *Journal of Abnormal and Social Psychology*, **49**, 595–7.

Rosenhan, D.L. and Seligman, M.E.P. (1989) *Abnormal Psychology* (2nd edn). New York: Norton.

Rosenman, R.H., Brand, R.J., Sholtz, R.I. and Friedman, M. (1976) Multivariate prediction of coronary heart disease during 8.5 year follow-up in the Western Collaborative Group study. *The American Journal of Cardiology*, **37**, 903–10.

Rosnow, R.L (1981) *Paradigms in Transition*. New York: Oxford University Press.

Ross, G., Kagan, J., Zelazo, P. and Kotelchuk, M. (1975) Separation protest in infants at home and laboratory. *Developmental Psychology*, **11**, 256–7.

Roth, S. and Cohen, L.J. (1986) Approach avoidance and coping with stress. *American Psychologist*, **41**, 813–19.

Rotter, J.B. (1966) Generalized expectations for internal versus external control of reinforcement. *Psychological Monographs*, **80**, whole no. 609.

Rutter, M., Colvert, E., Kreppner., J., Beckett, C., Castle, J., Groothues, C., Hawkins., A., O'Connor, T., Stevens, S. and Sonuga-Barke, E. (2007) Early adolescent outcomes for institutionally-deprived and non-deprived adoptees: I: Disinhibited attachment. *Journal of Child Psychology and Psychiatry*, **48**(1), 17–30

Rutter, M., Quinton, D. and Hill, J. (1990) Adult outcomes of institution-reared children: Males and females compared. In L. N. Robbins and M. Rutter (eds), *Straight and Devious Pathways From Childhood to Adult Life*. Cambridge: Cambridge University Press.

Sarason, I.G., Johnson, J.H. and Siegel, J.M. (1978) Assessing the impact of life changes: development of the life experiences survey. *Journal of Consulting and Clinical Psychology*, **46**, 932–46.

Schaffer, H.R. and Callender, W.M. (1959) Psychologic effects of hospitalization in infancy. *Paediatrics*, **24**, 4, 528–39.

Schaffer, H.R. and Emerson, P.E. (1964) The development of social attachments in infancy. *Monographs for the Society for Research in Child Development*, **29**, 3, serial no. 94.

Schaffer, R. (1996) *Social Development*. Oxford: Blackwell.

Schindler, P.J., Moely, B.E. and Frank, A.L. (1987) Time in day-care and social participation of young children. *Developmental Psychology*, **23**, 255–61.

Schooler, J.W., Gerhard, D. and Loftus, E.F. (1986) Qualities of the unreal. *Journal of Experimental Psychology: Learning, Memory and Cognition*, **12**, 171–81.

Schweickert, R. and Boruff, B. (1986) Short-term memory capacity: magic number or magic spell? *Journal of Experimental Psychology: Learning, Memory, and Cognition*, **12**, 419–25.

Sedikides, C. and Jackson, J.M. (1990) Social impact theory: a field test of source strength, source immediacy and number of targets. *Basic and Applied Social Psychology*, **11**, 273–81.

Segerstrom, S.C. and Miller, G.E. (2004) Psychological stress and the human immune system: a meta-analytic study of 30 years of inquiry. *Psychological Bulletin*, **130**(4), 601–30.

Seligman, M.E.P. (1971) Phobias and preparedness. *Behavior Therapy*, **2**, 307–20.

Selye, H.S. (1956) *The Stress of Life*. New York: McGraw-Hill.

Shah, P. and Miyake, A. (1996) The separability of working memory resources for spatial thinking and language processing: an individual differences approach. *Journal of Experimental Psychology: General*, **125**, 4–27.

Shallice, T. and Warrington, E.K. (1970) Independent functioning of verbal and memory stores: a neuropsychological study. *Quarterly Journal of Experimental Psychology*, **22**, 261–73.

Shekelle, R.B., Hulley, S.B. and Neaton, J.D. (1985) The MRFIT behaviour pattern study. II. Type A behaviour and incidence of coronary heart disease. *American Journal of Epidemiology*, **122**, 559–70.

Shepard, R.N. and Feng, C.A. (1972) A chronometric study of mental paper folding. *Cognitive Psychology*, **3**.

Sherif, M. (1936) A study of some social factors in perception. *Archives of Psychology*, **27**, 187.

Simon, H.A. (1974) How big is a chunk? *Science*, **183**, 482–8.

Shorter, E. (1997) A *History of Psychiatry: from the Era of the Asylum to the Age of Prozac*. Chichester: John Wiley & Sons.

Skinner, B.F. (1974) *About Behaviourism*. New York: Knopf.

Smith, E.R. and Mackie, D.M. (2000) *Social Psychology*. Hove: Psychology Press.

Skuse, D. (1984) Extreme Deprivation In early childhood – II. Theoretical issues and a comparative review. *Journal of Child Psychology and Psychiatry*, **25**, 4, 543–72.

Smith, P.B. and Bond, M.H. (1993) *Social Psychology across Cultures: analysis and perspectives*. London: Harvester Wheatsheaf.

Sperling, G. (1960) The information available in brief visual presentations. *Psychology Monographs*, **74**, 11, 498.

Stang, D.J. (1976) Group size effects on conformity. *Journal of Social Psychology*, **98**, 175–81.

Steele, H. (2001) Inter-generational patterns of attachment: recent findings from research. In L. Dryden, R. Forbes, P. Mukherji and L. Pound, (2005) *Early Years*. London: Hodder and Stoughton.

Stone, A.A. and Neale, J.M. (1984) New measure of daily coping: development and preliminary results. *Journal of Personality and Social Psychology*, **46**, 892–906.

Szasz, T. (1972) *The Manufacture of Madness*. London: Routledge & Kegan Paul.

Tajfel, H., Billig, M., Bundy R.P. and Flament, C. (1971) Social categorisation and intergroup behaviour. *European Journal of Social Psychology*, **1**, 149–77.

Tanford, S. and Penrod, S. (1984) Social influence model: a formal integration of research on majority and minority influence processes. *Psychological Bulletin*, **95**(2), 189–225.

Tanford, S. and Penrod, S. (1986) Jury deliberations: discussion content and influence processes in jury decision making. *Journal of Applied Social Psychology*, **16**(4), 322–47.

Tennen, H., Affleck, G., Armeli, S. and Carney, M.A. (2000) A daily process approach to coping: linking theory, research and practice. *American Psychologist*, **55**, 626–36.

Throne, L.C., Bartholomew, J.B. and Craig, J. (2000) Stress reactivity in fire fighters: an exercise intervention. *International Journal of Stress Management*, **7**, 235–46.

Tolpin, M. (1993) The unmirrored self, compensatory structures, and cure: the exemplary case of Anna O. *The Annual of Psychoanalysis*, **21**, 157–77.

Tomes, J.L. and Katz, A.N. (1997) Habitual susceptibility to misinformation and individual differences in eyewitness memory. *Applied Cognitive Psychology*, **11**, 233–51.

Tuckey, M.R. and Brewer, N. (2003) How schemas affect eyewitness memory over repeated retrieval attempts. *Applied Cognitive Psychology*, **7**, 785–800.

Turner, J.C. (1991) *Social Influence*. Buckingham: Open University Press.

Uchino, B.N., Cacioppo, J.T. and Kiecolt-Glaser, J.K. (1996) The relationship between social support and physiological processes: a review with emphasis on underlying mechanisms and implications for health. *Psychological Bulletin*, **119**, 488–531.

Ucros, C.G. (1989) Mood state-dependent memory: a meta-analysis. *Cognition and Emotion*, **3**, 139–67.

Vaillant, G.E. (2003) Mental health. *American Journal of Psychiatry*, **160**, 1373–84.

Van der Doef, M. and Maes, S. (1998) The job demand-control (-support) model and physical health outcomes: a review of the strain and buffer hypotheses. *Psychology and Health*, **13**, 909–36.

Van IJzendoorn, M.H. and Kroonenberg, P.M. (1988) Cross-cultural patterns of attachment: a meta analysis of the Strange Situation. *Child Development*, **59**, 147–56.

Vitaliano, P.P., Maiuro, R.D. and Russo, J. (1990) Coping profiles associated with psychiatric, physical health, work and family problems. *Health Psychology*, **9**, 348–76.

Vogt, T.M., Mullooly, J.P., Ernst, D., Pope, C.R. and Hollis, J.F. (1992) Social networks as predictors of ischemic heart disease, cancer, stroke and hypertension: incidence, survival and mortality. *Journal of Clinical Epidemiology*, **45**, 659–66.

Watamura, S.E., Donzella, B., Kertes, D.A. and Gunnar, M.R. (2004) Developmental changes in baseline cortisol activity in early childhood: relations with napping and effortful control. *Developmental Psychobiology*, 125–33.

Watson, J.B. and Rayner, R. (1920) Conditioned emotional reactions. *Journal of Experimental Psychology*, **3**, 1–14.

Watson, S.L., Shiveley, C.A., Kaplan, J.R. and Line, S.W. (1998) Effects of chronic social separation on cardiovascular disease risk factors in female cynomolgus monkeys. *Atherosclerosis*, **137**, 259–66.

Wells, G.L., Small, M. and Penrod, S. (1998) Eyewitness identification procedures: recommendations for lineups and photospreads. *Law and Human Behaviour*, **22**, 603–47.

Williams, J. and Warchal, J. (1981) Relationship between assertiveness, internal-external locus of control and overt conformity. *Journal of Psychology – Interdisciplinary and Applied*, **109**(1), 93–6.

Wolpe, J. (1958) *Psychotherapy by Reciprocal Inhibition*. Stanford: Stanford University Press.

Zimbardo, P.G. (2006) On rethinking the psychology of tyranny: the BBC prison study. *British Journal of Social Psychology*, **45**(1), 47–53.

Zimbardo, P.G., Banks, P.G., Haney, C. and Jaffe, D. (1973) Pirandellian Prison: the mind is a formidable jailor. *New York Times Magazine*, 8 April, pp38–60.

Zimmerman, P., Becker-Stoll, F., Grossman, K., Scheurer-Englisch, H. and Wartner, U. (2000) Longitudinal attachment development from infancy through adolescence. *Psychologie in Erziehung und Unterricht*, **47**(2), 99–117.

Index